The Sciences Po Series in International Relations and Political Economy

Series Editor, Christian Lequesne

This series consists of works emanating from the foremost French researchers from Sciences Po, Paris. Sciences Po was founded in 1872 and is today one of the most prestigious universities for teaching and research in social sciences in France, recognized worldwide.

This series focuses on the transformations of the international arena, in a world where the state, though its sovereignty is questioned, reinvents itself. The series explores the effects on international relations and the world economy of regionalization, globalization (not only of trade and finance but also of culture), and transnational flows at large. This evolution in world affairs sustains a variety of networks from the ideological to the criminal or terrorist. Besides the geopolitical transformations of the globalized planet, the new political economy of the world has a decided impact on its destiny as well, and this series hopes to uncover what that is.

Published by Palgrave Macmillan:

Politics in China: Moving Frontiers
    edited by Françoise Mengin and Jean-Louis Rocca
Tropical Forests, International Jungle: The Underside of Global Ecopolitics
    by Marie-Claude Smouts, translated by Cynthia Schoch
The Political Economy of Emerging Markets: Actors, Institutions and Financial Crises in Latin America
    by Javier Santiso
Cyber China: Reshaping National Identities in the Age of Information
    edited by Françoise Mengin
With Us or Against Us: Studies in Global Anti-Americanism
    edited by Denis Lacorne and Tony Judt
Vietnam's New Order: International Perspectives on the State and Reform in Vietnam
    edited by Stéphanie Balme and Mark Sidel
Equality and Transparency: A Strategic Perspective on Affirmative Action in American Law
    by Daniel Sabbagh, translation by Cynthia Schoch and John Atherton
Moralizing International Relations: Called to Account
    by Ariel Colonomos, translated by Chris Turner
Norms over Force: The Enigma of European Power
    by Zaki Laidi, translated from the French by Cynthia Schoch
Democracies at War against Terrorism: A Comparative Perspective
    edited by Samy Cohen, translated by John Atherton, Roger Leverdier, Leslie Piquemal, and Cynthia Schoch
Justifying War? From Humanitarian Intervention to Counterterrorism
    edited by Gilles Andréani and Pierre Hassner, translated by John Hulsey, Leslie Piquemal, Ros Schwartz, and Chris Turner
An Identity for Europe: The Relevance of Multiculturalism in EU Construction
    edited by Riva Kastoryano, translated by Susan Emanuel

The Politics of Regional Integration in Latin America: Theoretical and Comparative Explorations
  by Olivier Dabène
Central and Eastern Europe: Europeanization and Social Change
  by François Bafoil, translated by Chris Turner
Building Constitutionalism in China
  edited by Stéphanie Balme and Michael W. Dowdle
In the Name of the Nation: Nationalism and Politics in Contemporary Russia
  by Marlène Laruelle
Organized Crime and States: The Hidden Face of Politics
  edited by Jean-Louis Briquet and Gilles Favarel-Garrigues
Israel's Asymmetric Wars
  by Samy Cohen, translated by Cynthia Schoch
China and India in Central Asia: A New "Great Game"?
  edited by Marlène Laruelle, Jean-François Huchet, Sébastien Peyrouse, and Bayram Balci
Making Peace: The Contribution of International Institutions
  edited by Guillaume Devin, translated by Roger Leverdier
War Veterans in Postwar Situations: Chechnya, Serbia, Turkey, Peru, and Côte d'Ivoire
  edited by Nathalie Duclos

War Veterans in Postwar Situations

Chechnya, Serbia, Turkey, Peru, and Côte d'Ivoire

Edited by
Nathalie Duclos

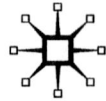

WAR VETERANS IN POSTWAR SITUATIONS
Copyright © Nathalie Duclos, 2012.

All rights reserved.

First published in French in 2010 as *L'adieu aux armes? Parcours d'anciens combattants* by Editions Karthala SAS, Paris, France.

First published in English in 2012 by
PALGRAVE MACMILLAN®
in the United States—a division of St. Martin's Press LLC,
175 Fifth Avenue, New York, NY 10010.

Where this book is distributed in the UK, Europe and the rest of the world, this is by Palgrave Macmillan, a division of Macmillan Publishers Limited, registered in England, company number 785998, of Houndmills, Basingstoke, Hampshire RG21 6XS.

Palgrave Macmillan is the global academic imprint of the above companies and has companies and representatives throughout the world.

Palgrave® and Macmillan® are registered trademarks in the United States, the United Kingdom, Europe and other countries.

ISBN: 978–0–230–34135–7

Library of Congress Cataloging-in-Publication Data

   War veterans in postwar situations : Chechnya, Serbia, Turkey, Peru, and Cote d'Ivoire / edited by Nathalie Duclos.
      pages cm.—(The sciences po series in international relations and political economy)
   ISBN 978–0–230–34135–7 (hardback)
    1. Disarmament—Case studies. 2. Armed Forces—Demobilization—Case studies. 3. Veterans—Social conditions—Case studies. 4. Postwar reconstruction—Case studies. 5. Peace-building—Case studies.
   I. Duclos, Nathalie.

JZ5588.W36 2012
305.9'0697—dc23   2011050342

A catalogue record of the book is available from the British Library.

Design by Newgen Imaging Systems (P) Ltd., Chennai, India.

First edition: June 2012

10 9 8 7 6 5 4 3 2 1

Printed in the United States of America.

CONTENTS

Preface   vii
Stathis N. Kalyvas

Introduction: Rethinking the Former Combatants'
Return to Civilian Life   1
By Nathalie Duclos

Part 1   Veterans' Habitus of War, Brutalization of Societies?

One   A "Chechen Syndrome"? Russian Veterans of the Chechen War and the Transposition of War Violence to Society   25
Anne Le Huérou and Elisabeth Sieca-Kozlowski

Two   The Return of the Conscripts—A Vector for the Construction of a National Security Regime in Turkey?   53
Sümbül Kaya

Three   Reintegrating Civilian Life after Combat: Between Invisibility and Resistance. The Experience of the *Ronderas* in Peru   73
Camille Boutron

Four   Paramilitary Demobilization and the Return of Violence in Colombia   95
Sophie Daviaud

Part 2   Process of Reintegration, Cultural Demobilization?

Five   A Veteran's Challenge: From the Test of War to the American Dream   117
Béatrice Richard

Six   The Position of Former Combatants, French Authorities, and Public Opinion Vis-à-Vis German Prisoners of War (1944–1949)   137
Fabien Théofilakis

Seven	The "Recycled" Militiaman: An Examination of the Postwar Reconversion of Four Former Members of a Serbian Armed Group *Samuel Tanner*	157
Eight	Museveni's Best Enemies: Dilemmas and Political Uses of the Reintegration of Former Lord's Resistance Army (LRA) Commanders in Northern Uganda *Sandrine Perrot*	177

Part 3 From Military Combat to Political Struggle: Reconversion or Continuity?

Nine	From the Great War to Democracy: Former Combatants and the Sardinian Autonomist Movement *Christophe Roux*	201
Ten	The Postwar Period in Chechnya: When Spoilers Jeopardize the Emerging Chechen State (1996–1999) *Aude Merlin*	219
Eleven	A "Warrior" Generation? Political Violence and Subjectivation of Young Militamen in Ivory Coast *Richard Banégas*	241

Conclusion 267
Nathalie Duclos

Bibliography 273

Contributors 287

Index 291

PREFACE

STATHIS N. KALYVAS
YALE UNIVERSITY

The end of the Cold War is associated with a significant shift in the way in which civil wars end. In the past, internal conflicts tended to end in decisive military victories, even when they lasted for a long time; nowadays, negotiated settlements between the warring parties, often facilitated, supervised, and financed by supranational institutions or international actors tend to be much more common than in the past. In the context of such settlements, the demobilization and reintegration of combatants becomes a central issue, one intimately related to both policy design and the theoretical understanding of concepts such as conflict and postconflict, violence, and peace. More specifically, the challenges posed by processes of transition from conflict to postconflict contexts are numerous and can be articulated most productively when arrayed around three related levels of analysis.

At the macro level, it is essential to understand the goals of the various actors involved in the conflict. For example, did they seek a social transformation of their society or just access to power for its own sake? Did they claim to represent the entire nation or particular social or ethnic groups? Given that civil wars take place primarily in poor countries, the transition away from conflicts calls for three intertwined giant projects: state-building, which entails the extension of state capacity to a state's entire territory, both in terms of security but also in terms of regional integration; national-building, which calls for the forging of a common identity and the introduction of representative institutions; and sustainable economic development. These projects are daunting in and of themselves; when undertaken together, they can easily undermine each other, generating a host of negative externalities.

At the meso level, it becomes necessary to pay close attention to the structure of the organizations that took part in the conflict. Were they cohesive or fragmented? Centralized or not? How exactly were their members recruited and socialized? What kind of relations did they maintain with the civilian population? How did they rule over it? Crucially, one must explore the dynamics of the war and the modalities of violence that took place. Unless we understand these processes it becomes very difficult to figure out whether it is preferable for demobilized combatants to abandon their former networks or remain embedded in them. Consider a common conundrum: on the one hand, it is extremely difficult to integrate atomized former combatants in a society that often treats them with disdain if not with outright vengefulness; however, the social embeddedness of these combatants into their former networks may facilitate both their remobilization (and, therefore, the possibility of a recurrence of the conflict) and the "organizational hijacking" of these networks into criminal activities. Clearly, "one model fits all" approaches to these issues are destined to fail, as are simplistic frameworks of the "new wars" kind.

Lastly, at the micro level, the focus must be on both the experiences of individual combatants and individual civilians. Questions of brutalization and traumatization should be investigated extensively, and the long-term effects of war on political and social behavior and identities calls for careful research. One of the most important insights of recent research on civil wars points to the "endogenous" effects of conflict: when exiting a conflict, individuals and communities do not revert to the status quo ante; they have been fundamentally transformed by the experience of conflict. Exactly how, is a question that to this day has not been investigated systematically. Clearly, the policies that are recommended or implemented must take into account explicitly the effects of conflict. This set of considerations must also be incorporated in debates of reconciliation and historical memory.

This brief overview suggests how difficult it is to trace the multiple paths available to former combatants during the transition from conflict to postconflict and, therefore, how challenging it is to design sensible policies. With its comparative and historical focus and its bold emphasis on combatants, *War Veterans in Postwar Situations* is a welcome contribution to the study of processes of demobilization and reintegration. Its originality is two-fold. First, it attempts to bridge the gap between present policy and past experience by stressing the historical and cultural modalities of the process of combatant "return" and reintegration. Second, by fully recognizing that war transforms society, all the way from individual brutalization to organizations and networks, and by placing this transformation squarely into the broader political and social context, it successfully integrates the micro, meso, and macro levels. In doing so, and in combining a subtle historical and contextual understanding of specific experiences with a broad comparative and theoretical perspective, this book marks a decisive improvement in our understanding of a problem at once vexing and fascinating.

Introduction: Rethinking the Former Combatants' Return to Civilian Life

NATHALIE DUCLOS

Abstract

The introduction examines research in the fields of history, political science, sociology, and anthropology concerning combat veterans of various armed conflicts, within and between states. Two research methodologies emerge which, though developed independently of each other, reflect a preoccupation with similar questions. The author proposes a third methodology, reformulating these questions in the aim of laying the groundwork for a political sociology of the ex-combatant's return to civilian life and their postwar trajectories. Critical of the view that the end of a war opens up a radically new era, the author suggests taking a closer look at the legacies of war, its postwar sociological and cognitive continuities and discontinuities, the possible difficulties involved in ex-combatants ridding themselves of a violent "mode," the effects, from that point of view, of policies aimed at them, and the strategies of individual veterans facing the deep sociological and political transformations of the postwar period. The career concept proposed by Howard Becker certainly helps to better understand and deal with ex-combatants' postwar itineraries.

This book constitutes an approach to a subject more prominent in Anglophone political science than in France and Francophone research. Our aim, in this comparative and multidisciplinary discussion of postconflict periods following a cease-fire, armistice, or signing of a peace plan, is to focus on the trajectories of the main actors in these conflicts, i.e., the ex-combatants—recruits called up for service, volunteers mobilized in an armed struggle movement, or combatants enlisted by force in an armed struggle group—with a view to analyzing their "contribution" to the ongoing pacification process. Given that the postconflict situation of ex-combatants is likely to facilitate or, on the contrary, undermine the transition from war to peace, our discussion will focus on their influence on the normalization process.

In the case of intrastate postconflicts, the situation of ex-combatants depends on an issue central to political science: having undergone war, the state faces the essential task of (re)monopolizing legitimate physical violence. Thus begins a period of "security transition," during which the institutions that have been (re)created are expected to ensure the transition from a situation of diffuse violence to a phase allowing the state to reclaim its monopoly on coercion. In all ends of war, ex-combatants pose another series of problems linked to their return to civilian life and how it affects social and political life. To what extent and under what conditions are they actually demobilized? Besides handing over their arms, they must also be reintegrated. How does reintegration operate, what are the various possible trajectories, and what are the sociological and political effects of their return?

Cases of armed remobilization are the most obvious indication that this process has failed and that there are obstacles to peace. However, our study has chosen to focus on the more frequent cases in which demobilization programs have apparently been successful, but in fact, while they allow the state to once again ensure security on its territory, they are in no way a guarantee that the various experiences of the ex-combatants' return to civilian life will not be a source of social destabilization.

These issues emerge from different levels of analysis—macro (state, national, and international public policies), meso (social and political organizations), and micro (individual)—but until now have been more or less left aside.

Postulating a similarity of issues, we have chosen to decompartmentalize the analyses of authors working on intra- and interstate postconflicts. The intra/inter distinction does not seem relevant, in the sense that it is the exit of the conflict that is important, in whatever space it takes place (or not). We will also confront the points of view of historians working on earlier conflicts with analyses of recent conflicts so as to obtain as well a relative view of the pertinence of analyses in terms of "new wars." Finally, we also wish to go beyond what seems to us an artificial disciplinary dichotomy between international relations and political sociology and attempt to compare the approaches of political scientists and historians. Until now both fields have in fact developed along parallel lines without sufficiently crossing.

On our subject, two analytical traditions have already been solidly built up: the first around political science research analyzing contemporary postconflicts, and the second around research by historians, in particular that related to social history and dealing with the two World Wars. In this introduction, we will attempt a rapid overview of the themes and issues that characterize this research, obviously without assuming any homogeneity of approach, and in the hope of rendering justice to the finesse of the various authors' analyses. We will then bring up a few issues common to both traditions on the basis of which it seems possible to establish a new research program on ex-combatants in the aftermath of armed conflicts.

Toward the Organization of a Dialogue between Historians and Political Scientists

The first tradition is represented here with studies by researchers in cultural areas, either by specialists in international relations or, more recently, by political scientists,[1] who, using the tools of political sociology, study issues that usually concern the international sphere.[2] Since the conflicts studied are intrastate in nature, many of the research works, following Max Weber, question the ability of the state to successfully (re?)claim the monopoly of legitimate physical violence. Thus they emphasize how seriously the states where these conflicts take place are challenged in their sovereign functions by contesting or separatist groups, often leading to the collapse of the state.[3] According to this approach, when a conflict seems to be over, what is most essential is to disarm these fighters, who most often belong to irregular groups, reconvert them, and lead them to return to civilian life in such a way that they cease defying the state. This preoccupation concerning the weakness or failure of the state brings many analysts to a study of the programs put in place for combatants and aimed at normalizing the after-war situation, namely the Disarmament, Demobilization, Reintegration (DDR) programs. Aside from their purely military aspect—recovery of arms and demobilization of ex-combatants—DDR policies are often based on the reconstitution of an army, or even a police force,[4] integrating former rebels and contributing thus to in-depth state reform. Thus it is a matter of encouraging new loyalties to state institutions and in that way cementing the legitimacy of the newly (re)born state. Putting in place a dynamic of "civilianization,"[5] which can be understood as a definitive return to civilian life combined with a change of identity that leads the ex-combatant to abandon the military reference and prefer a civil identity,[6] is generally considered an essential step in the normalization of political life. These DDR policies are more and more often carried out under the auspices of multilateral organizations, in particular the UN and two of its agencies, the World Bank and the United Nations Development Programme (UNDP),[7] which tend to follow the same policy from one country to another.[8] Much is at stake in DDR programs. Many research works underscore the need to give as much importance to the R of DDR (that is to say, the longer-term reintegration process of former combatants) as to the two preceding phases of disarmament and demobilization[9] so as to lay the groundwork for a durable peace and not aim solely for a "negative peace,"[10] which more often than not gives rise to armed conflict. In the case of Africa, Kees Kingma stresses that reintegration is part of a "broader process of reconciliation, of construction of the nation and strengthening of civil society,"[11] and that it is urgent to improve links between development issues and DDR policies.[12] The reintegration process thus seems particularly complex, since it concerns both socioeconomic development issues and security issues.[13] Thus it would seem more worthwhile to go beyond DDR "minimalist" programs narrowly centered on security and think in terms of "maximalist" programs that would encompass a socioeconomic approach and work from an overall perspective of peace-building.[14] Several authors emphasize the error that consisted in seeing the DDR as a primarily technical program. This resulted in policymakers forgetting about its fundamentally political dimension,[15] in the sense that DDR programs were an essential feature of the new postconflict social pact. For most authors, it is a challenge to find a solution that satisfies ex-combatants—whose acceptance of peace is a key to success—without giving a bonus to those who bore arms and depriving victims of their desire for justice.[16] There are numerous obstacles to normalization, many of them having to do with the nature of contemporary conflicts, described by some as "new wars."[17] In some cases, it is a matter of the weakness of the state itself, incapable of ensuring its regulatory role over the whole of the territory (*failed states)*,[18] or of the disruptive actions of "spoilers," i.e., those who "believe that peace emerging from negotiations threatens their power, worldview, and interests, and use violence to undermine attempts to achieve it"[19]; they therefore find it more advantageous to continue war than to end it. According to some authors, rebels are motivated more by greed than by (possibly legitimate) grievances, their combat being a sort of predation, of organized criminality, since it is determined by the sole pursuit of economic interests.[20] In addition, the post–Cold War period enabled a scattering of arms and munitions that facilitated the continuation of combats for actors of these "low-intensity conflicts." Sometimes, difficulties in normalization also seem to stem from the conditions in which a war ended. Three case types are usually distinguished: political accord between belligerent parties, victory of one party, and peace imposed by an outside party.[21] Some analyses consider the victory of one of the belligerent parties as creating a context that facilitates peace, while in the first case the "security dilemma" is most intense. In some studies, beyond peace from on top, reconciliation of former adversaries is primordial,[22] which raises the question of the role of justice in these after-war contexts and the place given to the victims of armed conflicts. Some international policies try to contribute to reconciliation, often by setting up new institutions (state building[23]), especially in the security sector, or putting in place a new social contract (nation building).

As for the research of historians, their studies focus mainly on the two World Wars. These were interstate wars with the resulting problem of demobilizing millions of recruits and returning them to civilian life in their respective countries. Research is also now concerning itself with the Algerian War.[24] In the wake of George Lachmann Mosse's work, which established a bridge between the First World War and the beginnings of Nazism in Germany in the 1930s,[25] some historians have examined the effects of the brutalization or *ensauvagement*[26] of societies induced by war. Mosse defines brutalization as a "continuation of wartime attitudes into peace," which "heightened indifference to human life."[27] Brutalization can be explained by an "attitude of mind derived from the war and the acceptance of war itself." Mosse analyzes the phenomenon as follows: "The outcome of the process of brutalization in the interwar years was to energize man, to propel him into action against the political enemy, or to numb men and women in the face of human cruelty and the loss of life." As a sign of the brutalization process taking place in Germany, "a new ruthlessness [which] invaded their politics" after the war, "the vocabulary of political battle, the desire to utterly destroy the political enemy, and the way in which these adversaries were pictured, all seemed to continue the First World War mostly against a set of different, internal foes."[28] One of the factors favoring brutalization was the refashioning of the war based on the construction of the "Myth of the War Experience," in which "the war was sanctified. Yet at the same time, [...] it became trivialized, notably by the many representations 'sanitizing' death"[29]: in literature and films, on everyday objects, toys, postcards, military cemeteries, and monuments to the dead. This brutalization was the product, after the war, of the *culture of war* internalized during the conflict. It can be described as a polarization of representations resting on a particularly negative vision of the enemy (diabolization, animalization, dehumanization, etc.) and a magnification of one's own camp (heroization, idealization of one's nation, sense of sacrifice, etc.). The culture of war would seem to have been an important factor in mobilization for war[30]: in France, for example, the fact that the French knew about atrocities committed by the Germans during the First World War was a determining element in the diabolization of the Germans during Second World War.[31] Such cultures of war often continue long after the war is over, since "cultural demobilization," as John Horne puts it, rarely takes effect concomitant with the armistice: "the demobilization process, rather than a condition for peace, becomes the main issue."[32] To show the importance of this phenomenon in the pacification process, the author stresses that "the impetus for mobilizing operated on another level [than military], that of values, representations and the imaginary of the populations concerned. This implies that the reestablishment of peace required another form of demobilization—that of the 'cultures of war' that had been a feature of collective life during the conflict."[33] In that context, although they rely essentially on the symbolic, rituals and commemorative ceremonies[34] appear to be of crucial importance, in that they offer an acceptable meaning to the sacrifices accepted by the combatants and in that sense, facilitate cultural demobilization.[35] These commemorations constitute a stage that also, paradoxically (?), facilitates reconciliation between former belligerents, since they answer to needs of recognition of what is perceived by ex-combatants—they who "gave" their lives and youth—as a major sacrifice.

Though at times traversed by the same questions, these two approaches have developed separately. In bringing together the contributions of both historians and political scientists, we hope to organize a dialogue to establish bridges between these two analytical traditions of postconflicts and the role of ex-combatants in such a way as to stimulate both fields of research. Let us first glance at two questions common to both approaches.

First there is the matter of "what survives" of the war in the after-war. This is the sense of Mosse's notion of brutalization, which supposes a transposition of the registers of war in the after-war (trivialization of violence, indifference toward human life) or the concept of "cultural demobilization," underscoring the fact that warlike images, and negative representations of the enemy in particular, can still be alive long after military demobilization is over. On their side, political scientists and sociologists question the "transformation of social statuses"[36] induced by the preceding combat period or changes in the construction of "social and cultural categories"[37]: new categories appear after the war, which are the product of the war; others have simply undergone a transformation due to the war. Another aftereffect of war is that legitimacy strategies are based on moral categorizations. As Laetitia Bucaille[38] observes, after-war narrations are highly structured by the preceding conflict and thus have a strong influence on postconflict recomposition.

Another point where the two approaches converge is in reconsidering, thanks to a "bottom up" approach to war, what constitutes the borderline between war and peace. Peacetime sociabilities continue into wartime[39]; the signing of a cease-fire is rarely synonymous with an immediate and overall end to combats (which sometimes intensify, as many historians have shown in the case of the First and Second World Wars[40]); combatants are still in possession of arms; situations vary from one part of the territory to another. Also, some anthropologists and political scientists claim that the war situation has been considered in a too monolithic way, as a "break in a state of being" between a before and an after, a tipping over into an anomic state, whereas war allows ordinary, routine situations to happen, albeit interrupted at times by violent episodes. Thus it cannot be apprehended as allowing irrationality to prevail, nor as a state of "disease."[41]

These questionings are valuable in that they break with a mistaken vision of the postconflict period and of former combatants. Postconflict periods, contexts of transition from war to peace, are generally seen in a too linear and inexorable fashion as periods of return to the ex ante situation. According to a traditional approach, the signing of a peace agreement is a turning point marked essentially by the laying down of arms, the return of the military to their barracks and the return of the other actors (militia, paramilitary, etc.) to their previous civilian activities. In such a case, the state's monopoly of legitimate physical violence would not be challenged and it would once again become the sole actor implementing the means of constraint. Peace would simply substitute for war.

Inversely, this book proposes to examine the postconflict period, the transition from war to peace, by calling into question the very idea of *after*-war and *transition* (in the sense of a certain transitology postulating the passage to something radically different).

Furthermore, our inquiry proceeds contrary to that in the literature of DDR programs. Rather than approaching these policies from the top and from the angle of "results," we prefer to start from the bottom with an examination of the trajectories of ex-combatants—whether or not they are enrolled in pacification programs. In other words, our approach focuses on the recompositions at work on return to civilian life. We feel that an analysis of these trajectories, based as often as possible on firsthand sources, can give us the most insight into the factors aiding or impeding the return to civilian life. Thus most of the following studies, rather than looking at the short-term, technical, and managerial considerations of disarmament and demobilization that constitute the majority of literature on DDR, take a medium- or long-term view of the "after-war," enabling us to shed light on the complex sociopolitical dimensions of these trajectories.

In this way we mean to avoid the two main stumbling blocks of a large part of the literature on DDR programs: normativeness and prescription.

Studies on DDR programs are often funded by entities that set up these programs and expect to improve their interventions via the accumulation of "lessons learnt." As a result, publications are largely prescriptive. This leads them to a major aporia: since their aim is to make a certain number of recommendations, they adopt an intellectual procedure, which consists in confining themselves to factual results and comparing them to objectives. For that reason, their approach is static, limited to a time T, and disregards political dynamics.[42] In so doing, as Norma Kriger rightly stresses, it also overlooks hidden agendas,[43] that is to say, agreements made in secret, often indispensable to the conclusion of a peace agreement.

These studies are also normative. They are based on the postulate that it is desirable to demobilize, disarm, and reintegrate ex-combatants, thus in a way hinting that their behavior is deviant.[44] What they advocate is a normalization of the situation. The notion of reintegration—one we intend to distance ourselves from—then becomes clear: the combatant is perceived as no longer integrated into "normal" life (which a number of fieldwork studies refute[45]), and he must leave behind the state of anomie and desocialization that supposedly characterizes war. According to this approach, the end of the war must simply be the opportunity for a return to the combatant's previous life (reintegration meaning return to the previous state of integration). We can see here, among DDR policymakers as well as observers and actors, a "white page temptation": as if a new page of history were being written,[46] as if a peace agreement erased all trace of the previous armed conflict. Thus war and its multiple consequences, in terms of sociological and cognitive transformations, constitute a blind spot[47]: as a phase of decomposition, it would be unworthy of analysis by the social sciences. This kind of thinking obliterates the history of the conflict, which is why we find practically no questioning on the political order or its possible injustices at the origin of the rebellion and the armed conflict. In the end, these approaches constitute a support for the peace process, i.e., the liberal peace of the UN.

Most of these approaches are influenced by the economic analyses of war, developed mainly in the work of Paul Collier, which prevents thinking in terms of the interrelated political dimensions of war,[48] DDR operations, and return to civilian life. In fact, DDR policies are not seen from the angle of their bargaining and negotiation dynamics since ex-combatants, supposedly moved by greed and not involved in political issues, are thought not disposed to compromise,[49] the peace agreement systematically considered detrimental to their material interest. In short, this makes it impossible for the DDR to be thought of as a "social contract" in the process of (re)negotiation. As a result, there is no analysis of the political dimensions of return to civilian life. This phase is nonetheless correlated to the political agreement that was reached, to its social and political acceptability. Return to civilian life is not only a matter of employability, as is assumed by training programs geared to professional competencies,[50] but a matter of consent to the new situation opening up with the peace agreement; depending on whether the new political, economic, and social order "promised" by the peace agreement seems more just, more acceptable by the ex-rebels, the latter will be more or less disposed to renounce combats definitively.

Avenues of Research for a Renewed Approach to Ex-combatants in the Aftermath of Armed Conflicts

The aim of this book is to reexamine periods of transition by questioning the continuities and/or discontinuities at work between war and "afterwar" periods. Its objective is to discover to what degree the past conflict induces transformations that we will distinguish in analytical terms as either sociological, "cultural," or "cognitive" in nature.

We will first study sociological changes caused by war in the sense that it disrupts preexisting social hierarchies. The veteran may come out of the war glorified for having participated in the "liberation" or "victorious defense" of a territory, or on the contrary, discredited for having been part of an organization that used methods considered "barbaric" and/or that caused harm to innocent civilians.[51] In the case of Peru, Camille Boutron (Chapter Three) shows the "benefits" of participation in self-defense committees, as these were a means of access to citizenship and social promotion for populations who in normal times were socially and politically relegated to the lower levels of society. Thus, the soldier home from the front is seen differently from how he was previously by those who did not fight. Crowned with the victory of his camp and his supposed courage or stigmatized for acts of violence and abuse or even for his defeat, he has to face society's new projections. The return of former combatants to civilian life must therefore be considered interactively, in the sense that reintegration is not a simple matter of moving from the front to behind the front, but varies according to the interaction occurring on return with those who did not fight.

In the after-war, combatants can avail themselves of new or transformed resources—possibilities for leadership, command and discipline, supervision and administration of a territory, the embodiment of prestigious figures (heroism, bravura, patriotism, etc.), social networks constituted during the war, and so on—allowing them to rebuild their situations in a renewed fashion compared to the prewar period. It is interesting to observe whether and how certain transfers of dispositions, structures, and organizations constructed during the war operate in the after-war. To what extent are competences acquired during the war reinvested in after-war activities? Do these new dispositions serve as a springboard for a new career? In her chapter, Sandrine Perrot analyzes in great detail how in Uganda, certain Lord's Resistance Army (LRA) officers enjoyed upward mobility and became success figures mainly because the government instrumentalized them to put an end to the armed rebellion (Chapter Eight). After-war periods provide very different possibilities for ex-combatants, favoring upward mobility for some and precipitating others downward.

On a meso-sociological level, one should also analyze how organizations of armed struggle were later able to constitute the core of a political organization involved in the democratic political game, as David Garibay has shown in the case of several former Latin American guerrillas.[52] There are many examples of political parties that originate in armed struggle organizations and adopt their hierarchical structure.[53] Also, to what degree do the social networks and structures of armed rebellion underpin after-war organizations engaged in (more or less covert) economic activities: some combatants groups reconvert into organized criminality, while private security agencies founded and headed by former combatants flourish.

It should also be of interest to study possible phenomena of "dual transposition" of social properties: from before-war to war, then from war to after-war. On the subject of Serbian militiamen, Samuel Tanner points out that certain leisure activities practiced before the war (combat sports) or others of a professional nature (involving the use of a knife) were reappropriated during the war (Chapter Seven). Richard Banégas shows that among the men, who, beginning in 2002, took up arms in self-defense groups in Ivory Coast, were roadblockers who had scattered during the perilous transition period following the death of Félix Houphouët Boigny in the second half of the 1990s; since the war, these young ex-militiamen have been able to exert new influence on the political scene and on land issues, using their experience during the conflict (Chapter Eleven).

We will also be examining, inspired by the work of historians, if and to what extent war also induces a number of "cognitive" transformations, viewed here as representations, perceptions, and "cultural categories," as termed by Xavier Bougarel et al., put forward and developed after-war, especially by former combatants. Do postconflict representations remain informed by previous animosity and depreciation? Fabien Théofilakis describes the gradual cultural demobilization that took place in France between 1944 and 1949 in his analysis of the changing relationship between public opinion and German war prisoners, who, after embodying the figure of the enemy, slowly became rehumanized (Chapter Six). To what extent does the war experience encourage assigning one's own identity and/or the other's to ethnic or national categories? Does it allow (ethno) nationalist entrepreneurs to mobilize groups according to their ethnic[54] or national belonging? From a more psychosociological point of view, we wonder about the degree to which veterans' thoughts and representations remain influenced, if not haunted, by the past war, making for a specific sociability among ex-combatants (in particular via veterans associations) and an incommunicability vis-à-vis family and close friends,[55] as shown by Béatrice Richard on the subject of former Canadian Second World War combatants (Chapter Five). Samuel Tanner emphasizes that although mythical violence, i.e., as fantasized by the thurifers of a Great Serbia, is often a subject of conversation among former militiamen and aids in the mythifying of their combat, they have difficulty remembering and talking about violence they have actually experienced (Chapter Six). We will also analyze the effects of war on ex-combatants' representations of their collective future, or on the vision they develop of the future of their country and of the world in a renewed context of "peace."[56] Thus combat experience in the Sassari brigade was a decisive factor in the politicization of Italians born in Sardinia and mobilized during the First World War, as illustrated by Christophe Roux (Chapter Nine): thanks to a renewed awareness of their regional identity and sense of responsibility, the brigade's ex-combatants in fact became the major actors first in veterans associations, then in the regionalist movement. Again, Jessica Schafer stresses the fact that sometimes the war experience favors "a feeling of solidarity that goes beyond the usual limits of community and loyalties,"[57] as was the case for the West-African soldiers who fought in the French colonial army and in that context developed a Pan-African and egalitarian feeling. By setting in motion a process of commitment and collective mobilization, the war experience can have sociopolitical effects on the whole of society.

Should we then consider war as a *continuum*, as Paul Richards[58] proposes, and consequently deny the exceptionality of war? One of our intentions in this book is to discuss this continuist hypothesis. Richards' aim is noble: reject the gratuitous, mindless character of war and admit that political projects are carried out via war. We cannot but agree on that point. Yet perhaps the notion of continuum involves the risk of trivialization, of in-differentiation of war in relation to peace. It is possible—and even necessary—to conceive of wars, including the supposedly new intrastate wars, as Clausewitz does, i.e., a strategic use of violence to achieve political aims and to apprehend these wars (with the usual tools of the social sciences) as a social reality. But does that mean we can or should think of wars as an experience comparable to all other social experiences? Does that make war a relatively insignificant, nonexceptional experience?[59] One objection would be that violence occupies a particular place,[60] generates great insecurity, and confronts all who are in any way involved with the presence of death[61] (one's own, that of relatives and friends, of "comrades of the trenches," of the enemy, caused by oneself). As a result, the emotional intensity of wartime certainly differentiates it from times of peace. From that point of view, war is a break, to a greater or lesser degree, depending on one's social origins and one's previous universe where death existed on a relatively predictable horizon and physical violence was not so preponderant. For that reason, it is important to differentiate former combatants according to whether they issue from pacified societies—civilized in the sense of Norbert Elias (the psychic economy dominated by mechanisms of self-control)—or societies where physical violence has not evolved toward control and rarefaction. Depending on whether one comes from one or the other, rupture with the previous universe will be greater or lesser. But there is one aspect in which the rules of war are in total opposition with those of peaceful societies, whatever they may be, and that is in breaking with the principle on which all social order is based, one of its fundamental prohibitions: "Thou shalt not kill." For this reason, we cannot consider the state of war as being indistinct from the previous state of peace. Proof of this nontriviality of the violence of war and the disappearances it results in can be seen in issues involving memories of war, issues that resurface sometimes decades later,[62] as well as issues of justice and mourning involving victims and their families,[63] in addition to the specificity of traumas due to the war.[64]

This book also aims to study the effects of war on after-war with regard to violence. Does the transition from war to peace presuppose, as historians say, the *déprise* of violence? This notion brings us to the issue of cultural demobilization but also to that of brutalization. For Mosse, brutalization refers mainly to a transformation on the cognitive level (he speaks of the attitude of mind that issues from war—indifference toward human life and sensitivity), which seems to authorize a change in behaviors (aggressive attitudes, combative energy, cruel beatings). War is seen as a process of breakdown[65] during which civilization, "a thin veneer underneath which nature courses, waiting for a chance to break through,"[66] is put in parentheses, if not altered, leaving space for an outbreak of aggressive and violent primary instincts that continue to torment the individual after the war.

We would like to try to sociologize this notion. First, by stressing that Mosse's thesis, or the interpretations thereof, lacks a differentiation between the multiple actors in a conflict. More intuitive than rigorous,[67] his work does not give us a clear idea of who is being brutalized. Discussion among historians differentiates brutalization of societies and brutalization of combatants,[68] but is it reasonable to assume that an entire society changes its state of being? Or would it be wiser to consider that those most concerned by brutalization are ex-combatants, having been exposed to the violence of war, the propaganda, and social control that usually go along with it. If we follow this line of thought, we must then propose a very subtle approach to the type of war in which former combatants found themselves. Obviously, questioning will not have the same validity depending on whether they were confronted with extreme violence and death or not or whether they endured combat over a long or short period of time. Even so, which way the correlation will work is not always evident. Antoine Prost emphasizes that the "*poilus*" (French soldiers in the First World War) who were on the front over a long period time found that their "disposition to kill" became dulled, whereas those most "avid to kill a *Boche* are often the newcomers [...] who arrive at the front steeped in a culture of back home, where patriotic exaltation and hatred of the enemy reinforce each other."[69] It is important to bear in mind that this was not a homogeneous group of men and that the practice of war violence can vary, depending on the length of time in the midst of a conflict, the combatant's status in the army organization, the location, the period during which he fought, etc. There are also important differences according to the combatant's type of commitment: whether he was a professional soldier or a recruit; a volunteer soldier or mobilized by force; a mercenary or a fighter acting out of conviction. It would be interesting to see the effects of the professionalization of soldiers and their belonging to a very structured, hierarchical organization, in contrast—to reason in an ideal type manner—to cases in which they received only brief training and were part of a loose structure. Doubtless, combatants cope with afterwars very differently depending on whether they were previously trained, that is, accustomed to the outbreak and use of violence and to death, or whether they found themselves on the battlefield only shortly after having left civilian life and with minimal background preparation.

Brutalization should secondly be approached in relation to different types of war. Without presenting the notion of radically different new wars as our own,[70] we nonetheless underscore certain tangible changes in war itself, in particular the growing exposure of civilians,[71] who today are war's main victims, thus undeniably creating a terrain that favors the brutalization of societies. Nowadays, the issue of the aftermath of war is raised in a new way for civilians, compared to certain interstate wars studied by historians where there was a clear distinction between a particularly bloody military front and the homeland at peace, at least so long as there was no bombing—excessively deadly for civilians—to blur the distinction. Thought should also be given to the impact of official terminology describing the conflict. Whether it is called a war or not, as is the case in Turkey (where they prefer to speak of a "struggle against terrorism," as Sümbül Kaya shows in Chapter Two) or in Chechnya (where Russian authorities claimed to be leading an "operation to restore constitutional order" between 1994 and 1996, then a "struggle against terrorism" beginning in 1999,[72] as Anne Le Huérou and Élisabeth Sieca-Koslowski explain in Chapter One), it has repercussions on those who fought, if only because after the war they are recognized as ex-combatants or not, and are proposed mechanisms for reintegrating civil society or not. Recognition of the war as such opens the way for both material and symbolic public policies for veterans, thus easing their return. Based on her experience as a therapist with veterans, Françoise Sironi believes that "when [...] the transition from the world of war to that of society is not organized correctly, there may result a specific psychopathology [...]. This psychopathology is liable to rebound on the whole of civil society." She adds that "we have observed a causal link between the development of psychopathological problems of a traumatic or depressive nature and the lack of recognition as a former combatant."[73]

Doubtless, to be able to approach brutalization empirically, it needs to be viewed as the transposition of a "repertoire of action" belonging to the preceding armed conflict. A set of learned and internalized war tactics, may be revived during peacetime, most likely in specific facilitating contexts—situations that replay the conflict's main actors, as was the case in Russia when veterans of Chechnya found themselves in conflict with Chechen émigrés, as illustrated by Anne Le Huérou and Élisabeth Sieca-Koslowski in their study of certain acts of violence committed after the Chechnyan war (Chapter One). The concept of *habitus* should help refine questioning on the impact of exposure to and/or practice of violence and its possible postconflict transfer. Introduced by Norbert Elias and reworked by Pierre Bourdieu, this concept can be understood as "a system structured by lasting dispositions that can be transposed onto different life situations; forged by socialization [...] it functions like a matrix of perceptions, evaluations and actions [...]." This book poses the question of a possible *war habitus* or *habitus of violence*. The war experience is certainly a socializing one, it contributes to a secondary socialization whose after-war effects deserve to be studied.[74] Research on secondary socialization indicates that we should examine the reconfiguration of identity caused by certain life experiences of adults.[75] What does the war experience produce in the after-war, i.e., what are the repercussions, particularly on ex-combatants, of the use of violence, the practice of combat, the experience of living side-by-side with death and causing the death of others? To what degree does war bring about a trivialization of violence and human life that is transposed in the after-war? If so, this would cause former combatants to view violence and death as something banal and lead to more frequent recourse to violent acts. An indicator of this could be the increase in criminality in countries just exiting from war.[76] Does the war experience lead to a greater propensity to use violence, to settle conflicts by force rather than by compromise? Do transfers of "brutal dispositions" operate, and if so in what ways? Has there been a change in scale because of these transfers of violence—meso- and macro-sociological collective war violence being transposed postconflict on the micro-sociological level of interindividual relations, in the form of social, even domestic violence, as shown by Camille Boutron in her analysis of acts of violence toward women in the secrecy of the home (Chapter Three)? Are former combatants the primary vectors of it, and if so, which former combatants? Can we note any difficulty, on the part of combatants, to renounce once and for all the attributes of the combatant (rhetoric, attitudes, bearing)? Analyses of discourse and ethnographic observations could bring valuable answers to these questions.

This necessarily means studying issues involved in ending violence and possible obstacles to doing so. Is it a process that passes through successive stages, facilitated by certain rituals? According to Bruno Cabanes, there are three phases in demobilization: during the separation period, the soldier "no longer has physical contact with the combat zone, loses the company of some of his comrades and the proximity of those who died on the 'champ d'honneur'"; then comes a second phase, the construction of a new identity, a "liminal phase," to be followed by a third phase, or aggregation, returning to civilian life and reimmersing in its codes and rules.[77] In a country like Mozambique, the carrying out of "cleansing" rituals made possible a relatively exemplary reintegration of former combatants, even though there were a great many of them (approximately 100,000)—when purged of the spirits by which they were supposedly possessed during the conflict, they were able to turn the page and once again be considered the same as other members of the community.[78] Contrary to the public policies of even the most sophisticated Western countries, such as the one implemented in Canada after the Second World War and analyzed by Béatrice Richard (Chapter Five), based on a mechanistic conception of the return to civilian life, these rituals were able to purge the former combatant of his warrior attributes and favor his return to civilian life. On the contrary, as Sümbül Kaya shows (Chapter Two), public policies that mythify past combats and sanctify martyrs, such as those deployed in Turkey in connection with the armed conflict against Kurd separatists, favor a moral armament of Turkish society against its "internal enemy," which helps legitimize the continuation of military operations in Kurdistan.

To take the opposite point of view, it is not infrequent that former combatants enter a process of civilianization without major difficulties, returning fairly easily to the lives they led before the war. The brutalization process observed by Mosse in Germany was in fact absent in France and Great Britain, where on the contrary, war encouraged pacifism[79]: the war experience would therefore have no single effect (the perpetuation of violence) and, inversely, can engender a refusal of the violence of war. National differences in the trajectories of former combatants also have a great deal to do with the victory or defeat of their country. From that angle, conflicts ending with neither winner nor loser are often propitious settings for the start of a new conflict, each side hoping to eventually win out over the other.[80] Concerning Chechnya, Aude Merlin demonstrates how the ambiguity of the Khasav-Yurt ceasefire agreement, signed in 1996, has been a factor of reengaging in combat. Thus the element of context is indispensable. It is possible that post-conflict political opportunities have a bearing on the itineraries of former combatants: a context of victory encourages the founding of a new, pacified political society, and personal investment in organizations supporting it (political parties and interest groups in particular). A context of strong economic development tends to undermine attempts at mobilization based on maintaining polarization and combative positions, making the advantages of personal investment in the economic sphere seemingly more tangible. In sum, actors' interests vary according to the context in which the end of the conflict occurs: when favorable, thanks to a dynamic economy and/or military victory, the continuation of conflict rationales seems less attractive, whereas defeat and a ruined economy are more likely to feed into rationales for the pursuit of conflict. Far from being "brutalized," former combatants seem to remain rational actors able to evaluate the advantages and costs of the various possible postconflict reintegrations, in any case, capable of thinking out strategies, which does not mean that these strategies are not informed by their past as combatants—the continuation of a conflict may rest on their calculation that to end it will engender frustrations in the rank and file. This was observed in two cases as different as that of Chechnya, analyzed by Aude Merlin (Chapter Ten), and Colombia by Sophie Daviaud (Chapter Four). In the first case, the feeling that the peace agreement signed by Mashkadov in 1996 deprived the Chechens of a victory that was close at hand and that would have given Chechnya its independence led spoilers to undermine the pacification process and the construction of a state. In the case of Colombia, the way in which the process of demilitarization of paramilitaries was carried out fostered the sentiment that far left guerrillas had gained more from peace than the self-defense groups, who then began to remobilize and resume the armed struggle.

Thus it is important to examine the factors at work in postconflict rationales. Some after-war activities can be seen as simple strategies for reconverting skills acquired during the war. This is the case with private security companies, which often proliferate after the war and are set up and managed by former combatants. Becoming involved in a political party or other organization in the public sphere can also be seen as capitalizing on notoriety gained during the war and proximity with a territory and population acquired thanks to one's own military location. The analysis of after-war partisan recompositions should pay close attention to the places occupied by ex-combatants and the resources they invest. Such commitments should then be seen in the long-term trajectories so as to gauge the extent to which resources acquired during the war furthered the combatants' political careers.

Ex-combatants are sometimes reintegrated via bargaining, in the context of national reconciliation policies or international DDR programs. This shows they are likely to opt for peace when it seems advantageous to do so and to resume war when it does not. The role of such bargaining deserves careful consideration, since it breaks with a "top down" vision of peace processes and gives preference to a relational approach concerned with how former combatants and their organizations use their own combat to consolidate their post-conflict positions in a political context in the process of recomposition.[81]

So far as method is concerned, the heuristic approach would consist in taking a longitudinal view of ex-combatants in order to answer some of the previous questions—the concept of "career" would prove extremely useful. We propose, in fact, after Howard Becker, to consider the trajectory of former combatants as a "career" organizing itself in a series of objective situations each time favoring a recomposition of subjectivities.[82] In particular, this would make it possible to differentiate the temporalities of ex-combatants, which are not the same just before the war as after reintegration into civilian life. If at one moment it may make sense to choose peace, at another it may be more opportune to choose war, choices not made by actors who are spoilers in themselves, but actors whose after-war possibilities vary according to a more overall and evolving political, economic, and social context. As a result, given that their evaluations of the comparative values of war and peace will change along with the overall situation, analyses based on the immediate after-war are insufficient, and it is preferable to view the trajectories of former combatants on the longer term. Translated by Judith Andreyev.

Notes

1. It is hardly our intention to express the idea that political science is not concerned with international relations. But in France, the development of international relations has been carried out, on the whole, relatively independently of the other branches of political science, political sociology in particular; the questions raised by political sociology and those of international relations remain rather foreign to each other. One of our aims here is in fact to bring greater convergence to these questions.
2. In this overview, we will sometimes include, perhaps too freely, publications which on the institutional level deal with fields other than political science stricto sensu: sociology and anthropology in particular, based on a broad concept of political science, understood as the social sciences of politics.
3. Understood by I. W. Zartman (ed.), *Collapsed States: The Disintegration and Restoration of Legitimate Authority* (Boulder, CO: Lynne Rienner Pub., 1995), as "a situation where the structure, authority (legitimate power), law, and political order have fallen apart [...]"(1).
4. It then becomes a question of Security Sector Reform (SSR). This in particular relies on a reformatting of coercion forces, which most often means reducing the size of the army, but also, at times, on employing ex-combatants in the army or the police. Concerning the action of the UN in Kosovo in this domain, see N. Duclos, *Le Kosovo Police Service, facteur de consolidation de la paix au Kosovo?* (Paris: IHESI, 2003). On DDR/SSR interrelations, see Alpaslan Özerdem, *Post-war Recovery: Disarmament, Demobilization and Reintegration* (London, New York: I. B Tauris, 2009), 187ff.

5. M. R. Berdal, *Disarmament and Demobilization after Civil Wars: Arms, Soldiers and the Termination of Armed Conflicts* (Oxford: Oxford University Press, 1996), 45ff.
6. A change in attitude whose importance is often emphasized, notably in the case of the transformation of rebel organizations into political parties. See J. de Zeeuw (ed.), *From Soldiers to Politicians. Transforming Rebel Movements after Civil War* (London: Lynne Rienner, 2008); João Gomes Porto, Chris Alden, Imogen Parsons, *From Soldiers to Citizens: Demilitarization of Conflict and Society* (Aldershot: Ashgate, 2007), 147ff.
7. In 2006, 7 out of 22 DDR programs were led by one state only, according to Özerdem, *Post-war Recovery*, 14.
8. According to B. Pouligny, *Les anciens combattants d'aujourd'hui: désarmement, démobilisation et réintegration* [*The Politics and Anti-politics of Contemporary: "Disarmament, Demobilization & Reintegration" Programs*] (CERI, SGDN, PESI, 2004), 43ff.
9. See in particular C. Alden, "Making Old Soldiers Fade Away: Lessons from the Reintegration of Demobilized Soldiers in Mozambique," *Security Dialogue* 33, no. 3 (September 2002): 349ff.; or J. Mc Mullin, "Reintegration of Combatants: Were the Right Lessons Learned in Mozambique?," *International Peacekeeping* 11, no. 4 (2004): 625–643. Also Joao Gomes Porto, Chris Alden, Imogen Parsons, *From Soldiers to Politicians*.
10. John Galtung, *Peace: Research, Education and Action* (Copenhagen: Ejlers, 1975), 109ff.
11. K. Kingma, "Demobilization of Combatants after Civil Wars in Africa and Their Reintegration into Civilian Life," *Policy Sciences*, 30, no. 3 (August 1997): 154.
12. K. Kingma (ed.), *Demobilization in Sub-Saharan Africa: The Development and Security Impacts* (Basingstoke: Macmillan, 2000), 4.
13. International Peace Academy, *A Framework for Lasting Disarmament, Demobilization and Reintegration of Former Combatants in Crisis Situations*, 2002, 2ff. The authors add that furthermore, the understanding of reintegration runs up against a methodological problem because of the difficulty of evaluating it quantitatively.
14. R. Muggah (ed.), *Security and Post-conflict Reconstruction: Dealing with Fighters in the Aftermath of War* (London/New York: Routledge, 2009), 3.
15. Berdal, *Disarmament and Demobilization*, 5; R. Marchal and C. Messiant, *Les chemins de la guerre et de la paix: fins de conflit en Afrique orientale et australe* (Paris: Karthala, 1997), 7ff. Almost all more recent publications agree on this point—university publications, at least. See in particular R. Muggah, M. Berdal, S. Torjesen, "conclusion" in R. Muggah *Security and post-conflict*, 2009, 271ff.; Özerdem, op. cit ; M. Berdal and D. H. Ucko (eds.), *Reintegrating Armed Groups after Conflict: Politics, Violence and Transition* (London/New York: Routledge), 2009.
16. International justice tries to give priority to satisfying these expectations, according to E. Claverie, "Les victimes saisies par le Tribunal pénal international pour l'ex-Yougoslavie" *in* S. Lefranc (ed.), *Après le conflit, la réconciliation* (Paris: Michel Houdiard, 2006), 152ff.
17. M. Kaldor, *New and Old Wars: Organized Violence in a Global Era* (2006; Stanford, CA: Stanford University Press, 1999); H. Münkler, *The New Wars* (Cambridge: Polity Press, 2005 [Trad. *Die neuen Kriege*, 2002]).
18. K. Holsti, *The State, War, and the State of War* (Cambridge: Cambridge University Press, 1996).
19. S. J. Stedman, "Spoiler Problems in Peace Processes," *International Security* 22, no. 2 (1997): 5. For a critical reading on the spoilers debate, see M. J. Zahar, "Reframing the Spoiler Debate in Peace Processes," in John Darby and Roger McGinty (eds.), *Contemporary Peacemaking: Conflict, Violence and Peace Processes* (New York: Palgrave Macmillan, 2003), 114–124.
20. P. Collier, *Economic Causes of Civil Conflicts and Their Implications for Policy* (World Bank, June 15, 2000); M. Berdal and D. Malone, *Greed and Grievance: Economic Agendas of Civil Wars* (London/Boulder: Lynne Rienner, 2000). For a review, see R. Marchal and C. Messiant, "De l'avidité des rebelles: l'analyse économique de la guerre civile selon Paul Collier," *Critique internationale* 16 (July 2002): 58–69.
21. Berdal, *Disarmament and Demobilization*, 6ff.
22. Lefranc, *Après le conflit*,; G. Mink and L. Neumayer (eds.), *L'Europe et ses passés douloureux* (Paris: La Découverte, 2007).
23. On this subject, see K. Hill Hawk, *Constructing the Stable State: Goals for Intervention and Peacebuilding* (Westport, CT: Praeger Publishers, 2002); B. Pouligny and R. Pouyé,

"Le *state-building* au secours de la sécurité internationale?," *RAMSES 2004* (IFRI): 51ff.; R. Paris, *At War's End: Building Peace after Civil Conflict* (Cambridge: Cambridge University Press, 2004); F. Fukuyama, *State-building : Governance and World Order in the 21st Century* (Ithaca, NY: Cornell University Press, 2004).
24. R. Branche, "La dernière génération du feu? Jalons pour une étude des anciens combattants français de la guerre d'Algérie," *in* B. Cabanes and G. Piketty (eds.), "Sorties de guerre au XXe siècle," *Histoire@politique* no. 3 (November–December 2007).
25. G. L. Mosse, *Fallen Soldiers: Reshaping the Memory of the World Wars* (Oxford: Oxford University Press, 1990).
26. Annette Becker proposes to replace the notion of *brutalization* with "ensavagement" (*ensauvagement*) to mark "the internalisation and trivialization of war violence making it possible to durably accept all its aspects, even the most paroxysmal, and to reinvest them in the political domain after the war" *in* "Compte rendu de la traduction française du livre de Georges Mosse," *Annales* 1 (January–February 2000): 181.
27. Mosse, *Fallen Soldiers*, 159.
28. Ibid., 160.
29. Ibid., 7.
30. Among historians, this thesis is fiercely debated: some, working with CRID 14-18, challenge the central role attributed to cultures of war in the participation in combats, preferring to insist on the tenacity of conscripts. See Nicolas Mariot, "Faut-il être motivé pour tuer? Sur quelques explications aux violences de guerre," *Genèses* 4, no.53 (2003).
31. J. Horne and A. Kramer, *German Atrocities* (London/New Haven, CT: Yale University Press, 2001).
32. J. Horne (ed.), "Introduction," and "Démobilisations culturelles après la Grande Guerre" in *14-18: Aujourd'hui, Today, Heute* (Paris: Editions Noésis, 2002), 46.
33. Ibid., 45.
34. G. Piketty, "Économie morale de la reconnaissance. L'ordre de la Libération au péril de la sortie de la Seconde Guerre mondiale," *in* B. Cabanes and G. Piketty (eds.), "Sorties de guerre au XXe siècle."
35. Horne, *Démobilisations culturelles après la Grande Guerre*, 49ff.
36. Marchal and Messiant, *Les chemins de la guerre*, 8.
37. X. Bougarel, E. Helms, and G. Duijzings, *The New Bosnian Mosaic: Identities, Memories and Moral Claims in a Post War Society* (Aldershot: Ashgate, 2007), 20.
38. L. Bucaille (ed.), "Reshaping Identities in Post-conflict Societies: Ex-combatants, Heroes and Exiles," *International Social Science Journal* 58, no. 189 (September 2006): 425–432.
39. S. Audoin-Rouzeau and A. Becker, *14-18, retrouver la guerre* (2003 ; Paris: Gallimard, 2000), 50.
40. B. Cabanes, *La victoire endeuillée: La sortie de guerre des soldats français (1918–1920)* (Paris: Seuil, 2004); Stéphane Audoin-Rouzeau and Christophe Prochasson (eds.), *Sortir de la Grande Guerre: le monde et l'après-1918* (Paris: Tallandier, 2008).
41. P. Richards (ed.), *No Peace, No War: An Anthropology of Contemporary Armed Conflicts* (Athens, OH: Ohio University Press, 2005), 3.
42. Rather than "the evaluative focus [...] on the achievement (or not) of programmatic targets," Kathleen M. Jennings recommends analyzing "how DDR plays out on-the-ground [...]," *Seeing DDR from Below. Challenges and Dilemmas Raised by the Experiences of Ex-combatants in Liberia*, Fafo-report no.3, 2008: 5
43. Norma J. Kriger, *Guerilla Veterans in Post-War Zimbabwe: Symbolic and Violents Politics 1980–1987* (New York: Cambridge University Press, 2003), 21.
44. One has only to remember the exclusively negative adjectives used by Stephen J. Stedman to designate ex-combatants as possible future spoilers: "In war, there are combatants, who can be identified in myriad ways—for example, rebels, bandits, pariahs, rogues, or terrorists [...]," in "Spoilers Problems in Peace Processes," 7. At no point does the author perceive ex-combatants in a favorable light, for example, as heroes, patriots, combatants for freedom, etc.

45. See in particular Jessica Schafer, *Soldiers at Peace. Veterans and Society After the Civil War in Mozambique* (New York: Palgrave MacMillan, 2007).
46. This is evidenced by many DDR policies, which, in the case of ex-combatants, who were previously farmers, simply assume they will go back to the land, disregarding the new competencies acquired during their war experience, distancing them from their social group and leading them to no longer identify with it. See C. Alden, "Making Old Soldiers Fade Away," 350.
47. This approach disregards the nonetheless real transformations induced by the experience of combat, one that varies, obviously, according to the length of the conflict, its nature (low intensity conflict or not), the nature of engagement in the combat (forced or not), the duration of involvement in the combat, the position occupied by the combatant, etc.
48. Following on the wake of new wars. For a salutary critique, see Stathis Kalyvas, "'New' and 'Old' Civil Wars: A Valid Distinction?," *World Politics* 54, no. 1 (October 2001): 99–118; Roland Marchal, Christine Messiant, "Les guerres civiles à l'heure de la globalisation: nouvelles réalités et nouveaux paradigmes," *Critique internationale* 18 (January 2003): 91–112.
49. Producing the effect of a self-fulfilling prophecy, Alexandra Guaqueta stresses along these lines that the political reintegration of a rebel group like the M-19 in the 1970s in Colombia, turned out to be easier than that of paramilitaries in the 2000s, in particular because unlike the recent conflict, M-19 rebels were seen as bearing legitimate political demands, "The Way Back in: Reintegrating Illegal Armed Groups in Colombia Then and Now," in M. Berdal and D. Ucko (eds.), *Reintegrating Armed Groups,* (Abingdon: Routledge, 2009), 11ff.
50. Postulating, in the wake of economic theories of war, that involvement in armed conflict is a feature of "young, uneducated males" who are idle as a result. See Paul Collier et al., *Breaking the Conflict Trap: Civil War and Development Policy* (Washington DC: The World Bank/Oxford University Press, 2003), 68.
51. On this point, the comparison of historian/political scientist approaches shows the great value placed on fighting action that dominates many analyses of the two World Wars, whereas inversely, today's combatants are more often than not considered suspect; moved essentially by the desire for monetary gain, their combat is devoid of the heroic qualities attributed to the former allied combatants of the two World Wars.
52. D. Garibay, *Des armes aux urnes: processus de paix et réinsertion politique des anciennes guérillas en Colombie et au Salvador,* Doctoral thesis, IEP de Paris, 2003.
53. For example, the prime minister of Kosovo, Hachim Thaci, who declared the independence of his country on February 17, 2008, is none other than the former head of the Kosovo Liberation Army (KLA)!
54. As the SDA in Bosnia is attempting to do vis-à-vis Muslims. See X. Bougarel, "Death and the Nationalist: Martyrdom, War Memory and Veteran Identity among Bosnian Muslims," *in* X. Bougarel et al., *The New Bosnian Mosaic,* 167ff.
55. Relational difficulties, in particular with spouses and causing numerous divorces, have often been underscored, but they should be observed more systematically.
56. This was the case for former combatants in France between the two wars. Their personal investment in veterans associations benefited the pacifist movement. See A. Prost, *Les anciens combattants (1914–1939)* (Paris: Gallimard, 1977), 85ff.
57. Schafer, *Soldiers at Peace,* 12.
58. Richards, *No Peace, No War,* 5ff. A continuist hypothesis adopted also by Mariot in "Faut-il être motivé pour tuer ?," 169ff.
59. The research of Jessica Schafer seems to go in this direction. The author in fact points out that Mozambican former combatants' main reasons for complaint are not so much the violence of combats and the fear of death, as it is the separation from the family, deprivations, and forced transfers, in short, elements that are not specific to combatants and to the war they fought but that concern all people living in a space undergoing civil war, in "Guerillas and Violence in the War in Mozambique: Desocialization or Resocialization?," *African Affairs* 100, no. 399 (April 2001): 224.

60. Violence brought to light by certain historians, in particular Audoin-Rouzeau and Becker, *14-18*. See also S. Audoin-Rouzeau, *Combattre: une anthropologie historique de la guerre moderne, XIXe-XXIe siècle* (Paris: Seuil, 2008).
61. An aspect particularly stressed by Prost, *Les anciens combattants (1914–1939)*, 13ff.
62. See how the emblematic case of Spain, which, for a long time, was presented as a "model of democratic transition" based on a pact of silence, has in the past few years reopened Pandora's box, in particular via the association for the recovery of historic memory. On this question, see D. Rozenberg, "Mémoire, justice et . . raison d'État dans la construction de l'Espagne démocratique," *Histoire@politique: Politique, culture et société* 2 (September–October 2007), online since October 18, 2007, at www.histoire-politique.fr. One should also keep in mind other European cases, such as that of the Germans and Sudetans, analyzed by Muriel Blaive in "De la démocratie tchèque et des décrets Benes," in Mink and Neumayer (eds.), *L'Europe et ses passés douloureux*. See the phenomenon of return of memory concerning conflicts and acts of violence "forgotten" during decades, both in Algeria and in relation to colonization, as evidenced in recurrent debates in France in the 2000s.
63. The case of the Plaza de Mayo Mothers (now grandmothers) in Chili, whose demands impeded the peace process, according to Daniela Cuadros Garland. See "La commission Rettig. Innovation, silences et contestations d'une mise en récit 'consensuelle' des violations des droits de l'homme au Chili," in Lefranc, *Après le conflit, la réconciliation?*, 208ff.
64. See the questions of post traumatic stress disorder (PTSD) concerning Vietnam veterans in particular. On this subject, see G. Boulanger and C. Kadushin, *The Vietnam Veteran Redefined: Facts and Fiction* (Hillsdale, NJ: L. Erlbaum, 1986).
65. For a presentation/discussion, see S. N. Kalyvas, *The Logic of Violence in Civil War* (Cambridge: Cambridge University Press, 2006), 55–58.
66. Hermann Löns in Mosse, *Fallen Soldiers*, 162.
67. Fleeting intuitions, says Becker in her "Compte rendu," 181.
68. A. Prost, "Brutalisation des sociétés et brutalisation des combattants" in B. Cabanes, E. Husson and O. Bartov (eds.), *Les sociétés en guerre. 1911–1946* (Paris: Armand Colin, 2003), 99ff.
69. A. Prost, "Les limites de la brutalisation. Tuer sur le front occidental. 1914–1918," *XXe siècle: Revue d'histoire* 81 (January–March 2004): 14.
70. On this point, we fully agree with the well-advised criticisms of R. Marchal and C. Messiant, "Les guerres civiles à l'ère de la globalisation. Nouvelles réalités et nouveaux paradigmes," *Critique internationale*, no.18, January 2003; and of S. N. Kalyvas, "Les guerres civiles après la guerre froide," *in* P. Hassner and R. Marchal (eds.), *Guerres et sociétés: État et violence après la guerre froide* (Paris : Karthala, 2003), 107 ff.
71. H. Münkler, op. cit.; Human security report 2005, *War and peace in the 21st century* (Oxford: Oxford University Press, 2005).
72. We are reminded, of course, of the fact that for many years France refused to speak of a war in Algeria, giving preference to the notions of "maintenance of law and order" or of "events." On the effects of this nameless war on French and Algerian societies, see B. Stora, *La gangrène et l'oubli. La mémoire de la guerre d'Algérie* (Paris: La Découverte Poche, 2005 [1998]).
73. F. Sironi, *Psychopathologie des violences collectives: Essai de psychologie géopolitique clinique* (Paris: Odile Jacob, 2007), 110 and 126.
74. From this point of view, the case of child soldiers is distinct from that of other combatants, since war intervenes in the primary socialization phase, the combatant milieu replacing the family. The impact of war experience on a child would therefore seem to be greater than on an adult.
75. Used by Claude Dubar to describe the effects of professional experiences, the notion of secondary socialization deserves being tested for other experiences, such as that of war. See C. Dubar, *La socialisation: construction des identités sociales et professionnelles* (Paris: A. Colin, 1995).
76. An avenue of research suggested by Mosse and considered with a great deal of precaution by Cabanes (*La victoire endeuillée,* 502), who emphasizes in particular the methodological difficulties. We observe nonetheless that several Latin American countries are concerned by these

phenomena of postwar rise in criminality, though it remains to be seen whether former combatants are at the source of it. According to Joanna Bourke, research by criminologists on acts of violence by former combatants concludes that they are no different from the rest of the population on this point. *An Intimate History of Killing: Face-to-Face Killing in Twentieth-Century Warfare* (London: Granta Books, 1999).

77. Cabanes, *La victoire endeuillée*, 278.
78. P. Granjo, "The Homecomer: Postwar Cleansing Rituals in Mozambique," *Armed Forces and Society* 33, no. 3 (April 2007): 382–395.
79. A phenomenon considerably underestimated by Mosse, if we agree with Antoine Prost, "Brutalisation des sociétés et brutalisation des combatants", *in* B. Cabanes, E. Husson and O. Bartov (eds.), *Les sociétés en guerre*, 104ff. Also in Sardinia, there was first a democratic mobilization after the First World War, under the aegis of former combatants (see Chapter Nine).
80. This observation leads some theoreticians of international relations to advise nonintervention and allow one camp to win out over the other, a victory of this kind seemingly a condition for peace. See Edward N. Luttwak, "Give War a Chance," *Foreign Affairs* 78, no. 4 (1999): 36–44.
81. This is the case in Kosovo, as I showed in my article "Pacification sans reconciliation," in Lefranc, *Après le conflit,* 271ff.
82. H. S. Becker, *Outsiders* (Paris: Métailié, 1985), p. 47.

PART 1

Veterans' Habitus of War, Brutalization of Societies?

CHAPTER ONE

A "Chechen Syndrome"? Russian Veterans of the Chechen War and the Transposition of War Violence to Society

Anne Le Huérou and Elisabeth Sieca-Kozlowski[1]

"During the Chechen campaigns, it was an error to call on police units normally in charge of maintaining public order. Policemen found themselves in a situation where they had to shoot people, to kill and be shot at. They returned home in a state of total psychological shock, and were expected to go back to maintaining public order. The "Chechen syndrome" is rife in the police force, transmitted from "policemen from Chechnya" to those who had no part in antiterrorist operations. This is evidenced in the many cases of abuse perpetrated against citizens by men in uniform."[2]

Ruslan Aushev, former president of Ingushetia, 2004.

Abstract

This chapter is a study of Russian veterans after the Chechen conflict and the trajectories both of demobilized soldiers and policemen returning to their previous law enforcement functions. The authors explore the hypothesis that the war experience is transposed into episodes of postwar violence. They also bring in related elements, such as prewar experiences in institutions where brutality is common (army, police) and government policies implicitly or explicitly authorizing violence.

The man who spoke these words was speaking from experience: previously in the upper ranks of the Russian army, the former Ingush president witnessed the gradual deterioration of the behavior of policemen sent to Chechnya. What he describes and what journalists and experts refer to as the "Chechen syndrome," calling to mind other individual and collective postwar traumas (Vietnam, Afghanistan, etc.), is one of the many facets of the itineraries of the Russian veterans of the Chechen wars. This chapter will focus on the men who in one function or another took part in military operations in Chechnya[3]; on one hand, it will examine the building blocks of these itineraries and, on the other, the institutional, political, and social context on which they depend.

Exactly what to call the situation in Chechnya in 2009—postwar, low-intensity conflict, regime of terror—would be the subject of another discussion. Yet at the same time, the inability to assign a name to the war is not unrelated to the acts of violence committed, both on the field and on return. Russians and Chechens still bear the scars of an "anti-terrorist operation," which continues to be deadly, with tens of thousands of victims, despite the fact that its official end was decreed by the Chechen president Ramzan Kadyrov on April 16. The Chechen war is one of those situations in which "the page has been turned without having been read,"[4] leaving its protagonists in the grip of individual and collective traumas produced by the war and the brutalization they carry within.

Our principal hypothesis is that "having been through Chechnya" both favors and authorizes acts of violence. Added to this is the role played by a propitious social and institutional environment, either in the content of political discourse or in what is kept silent. While the particularly brutal violence that took place in Chechnya is typical of an extreme situation, it also reflects the export onto military terrain of forms of violence preexisting in society and institutions, notably in the police force and the army, the main suppliers of participants in operations. We will therefore try to understand how these rationales work together in a phenomenon of dual transposition.

Rather than unwind the thread of a direct causal relationship between the war experience and the violence in Russian society, we will examine a combination of *micro* factors (the socialization of the individual), *meso* factors (the war experience and the institutions frequented by the veteran before, during, and after), and *macro* factors (the war in the Russian political context). In our view, a variable combination of these three factors, rather than each one taken separately, will give us the most accurate picture of this dynamic of transposition. We will observe how the "Chechen syndrome" feeds on war violence as a "propitious terrain," before discussing the significance of state policies concerning veterans.

Is the Chechen War Experience a Factor in The Brutalization of Veterans?

Is There a "Chechen Syndrome"?

Since the beginning of the 2000s, Russian publications have used the term "Chechen syndrome"[5] to describe the reproduction of war experiences by Chechen veterans, whether it concern their transposing of repressive methods similar to the "clean-up operations" executed by law enforcement officials or scattered acts of violence aimed at Chechens or other minorities living on Russian territory. Psychological in nature and recalling the Vietnam War, the term is used to describe a *transposition* of the violence of the Chechen conflict, repressive methods in particular, to other regions of Russia and other categories of the population. The following episodes and facts illustrate these transpositions,[6] though we will guard against generalizations and single interpretations.

Violent Acts Committed by "Veterans in Uniform"

Although most veterans of Chechen operations come from the federal army, if we wish to gain insight into the veteran question in Russia today and its impact on society, it is important to look at the whole of this multifaceted population: part of its forces, on return to normal life, are in direct contact with the population—for example, local community policemen, who make up the core of the public security forces in Russia, or road police, or the troops of the Justice Ministry—whereas the other part returns to its training and special missions (federal army forces, special forces of the Defense Ministry), where they have less contact with the overall population. Between the two, there is the particular question of the OMON (special troops), who are an integral part of the public security police but were created only recently (in the 1980s) to counter political manifestations, before being widely used at "hot spots."

The violent acts committed in Blagoveshchensk illustrate one aspect of the Chechen syndrome featuring a large number of professional policemen serving in alternation in Chechnya. In December 2004, under the pretext of an operation to fight against delinquency ("a preventive measure for restoring public order"), an order given by the Ministry of Internal Affairs of the Republic,[7] this city in Bashkortostan (an autonomous republic in the Volga region) was the scene of massive acts of abuse on the part of special police units. Over a period of five days, they raided the entire city and held nearly a thousand inhabitants out of Blagoveshchensk's 30,000, using surrounding techniques and mass arrests characteristic of the cleanups that took place in Chechnya, to the extent that one of the victims' lawyers referred to the infamous Chechen "filtration camps."[8] The Ministry of the Interior's special troops (OMON), who took part in this operation, as well as some local police who went along with them, had returned from a mission in Chechnya. In this particular case, the individual and collective experience acquired and practiced as policemen in Chechnya seems to have been reenacted in what should have been a simple police operation. Many similar instances have been recorded, mainly by journalists and associations.[9]

The brutal behavior of the OMON during political gatherings and meetings of the opposition[10] also reveals a certain *continuum* established by the policemen themselves between enforcing the law in Chechnya and supervising these meetings, which in their view required the professionalism of special forces. Thus an OMON declared: "Who else can we call on in such cases?"[11] An officer of these special forces describes the same mechanism—he deplores it, but can do nothing about it. "Try to understand me. Do you have any idea what we do in Chechnya?[12] Do you realize what we do there, how we arrest people? And after that, as soon as we get back, they send me and my detachment to patrol the streets, to arrest tramps and alcoholics at night. You can imagine how we carry out these detentions—they shouldn't let us come anywhere near living people..."[13]

Comments like these were reported by researchers from the Demos Center in five Russian regions[14] during a study aimed at analyzing the mechanisms through which the war experience is carried over into policemen's everyday professional functions after their return. The study focuses less on the psychological aspects of individual trauma and more on its consequences on daily relationships with the population, the hierarchy, colleagues, and others. The border line between terrorists, persons disobeying the law, and ordinary civilians seems completely blurred on the field and distorted by fear. On their return, and for lack of any rehabilitation other than a few days off work, the men most often continue to apprehend those they have to deal with in this same mode of blurredness.[15] One notable result of this widely observed brutalization is a deprofessionalization: policemen become isolated and marginalized by society; little by little they lose interest in the public good, which normally guides them in their profession, and, at least when not totally withdrawn into themselves, they seek by all possible means to get back to the field of operations, since only combat experience continues to give meaning to their profession.[16]

Many testimonies, including criminal cases, recorded by lawyers and associations for the defense of human rights emphasize acts of violence committed in police stations against Chechens living in Russia.[17] In some cases, the policeman himself makes the connection: "I killed the likes of you in Chechnya." Hierarchical superiors can then use the fact of having been through Chechnya as an explanation or an excuse: one woman in charge of an association for human rights, who intervened during a brutal police check in the street was insulted by the policeman in charge of the control and summoned to the commissariat. The superior said to her: "You have to excuse him, he's back from Chechnya, he doesn't like Chechens, Uzbeks, Jews and other Caucasians."[18]

Similar testimonies can be found in Tatarstan, where members of orthodox Muslim groups were accused and often imprisoned in the framework of anti-extremist and anti-terrorist laws in Russia. Often victims of maltreatment and torture or their families and friends claim that policemen, detention center guards, and investigating officers of the prosecution often mention the fact of having fought in Chechnya.[19] In a way, the image of the potential terrorist that the authorities have maintained since autumn 1999, when the war resumed around the "wahhabi" fighter and his supposed links with a vague Islamic conglomeration operating in several Russian regions with a view to setting up a caliphate, was extended to regions with strong Muslim minorities. In a context of reinforced federal control over the regions and in the aim of demonstrating their loyalty to Moscow, police authorities are keen to show how efficient they are in the fight against terrorism.

Acts of Violence Committed by Veterans Returning to Civilian Life
Most veterans of the second Chechen conflict were volunteers; their situation thus differs from that of 1996 or Afghanistan veterans, made up of entire classes of recruits of a specific age at a time when young men were only rarely able to escape military service and when draft and dispatch to Afghanistan affected all social categories, including university graduates. This was seldom the case in the second Chechen war. Does that mean that different sociological profiles had different postconflict itineraries? Such a hypothesis would be impossible to prove or disprove, if only because the chronology of the conflict and the overall context in Russia differed from those of the Afghan conflict.

Itineraries of return to "civilian" life do have a few points in common however, particularly as concern jobs in private security companies. From the start of their existence, these companies were a choice refuge for Afghanistan veterans and have remained so for Chechen veterans. They are often the source of violent incidents—in Kaliningrad, the security service of an enterprise beat up migrants from Central Asia with the words "they killed our guys in Chechnya, now we'll get our revenge."[20]

The Kondopoga episode—which left its mark on people's minds in the autumn of 2006, to the point of generating changes in migratory policies as well as hot debates in Parliament and the media on the notion of a "tolerance threshold" vis-à-vis foreigners—is different in the sense that it pitted young Russians against young Chechens living in a crisis (monoindustry) city in the northwest of Russia in what bore a closer resemblance to a riot than to a police operation. In this small city of the Republic of Karelia located on the Finnish border, a brawl in a bar held by Caucasians degenerated into a riot that lasted several days; the local situation, already tense, was fuelled by official discourse and by the arrival, for reinforcement, of DPNI militants (movement against illegal immigration), a far-right group known for its many racist attacks. In what was often presented as the first large-scale, interethnic riot in Russia, young Chechens living in the region fought against recently demobilized parachutists with whom they had earlier enjoyed occasional neighborly friendships: the presence of a heavily militarized patriotic club obviously favored the explosion of violence, but the club included in its members both young Chechens and young veterans. Here again, we cannot be sure of the part played by the "Chechen syndrome" in relation to other, more structural social factors.

The nature of the combats and acts of violence perpetrated by the various forces present in Chechnya allow us to put together a first set of links between the "Chechen syndrome" and the terrain of the Chechen war.

A Particularly "Brutalizing" War?[21]

After a first conflict that lasted from December 1994 to August 1996 and numbered between 50,000 and 100,000 victims, the war resumed in late summer 1999 after three years of de facto independence—a period marked by economic and political chaos, an increase in hostage-taking, and a growth of radical movements challenging the authority of the elected president, Aslan Maskhadov. The invasion of Dagestan and a series of deadly explosions in Russia headed by two warlords, Khattab and Basayev allowed the latter to launch a new military intervention. After a first phase of deadly and indiscriminate bombings that led to a sizeable exodus of refugees, massive "clean-up" operations followed by more targeted retaliation operations began in 2004. The Russian forces then gradually withdrew to be replaced by special forces or Chechen militia.

The two conflicts gave rise to acts of extreme violence, both in the treatment of Chechen fighters and toward the civil population. As many as 140,000 armed men—troops of the Defense Ministry, special police forces, and various security services—were massively present on a territory the size of three French departments. In 2007, with normalization, as well as the transfer of operations to Chechen forces already well under way, there were still 80,000 Russian soldiers and policemen in Chechnya. These forces led systematic operations of repression, during which they massively and repeatedly violated human rights. Russian forces systematically practiced illegal detentions, torture, disappearances, summary executions, and collective massacres of both the civil population and combatants. These violations were committed in legal detention centers, such as the ORB-2 bureau in Grozny, or in illegal and thus officially nonexisting places such as the Chernokozovo filtration camp.[22] Their brutality and systematic character were made possible by official discourse that not only failed to condemn but also authorized and even encouraged recourse to violence against the whole of the Chechen population, designated as potential terrorists. This amalgamation greatly contributed to forging the "image of the enemy," both in the military on the terrain and in the whole of Russian society as well.

On the military level, the massive use of heavy artillery made this conflict one of the most brutal to take place in an urban environment—American military specialists consider urban guerrilla combat to be the most traumatic type of combat.[23] In 1996, a study[24] made by a Russian military psychiatrist of Russian recruits having participated in the first Chechen war showed that proportionally, there had been more victims of psychiatric disorders in Chechnya than in Afghanistan (a war in a mountainous terrain). The author describes the various pathologies and neurological disorders recorded in Chechnya, and observes that out of 1,312 soldiers examined, "28% are in good health, whereas 72% suffer from psychic disorders such as insomnia, lack of motivation, intense anxiety, neuro-emotional stress, fatigue and hypochondriacal obsessions."

The conditions under which the fighting took place were arduous and stressful. The configuration of Grozny itself, with its vast network of linked-up cellars and caves, gave the guerrillas the advantage of surprise—at least at the start of the first war—enabling them to shoot up anywhere at any moment and attack the Russian forces. Badly planned and carried out in difficult climatic conditions, combat revealed the insufficient training of the Russian troops. Poor coordination resulted in numerous cases of friendly fire; thus, in August 1996 in Grozny, the troops of the Ministry of Internal Affairs were caught in a trap and bombed massively by the Russian federal army.[25] Russian forces found themselves faced with enemies who spoke their language, whereas they themselves understood no Chechen; many Chechen guerrillas, having earlier spent three years in the Russian army, knew Russian military tactics and culture and were able to foresee the movements of Russian troops[26] and even intercept their radio messages.

Combats thus took place in an atmosphere of permanent suspicion toward any and all individuals, men, women, and children, an atmosphere intensified by the declarations of General Kazantsev, designating all Chechens between the ages of 10 and 65 as potential terrorists.[27] The mutilations and tortures inflicted on Russian prisoners, whose bodies were found decapitated, increased the stress and fatigue of combats.

How the war evolved can be seen in the changes in composition of the forces. During the first conflict, the 45,000 men present on the terrain included soldiers from the federal army, troops from the Ministry of Internal Affairs, the special forces of the Military Intelligence,[28] and the FSB (Federal Security Service—former KGB). The contingent of the first two was essentially made up of recruits from a segment of the population unable to escape military service because unconnected to networks that could help them get round it—many had dropped out of school and were in poor health.[29] Furthermore, with the exception of the special forces, their training was rough and failed to prepare new recruits to control their reactions on the terrain, thus increasing stress, fear, and the indiscriminate and disproportionate use of force.

During the second Chechen war, much more diversified, combined forces were being used; besides the regular federal army troops (still made up of recruits, at least at the beginning of the war), there were troops from the Internal Ministry (MVD), elite troops, and police forces of the

Internal Ministry,[30] some members of the road police, troops from the Federal Border Service, from the railroads, special forces from the Justice Ministry,[31] troops from the Ministry of Urgent Situations (MTchS), members of the reserves, and *kontraktniki* (military under contract recruited in the context of the professionalization of the Russian army). When combat was at its most intense, 60,000 members of the armed forces were present on the terrain, with an estimate of some 40,000 more from the MVD— the exact numbers have never been disclosed.

The multiplicity of forces engaged was in itself a factor favoring disproportionate acts of brutality, due to the long-time vagueness in the command chain and the resulting dilution of responsibility. On the terrain, soldiers often felt left to their own devices and as a result there was no real supervision of the group's behavior. However traumatizing and brutalizing the experience of the war, that alone was not responsible for the violence observed; to a great extent, the "Chechen syndrome" was also favored by elements upstream of the war.

A "Propitious Terrain" for Brutalization

Aside from the aforementioned factors, what we mean by "propitious terrain" is an overall context, which, on *meso* and *macro* levels, resonates and interacts with the war experience; rather than distancing or confining it, it feeds into it *upstream* and favors violence *downstream*.

Examining *upstream* factors means first and foremost underlining the importance of violence in the internal socialization process in military and police institutions and in the daily practices of these institutions: vis-à-vis soldiers inside the army and citizens as concerns of the various police forces. In our view, the violence proper to all institutions of control and coercion seems in the case of Russia, to have been trivialized to the point that it can be considered a founding principle of both "professional practice" and an attitude toward the population in general.

Within the army, *dedovshchina*, brutal and humiliating hazing practiced on young recruits and responsible in peace time for many deaths and suicides among draftees,[32] is at the source of numerous psychic disorders among recruits and testifies to the culture of violence that reigns in the officers' corps. Some conscripts were forced by their superiors to sign engagements for several years in the army using such techniques. Presented as a measure designed to speed up the professionalizing of the army, *dedovshchina* also made it possible to find "volunteer" conscripts to serve as *kontraktniki* in Chechnya.[33]

Acts of violence among the military, especially on the part of officers or the more experienced *kontraktniki*, against newly arrived recruits should also be mentioned as a contributing factor to heightened war violence. Soldiers who had been beaten up or abused by their superiors in the barracks before their departure for Chechnya often tended to reenact these same procedures vis-à-vis the Chechen population— their own violence being a reflection of what they had been subjected to. These concomitant phenomena were also observed on the terrain when soldiers were put by their superiors in underground prisons *(zindan)* along with Chechen civilians.

Recourse to torture to obtain confessions is widely practiced in police stations throughout the country. Various studies and inquiry reports, opinion polls, and some official denunciations are testimony to the massive nature of the acts of violence perpetrated by law enforcement agents[34] and the various "entrepreneurs of violence."[35] The habitus of violence thus existed previous to the war experience and was related to the socialization of the policemen and soldiers. Whether it was a question of socialization previous to their entry into the institution or acquired during their professional apprenticeship is yet another question, rooted in two different theoretical concepts of closed institutions—the first involves specific production places for a violence of "extreme groups,"[36] and the second consists of "small societies" that replicate a "large society"[37] marked by the violence of its history—imprisonment in Stalinist camps, for example. In his desire to protect veterans as a social group that he feels is basically a victim, the veteran and writer A. Babchenko[38] agrees with this hypothesis —when he speaks of the brutalization of society that preexisted the war and that would explain the violence committed later, as much as the reverse relation.

On their return, will policemen use the war experience to justify in their own eyes the violence they perpetrate, to frighten the accused by explicit reference to a conflict known for its brutality? Or did Chechnya serve as an apprenticeship for brutal methods, which would be that much easier to put into practice later on, when the person, or target-group, was presented in a similar light to the Chechen enemy? Do these "entrepreneurs of violence" operate only on that single level? Violent deaths of all kinds occur in Russia. Its population is half that of the United States, yet in 2003, it had twice as many violent deaths.[39] Other variables also come into play inside the institution, in particular, signals emanating from the hierarchy. On the basis of data gathered in the Demos inquiry, A. Novikova emphasizes the importance of command, both in matters involving soldiers' behavior in Chechnya and in law enforcement operations.[40]

However, the downward spiral often associated with trauma, war/drugs or alcohol/delinquency, and violence can also work in the other direction, as illustrated by the testimony of one policeman questioned, who chose the profession so as to "escape the fate of fellow schoolmates who were either dead, alcoholic, or in prison." The same question arises in relation to the documentary by Manon Loizeau, *Les âmes perdues de l'armée russe* [The Russian Army's Lost Souls], the story of the impossible return to civilian life of veterans of the Urals—did the desocialization, the lack of moral and ethical standards, the latent or actual violence exist prior to the war experience? Or should we see them as factors that favored going to Chechnya?

Thus the "Chechen syndrome"—a causal relation between police violence and the fact of having been through Chechnya—may not always be relevant and may cover up more important, structural problems related to the institution of the police itself. The amplitude of acts of police violence committed in the Tver region suggests such a possibility: grave incidents took place shortly after Blagoveshchensk, but no explicit link was made between the policemen responsible for these acts and their having been through Chechnya. The incident itself, however, was immediately likened to Blagoveshchensk, and therefore to the "Chechen syndrome."[41] Similarly, the inquiry carried out by a team of sociologists who specialized in the police and the Nizhni-Novgorod Committee Against Torture[42] does not mention having been through Chechnya among the causes of police violence cited.

While we cannot determine with any certainty the direction of the relation, we can say that the experience of war violence is widely trivialized among veterans and revived during their frequent friendly and informal get-togethers, as during official commemorations.[43] Furthermore, the very fact that they refer to Chechnya when they think about or commit acts of violence or torture in another context that seems to show that the war experience has its fallout, even if in words only.

The second component of the "propitious terrain" consists of a combination of institutional mechanisms and official rhetoric widely relayed by the media and mass culture, along with a frame of mind on the part of the population, which all together create an environment particularly favorable to a continuum between war experience and practices implemented on return. The "Chechen terrorist" was an excellent crystallizer of the image of the "enemy,"[44] before being gradually replaced by other inside enemies present to threaten the Russian population, its regained well-being, its purity, traditions, and power.

These elements doubtlessly fuelled violence on the terrain, at least by implicitly authorizing it and at times encouraging it; all the more so as the crimes enjoyed broad impunity and continue to do so, the lenience of justice has run into no opposition from public opinion, neither indifferent to nor tolerant of such violence.[45] Needless to say, instances of mistreatment and torture, as were perpetrated by American soldiers in Afghanistan and Iraq, are a reminder that even military institutions that boast a well-tried discipline and code of ethics are not safe from abuse of power. In the global fight against terrorism, they too are part of the generally propitious environment. However, such slippages are far more systematic and far greater in the case of Russia and the Chechen war due to the lack of any institutional or societal counterweight.[46] Continually present in Russia, they have also contributed to the transposition of these behaviors and practices from the terrain to civilian life, as witnessed by the multiplication of xenophobic and racist acts in Russia in the 2000s.[47] This phenomenon is not simply the legacy of Chechnya but part of an overall climate starring an official discourse that relays, or at least does not counter the fabrication of an image of the enemy and favors the slippage from one target to another.

Whether the above phenomena mean that war violence transposes directly into civilian life or that it is part of a more complex circuit up or downstream from the Chechnya experience, there is clearly a continuum linking together the various factors mentioned: an initial tolerance of mistreatment within police and prison institutions; the fact that the practice and observation of acts of violence and torture in Chechnya were, if not encouraged, at least left unpunished; the fabrication of an enemy figure whose extension beyond Chechnya has been maintained thanks to the anti-terrorist rhetoric of the authorities, and integrated all the more successfully given that the forces of public order in charge of applying this policy have been through Chechnya themselves.

We will now turn to the Russian state's policies concerning veterans and to the effects of its stance in relation to the war.

The State Confronted with the War and Its Veterans

Our second aim will be to show that the state's denial, confronted with the war and its veterans, is an essential element in the nonreintegration of former combatants. Our demonstration will be supported by the research of Françoise Sironi that establishes a "causality between the development of psychopathological problems of a traumatic or depressive native and the lack of social recognition as former combatants," notably in the case of veterans of Afghanistan.[48] The clinical approach therefore shows that psychological troubles do not result solely from wars. In the case of wars that were lost or not acknowledged as such, "the impact of the *non-thought* and *non-organized* transition from combat life to civilian life" is to be taken into consideration, as it is the cause of a specific suffering.[49]

Nonrecognition of a War: The Eclipse of Violence, a Factor in the Trivialization of That Violence

One cannot discuss the issue of Chechen veterans without examining state policy toward them. The status of veterans and the social policy concerning them depends to a great extent on how the state defines war: if it refuses to call a conflict a "war," then the war does not exist and there are no veterans. The official aim of the first Chechnya conflict was to "restore constitutional order" and the second, beginning in 1999, was fought in the name of the "struggle against terrorism." It was only in 2002 that an addition to the previously cited law of 1994 put Chechnya on the list of "veterans of operations outside Russian borders" and granted veterans a legal status, along with rehabilitation measures and financial compensation. As noted by Serguei Oushakine, before the publication of this addition, veterans of Chechnya were handed documents in which they were categorized as invalids of the Great Patriotic War.[50]

The "absence" of war brought about a denial of the existence of veterans and their sufferings, and therefore a belated system of care for this population (more systematic care began in the army in 2000 and in the police in 2002). The announcement of the official end of operations in Chechnya in 2006 was another blow—from then onward, policemen have continued to be sent to Chechnya on missions of public order and assistance in the training of Chechen police, while remaining the target of attacks. But since they are considered as operating in a peaceful context, their real experience is the subject of an even greater denial.

Whereas the state refuses the word "war," policemen unanimously use it. This institutional denial, along with the numerous obstacles encountered in the exercise of justice in Russia, has contributed to the fact that the large majority of those who commit crimes against the civilian population go unpunished. The notable exceptions to the rule, such as the trials of Budanov or Ulman, also confirmed it, in the sense that they aroused sympathy in favor of the accused rather than the victims.[51] And despite the fact that the many cases brought before the European Court of Human Rights have all condemned the Russian state, the latter has never prosecuted the military officers responsible for the offences. This impunity contributes in a large measure to the trivialization of the violent acts committed and to their extension outside the territory and context of the conflict, as we have seen in the case of Blagoveshchensk or in the abusive remarks made in police stations.

The state delegates the problem of caring for veterans, for whom they have no exact numbers, to associations and to society. There is no official data on the number of victims in the Russian army for the Chechnya wars.[52] Although veterans associations estimate that the counting of the missing and dead in Afghanistan is not finished, official figures that have nonetheless been published (listing the number of dead, wounded, missing, invalids by category, etc.)[53] tend to agree with Western estimates.[54] The situation is completely different for the Chechnya campaigns: the only estimates are those made by Russian military journalists or Western military specialists. In 2007, they estimated that when the conflict was at its height, there were 100,000 men on the terrain, which means that in 12 years, according to the principle of rotation, 1.8 million men would have been on the terrain, without counting the missions of special or combined units.[55] The rare figures published by the official military press encompass all veterans, from the Great Patriotic War to the present, and estimate the figures at a total of one million, of whom 117,000 veterans of the Great Patriotic War.[56] Such enormous discrepancies make it impossible to evaluate needs.

Some veterans associations, in particular the organization Boevoe Bratstvo (Combat Brotherhood), have set up a data base to count the number of victims in Afghanistan and Chechnya so as to pay tribute to all these men—living, dead, or missing[57]—one more failing on the part of the state, which they have taken on themselves to overcome.

From Irresponsibility to Disengagement

Random and Occasional State Aid

Beginning in 1992–1993, in the context of a federalist crisis with regional powers challenging the authority of the central government, the economic burden of the army was transferred to the local authorities. The regions thus found themselves in charge of the social protection of veterans, whose pay would thus depend largely not only on the region's resources but also on the extent to which the local head of government took an interest in their welfare, which explains significant regional inequalities.

Thus we find Boris Gromov at the head of the Moscow region. Former armed forces commander during the first Chechen campaign, president of the veterans association Boevoe Bratstvo, deputy to the Duma, member of the Yedinaya Rossiya party, Boris Gromov was particularly attentive to the needs of veterans of local wars. One of his main measures in favor of soldiers' families was the payment of 7,000 rubles to each parent of soldiers killed in combat during the Chechen campaigns.[58]

As for veterans associations, they were left on their own, with no financing and no state aid to help them solve problems in connection with medical treatment, psychological rehabilitation, or lack of housing. The press of these veterans associations overflows with examples of individual aid granted by one association or another to an invalid or to the mother of a Soviet hero.[59] But testimonials agree that these aids are only one-offs and rarely involve Chechen veterans, to whom little attention is paid. Furthermore, the latter seem not too well organized and without any strong ties with veterans associations, although a few organizations of former Chechen combatants have joined with associations of Afghanistan veterans.[60] However, their quasi-absence on the premises when we met with representatives of veterans associations in Moscow is an indication of their lack of participation in associative work.

There is no government administration in charge of issues related to veterans. None of the so-called "power" ministries devote a percentage of their budget to their care. Concrete measures in their favor are therefore extremely rare. In the absence of allocations from the state, funds have been set up to help veterans who fought in the North Caucasus. Their commercial activities make it possible to earn enough to meet veterans' most urgent needs, but only on a very small scale.[61]

In 2007, Ivan Shilov, president of the Council of Veterans at the MVD, noted that 80 percent of veterans earn their own material aid. The rest comes from various associations or funds, as, for example, the "Veterans of the MVD" foundation, which raises funds through a lottery![62] Resourcefulness is the key. Civil chamber tenders (*Obshchesvennaia Palata*) are another possibility of funding for veterans associations, though their aid is relative, often just enough to equip the main office with computers or to pay a secretary.[63] More than funding, it is a form of recognition that these associations are looking for when they participate in such contests,[64] since the tenders they answer most often involve patriotic education.

Delegating the Social Integration of Veterans

The attempt in 2005 on the part of the Ministry of Internal Affairs to reintegrate veterans in its structures by giving them jobs in exchange for a symbolic salary[65] was not enough to cover up the state's disinterest in this category of the population, nor its will to delegate the overall care of veterans to associations and to society.

With the twentieth anniversary of the withdrawal of troops from Afghanistan in view, orders became more explicit as to the roles of society and the various veterans organizations in the reintegration of ex-combatants. Concerning jobs, recommendations were unchanged: "The measures taken at the time of the jubilee must motivate citizens of the Russian Federation for patriotic education, increase the authority of the armed forces and the prestige of military service."[66] But concerning the material and social responsibility for veterans, the state would rely on society: "Veterans of Afghanistan certainly remember that in that war, like in no other contemporary war, the principle 'the people and the army' was put in practice." This was a reference to the patronage or sponsorship (*shefstvo*[67]) of military units by enterprises, scientific departments, and kindergartens at the end of the Afghanistan war, as well as to the aid in terms of housing and jobs contributed by the regions and territories. Today, we must "adapt this experience to present conditions."[68] As for veterans associations, "it is positive that organisations of the veterans of Afghanistan rally around themselves the young veterans of combats in Chechnya and other 'hot spots' of the ex-USSR, that they help them socially and co-opt them for the job of patriotic education. This tendency must absolutely be developed."[69]

A State That Renounces Responsibility

In January 2005, a regional court of the Orel region overruled a decision of a lower court constraining the Ministry of Defense to compensate Gennady Uminsky, a contractual military gravely wounded during an attack in Grozny during the first Chechen war.[70] Under siege in a cave, his section remained blocked there until the end of the war. Left for dead, Uminsky and his companions survived—although they were officially declared "killed in combat." In the hospital for a year, when released, he was diagnosed as an "invalid of the second group," implying that he would be in need of constant medical supervision. After having tried in vain to obtain a pension from the Ministry of Defense, Uminsky went to court. By annulling the judges' decision, not only did the court of Orel release the Defense Ministry from any responsibility in the wounds inflicted on Uminsky but set a precedent. According to the judges' decision, no link could be established between the federal army and the wounds received by the plaintiff. No compensation could therefore be awarded.

Faced with the incapacity of the Defense Ministry or the Ministry of Internal Affairs to pay pensions or combat compensations, other cases went to the courts. Some plaintiffs demanding compensation for war wounds were asked to provide proof that the federal army was responsible for them. In the end, they were told to request compensation from the Chechen combatants—those in fact responsible for the wounds. On the basis of these arguments, decisions favorable to veterans were revoked on appeal by the state.[71]

The reaction of the court of Orel—this outrageous rationalizing of a taboo situation—is a symptom of the state's incapacity to recognize and to politically assume and take financial responsibility for the consequences of a conflict with no status. It brings in a completely new element: the idea that veterans are responsible for their acts and their war and that the state cannot be held responsible for their suffering.

Very Limited Recognition and Aid Given to Veterans Suffering Psychologically

In addition to the state's lack of responsibility for physical suffering, in our view, another form of institutional violence contributes to the brutalization of the behavior of former combatants. In this case, it is the incapacity on the part of the state and the Ministry of Internal Affairs to put in place an efficient system of professional and psychological rehabilitation that would function on the return of soldiers to civilian life.

Françoise Sironi writes that "wars always involve a 'fabrication' or 'fashioning' of those who are fighting the war."[72] "Fabricated" by the violence of combat and by a demonization of the enemy leading to a state of complete "dis-empathy," the veteran returns home, bearing within a shocked and disorganized psyche ready to be awakened by any trauma. According to Françoise Sironi, the individual is then in a psychic state in which any frustration, vexation, or difficult situation sends him back to the war context and to the fighter's reflexes and violence.[73] Such a state demands the kind of psychological care that will allow him to "deconstruct" this "dis-empathy" and gradually defuse the violence always on the verge of explosion. In some cases, for example professional military or policemen, reorientation or professional rehabilitation should be considered, since the pursuit of missions similar to those having produced the trauma (combat, confrontation, armed tension) is liable to reawaken the conditioned reflexes of the combatant, policeman, or soldier.

In the case of the personnel of the Russian Ministry of Internal Affairs, it would not be an exaggeration to say there is no system of professional rehabilitation, while psychological rehabilitation is as yet embryonic, having been set up very late and being marked ideologically.

The psychological services of the Ministry of Internal Affairs date officially from the mid-1990s but have only been in place since 2000.[74] The interviews by Asmik Novikova for the study mentioned earlier of policemen veterans of Chechnya shed new light on the evolution and practice of psychology in a closed institution like the Ministry of Internal Affairs.[75] Besides the fact that, until 2006, MVD psychologists were not required to have had psychological training (any studies in the humanities or social sciences would do[76]), and that the notion of confidentiality concerning the information gathered was nonexistent, these interviews show that the psychologists in charge of veterans occupy an ambiguous position inside the institution: on the one hand, they belong to the same grade system as their colleagues and can be called on to take part in patrols if there is a police alert; however, they depend on the senior administrative directorate and as such are in charge of deciding who can be hired for senior positions in the police department and who can be discharged—policemen thus hesitate to confide in them. Finally, the system of psychological expertise is deeply marked by a historically Russian and ideologically Stalinist concept of the individual and his psychic state,[77] which considers trauma to be a personal weakness. The job of MVD psychologists is thus to spot potential weaknesses in candidates before sending them to the field of operations, which means that for psychologists, any manifestation of posttraumatic stress is proof in itself of professional incompetence. It is therefore not surprising that MVD psychologists detect a minimal number of posttraumatic syndromes each year.

Nonetheless, since 2007 the specialized press of the Ministry of Internal Affairs has shown a considerable opening onto issues involving the psychological balance of its collaborators. In one 2007 issue, at the same time, the review *Professional* announced the creation of new centers of medical and psychological care for MVD personnel,[78] launched a debate on professional rehabilitation,[79] and fiercely denounced the way in which psychologists were selected in the Ministry.[80] In early 2008, the "military" and potentially traumatic nature of the missions of the Ministry's forces in Chechnya was recognized for the first time.[81] Moreover, whereas the therapeutic arsenal formerly proposed by the MVD specialized revues included only various relaxation techniques,[82] as for example those used by cosmonauts to evacuate stress,[83] the introduction in the same year of talking as a mode of therapy was an indication of progress within the MVD.

While remaining ambiguous and often indifferent toward ex-combatants, the Russian state also set up a series of mechanisms aimed at using veterans to put in place a patriotic program the authorities hoped would cement a new social contract.

Are Veterans Being Instrumentalized for a Militarist and Patriotic Project?

Since the coming to power of Vladimir Putin, there has been renewed use of veterans in the service of a state patriotic project; in Russia today, the role of the state so far as veterans as a social group are concerned can be seen less in its sense of responsibility toward these men and in the definition of their status than in an official ideology that allows the state to instrumentalize them. Thus the enlistment of veterans of the Russo-Chechen and Afghan conflicts in a social project under the Patriotic Education Program[84]—alongside the social disengagement of the state—bears witness to its ideological priorities, to its will to redirect a population that already carries a *memory* of violence, and to put the population on familiar terms with the military environment.

The Publicizing of a Social Military-Patriotic Ideal in Civil Institutions (Media, Schools, Museums, etc.) and the Instrumentalizing of Veterans

The importance of the anniversary of the Great Patriotic War—the only reference war—and the educational mission (primarily for the young) assigned to Afghanistan and Chechen veterans contribute to the perpetuation of the latter as a distinct social group and to the diffusion throughout Russian society of a culture of violence that veterans carry within and consider their heritage. Their instrumentalization makes it possible both to spread the word of the military and to trivialize conflict and violence.

Veterans in Post-Soviet Society: In Continued Service to the State

That veterans have duties toward the Russian state but no rights is a fact that veterans of the Great Patriotic War found out a few weeks after they were demobilized, when government aid dwindled and official propaganda exhorted them to get back to work as soon as possible.[85] Likewise, Afghanistan and Chechen veterans found out the same thing with the publication of the two Patriotic Education Programs implemented by Putin in 2000 and 2006.

In substance, this is what the second Patriotic Education Program tells the entire Russian veteran community as it calls on them to work hand in hand with the program's partner ministries[86] in a societal project based on the patriotic-military education of the population, youth in particular, in exchange for the esteem of the Russian state. As if it were not enough to have sacrificed their lives at the service of the homeland, they discover on return that they owe a debt to the state and that having a place in society is linked to continued service.

Social advantages and potential state aid are presented as a gift for which they owe additional service. Having served their country on the battlefield—with the sacrifice inherent in that service—veterans learn that they continue to have obligations to the state.

If we analyze the measures taken in the context of the application of the Patriotic Education Program by the Interior and Defense Ministries, the main providers of veterans in Russia (creation of commissions or structures within the MVD and MO⁸⁷ in charge of carrying out the Patriotic Education Program⁸⁸), as well as their publications, we find a rhetoric similar to that which followed the Second World War⁸⁹: the veteran must be a model of organization and discipline, and must inspire heroic acts in the younger generations (by spreading the "propaganda of the Russian people's heroic traditions and the army," and by dispensing "lessons in courage" to the young⁹⁰). He must organize military education to ensure the production of a new generation of defenders of the homeland (for veterans of the armed forces) or must himself (if a veteran of the MVD forces) be in the reserves of the law enforcement department.⁹¹ Finally, he must participate in the patriotic education of young people by sponsoring activities in schools and teaching establishments.⁹²

The Mechanism Put in Place by the Public Authorities

The creation in November 2005 of a Central Council for Veterans Affairs (TsSDV) with the Ministry of Defense could legitimately have been perceived by veterans as an answer to their expectations in terms of aid. However, the creation of this council on the initiative of the Defense minister of the time—just after the demonstrations prompted by federal law no. 122 on the suppression of advantages in kind—did not answer them. The founding meeting of the Council was devoted to the increase in the role of veterans' organizations in the training of "high performance" soldiers.⁹³ In this respect, the record of this meeting⁹⁴ is significant: emphasis is put on the strengthening of the role of veterans in the tasks set by the 2006–2010 patriotic program, notably in the domain of patriotic/military education (in schools, support to school patriotic youth movements), in the spread of their know-how among the young generations of future military by a form of student "coaching" (in military schools and academies, recruits, and officers) as well as the organization of the draft. The Council's organization and work directorates are oriented essentially toward the "consolidation of this social group around the President [Putin]," whereas the social support program remains evasive, promising to study the question in the near future.

Concretely, the actions put in place by the Council are mainly of a propagandist nature: thus in February 2006, the Ministry of Defense launched a program of common action with the Union of Veterans of Afghanistan, entitled "Serving is not so terrible" (*Sluzhit' ne tak strashno*)—a campaign aimed at reassuring future recruits and dissuading them from trying to avoid military service.⁹⁵ Other actions of this type were to follow.

Over the years, the military press has continued to make a point of veterans' obligations:

> Veterans must take part in the organisation of special days for conscripts, in competitions for the best preparation of citizens for military service, in the organisation of the draft in municipal

establishments and schools. They must to the best of their ability aid ROSTO (DOSAAF) (organisation that prepares young people for military service) in the training of youth for military service. They must organise the implementation of the State Programme in the Armed Forces 'Patriotic Education of Citizens of the Russian Federation, 2006–2010.' It is also evident that they must contribute to the preparation and organisation of manifestations linked to the 65th anniversary of various events of the Great Patriotic War of 1941–1945.[96]

...while remaining extremely evasive on fundamental issues:

Concerning the most serious social problems, the proposals emanating from veterans associations [...] will be generalised and transmitted for examination to the federal organs of executive power and to the military authorities concerned. Decisions have already been adopted, and some proposals are in the process of being adopted, as for example the allocation of indemnities for the purchase of food rations.[97]

Thus the veteran of the Ministry of Defense must be a "model" for society—generous and altruistic.

The MVD decree no 875 of November 2006 on the cooperation of MVD organs and units with the veterans organizations of the Ministry of Internal Affairs defines how these veterans' organizations work within the MVD system.[98] Benevolently, or on contract (3,000 rubles), veterans are called on to put their experience at the service of the young (tutoring or a form of "coaching," *nastavnichestvo*) but not only: they can also be in charge of carrying out inquiries and arresting criminals. Every year in fact, the Council of Veterans draws up a precise list of its achievements in an internal publication: the number of arrests and affairs settled thanks to its help, the number of works published, films made, conferences given, scenarios written, television and radio programs broadcast thanks to their participation.[99]

A Convergence of Interests for Veterans and the State: Making the Military a Normal, Everyday Feature of Society

Although a large part of the actions of the Ministry of Defense and the Ministry of the Interior for military-patriotic education concern only these institutions and are mainly propagandist in character, a last category of actions entails the mobilization of the entire population and is made up of sports activities and military training exercises. Veterans are expected to play an active part in the organization and realization of this type of mobilization.

Mobilization around Sports

The army, the ROSTO association (Russian Defence Sports-Technical Organization) and military commissariats all agree that military-patriotic games "strengthen young people's motivation to defend the homeland, to serve in the army and enter into the high-level military schools."[100] All these entities (army, ROSTO, and military commissariats) are at the origin of sports games, organized on the model of *Zarnitsa* or *Orlenok*, military sports games, which were very popular during the Soviet era, during which child volunteers spent two weeks in army barracks, where they were transformed into defenders of the homeland.

Some power ministries (Defense, Interior, Emergency Situations), as well as the ROSTO association, also organize holiday sports camps of a military kind. The Russian Orthodox Church is often associated with these initiatives. The targeted population is young—from the age of 5—and often disadvantaged: wayward children from broken homes, orphans, and veterans' children constitute the majority of children in these state-subsidized camps. The former combatants who are attracted to these camps are solicited to collaborate in activities aimed at the young.

Wartime Mobilization

The population is expected to mobilize and prepare itself militarily. The first sign of this mobilization occurred during the autumn of 2000. On the initiative of General G. Troshev, commander of the North Caucasian military region, high-level civil servants of southern Russia were made to follow military training (shooting, grenade-throwing, physical exercises, etc.) near Rostov-on-the-Don. This initiative served as an example and since 2001 has been extended to several other regions,[101] as well as to deputies, called up once or twice a year for military training. In the autumn of 2002, exercises in general mobilization were also brought back: the first took place in the region of Ulyanovsk under the direction of Governor Vladimir Shamanov[102] (former commander of Russian forces in Chechnya) and were the first such large-scale exercises in post-Soviet Russia.[103] More recently, in 2003, Vladimir Putin signed a decree, calling citizens of the Russian Federation in the reserves to participate in summer training camps. These camps, a fairly common practice during the Soviet era—reserve soldiers obliged to leave their families and jobs were called "partisans" by the professional military—had practically disappeared since the fall of the USSR[104] but were reinstituted two years ago, with a two-month limit on the length of service. The number of reservists remains classified as a "defense secret." However, due to the material impossibility of participating in all such training and mobilization actions, the army once again calls on veterans for assistance.

Veterans seem to accept these tasks willingly, all the more so as they and the state have common interests. They identify with the army reserves and define patriotic-military work with youth as their "mission." The repertoire of the collective actions of Afghanistan and Chechen veterans in the mid-1990s, even before the publication of the patriotic programs, is proof of their readiness to cooperate in programs in which their own interests converge with those of the state: festivals of patriotic and military songs, recordings of war songs,[105] the opening of camps for military training and preparations, or clubs for children and young adolescents,[106] students or businessmen,[107] patriotic education courses in schools, sponsorship of schools or classes by veterans associations,[108] "lessons in courage" in schools for general studies,[109] and so on are a few of the activities organized spontaneously by former combatants on return from the war. Moreover, the job choices of Chechen veterans are clearly determined by their military training and the internalization of the military function: contractuals in the army, integration into the police force, private security services, creation or participation in military preparation camps for children. Anti-war actions or actions aimed at preventing war are few among this section of the population. War remains an activity that Chechen veterans continue to identify with when the war is over.

This mobilization on the part of the authorities may also have other intentions. Besides the project of transmitting patriotic values via educational and paraeducational mechanisms, there is also the need to channel the *chechentsy* by federating them and keeping them busy and *that*, in the same way as the *Voenno-Patrioticheskoe Vospitanie* (VPV), the patriotic education network offering a framework for Afghanistan veterans on their return from combat, giving them work and the opportunity to collaborate with the authorities.[110] As a way to attract them, the state offers them a few jobs related to patriotic education and reserve training, as well as the opportunity to put their know-how at the service of the nation.

Patriotic education has thus a dual aim: to federate veterans around the central authorities by using them as a propaganda network, and to channel a population that escapes government control and whose violence on return to civilian life (violence toward the population in the context of their function, Ministry of Internal Affairs veterans in particular) have darkened the image of the "power" ministries. Due to a lack of attention to its social, professional, and psychological needs, this population, which has difficulty structuring itself, falls easily into marginalization and *proizvol* (arbitrariness) unless taken in hand.

This aspect offers food for thought with which to temporarily conclude: what has been said shows the considerable weight of the military in society and its influence on youth in particular. Moreover, as in Soviet times, the uniform and the "military phenomenon" in general are everyday features of society, if only because of their omnipresence in the public space and in the population's network of relations. It could even be said that there is an overall militarization of society, which, thanks to war and to the state's patriotic-military programs, generates violence in its own way.

At this point, a distinction should perhaps be made between brutalization and militarization: military patriotic programs and the use of veterans also testify to a will to channel the latter and bring them in some way back into the bosom of the state, to ensure the values of order and obedience, and oppose uncontrolled violence. Some camp directors sincerely wish to save young people both from the corrupting influences of the West and the temptations of joining the nationalist and racist far right, to which an army that defeated Nazism remains strongly opposed.

All of which, in the case of Russia, encourages us to temper the hypothesis proposed by Georges Mosse—war as the vector of brutalization—and think in terms of a complex spiral of brutalization, fed by diverse experiences and favored by a propitious environment. If a continuum and syndrome do exist, they are more likely to originate in the indisputable trauma of war and the transformation it imposes on political discourse and society—than in a more or less direct reactivation of the trauma of war in individual and collective practices that repeat the violence of the terrain. Translated by Judith Andreyev.

Notes

1. The interviews conducted by Elisabeth Sieca-Kozlowski were carried out thanks to a research grant awarded by the *Centre franco-russe de recherches en sciences humaines et sociales de Moscou* (USR 3060, CNRS-MAE), October 2008.
2. Statement made by Ruslan Aushev, president of the Committee for Internationalist Fighters Affairs with the Council of Heads of Governments of the CIS member states, in an interview given to Nezavisimoe Voennoe Obozrenie (NVO), February 13–19, 2004, 1, 6.
3. The authors wish to express their gratitude to Nathalie Duclos, editor of the book, as well as anonymous referees, for their remarks and careful rereading.
4. See S. Lefranc, "Vérité, justice, réconciliation ou comment concilier l'inconciliable" [Truth, justice, reconciliation, or how to reconcile what cannot be reconciled], *Mouvements* 53 (May–June 2008), and "Les dilemmes de la justice transitionnelle," http://www.mouvements.info/spip.php?article276.
5. E. Rubin, "Down in the Dark hole of Chechnya," *New York Times Magazine* (July 8, 2001); Y. Zakharovich, "Chechnya's Walking Wounded," *Time Magazine* (September 28, 2003). It is also used by the Russian military institution to explain a state of mind of humiliation and a feeling of betrayal of the military after the first conflict (1994–1996), a feeling that the resumption of combats in 1999 allowed them to overcome. See the talk in French by Mme Arbatova, head of the department of European Political Studies at the World Economy and International Relations Institute in Moscow, before French officers.
6. J. Corwin, "Russian Police's 'Clean-up Operations' Extending beyond Chechnya?," *Radio Liberty*, March 24, 2005.
7. Moscow Helsinki Group, *Special Operation by MVD of Bashkortostan, Events, Facts, Assessments, Findings*, http://www.mhg.ru/files/knigi/bashkor.doc; N. Nougayrède, "Rafles, tortures, intimidations: les dérapages des forces spéciales russes à Blagovechtchensk" [Raids, torture, intimidation: abuses of power by Russian special forces in Blagoveshchensk], *Le Monde* (March 17, 2005); Il'dat Issangulov, *U Posledney Cherty, Dokumenty i fakty o deiatel'nosti mafii v Respublike Bashkortostan* (Mosco: Izdatel' "Gainullin," 2006).
8. S. Markelov, *The Chechnya Syndrome and the Blagoveshchensk Case*, http://www.robertamsterdam.com/2007/04/stanislav_markelov_russias_fil.htm. Stanislas Markelov was assassinated in Moscow January 19, 2009. He had just appealed the early release of Colonel Budanov, sentenced for the rape and murder of a young Chechen girl in 2000.

9. Anna Politkovskaya, the journalist of *Novaia Gazeta* who was assassinated in October 2006, had inquired specifically on this question, as did the Sova Center, which on several occasions drew attention to racist and xenophobic acts perpetrated by Chechen veterans. See Corvin, "Russian Police's 'Clean-up Operations' Extending beyond Chechnya?"
10. In particular, during the "Disagreement Marches" organized since 2006. The ombudsman of the Russian Federation for Human Rights, Vladimir Lukin, himself has acknowledged abuse by policemen and suggested to victims that they lodge a complaint. http://www.bilingua.ogi.ru/bbs/2007/04/16/serv_print.html
11. A. Novikova, "Sovremennyi Omon. Ot sebia ne ubezhish'," *Militsiia mezhdu Rossiei i Chechnei. Veterany konflikta v rossiiskom obshchestve* (Moscow: Demos, 2007).
12. At the time of the interview, he had been sent to Chechnya five times.
13. Comments recorded by Tanya Lokshina, Head of the Demos Center at the time, from an interview published in the online review *The Journal of Power Institutions in Post-Soviet Societies* 6 (2007): http://www.pipss.org/index772.html.
14. *Policemen in Limbo: Veterans of the Chechen Conflict in Russian Society* (Moscow: Demos, 2007). The study encompasses 80 in-depth interviews in five Russian regions of professional policemen veterans of Chechnya.
15. In military and police psychological jargon, this state is known as *"Povyshenie i obostrenie vospriiatiya opasnosti"* [reinforced argumentation and acuity in the perception of danger].
16. Interviews by Anne Le Huérou with Asmik Novikova and Olga Shepeleva, researchers at the Demos Center, Moscow, March 2008. The authors are indebted to them for the precious data and analyses resulting from their research and transmitted during the interviewing process.
17. See in particular the annual reports established by the Civic Assistance Committee on the situation of the Chechens living on Russian Federation territory. http://www.refugee.ru/.
18. Testimonies recorded by A. Le Huérou in Moscow, February and March 2008.
19. Testimonies recorded by A. Le Huérou in Kazan and Naberezhnye Chelny, February 2008.
20. I. Orekhov, "Gastarbaiterov izbivali beisbol'nymi bitami," *Komsomolskaya Pravda*, Kaliningrad, June 14, 2006, http://www.kaliningrad.kp.ru/2006/06/14/doc120833.
21. We use the term developed by G. Mosse, in whose view the acts of violence of the First World War were in part responsible for the brutalization of European societies that favored the installation of totalitarian regimes: *De la Grande Guerre aux totalitarismes, la brutalisation des sociétés européennes* (Paris: Hachette, 1999). For an approach applied to the Russian context, see P. Holquist, *Making War, Forging Revolution: Russia's Continuum of Crisis, 1914–1921* (Cambridge, MA: Harvard University Press, 2002).
22. These facts have been reported by all the big international organizations for the defense of human rights, such as Amnesty Human Rights Watch and the International Federation for Human Rights, by Russian associations such as Memorial, and attested by international organizations, such as the Council of Europe, the Committee for the Prevention of Torture, and special representatives of the UN.
23. L. W. Grau and T. L. Thomas, "'Soft log' and Concrete Canons: Russian Urban Combat Logistics in Grozny," *Marine Corps Gazette* (October 1999): http://www.globalsecurity.org/military/library/report/1999/991000-softlog.htm; T. L. Thomas and C. P. O'Hara, "Combat Stress in Chechnya: 'The Equal Opportunity Disorder,'" *Army Medical Department Journal* (January–March 2000): http://fmso.leavenworth.army.mil/documents/stress.htm.
24. Quoted in T. L. Thomas and C. P. O'Hara, "Combat stress in Chechnya," *Voennyi Meditsinksii Zhurnal* 4 (April 1996): 37–40.
25. P. Felgenhauer, "Russia's Forces Unreconstructed," *Perspective* X, no. 4 (March–April 2000): http://www.bu.edu.iscip/vol10/Felgenhauer.html
26. Thomas and O'Hara, "Combat stress in Chechnya."
27. This was the sense of the ultimatum posed to the inhabitants of Grozny at the beginning of December 1999: either they left the city within 48 hours or those who remained would be considered terrorists.
28. *Spetznaz* of the GRU (*Glavnoye Razvedyvatel'noye Upravleniye*), foreign military intelligence directorate of the General Staff of the Armed Forces of the Russian Federation.
29. Human Rights Watch Report, *To Serve Without Health*, November 2003, available at: http://www.hrw.org/sites/default/files/reports/russia1103.pdf.

30. Special forces OMON and SOBR (the Ministry of the Interior's special troops), GUVD (The Main Interior Office), and UVD police (The Interior Office).
31. Forces in charge of suppressing revolts in prisons.
32. F. Daucé and E. Sieca-Kozlowski (eds), *Dedovshchina in Post-Soviet Military. Hazing of Russian Army Conscripts in a Comparative Perspective* (Stuttgart: Ibidem-Verlag, 2006).
33. See P. Felgenhauer, "Russian Military: After Ivanonov," *Perspective* 17, no. 3 (May–June 2007): http://www.bu.edu/iscip/vol17/felgenhauer2.html.
34. Human Rights Watch, *Confessions at Any Cost: Police Torture in Russia*, New York, November 1999, http://www.hrw.org/legacy/reports/1999/russia/; *Sociology of Violence: The Arbitrariness of Law Enforcement Bodies in the Eyes of the People*, report and sociological inquiry of the Committee Against Torture, Nizhni-Novgorod, 2006, http://www.pytkam.net/web/files/sociological.doc; See also the work of Amélie Cook: *Les violences policières en Fédération de Russie: les pratiques policières violentes en Russie post-soviétique et leur constitution en enjeu politique et social*, Research thesis for a Master, directed by G. Favarel-Garrigues, Paris, IEP 2005.
35. See V. Volkov, "Violent Entrepreneurship in Post-Communist Russia," *Europe-Asia Studies* 51, no. 5 (1999); G. Favarel-Garrigues and A. Le Huérou, "State and Multilateralization of Policing in Post-Soviet Russia," *Policing and Society* 14, no. 1 (January 2004): 13–30.
36. K. Bannikov, *Antropologiia ekstremal'nykh grupp. Dominantnie otnoshenie sredi voennosluzhashchikh srotchnij sluzhby Rossiiskoi Armii* (Moscow: RAN, 2002); K. L. Bannikov, "Regimented Communities in a Civil Society," *The Journal of Power Institutions in Post-Soviet Societies* 1 (2004): http://www.pipss.org/index40.html.
37. A. Oleynik, "'Dedovshchina' as an Element of the 'Small Society': Evidence From Russia and Other Countries," *The Journal of Power Institutions in Post-Soviet Societies* 1 (2004): http://www.pipss.org/index136.html.
38. Interview by A. Le Huérou, Moscow, March 2008.
39. INED, "Les morts violents dans le monde" [Violent Deaths in the World], *Population et sociétés* 95 (November 2003).
40. She cites the example of a Gay Pride attempt in Moscow, during which the OMON more or less protected the demonstrators against groups of skinheads, because the order had been given to them in the aim of avoiding incidents, and this was despite the official prohibition of the demonstration. Interview by A. Le Huérou, Moscow, March 2008.
41. "V Tverskoi oblasti otmecheny vspyshki nasiliia militsii v otnoshenii grazhdan," www.regnum.ru/news/421898.html (accessed on March 16, 2005).
42. *Sociology of Violence*.
43. Cf. the documentary film produced by the Capa Agency and directed by Manon Loiseau "Les âmes perdues de l'armée russe."
44. The category of the inside enemy and its link with violence are taken up by R. Lew in "L'ennemi intérieur et la violence extrême: L'URSS stalinienne et la chine maoïste," *Cultures et conflits* 43 (2001): 127–139.
45. A. Merlin (ed.), "La société civile en Russie face à la guerre en Tchétchénie," *Où va la Russie?* (Bruxelles: Presses Universitaires de Bruxelles, 2007).
46. See A. Le Huérou and A. Regamey, "La guerre russe en Tchétchénie: discours anti-terroriste et légitimation de la violence," *Critique internationale* 41 (2008).
47. See in particular all the publications of the Sova center: http://xeno.sova-center.ru/
48. F. Sironi, *Psychopathologie des violences collectives. Essai de psychologie géopolitique clinique* (Paris: Odile Jacob, 2007), 126. Françoise Sironi, clinical psychologist and researcher in psychology, has worked with veterans of numerous conflicts, from Algerian draftees to child soldiers in the recent wars in Africa, and in the 1990s led a project with Russian veterans of the Afghan conflict in the region of Perm.
49. F. Sironi, "Les vétérans des guerres perdues—contraintes et métamorphoses," *Communication* 70 (2000): http://www.ethnopsychiatrie.net/actu/Communic.htm
50. See the chapter "Subjected to War: Military Brotherhood in Search of Recognition" in the doctoral thesis of Serguei Oushakine, entitled *The Patriotism of Despair: National Memory, Symbolic Economics, and Communities of Loss in a Russian Province* (New York: Columbia University, 2005).
51. In addition to numerous reports by international organisations, see A. Regamey, "L'opinion publique russe et l'affaire Boudanov," *The Journal of Power Institutions in Post-Soviet Societies* 8 (2008): http://www.pipss.org/index1493.html.

52. *NVO*, no 25–31, October 2002, 1 and 8.
53. "Voina uchastvuet vo mne," *Novaia Gazeta*, no 22, March 29, 2007; *Rossiia i SSSR v voinakh XX veka: statisticheskoe issledovanie* (Moscow: Olma-Press, 2001); interview with Ruslan Aushev, *New Times*, July 2005.
54. In ten years, 620,000 men were sent to Afghanistan, 15,400 were killed, 39,000 wounded, and 270 reported missing. We also have figures for the number of invalids, according to the various categories. See M. Galeotti, "Veteran Society," in *Afghanistan: The Soviet Union's Last War* (London: Frank Cass, 1995).
55. "Voina uchastvuet vo mne."
56. S. Troshin, "Traditsii deval'vatsii ne podlezhat; S pervogo soveshchaniia veteranskogo aktiva vooruzhennykh sil RF," *VPK voenno-promyshlennyi kur'er* 14, no. 180, April 11–17, 2007; http://www.vpk-news.ru/print.asp?pr_sign=archive.2007.180.articles.army_s02.
57. Interview by E. Sieca-Kozlowski with the head of patriotic education for the Boevoe Bratstvo association, G. S., Moscow, October 9, 2008.
58. Interview by E. Sieca-Kozlowski with N. S., former director of the review *Boevoe* Bratstvo, publication of the association of the same name, Moscow, October 9, 2008. Seven thousand rubles are the equivalent of 200 euros.
59. *Boevoe Bratstvo Lug Podmoskov'ia* 3, no. 17 (2007): 3.
60. Ibid.
61. Vadim Udmantsev, "V ozhidanii 'neoplatnogo dolga'. Tysiach invalidov voiny v Chechne obrecheny gosudarstvom i obshchestvom na polugolodnoe vyzhivanie," *NVO*, no. 9 (March 22–28, 2002): 3.
62. I. Shilov, "Veteranskoe dvizhenie i vospitatel'naia rabota," *Professional*, no 5, 2007; http://www.ormvd.ru/press/mag/256/260/1003.
63. Interview by E. Sieca-Kozlowski with I. A., deputy president of the Council of Veterans of the MVD, Moscow, October 17, 2008; interview by E. Sieca-Kozlowski with V. K. and V. V., deputy presidents of the central administration of the Union of Veterans of Afghanistan (RSVA), Moscow, October 6, 2008.
64. Interview by E. Sieca-Kozlowski with I. A.
65. Shilov, "Veteranskoe dvizhenie i vospitatel'naya rabota."
66. K. Trofimov, "20 let posle Afgana. Zasedanie tsentral'nogo soveta MO RF po delam veteranov," *VPK Voenno-promyshlennyi kur'er*, 44, no. 260 (November 10–12, 2008).
67. The term *shefstvo* applies to organizations, factories, and enterprises that "adopt" army units and ensure moral and material support. See E. Sieca-Kozlowski "Les liens indestructibles entre la société et l'armée en Russie post-soviétique ou la résurgence du *chefstvo* de Boris Eltsine à Vladimir Poutine," in A. Le Huérou and E. Sieca-Kozlowski (eds.) *Culture militaire et patriotisme dans la Russie d'aujourd'hui* (Paris: Karthala, 2008), 147–170.
68. Trofimov, "20 let posle Afgana."
69. E. Nesterovich, "Boevoi opyt vostrebovan. Sozdana edinaia organizatsiia veteranov vooruzhennykh sil Rossijskoi federatsii," *VPK Voennopromyshlennyi kur'er* 46, no. 262 (November 26–December 2, 2008).
70. For more details on this case, see the chapter "The Patriotism of Despair: National Memory, Symbolic Economics, and Communities of Loss in a Russian Province" in the doctoral thesis of S. Oushakine, 1–4.
71. "Court Challenges Unprecedented Compensation award for Chechen War Veteran," RFE/RL Russia, September 29, 2003.
72. Sironi, *Psychopathologie des violences collectives*, 99.
73. Interview by A. Le Huérou and E. Sieca-Kozlowski with F. S., Paris, January 22, 2009.
74. *Normative act* no. 770 of June 26, 2000: "Ob utverzhdenii polozheniya o poriadke organizatsii psikhologicheskogo obespecheniya sotrudnikov organov vnutrennykh del rossijskoj federatsii."
75. See the chapter of A. Novikova, "Psikhologicheskaya sluzhba MVD" in *Militsiya mezhdu Rossiej i Chechnej*, 60–75.
76. Ibid., 43.
77. C. Merridale, "The Collective Mind: Trauma and Shell-shock in Twentieth Century Russia," *Journal of Contemporary History* 35, no. 1 (January 2000): 39–55.
78. D. Morozov, "Aktual'nye voprosy meditsinskogo i sanatornokurortnogo obespecheniya v MVD Rossii," *Professional* 1 (2008): 31–33.

79. I. Amel'shakov, "Sovershenstvovanie sistemy professionalnoj podgotovki, perepodgotovki i povysheniya kvalifikatsii," *Professional* 1 (2008): 39–41.
80. A. Adaev, "Problemy organizatsii psykhologicheskogo obespecheniya deyatel'nosti organov vnutrennykh del," *Professional* 1 (2008): 42–44.
81. The term *spetsificheskie sluzhebno-boevye zadachi* [specific combat missions linked to service], taken up by the MVD medical review the same year, appeared here, as well as the notion of posttraumatic stress, also introduced for the first time by the aforementioned psychologist. V. Zlenen'kij, "Moral'no-psikhologicheskoe obespechenie vypolneniia lichnym sostavom sluzhebno-boevykh zadach," *Professional* (Popularno-pravovoi al'manakh MVD Rossii), 1 (2008): 7–9; D. Morozov, A Kalyaev, and G. Shutko, "Aktual'nye voprosy sostoianiia zdorov'ia sotrudnikov spetsial'nykh prodrazdelenii militsii," *Meditsinskii vestnik MVD*, 3, no. 34 (2008): 1–4.
82. A.V. Kapeev, "Terapevticheskaia pomoshch v meditsinskikh uchrezhdeniiakh sistemy MVD Rossii: Itogi desiatiletiia, Osnovnye tendentsii razvitiia i puti sovershenstvovaniia," *Meditsinskii vestnik MVD* 2 (2007).
83. Interview with K. A., director of the Center for Protection Against Stress, "'Klyuch, kotoryi vsegda s toboi," *Sodruzhestvo* (review of the Council of Interior Ministers of the CIS) 1, no. 3 (2007): 47–51.
84. The first stage was put in place in 2000 and ended in 2005. The second stage began in 2006 and ran until 2010.
85. On this subject, see the remarkable work of Mark Edele, *Soviet Veterans of World War II: A Popular Movement in an Authoritarian Society, 1941–1991* (Oxford and New York: Oxford University Press, 2008).
86. All power ministries are part of this program.
87. Order no 120 of the MVD of February 1, 2007, recommending several measures to encourage the participation of veterans in patriotic education work; order no 859 of December 30, 2007, "O privlechenii pensionerov k rabote v systeme MVD Rossii."
88. For example, concerning the transport police, see the interview with Viktor Molchanov, president of the Veterans Council of the UVDT of North Caucasian, Transport Police, "Ne prervetsya sviaz' pokalenij," *Militsiya* 8(2007): http://www.ormvd.ru/press/mag/332/336/8991.
89. Edele, *Soviet Veterans of World War II*.
90. Shilov, "Veteranskoe dvizhenie i vospitatel'naya rabota."
91. I. Shilov, "Vzaimodeistvie veteranskikh organizatsij s organami vnutrennykh del i porazdeleniyami vnutrennykh vojsk," under the section "Vospitatel'naya rabota: shagi reformy," *Professional* (Popularno-pravovoj al'manakh MVD Rossii) 6 (2007): 17–19.
92. Ibid.
93. V. Mukhin, "Politicheskaya nota veteranskogo prizyva," *Nezavisimaya Gazeta*, April 4, 2007, http://www.ng.ru/printed/76993.
94. The minutes of the meeting of the TsSDV of the Defense Ministry of November 2, 2005, can be found at http://old.mil.ru/print/articles/article12486/shtml.
95. *Gazeta*, no 30, February 22, 2006.
96. S. Troshin, "Traditsii deval'vatsii ne podlezhat; s pervogo soveshchaniya veteranskogo aktiva vooruzhennykh sil RF."
97. Ibid.
98. In order to do this, Coordination Councils were set up in the seven federal regions. They are made up of regional representatives of Veterans Councils, vice-ministers of the Interior of the subjects of the Federation, heads of the GUVD, UVD, UVDT , and the Interior forces of the MVD of Russia.
99. Interview by E. Sieca-Kozlowski with I. A., Deputy President of the Council of Veterans of the MVD, Moscow, October 17, 2008.
100. *Voennye Komissariaty* 3 (2008): 31.
101. "Military training for civil servants," *Gazeta.ru*, February 9, 2001; see interview with the Head of the Department of Teaching and Science of the Regional Administration of Lipetsk, Yurij Taran, presented as returning from the previous day's exercise of general mobilization in the company of the heads of the local administrations and all the directors of the region, *Voennye Zaniia* 9 (2004): 10–11.
102. General Shamanov, accused of violent acts in Chechnya, is the former governor of the region of Ulyanovsk (2000–2004). Since March 2006, he has been advisor to the Defense Minister

and in November 2007 was appointed responsible for the moral training of officers. He is now in charge of the current military reform.
103. V. Silantyev, "If War Comes Tomorrow," *Narodnaia Gazeta* (Ulyanovsk), November 15, 2002, 1 and 6, *via WPS Defence and Security* 136, November 25, 2002.
104. According to the law "on military function and military service," a reservist can only be called up for training in his specialty once every three years; the length of service cannot go beyond 12 months.
105. Interview by E. Sieca-Kozlowski with the secretary of Kontingent, Association of Veterans of Afghanistan, Moscow, October 1, 2008.
106. Poliarnaia Pravda, quoted by G. Hønneland and A.-K.Jørgensen, in *Integration vs. Autonomy: Civil-Military Relations on the Kola Peninsula* (Ashgate: Alderchot, 1999), 167.
107. K. O'Flynn, "Join the Russian Army. Veterans of Chechnya set up a boot camp for tourists," *Newsweek,* August 8, 2005.
108. Hønneland and Jørgensen, *Integration vs. Autonomy.*
109. Ibid.,168.
110. Galeotti, *Afghanistan: The Soviet Union's Last War,*104–107.

CHAPTER TWO

The Return of the Conscripts—A Vector for the Construction of a National Security Regime in Turkey?

Sümbül Kaya

> **Abstract**
>
> This chapter analyzes the situation of Turkish soldiers who participated in the Kurdish conflict during their military service. It questions the extent to which the return of ex-combatants has been instrumentalized by the Turkish authorities, in particular through a mythification of past combats and sanctification of martyrs. This accounts for the expansion of a secutarian way of thinking within the society and thus facilitates a redeployment of the security regime in the social structures. Indeed, the return of the veterans to civilian life seems to play a role in the security ethos. Furthermore, the spread of this mode of thinking engenders an attitude of "moral armament" toward the Kurdish conflict.

Since 1984, the Turkish army and the Kurdish nationalist movement (Kurdistan Workers' Party) have been confronting one another, principally in southeast Anatolia. The arrest of the movement's leader, Abdullah Öcalan, had led to a ceasefire in 1999. The intervention of the Turkish army in northern Iraq in 2007, subsequent to the counteroffensive by Turkish Kurd guerrillas (PKK/Kongra-Gel), is illustrative of the resurgence of conflict and violence. The Turkish authorities justify the permanent presence of the Turkish army in the mountains of the Southeast by the need to combat "terrorism"—and this during a period of ceasefire.[1]

Regulars and conscripts are sent to the predominantly Kurdish zones on a regular basis to carry out military operations, but this chapter will deal only with conscripts. Large numbers of conscripts, who are aged between 19 and 22, are sent to the southeast, even though they are not war and combat professionals. They are generally recruited from among the lower classes—though not systematically.[2] Some of them receive only two or three months commando training in class, and then spend 15 months in the military.[3] These commandos' military service is very particular, as they make up the principal forces sent out on land operations. These conscripts fully take part in the war and are confronted with violent fighting. They therefore do not return unscathed to civilian life, and often have to confront difficulties in readapting when they return.[4] This chapter will study the processes and difficulties encountered in reintegrating into civil life and the effects their fighting experience has on their lives after the war.

War contexts have at times resulted in the militarization of society, where this term is used by Uri Ben-Eliezer when referring to the Israeli situation as meaning that "the population is constantly mobilised—either directly or indirectly—to wage war."[5] Alain Dieckhoff uses the term in the sense of "the generalised propagation of a security mindset,"[6] arising from the absence of any demarcation between the political and the military. In the case of Turkey, it seems preferable to base our analysis on the concept of "national security" (*Millî güvenlik*),[7] resulting in an emphasis on the drift toward security measures that has been operative for several years now. According to Gilles Dorronsoro, "national security" emerged "as the founding ideology of the regime after the coup in 1980," with the result that the regime "justifies the intervention of security institutions into practically every domain of social activity."[8] Ahmet Insel for his part describes the Turkish regime as a "national security regime"[9] based primarily on defending the essential characteristics of the Turkish state and its loyalty to the nationalism of Ataturk and the Kemalist ideology of the indivisibility of the land and nation.

This chapter will analyze to what extent the Turkish authorities make use of the return of former combatants to propagate a security mindset within society, and thus encourage the redeployment of the security regime in social structures. The hypothesis tested here is that this propagation of a security mindset provides the Turks with "moral arms" against the Kurdish conflict. This study is based on interviews of conscripts and former conscripts[10] carried out in Kayseri, one of the districts in Anatolia, between 2005 and 2007, on observation of the funerals of "martyrs" and rites on the return of conscripts, and on analysis of the local and national press.

The first part of this chapter will study the dynamics unleashed by the return to civil life of conscripts who have taken part in war operations. It will be suggested that their return to civilian life partakes in the propagation of a security ethos.[11] A second part will show how a "war myth" is built up, based both on national historiography and on the figures of the "martyrs" and "veterans," helping to consolidate the national security regime.

The Role Played by Demobilized Conscripts in Propagating a Security Ethos

The notion of a former combatant (*eski savaşçı*) is one that is never used by the Turkish authorities to describe combatants in the Southeast, because the operations carried out there are not considered to be part of a war. While the conscripts who come back "safe and sound" are not officially former combatants, they will be considered to be so here insofar as they have often directly taken part in war.[12] Conscripts and their families and close relations are attuned to the war—directly for conscripts, indirectly for their entourage. The "social construction of the war" passes via the vectors constituted by the returning soldiers and their entourage. The return of demobilized conscripts takes place without any involvement by the military institution, and their situation is thus unlike that of war veterans and the families of martyrs. In particular, no institutional assistance is available for the many psychological disorders caused by their experience of war. The fact that they return to civilian life without any support or backup from the specialized units in the Turkish armed forces no doubt makes it more difficult for them to readapt.

The question of the effects of war on conscripts, and on regulars too, is still a taboo subject in Turkish society. Those who might be tempted to speak are silenced by the obligation of confidentiality incumbent on people having taken part in "operations to combat terrorism." Some interviewees referred to "South-East syndrome" ("*Güneydoğu Sendromu*") to describe the psychological disorders specific to those combatants in the Kurdish conflict. What effect does their experience as combatants have on the conscripts' return to civilian life? Can the return of former combatants to civil society encourage the propagation of a security mindset? It will be argued here that their involvement partakes in the moral arming of Turkish society against Kurdistan Workers' Party (PKK) guerrillas, thus contributing to the social construction of an "enemy within."

Social Science,[13] a textbook used in secondary schools, presents the end of military service as a moment of festivity when the conscripts, surrounded by their family and friends, celebrate their return to civilian life. Field observations carried out showed that these returns were far less celebratory than the textbooks, interviewees, and families claim. In general, a few members of the family and friends go and pick up the person up at the bus station and take him back home. Often this is when conscripts make certain revelations, as some hid from their family the fact that they have been in the Southeast, where most of the fighting is, so as not to worry them. Over the course of the first two weeks, friends and family members come and visit the conscript's family. Codes of politeness demand that the guests tell the parents of the former combatant that they are "delighted to know it is behind you now." As their child escaped death, a sheep is sacrificed in accordance with Muslim rites and in reference to Abraham's sacrifice.[14] In Kayseri, the conscripts' families give pieces of mutton to their entourage and to needy strangers. Often people in Kayseri accompany this rite by giving sweets and chocolates to children from disadvantaged families.

It is true that the return of the conscript does initially give rise to the attention of his family and friends. National service gives him a new status within society, and the conscript is now a man in his own right.[15] But interviews show that after this period of welcome, and once they are no longer the center of attention, conscripts suffer from a feeling of emptiness and malaise. Talking about the state of mind of French conscripts who survived the First World War, Odile Roynette refers to a "nostalgia for the front."[16] The main effect of the return to civilian life is the loss of bearings conscripts had internalized during their military service, probably causing the feeling of emptiness. The norms and codes that hold in the military and civilian worlds are very different, obliging the conscripts to make an effort to adapt. Ali is 20 years old and has just gotten back from his service. The evening of his return, he spoke of what he felt: "I can't believe it's all over. I feel that I'm going to go back. I can't get used to it. I call my father 'Sir!' and I miss the friends I left behind. My mind is still back there."[17] In order to explain this feeling of emptiness, it is necessary to take into account the break that takes place with regard to the military rhythm imposed by the institution, and which minutely controlled the conscript's schedule throughout his military service. Behavior in daily civilian life includes skills and habits, which were not put into use during service. The conscript has interiorized the norms of his new military world and developed new habits in this "total institution," and so norms and routines of civilian life not repeated or carried out on a daily basis have been put on standby, as it were. Furthermore, the disciplinary measures, which are effective in barracks, reinforce the incorporation of the military ethos by the conscripts.[18]

Losing this rhythm can have a destabilizing effect for a certain time, leading the conscript to a certain degree of inactivity while seeking to reintegrate into the working world. Organization within the army, and in particular time management, did not leave the conscript any opportunity to reflect on his actions, since he had to obey orders and his schedule was minutely organized. But he is now free and in charge of his own life. What's more, conscripts also have to cope with changes that took place during their absence, such as births, deaths, and moving houses. Kahraman's story is evocative here: "But what do you expect? I came back and went around emptily like some idiot and without any money. There's nothing to do. And on top of that our house had been repossessed and destroyed. We now live in a little house near the hospital. I thought it was far too small. I wondered how we were going to cope with living there."[19] The conscript's return to civilian life obliges him to confront a world that is no longer familiar and he may at times experience it as strange, as some explain.

For certain former combatants, the return to civilian life is more difficult than military service was: "Reality kicks in after your service. I can't manage to forget what happened. But if I had to do it again, I would happily go back."[20] They often admit that they went through a difficult period adapting to civilian life. In general conscripts do not immediately work on returning. Certain basic things have to be learnt once again—washing, shaving, walking on metalled roads, drinking in a glass instead of a plastic cup, getting used to female company once again, and so on. Alice Kaplan underlies the fact the combatants need to relearn a "form of corporal economy," re-conquer their self-image, and discover "hygiene and propriety" once again.[21] They can find certain practices they integrated during their experience as a combatant hard to get rid of. Duran, for instance, kept all his cigarette butts during the interview we had with him, as in the mountains he had got used to not leaving any traces of his presence. And his way of holding his cigarette in his hand meant that it was totally hidden.

A few months of readaptation, the return to work, and the carrying out of new projects—getting married, engaged, or else other things—help the conscripts to rebuild their sense of self, with the material and affective support of their entourage. But while some conscripts manage to relaunch a new life, others never get over what they have been through. Families are obliged to look after sons who have not come back "in a normal state," who are unable to cope on their own and who display significant psychological disorders that were either produced or brought to the surface by war. It is not rare to hear people say "ever since he came back, he's been mad."[22] No support is provided by the military in this case, for only the physically wounded are deemed to be war veterans. The family and friends blame the PKK for the state of the conscript, and sometimes the Kurdish population even. It seems to them that Kurdish claims and behavior have harmed the integrity of the nation, i.e., their son. The Kurds are thus deemed to be responsible for the consequences of the war on conscripts sent to war. This leads certain families to adopt a racist stance. The return of the conscript therefore takes part in what could be called the "moral arming" of the families against the PKK and Kurdists (i.e., those who support the Kurdish cause). Certain mothers even adopt a violent attitude, such as the mother who explained to us that she asked her son to "bring back the head of Abdullah Öcalan."[23]

Language enables these former combatants to pass on the tales of their experience to people who have not taken part in war. It is thus a means of propagating the experience of war among the social environment of the former combatant. But it is important to distinguish between those who never want to talk about this experience again (and who resort to repressing their trauma and to silence), and those who spend many hours telling the tale of their military service, while deforming or exaggerating certain aspects of it.[24] Ziya tried to find out what things were like before going to the Southeast and explained that "some people told me about their experiences, but it wasn't really like that. If we started telling people what really happens there, nobody would want to go and do their service."[25] And as for Nedim, who we interviewed prior to his departure, he never wants to talk about the subject and wants to forget it as quickly as possible. Ahmet, who we met the day he got back, briefly referred to the fact that he had killed two people in combat and had received a bonus for that. He was to be monitored by the army's psychological unit since two months after these operations he was seeing in his dreams the people he had killed. Administering a medicinal treatment would help him to feel a bit better. He described scenes of torture in detail: "We caught a terrorist. He didn't want to talk so we gave him electroshocks and stuff. We hit him. The officer got an insect and put it in his ear. He ended up talking. So we set him free. He got a couple of meters and we shot him. We keep registers in the barracks, and it was essential he didn't appear in them, you see?"[26] Then he explained that from time to time in the mountains in the Southeast he had smoked drugs and sniffed glue. Paradoxically, given the problems revealed during the interview, he took the opportunity to proudly show off the three certificates of congratulation hanging in the living room (one for marksmanship, one for his motivation, and a more general one), as well as the photos of the party that had been held just before he had left for the front. He did not censor what he said as he had just got back, and so had not had time to distance himself from his experience.

The conscript's experience as a combatant affects the entire family and his personal and professional environment. Parents are proud that their child fought in the East and came back safe and sound. They find it normal that other young men go off to defend their country. The return of these young men who are neither "martyrs" nor "veterans" thus makes the war acceptable and legitimizes the fact that other families must take the same risk. This experience of the barracks and operations carried out in the Southeast thus has an effect on social issues. The stories are passed on to women (the mother, wife, fiancée, girlfriend, sister), even though they are excluded from combat experience. And so the stories of this traumatic experience help nourish subjectivities on the subject of the "enemy within" and the need to send combatants to the Southeast. The fact that conscripts adhere to the discourse of the central authorities can encourage the conscript's family to copy him and interiorize it. These young combatants have been exposed to daily violence throughout their service. They have been both victims of violence (the violence of their hierarchical superiors and the violence between conscripts) and perpetrators of this violence (toward supposed terrorists and other conscripts). Having experienced extreme situations and the death of other conscripts, they appropriate the discourse about "enemies within" driven by the military institution and adhere to military intervention and legitimize it. Systematic recourse to physical and verbal violence means that violence is internalized and trivialized, to a certain extent, since it is the norm in the barracks.

Yet violent and warlike predispositions integrated during their experience as a combatant are not automatically transferable to other contexts in civilian or nonmilitary life. In her work *Mehmedin Kitabı*, Nadire Mater refers to the fact that on returning to civilian life, some former combatants carry out criminal acts.[27] Her final chapter is about those "who are no longer able to speak." Her analysis of press reports in Turkey enables her to emphasize that certain conscripts who did their service in the southeast of Turkey go on to perpetrate violent and criminal acts. The example of the hijacking of a Turkish Airlines plane by İhsan Akyüz six months after returning from the Southeast, and that of Orhan Kara who killed his mother, sister, and brother three months after coming back from his service in Diyarbakır, enable her to reveal the mental suffering of these former combatants.[28] While it cannot be scientifically asserted that these conscripts reactivated their predispositions with regards to war and violence at the moment of perpetrating their acts, it may be noted how traumatizing these experiences of war can be and how they may lead to destructive acts. Nadire Mater quotes İhsan Akyüz's father: "Those who die become martyrs, those who become handicapped are veterans, but what are we going to call these children who come back disturbed?"[29] This sort of dramatic situation is revelatory of the problem of rehabilitating former combatants in Turkey. But the question of the nonrecognition of the social status of these conscripts, and the absence of care for posttraumatic disorders that some of them suffer from, are not publicly denounced or discussed.

Overall, the experience of socialization to the military order and to violence has complex effects on these conscripts. Despite difficulties in reassuming their place, some of them have integrated the norms and values of the military institution and central authorities, and act as vectors for them within society. The participation of conscripts in combats and operations carried out in the predominantly Kurdish zones, the involvement of their entourage, and the transmission of their tales of war can contribute to the propagation of a security mindset that legitimizes the Turkish national security regime. Others, however, bear the scars of their time spent in the army, and their close circle experiences the traumas of war with them.

While the return of conscripts is not accompanied by any support from the military or state authorities, the situation is wholly different for "martyrs" and "veterans" who benefit from very significant levels of support and are susceptible to encourage their family circle to accept the war. A particular place is accorded to soldiers who die on service, who are qualified as *şehit* by the law relating to the fight against terrorism, that is to say as "martyrs."[30] It is interesting to note that the figure of the "martyr" is meaningful both in the religious sphere and in the state and social sphere. Paradoxically, the ideological differences separating the Kemalists, who champion the secularity of the Turkish state, from the Islamists are erased here, and they agree in conferring on "martyrs" an exceptional status. *All* the population (including the "secular-minded") is convinced that "martyrs" continue to live in heaven. This is in reference to a verse in the Ali-i-Imran sura of the Koran—"Think not of those who are slain in the way of Allah as dead. Nay, they are living"[31]—and applies to the case of combatants in the Southeast. In religious circles, the Turkish armed forces are often referred to as the "home of the Prophet," *peygamber ocağı*. If soldiers die during operations in southeast Turkey, they are deemed to have been operating in the home of the Prophet and in the cause of Allah. "The martyr does not die," he is glorified. It is a means of giving him another meaning that transcends his physical existence and places him within a meta-community where his life continues in meta-history. Furthermore, the fact that the soldier achieves immortality doubtlessly makes the situation easier to accept for his close circle. As for the conscripts, the same law relating to the fight against terrorism states that they become "war veterans" if they are wounded while exercising their duties. "War veterans" (*ghazi*) and the families of "martyrs" receive compensation from the Turkish armed forces. The term also makes sense in religious circles as originally *ghazi* means someone who took part in an "operation to fight the Infidel, in other words, a Jihad operation."[32] As will be seen, the veneration of "martyrs" and "veterans" is a central element in the social and political construction of a "war myth" reinforcing the national security regime.

Constructing a "War Myth" and Reinforcing the National Security Regime

This part will analyze the various elements involved in the social and political construction of a "war myth" conjointly based on national historiography and the figures of "martyrs" and "veterans." The army, and the public authorities in general, make use of veterans and martyrs to help legitimize the war and designate the "enemies within." It will also be seen how the current mythologization of former combatants in the Kurdish conflict reactivates older representations of national heroes, and how national historiography plays an important role in propagating the security mindset.

National historiography, especially in Turkey due to the circumstances in which the Republic emerged, creates an affective relationship to the past by presenting former combatants of the early twentieth century as heroes. Current ideas about the Turkish nation depend heavily on the past and the context in which the Republic was created. The defeat of the Ottoman Empire, on the losing side in the First World War, led to its dismantling and a loss of public confidence. Mustafa Kemal Atatürk is considered to be the liberator and founding father of contemporary Turkey, as he called on the Anatolian populations to reconquer their lost territories. In his analysis of nationalist historiography from 1931 to 1993, the historian Étienne Copeaux underlines to just what extent it produces a "discourse of justification intended to give back to the Turks their confidence and pride, to correct their image, to prove the continuity and grandeur of their culture, and establish how long-standing and legitimate their presence was in Anatolia, and their ability over the millennia to devise State structures."[33] He argues that "the attachment to the Anatolian soil is expressed by glorifying sacrifice, frequent references to the enemy threat, and the call for cohesion and concord."[34] He considers this discourse to be a response to anti-Turkish feeling in the early twentieth century. From this perspective, "the aim of history teaching is as much to create an affective relationship to the past as it is to inform about it."[35] Great value is attached to the figures of the martyr and war veteran in Turkish national history, as they are held to have reinstated Turkey's honor and territory. They are called the heroes, "*Kahramanlar.*" Numerous commemorative speeches refer in particular to the martyrs and veterans of the Dardanelles War (1915–1916) and the "War of Independence" (1919–1922), which are officially viewed as the basis for current social peace and the existence of the Turkish nation.

The current conflict in the Southeast reactivates representations of these heroes of the past in the collective memory, and the martyrs and war veterans of today are reminiscent of these former combatants of the early twentieth century who sacrificed themselves for their country. As Xavier Bougarel argues, the hermeneutic grids for interpreting the conflict were already in place at the beginning of the war in the Southeast.[36] Past and present are caught up together, and national sentiment and/or national identity are reactivated within a society whenever it is led to believe, as Gérard Noiriel suggests, that its interests are "'threatened' by other national groups."[37] Rhetoric about the enemy without and enemy within, sacrifice for the nation, and the indivisibility of the Turkish nation and territory are very similar in the past and in the present. National historiography is thus a means of glorifying soldiers who died in the past or present and of viewing the present through the hermeneutic grid afforded by the past.

Collective memory is kept alive principally via commemorations, which encourage the assimilation between past and present. Government and state institutions devise commemorative ceremonies, which glorify martyrs and war veterans and which are thus involved in the social construction of the war and of a Kemalist national identity. These commemorative ceremonies are put in place both by central authorities and more locally. A law of June 27, 2002,[38] obliges institutions and government institutions to organize commemorative ceremonies on March 18 each year to pay homage to martyrs[39] and on September 19 for veterans. These ceremonies include associations and the population. Thus many ministers and the President of the Republic gave speeches on September 19, 2008, similar to that below, paying tribute to veterans, in which they also referred to martyrs. The Chief of General Staff, İlker Başbuğ, declared:

> The combat launched in order to protect the country and its independence, to protect the indivisibility of the Turkish nation, our national unity, and the possibility of living together, will never be forgotten thanks to your sacrifice and heroism [...]. If the Turkish nation is able to live freely, independently, and in unity today, it is thanks to our holy martyrs and our heroic veterans. A blessing upon our sublime leader Mustafa Kemal Ataturk first and foremost, and his companions in arms, and our holy martyrs and heroic veterans.[40]

The President of the Republic, Abdullah Gül, also gave a speech associating martyrs and veterans of the past to those of today:

> For the Turkish nation, it is 'martyrism' and 'veteranism' that places the nation above everything else. We have inherited this heavenly homeland from our martyrs and our veterans [...]. Our security forces are now helping in a fight against terrorism. The heroic veterans of this combat, sacrificing their all for their country, are the finest example of patriotic love. [41]

It is very interesting to note that the President's speech refers both to the past, by including former combatants of the War of Independence, and the present day, underlying the participation of Turkish armed forces in the fight against "terrorism." The speech by the Chief of General Staff refers more to the former combatants of the past, but his references to the "indivisibility of the Turkish nation," to "national unity," and to "the possibility of living together" also make sense in collective representations of the conflict in the Southeast. Associating past and present conflicts in this way can affect and move the population, and thus activate the national habitus.[42] Gérard Noiriel further argues that the traumatic events and sufferings undergone play a very important role in fixing the national habitus due to "the place taken by the affective dimension in the process of internalizing state norms and structures."[43] For Noirel, "armed conflicts, collective violence, are determining factors for the propagation of the feeling of belonging to the nation at all levels of society."[44] In the case under study here, the Turkish authorities, by making use of references to the War of Independence, which gave rise to the Republic, help reinforce the feeling of national belonging.

Legislation relating to commemorative ceremonies also has to be respected by local public authorities. Their proximity to the population can facilitate the activation of the national habitus and the recognition of the legitimacy of government interventions in the Southeast. In various districts the families of martyrs are invited to dinners laid on by the local public authorities. In Kayseri, the prefect invited the families of martyrs to a Ramadan meal, together with the rector of the University, politicians, the mayor, and administrative representatives. The photo alongside the article in the local press shows the leading figures of the town praying at the table with the Turkish flag, a photo of Mustafa Kemal Atatürk , and the emblem of the police hanging on the walls. During the meal the Prefect declared: "You are the people who have given their lives to the country. These martyrs are also our soul. Even if we don't often manage to get together, we are proud to be gathered together here today."[45] These events bringing together the families of the martyrs and various leading local figures receive extensive media coverage, which means that these images and speeches reach all of the district's inhabitants. It would seem that there are ever more commemorative practices. For instance, the prefecture in Kayseri has set up a space dedicated to the martyrs on its web site,[46] listing the last and first names of the martyrs "given" by the district of Kayseri (251 in all).[47] Visitors to the web site may also see a large number of photos taken during commemorative days (2007, 2008, and 2009). In addition to this, the funerals of "martyrs" of the Kurdish conflict tend to take place locally, since when a member of the commando dies during his military service his body is sent back to his place of residence. In this way the conflict in the Southeast is made visible and exported to the various Turkish districts. The local public authorities thus become involved in managing the effects of the war on wounded or dead soldiers. The "veterans" and "martyrs" are made use of, so as to help in turn with constructing the national security regime.

The veneration of martyrs and veterans can activate homogenous representations of the enemy and a conception of the nation and national identity conforming to the Kemalist ideology of the Turkish state. The mythologization of the figure of these former combatants by the authorities helps to make this war acceptable, even though the population's first reaction is to hold it to be scandalous (since their young men die in combat).

Observation of funeral ceremonies[48] makes it possible to assess how emotionally charged the death of a soldier described as a martyr is. The funeral rites are highly codified by the Turkish armed forces. The way the funeral is carried out, laid down by the institution, seeks to exalt and conceal the war. Describing a funeral ceremony attended by the present author[49] will bring out to just what extent the feeling of national belonging is reinforced. In Kayseri, the martyr's body is placed beneath a camellia in the gardens of the Grand Mosque. A crowd of people gradually gathers around the coffin of the deceased, surrounded by soldiers. They all wait for the end of the prayer , which is transmitted by loudspeakers outside the mosque and pronounced by the district leader of religious affairs (*Müftü*) working for the prefecture. At the end of the religious ceremony, the martyr's body is transported from the mosque to the cemetery. Leading local figures, the Mayor, the Prefect, the officer in charge of the Kayseri garrison, the *Müftü*, and the relatives of the departed, gather in front of the coffin. Then, after the prayer, there is a cortege. The cortege is led by 50 marching soldiers, who are followed by the military band, soldiers carrying wreaths of flowers, then the lorry followed on which is the body of the dead solider, followed in turn by the relatives, high-ranking officers, and, at the tail of the cortege, a crowd of citizens either waving the Turkish flag or else simply following the procession. Martyrs' funerals combine religious and military symbols in the same place, though they are often antagonistic within Turkish society.[50] The relatives may choose between a funeral at the barracks where the soldier was posted, or repatriation by the Turkish armed forces of the soldier's body to the mosque where he lived.[51] In both cases martyrs are entitled to a military and religious funeral, which are complementary. The soldier is buried in a special martyrs' cemetery with a soldier on guard, and the tombs of the martyrs of the Kurdish conflict lie close to the guardhouse. They are arranged by date of death, with the earliest dating from the War of Independence, followed by many tombs from 1993 and 1997[52] and more recent ones of 2007. The funeral rites for martyrs differ significantly from those of the average citizen. The coffin, normally covered by a green fabric, green being the color of Islam, is covered by a Turkish flag offered by the highest-ranking officer to the wife or oldest child, or else to the parents, brothers, and sisters. A high-ranking officer gives a medal to one of the members of the family. Martyrs' funerals attract great media coverage and are attended not only by the relatives in mourning but also by a large number of onlookers, who came to see this dramatic event, from tanks and soldiers in uniform taking over the mosque in the town center to the sound of a military band.

The broadcasting by local and national media of certain stereotypical images, such as the high-ranking officer kissing the hand of an old peasant woman wearing a veil, is intended to touch and move all of society. Soldiers give out safety pins and a photo of the martyr to the whole crowd, and everybody pins it to their heart. The crowd is deeply moved and soon becomes angry, and as they follow the body of the martyr from the mosque to the cemetery, they chant slogans against the PKK, "Curses on the PKK," or religion slogans, "Allah is great," or else "the fatherland is indivisible and martyrs do not die," "the greatest soldier is our soldier," and so on. People attending might be hesitant about the order in which to chant the slogans, but those cited above are heard at the majority of funeral ceremonies. The way the event is carried out, laid down by the institution, no doubt seeks to channel the anger and emotions of the participants.

State financial support for the families of martyrs and veterans is particularly sophisticated. It creates a link of dependency between the family and the Turkish armed forces that no doubt encourages the allegiance of

Figure 2.1   Legend: Funeral ceremony for a martyr, Kayseri, August 6, 2007

the families concerned. Article 61 of the Turkish Constitution stipulates that the state has an obligation to protect the families of martyrs who died at war, for the state, or in carrying out their functions, as well as the families of veterans, and to ensure they enjoy good living conditions. For in Turkey it is possible to die for the state. The law relating to the fight against terrorism sets out the rights of veterans and martyrs. The Turkish armed forces accord certain rights to the family of the deceased—to his wife, if he was married, or otherwise to his parents, brothers, and sisters—so as to relieve their suffering a bit and provide minimal support to those who have lost a relative. The Mehmetçik Foundation, set up on May 17, 1982,[53] by the Turkish armed forces, administers economic and social aid for families of conscripts, be they martyrs or veterans.[54] The role of the foundation is to pay out death and invalidity allowances to soldiers and their families, to provide educational assistance and continuous care for veterans' families, and to organize social programs bringing together veterans and their families, martyrs' families, and donors. Material support for the families of martyrs and for veterans consists in a lump sum[55] plus a monthly pension.[56] A text glorifying martyrs and veterans may be read on the foundation web site: "Soldiership is the most sacred value and source of honour in the Turkish tradition [...]. We say that martyrs are luminous, that is to say that they have pronounced religious and spiritual qualities and that the veteran is an honoured solider."[57] This official discourse of the foundation involves the sacralization of the soldier. Does the war thereby take on a sacred character?

In European societies, the veneration of dead soldiers is at the heart of the "war myth" at work during the First World War, as described by George L. Mosse. He argues that for France and Germany, the "Myth of the War," that is to say the transformation process of the reality of war to make it into "a meaningful and even sacred event,"[58] made it possible to transcend "the horror of war and at the same time supported the Utopia which nationalism sought to project."[59] This veneration is also said to take part in trivializing violence and war,[60] thus contributing to the "brutalisation of European societies." In the context under study here, does veneration of the dead soldier also result in violence and war being trivialized?

In Turkey the same phenomenon of transforming the reality of war into a sacred event may be observed. In addition to the role played by national historiography in exalting Turkish national identity, the veneration of dead soldiers and war veterans via commemorative ceremonies and speeches, the almost daily broadcasting of martyrs' funerals by the media, and the video films placed on websites by their families, all help build up a certain "war myth" in Turkey.

The sacralization of the war also feeds the ideological discourse of the far right, which is becoming more radical and no longer dissociates the Kurdish population from the PKK guerrillas.[61] Turkish ultra-nationalists do not hesitate to refer to the superiority of the Turkish race, even referring to Hitler and Nazism[62] to reinforce their ideology. They also accuse the Western countries of supporting the PKK, implying the complicity of foreign powers to divide the country from within.[63] As Gilles Dorronsoro suggests, the concept of "national security" guides "the main social and political questions... towards searching for an enemy within—possibly related to foreign powers—working to destroy Turkey."[64] Dehumanizing observations about the PKK guerrillas and sometimes about the Kurdish population were also made during interviews: "we call them the pigs,"[65] "they're baby killers,"[66] "we need to be wary of the most integrated who infiltrate our institutions."[67] Kurds represent "fifth columnists." In this way it would appear that violence and war tend to be trivialized.

Even if there are similarities between the process described by George L. Mosse and Turkey, there are nevertheless differences. Among the similarities is the fact of deploying a syntax of hegemony enshrined by the sacred and by the feeling of national belonging. National historiography, commemorative ceremonies and speeches, the way funerals are organized as laid down by the institution, and economic support for the families of martyrs and war veterans, all work together to mythologize combat and derealize the violence of the conflict. However, it would seem to be empirically impossible to prove that the Turkish people have become accustomed to "a certain level of visual and verbal violence."[68] Such a generalization seems unwarranted: how could one empirically prove that people get used to the "awesome and frightening," as George L. Mosse suggests? But it may nevertheless be stated that, with regard to discourse, a favorable feeling toward the Turkish armed forces is developed, and that the length of the conflict creates a feeling of insecurity among the population who, in return, consider operations to fight against "terrorism" to be legitimate. Ahmet Insel thus underlines the determination of "praetorian forces" to maintain their position of power: "By permanently pointing out the perils threatening the unity and integrity of the Republic, the praetorian forces regularly seek to reproduce the conditions for a national security regime in which the exceptional nature of the situation authorises the extending of the exceptional nature of certain tutelary powers."[69]

The veneration of martyrs and veterans, and the discursive production of a dehumanized representation of the enemy, foster the process of moral arming against the PKK guerrillas. The social construction of the war and designation of "enemies within" are certainly at work. The veneration of martyrs and veterans reinforces a national identity conforming to the Turkish state's Kemalist ideology, and stigmatizes the figure of the enemy of the nation. The Turkish population is permanently called upon, either directly or indirectly, in this conflict. For instance, the death of a soldier affects all of society. He could be anyone's son. Everybody feels concerned, and everyone knows someone who was sent to the predominantly Kurdish zones on their service. The involvement of conscripts and their entourage in this conflict also takes part in the propagation and internalization of a security mindset.

The military institution thus derives a certain social legitimacy from this. It is not unusual to see parents walking around with their son dressed in military uniform, which can be bought on markets in the same way as traditional costumes can. In the commando market in Kayseri,[70] where conscripts go to study, anyone can buy postcards showing caricatures of barracks' life, with what looks like real grenades set out in such a way as to spell "I love you" or "I'm not dead yet, Mum." While these objects are indeed a reminder of war, it does not thereby follow, as George L. Mosse suggests, that "war is seen as a game,"[71] and that the experience of war is thus trivialized. Instead it needs to be underlined that, as a social construct, individuals perceive this war in varying ways. Even though state institutions seek to influence the way the war is seen by using former combatants, as seen above, this does not confirm the hypothesis that violence is trivialized. Furthermore, even if there is a consensus in regards to the glorification of martyrs and veterans, that does not engender a generalized acceptance by Turkish society of war and violence, as the existence of anti-war movements illustrates.[72]

Conclusion

The sacralization of martyrs and war veterans, the commemorative ceremonies and speeches, the funeral ceremonies of martyrs and their media coverage, as well as the return of combatant conscripts to civilian life, all take part in the moral arming of Turkish society with regard to the Kurdish conflict. These practices enable the Turkish state to invest in social structures and legitimize the national security regime. The security discourse is thus a resource for the Turkish regime. Yet its effects on society can be ambivalent. Élizabeth Picard underlines that "security discourse lies at the heart of authoritarian measures to stigmatize the enemy and construct a shared normative ethos, even though this has the effect of exacerbating identity differences within the national community (by designating offending individuals and groups, or by building up the figure of the enemy within), thus feeding state violence."[73] In the case under study here, the "shared normative ethos" is the Turkish state's Kemalist ideology. The state makes use of former combatants to stigmatize the "enemies within," either Kurdists or Islamists. Overall, it succeeds in mobilizing society around the figures of the martyr and the former combatant, by celebrating them within the long time frame of Republican history, thus legitimizing its security ideology. The reverse side of making use of the return of conscripts in this way may, however, be observed in the difficulties they experience in reintegrating into society and in the propagation of violent emotions and reactions within their environment, to the point where illegal armed actions are carried out in the name of security imperatives.

Since October 20, 2008, the "Ergenekon" trial has been taking place, implicating very high-ranking officers in the Turkish armed forces, as well as journalists and businessmen, in the activities of a terrorist, ultranationalist organization. This affair shows that security discourse is not the exclusive prerogative of the state in Turkey. The indictment states that members of this organization wanted to defend "national interests" and felt that "the State could not be governed in a safe and certain manner with constitutional laws."[74] Their intention was to sow terror in the country so as to be able to seize power and eject the government of the Justice and Development Party, which they consider to be insufficiently secular. This shows that the violence of war has indeed contaminated political life in Turkey. Translated by Adrian Morfee.

Notes

1. For details about the history of the conflict, see H. Bozarslan, *Les Kurdes. L'autre front du Proche-Orient* (Paris: Autrement, 2009); *Histoire de la Turquie contemporaine* (Paris: La Découverte, 2004); and *La question kurde: États et minorités au Moyen-Orient* (Paris: Presses de Sciences-Po, 1997).
2. Observations and interviews carried out at the Kayseri commandos market confirm the idea that the commandos come mainly from the lower classes.
3. S. Kaya, "La fabrique du 'soldat-citoyen' à travers la conscription en Turquie," *European Journal of Turkish Studies* 8 (2008): http://www.ejts.org/document2922.html.
4. These difficulties were referred to by the people interviewed. Also see the book by Nadire Mater, *Mehmedin Kitabı* (Istanbul: Metis Yayınları, 2001).
5. Translated from the French, U. Ben-Eliezer, "L'armée, la société et la nation-en-armes," *Les Cahiers de l'orient* 54 (1999): 161.
6. Translated from the French, A. Dieckhoff, "Où va Israël?" *Critique internationale* 16 (July 2002): 33.
7. The 1982 Turkish Constitution refers nine times to this concept: http://www.tbmm.gov.tr/Anayasa.htm. What is more, the National Security Council (*Milli güvenlik kurulu*) played a dominant role in the world of politics until 2003.
8. Translated from the French, G. Dorronsoro (ed.), *La Turquie conteste. Mobilisations sociales et régime sécuritaire* (Paris: CNRS Éditions, 2005), 24.
9. According to Ahmet Insel, "until 1997, the national security regime was in place primarily to handle the Kurdish problem" and he describes the regime from February 28, 1997, on as a "National Security Council and permanent coup regime," for "security management expanded from the Kurdish problem to that of political Islam" (translated from the French). Ahmet Insel, "'Cet État n'est pas sans propriétaires!' Forces prétoriennes et autoritarisme en Turquie," in O. Dabène, V. Geisser and G. Massardier (eds.), *Autoritarismes démocratiques et démocraties autoritaires au XXe siècle,* (Paris : La Découverte, 2008), 147.
10. This research is based on semi-guided and open interviews (narratives of their military experience). The corpus of interviews falls into three groups: men getting ready to do their military service, those doing it, and those who had come back from it. For certain interviewees it was possible to carry out all three successive stages. A sample was established representing different social and professional categories, different places of residence (urban/rural), and different political and ideological sensibilities. In some instances the interview was supplemented by contributions from the mother or wife of the interviewee. Officers in charge of training conscripts were also interviewed, and observations carried out in barracks.
11. For Bourdieu, the word ethos means "an objectively systematic set of dispositions with an ethical dimension, and practical principles" (translated from the French). See P. Bourdieu, *Questions de sociologie* (Paris: Minuit, 1984), 133. The term security ethos will be used to refer to the set of security measures and practices.
12. This chapter will draw on interviews of men who took part in combat as commandos during their military service, or who did their service in police stations, prisons, etc. in southeast Turkey. Some of them took part in combats, and others carried out surveillance or information-gathering work. These interviews were conducted outside the barracks, sometimes several years after their return from military service.
13. D. Yıldırım, Özkül Çobanoğlu, and M. Özarslan, *Liseler için, Halk Bilimi* (Istanbul: Devlet Kitapları, 2004), 132–133.
14. Abraham is said to have accepted to sacrifice his son out of obedience to God, but God allowed him to sacrifice a sheep in his place.
15. Military service may be considered as a "rite of passage" with the conscript losing his status as a child and becoming a man. For a definition of the rite of passage, see A. Van Gennep, *Les rites de passage* (Paris: Editions A. & J. Picard, 1981).

16. O. Roynette, "La nostalgie du front," in B. Cabanes, G. Picketty (eds.), *Retour à l'intime au sortir de la guerre,* (Paris: Tallandier, 2009), 51–65.
17. Interview carried out with Ali, on July 25, 2007, in Kayseri.
18. See Kaya, "La fabrique du 'soldat-citoyen.'"
19. Interview carried out with Kahraman on March 22, 2006, in Kayseri.
20. Interview carried out with Yakup on July 12, 2007.
21. Translated from the French, A. Kaplan, "Espaces publics, espaces privés, espaces intimes en sortie de guerre," paper given at the international conference organized by the Sciences Po History Center on "The Return to Private Life after the War, from the First World War to the Current day," June 19–20, 2008.
22. Interview carried out on April 19, 2006, in Çiraz (a small village in the district of Kayseri) with the family of a former combatant.
23. Interview carried out with Fatma on March 14, 2006, in Kayseri.
24. It is possible to avoid certain blockages by taking into account the moment when they speak. The men spoke more readily in interviews shortly after their return, and when the interview was not being recorded. The greater the lapse of time since their return, the more they repress their emotions, fears, and anxieties. What is more, the soldiers were silenced by the obligation of confidentiality regarding operations carried out during their service.
25. Interview carried out with Ziya on March 25, 2006, in Kayseri.
26. Interview carried out with Ahmet on July 24, 2007, in Kayseri.
27. Mater, *Mehmedin Kitabı.*
28. Ibid., 246–256.
29. Ibid., 246.
30. The law relating to the fight against terrorism no. 3713 was adopted and officially published on April 12, 1991. It may be consulted on the official web site of the Ministry of the Interior devoted to martyrs and war veterans: http://www.sehitlervegaziler.gov.tr.
31. Verse of the Ali-i-Imran sura: "Think not of those who are slain in the way of Allah as dead. Nay, they are living. With their Lord they have provision. Jubilant [are they] because of that which Allah hath bestowed upon them of His bounty, rejoicing for the sake of those who have not joined them but are left behind: that there shall no fear come upon them neither shall they grieve." Source: http://www.yabiladi.com/coran/.
32. Translated from the French, J. and D. Sourdel, *Dictionnaire historique de l'Islam* (Paris: Presses universitaires de France, 2004), 313.
33. Translated from the French, É. Copeaux, *Espaces et temps de la nation turque. Analyse d'une historiographie nationaliste 1931–1993* (Paris: CNRS Éditions, 1997), 33.
34. Ibid., 339.
35. Ibid.
36. X. Bougarel, "Guerre et mémoire de la guerre dans l'espace yougoslave," in S. Yérasimos (ed.), *Le retour des Balkans 1991–2001,* (Paris: Éditions Autrement, coll. Mémoires, no. 78, 2002).
37. Translated from the French, G. Noiriel, *État, nation et immigration. Vers une histoire du pouvoir* (Paris: Belin, 2001).
38. Law no. 4768 of June 27, 2002, officially published on July 3, 2002.
39. The date of March 18 is that of the destruction of Allied shipping by the Turks in the Battle of the Dardanelles.
40. Speech on September 19, 2008, available on the web site of the Turkish armed forces: http://www.tsk.mil.tr.
41. Official Turkish government martyrs and veterans web site: http://www.sehitlervegaziler.gov.tr.
42. Norbert Elias gives the following definition of the national habitus: "What we call the 'national character' is a stratum of the social habitus that is very deeply and very solidly anchored within the structure of the individual's personality [...]. The deep rooting of various national characters, and the awareness of one's own national collective identity which is very closely bound up with this character, could be a fairly clear example of the way the social habitus of the individual acts as the ground on which purely personal individual differences develop." (translated from the French), *La société des individus* (Paris: Fayard, 1991), 273.
43. Noiriel, *État, nation et immigration,* 136.
44. Ibid.
45. "Şehit ve gazi ailelerine iftar yemeği," *Kenthaber,* December 24, 2008.

46. Kayseri prefecture web site: http://www.kayseri.gov.tr/.
47. The Kayseri prefecture also took part in producing an album called "2007 album of martyrs and veterans of Kayseri."
48. Observations carried out in Kayseri on August 6, 2007, and studies of many videos on YouTube and on Dailymotion.
49. Observation carried out in Kayseri on August 6, 2007.
50. Secularism is one of the characteristics of the Turkish state (article 2 of the 1982 Constitution). The measures set out in article 2 cannot be modified.
51. In practice, the body of the dead solider is repatriated most of the time to the mosque where he lived.
52. The period when operations in the southeast became more intense.
53. Same day the Constitution drawn up by the military was adopted, subsequent to their coup on September 12, 1980.
54. Foundation web site: http://www.mehmetcik.org.tr.
55. The death allowance is paid to the families of "martyrs" and conscripts who die while carrying out their functions. The invalidity allowance is paid to soldiers who have become war veterans or who were wounded during their service. A death allowance is paid in the event of the death of the war veteran or wounded soldier. A birth allowance is paid if the veteran or wounded soldier has a child during their military service. A child's death allowance for the offspring of martyrs, veterans, and wounded soldiers is paid in the event of the death of their child.
56. Care benefit is paid monthly to the veteran or wounded soldier. A monthly benefit is paid for the education of the offspring of martyrs, war veterans, and soldiers wounded during their military service. For martyrs and veterans who were not conscripts but regulars, the benefits are substantially higher. The Turkish armed forces accord financial assistance to one of the martyr's—funeral costs, financial compensation, an educational benefit for children—and the general directorate of the Turkish Republic's pension fund also accords them a monthly salary. The families are also entitled to a series of advantages: reduced electricity bills, exoneration from land tax, social security protection, a Turkish armed forces ID card, access to specialized training centers, free public transport, free car parking, access to military officers' clubs, the excusing from military service for the martyr's brother, recruitment as a civil servant for one of the relatives of the deceased person, exoneration from higher education enrollment fees for the martyr's children, and free access to specialized educational establishments. Martyrs' children take priority for lodging and credits when they are students and for entering a military school.
57. The foundation's values include, among others, honesty, respectability, respect for national values and Atatürk's principles, responsibility, transparency, creative participation, and neutrality. http://www.mehmetcik.org.tr.
58. George L. Mosse, *Fallen Soldiers: Reshaping the Memory of the World Wars* (New York: Oxford University Press, 1990), 7.
59. Ibid., 106.
60. According to George L. Mosse, "The public remembrance of war appropriated religion and nature, forces which had always served to uplift men and women. The memory of war was also appropriated through a process of trivialization, cutting war down to size so that it would become commonplace instead of awesome and frightening [...]. Trivialization was one way of coping with war, not by exalting and glorifying it, but by making it familiar, that which was in one's power to choose and to dominate." Ibid., 126.
61. Interview with Ali on July 3, 2008, in Kayseri.
62. Ibid.
63. These arguments crop up in numerous interviews: "Foreign powers are at work to divide Turkey from within."
64. Dorronsoro, *La Turquie conteste*.
65. Interview carried out in Kayseri with İhsan on July 15, 2007.
66. Informal, anonymous document about the "Sun" operation carried out by Turkey in northern Iraq against the PKK/Kongra-Gel since February 21, 2008.
67. Informal conversation with a Kayseri journalist, March 29, 2006.
68. Mosse, *Fallen Soldiers*, 181.
69. Insel, "'Cet État n'est pas sans propriétaires!'"

70. The Kayseri commando market is a place where businesses specialized in the military sector can be found grouped together. Barbers, hairdressers, photographers, and bookstores are used by conscripts studying in Kayseri.
71. See Mosse, *Fallen Soldiers*, 142.
72. See the web site of those opposed to the war: http://www.savaskarsitlari.org.
73. Translated from the French, Elizabeth Picard, "Armée et sécurité au Coeur de l'autoritarisme" *in* O. Dabène, V. Geisser and G. Massardier (eds.), *Autoritarismes démocratiques et démocraties autoritaires au XXe siècle*, 308.
74. Indictment (*Ergenekon İddianamesi*) in Turkish, available on the web site of the *Milliyet* newspaper: http://i.milliyet.com.tr/ergenekon/iddianame.aspx?sayfa=49.

CHAPTER THREE

Reintegrating Civilian Life after Combat: Between Invisibility and Resistance. The Experience of the Ronderas in Peru

CAMILLE BOUTRON

> **Abstract**
>
> Between 1980 and 2000, Peru was shaken by violent armed conflict causing the death of more than 69,000 people. In collaboration with the army, civil defense patrols were set up in the peasant communities hardest hit by political violence. Known as *Comités de Autodefensa*, these organizations armed themselves to protect their communities. Although the majority of their members were men, women made a significant contribution to self-defense activities. Their participation, however, has been obliterated from the memory of the communities. Moreover, incidents of domestic violence against women have increased sharply, a fact interpreted by the author as due to the continuation of a "warrior habitus" in peacetime.

Between 1980 and 2000, Peru was shaken by a violent armed conflict that resulted in the death of more than 69,000 people.[1] Two left-wing political parties, the Maoist Shining Path-Communist Party of Peru (PCP-SL) and the Tupac Amaru Revolutionary Movement (MRTA), inspired by the Cuban and Sandinista revolutions, in turn declared their armed opposition to the Peruvian state, which was then undergoing its transition to democracy. Paradoxically, it was with the return of authoritarianism incarnated by Alberto Fujimori's rise to power that subversive actions waned, beginning in the early 1990s with the arrest of the main leaders of the armed rebel groups.

Following the resignation of President Fujimori at the end of 2000 and the establishment of a transitional regime with the responsibility of ensuring a return to democracy, a genuine national reflection emerged on these 20 years of political violence. This was symbolized by the creation of a Truth and Reconciliation Commission (*Comisión de la Verdad y Reconciliación*—CVR), whose final report was made public at the end of August 2003. While the principal militants of the PCP-SL and the MRTA were condemned to serve long prison sentences, the main nongovernmental organization (NGO) type civil society organizations turned their attention to the victims and their families, in order to obtain the establishment of mechanisms of transitional justice. Any form of negotiation with the rebels had been pushed back, along with all possible demobilization, disarmament, and reconciliation programs (DDR *process*). However, the criminalization of subversive groups was not the only strategy adopted by the state. During the 1980s it also relied upon the civilian self-defense committees (SDCs), which were formed in the rural areas most affected by the conflict. Indeed, armed conflict in Peru also led to a militarization of certain sectors of civil society. Regular collaboration with the armed forces, manifest in the establishment of military bases in the regions most affected by political violence, influenced the social and political organization of rural communities to the point where the persistence of military culture is remarkable, even long after the intensity of the conflict has declined.

Although a large number of studies have been devoted to these armed groups (particularly the PCP-SL but also the Self-defense Committees), few of them have chosen to explore the issue of gender—which is generally "reserved" for questions dealing with the transitional justice process, peacekeeping, or development in postconflict society. Yet an estimated 40 percent of militants in the PCP-SL were women, and women were also very involved in the MRTA. Similarly, the self-defense committees relied on the contribution of the women of the communities concerned, through activities designed to complement and support those carried out by the self-defense patrols. Despite this, the title of "combatant" is rarely attributed to these women, either by the men of their communities or by representatives of civil society on the field. Women are more commonly reduced to "supporting" roles: fulfilling the daily needs of the armed groups during the conflict and then participating in the reconstruction of social ties in their communities when peace returned. In the wake of the conflict, they found themselves excluded from the various processes of construction and reproduction of a collective memory of the conflict within their communities.

This chapter focuses on the experience of women in these organizations, insisting above all on the process of invisibilization they are subject to with the return of peace. This invisibility manifests itself in a certain marginalization of women from public affairs in the community, and in their absence from the collective memory constructed around the role of the self-defense committees in the counter-subversive struggle. In mobilizing these actors, who have been largely ignored up until now, we hope to propose a different perspective on the reinsertion of former combatants. We use gender as a tool to provide an alternative interpretation of these processes.

We begin by observing that women's participation in self-defense activities opens up a path to new spaces of collective action, but also to activities generally reserved for men. These changes have the effect of blurring the cultural boundaries that constructed gender identities in the community, which may cause problems with the arrival of peacetime. Indeed, we then go on to show how the withdrawal of women from self-defense activities is accompanied by an increase in and a transformation of domestic violence, which can be interpreted here as a continuation of armed violence. We will also argue that this type of violence in a postconflict society should not only be considered a possible expression of posttraumatic scarring from armed violence but should also be seen as the expression of social, political, and cultural tensions and upheavals resulting from the normalization of self-defense activities in the community's agenda.

The Engagement of Women in Self-defense Committees and Its Effects

The Emergence and Role of Self-defense Committees during the Peruvian Armed Conflict

Self-defense committees (SDCs) take the form of collective organizations bringing together members (generally men) of one or more communities in order to fight against attacks perpetrated by subversive groups in rural areas.[2] These organizations were either born of the community members' own initiative or set up under the auspices of the army, according to the model of counter-subversive struggle inherited from the American experience in Vietnam.[3] Moreover, SDCs represent a sort of hybrid organization to the extent that on one hand, they can be considered a phenomenon directly produced by the conflict, and on the other, they are part of historical preexisting rural practices. In the second half of the nineteenth century, the *ronda campesina,* or peasant rounds, were active in the north of the country, with the objective of protecting the community against cattle thieves and insecurity in the countryside.[4] The SDCs that were formed during the 1980s broke with this tradition however; it was no longer a matter of defending the village from possible pillage but rather of organizing the whole community around self-defense activities in collaboration with the armed forces present in the area. As a result, the committees underwent a process of militarization that was without precedent in the history of rural Peru and were recognized as actors in their own right in the counter-subversive struggle from 1991. In the rural communities, the terms *la ronda* or *la autodefensa* are often used to designate the organization itself, while its members are called *ronderos*.

The formation of SDCs initially concerned those regions most affected by the conflict, i.e., the areas of Ayacucho, Huancavelica, Apurímac, and Junín, before gradually spreading to the rest of the national territory. The most representative committees are those of the valley of the Apurímac and Ene rivers (VRAE), which run along the northern part of the Ayacucho region. The first of these structures were officially established in May 1984 and were referred to as Counter-subversive Civilian Defense (Decas). They were the first self-defense organizations that succeeded in setting up a network across a whole regional area.[5] They are particular in that they were organized relatively independently of the army (although the constant collaboration between the soldiers and the *ronderos* is clear). The VRAE is identified as being one of the most marginalized areas of the country, in which drug-trafficking is widespread. The SDCs thus also filled a void in power while gaining legitimacy by their counter-subversive activities.

In other instances, it was the army that was behind the formation of the SDCs. In 1983, in the Huanta province, also in the area of Ayacucho, the army successfully organized more than 600 families into self-defense at the "multi-community" base of Ccarhuahurán.[6] Further south from the regional capital, in the Ayacucho and Huancasancos provinces, the first SDCs were formed from 1984 onwards, when farmers began to rebel against the Shining Path guerrillas, whom they had previously welcomed. In fact, the members of the rural communities did not take kindly to their traditional authorities being replaced by militants of the PCP-SL, who combined personal and family interests with politics, thereby exacerbating micro-conflicts within the communities.[7]

The end of the 1980s saw the SDCs spread to all areas of the national territory affected by political violence. The Decas of the VRAE area extended their influence to the Andean communities, and set up a system of remuneration for the *ronderos*, which completed the formalization of the SDCs. In March 1990 the Central Committee of the Peasant Rounds of upper and lower Tulumayo in the region of Junín was set up. The phenomenon then spread to the neighboring region of Huancavelica and those in the south (the areas of Puno and Cusco), as well as the traditional peasant rounds in the Piura and Cajamarca regions in the north. It thus became the expression of a new kind of social movement. According to Aldo Olano, in 1993 there were more than 4,200 SDCs bringing together more than 230,000 *ronderos* across the country—which at that time had a population of 23 million people (according to the Peruvian National Institute of Statistics).[8] Although these committees were born of the need to fight against attacks by subversive groups, their members ended up gaining strong influence within their communities. This led them to take on roles beyond those of self-defense, particularly in areas under the prerogatives of public authorities. Ponciano del Pino, therefore, shows how, in certain communities, the SDCs take part in the administration of justice, resolution of family disputes, or intracommunity conflicts—or even represent the demands of their communities at state level. This was the case for example in April 1992 when the president of the Palmapampa SDCs travelled to Lima in order to demand medicines following an outbreak of cholera.⁹

Although the SDCs were active from the very first years of armed conflict, they were only legalized at the end of 1991, with the passing of Parliamentary Decree 741, which established their code of conduct. This came, however, at the same time as the question of the demilitarization of rural areas engaged in counter-subversive struggle was being raised. Indeed, far from having disappeared with the end of armed violence, this organization paradoxically emerged as a key actor in civil society. As evidence of this, the SDC representatives of the VRAE regions are regularly called upon during debates preceding the implementation of public policy, as was the case with the "Peace and Development" plan, which involved an investment of some 150 million dollars by the Peruvian state.¹⁰

Different Forms of Women's Engagement in the Self-defense Committees

Self-defense committees are generally presented as structures in which the specific activities consist of patrolling around the village to ensure its security. In reality, however, it seems that self-defense is rarely limited to simple patrols; the whole community is involved in one way or another in self-defense activities. Community members might thus be involved in surveillance tasks or other chores that, although they might not look like self-defense tasks, are nonetheless related (such as the preparation of meals for the *ronderos* or healing the wounded). Moreover, they might also be involved in less traditional activities such as interacting with soldiers or taking responsibilities for tasks that they were not traditionally responsible for. The SDCs were thus behind a radical shift in the relationships between individuals; gender—or at least the references associated with gender—was a decisive factor in these changes.

The place of women in the SDCs is worth exploring in detail. Some were heads of commando units such as T. R. who was put in place by the army at the head of a group of 30 women in the Ticllas community. We could also evoke the example of H. a Huanta shopkeeper originally from a neighboring community, who after being initially persecuted by the army, was appointed by them at the head of a commando covering some 20 communities:

> And finally things changed, they started to reform the commandos and then the army appointed me head of the commando, of 26 commandos in the district [...] they appointed me head of the commandos of the whole base! [...] one day the soldiers decided to get us all together and they called me. They called me by my name, and they

said "you'll be the head of the commando," even though the people had chosen someone else. So I said that I didn't want to, because I had my children to look after and I lived in Huanta. But they forced me to accept.[11]

I., from a village to the north, did not wait to be forced by the army before forming a commando so that other young girls of her community could mount a patrol. For several years, while other communities took advantage of the chaos generated by the conflict to attack her village, she directed a self-defense unit entirely composed of women, before it was finally dispersed at the end of the 1990s:

It was in 1992–1993, and they (the SDCs of the neighboring communities) were starting to mistreat us. When we arrived they wanted to hit us, punish us, and we, the young ones, we rebelled against them, and we said "we're going to form a women's commando," and we did, we set up a commando of 15 women, all young, and they picked me as their leader. After that, we started working, going out on patrol when it was our turn with the men commandos, because when people from another community arrived, they treated us badly, they came in the night and they took us out of the house, and they punished us in all possible ways... That's why we had to fight back against the other communities.

Yes, we women participated, they even gave us weapons. For the self-defense committee in each community, we had to collect money to buy weapons, or in other cases the state gave them to us. For example, the machine guns were brought through the forest. We bought lots of weapons like that. Everyone had their gun, and I had one. When there was the slightest alarm, we went out straight away on patrol, we defended the village well. We did what we had to do to defend ourselves.[12]

On the other hand, the testimony of R. whose husband (a commando leader) was killed by PCP-SL militants, shows how the smooth running of the counter-subversive activities conducted by the communities involved all their members:

There were other women who were active participants, young women. And we were all part of the *ronda*, we didn't live in our houses anymore, we all slept in the same place. For example, we'd say "tonight we'll sleep here," and so while we got together the men patrolled. Then we built small huts so we didn't have to sleep in the houses, because that was certain death. At night the soldiers come and they kill you, and the terrorists come and they kill you. But during the day we'd go back down to the village and work in the fields. But those who didn't participate in the *ronda* were punished and the soldiers always came for roll call. Whether it was raining, too cold or too hot, they did roll call. So my husband's role was always to keep people together.[13]

At the same time, the women also responded to the insecurity caused by the conflict by increasing their collective organization initiatives, such as the "mothers' clubs" which emerged in the first years of conflict. In addition to her self-defense activities, I. was also behind the formation of the first mother's club of her village:

> [W]hen I saw how many mothers there were, how many widows, or poor children, who cried every day, when we saw that, we thought of making our own organization to pool our resources, to help the young people, in all this blood, and that's why we're attached to our organization. [...] because there were sons, fathers, brothers, men yeah, who were taken away. They [the soldiers] just made them disappear. That's where the women came in, with our children on our backs, we sat in front of the door to the police station at the military base, and well they couldn't touch us because we made a hell of a racket. [...] So the organization was looking for support, to look after the children, and to make the region peaceful again. Within our district we pretty quickly had thirty-five mothers' clubs and we had leaders in each community.[14]

This type of organization revealed itself to be a key place for learning about politics, for actors who were normally excluded from the political sphere. The mothers' clubs, which were trying to provide a response to the immediate needs of the rural communities, gradually became established institutions. In 1988 the Provincial Federation of the Ayacucho Mothers' Clubs was born, and other survival organizations followed, until eventually a Regional Federation of Mothers' Clubs was formed, covering the whole of the region (Fedecma[15]). According to Isabel Coral, the women of the Ayacucho region achieved a redefinition of their roles in both the public and private spheres, most notably through the collectivization of domestic work and responsibilities.[16] They also succeeded in imposing themselves as interlocutors between the SDCs and their communities; negotiating the conditions of men's participation in self-defense, managing to limit the recruitment by the SDCs to one man per family, and seeking to contain the expanding sphere of action of the SDCs.

In most instances, women supported the war effort by taking on new roles and functions previously reserved for men. This was how women came to be appointed *regidoras* in certain villages, in order to replace the traditional authorities who may have fled before the threat of the PCP-SL. There were women who became veritable local legends for having taken up "risky" public positions. One of these was R. L. who replaced the Mayor of her village in Huanta province (in the Ayacucho region) after he fled to Lima; another is H. M. in one of the communities of the VRAE region.[17] These women were either elected by the people who had not fled the community or were appointed by the local SDC and received the support of all their fellow citizens. The development of self-defense activities provoked radical changes in the social relationship between the sexes. Thus, we might consider this a privileged interpretative space for the analysis of the demobilization of the SDCs and the reinsertion of their members, both men and women, into civilian life.

Gender Confusion and Transformations in Social Sex Relations

The activities that the women of the communities developed during the conflict manifest a certain "gender confusion." This is primarily explained by the demographic changes provoked by the violence that affect individuals differently depending on their gender. Although the majority of fatalities in the conflict were male, women represented other specific targets, notably in the case of sexual violence. They nonetheless made up the majority of survivors and thus had to deal with the absence of a masculine labor force. Moreover, because they were traditionally in charge of reproductive work, women were the first to have to show initiative in developing new survival strategies, both on a material and social level. The need to take care of children orphaned by the conflict, to resolve food shortages produced by the abandonment of agricultural work or pillaging in many communities, or to search for missing persons, pushed them to join forces and work collectively. Meanwhile the organization of daily life was to be transformed in response to new requirements imposed by self-defense strategies.

Many of the women who took on self-defense tasks were also women "without men," i.e., widows or unmarried women. Indeed, those who could not be "represented" by a man, whether by their husband, brother, or a son old enough to participate in self-defense, had to occasionally take up these self-defense tasks themselves. M.[18] who runs the mothers' club in the neighboring village to I.'s, thus tells of how toward the end of the 1980s, militants from the PCP-SL conducted a raid on her community and forcibly enlisted everyone considered able to fight—including her husband. Only old people, widows, and young children were spared. When the army arrived in the village shortly afterwards to set up a self-defense committee, they were obliged to give weapons to the elderly, essentially widows because there were not enough men to form a patrol. María says she was recruited just as if she had been a man and obliged to participate in surveillance activities around the village. Although she talks about the suffering that the conflict has caused the members of her community and her own difficulties dealing with everyday life during this period, she did not question her obligation to participate in the self-defense activities in preparing for possible confrontation if ever the PCP-SL should return. The idea of carrying a weapon, or at least the military aspect of everyday life, observed in the interviews quoted above, appear to be events that were impossible to avoid during this period.

A shift had thus occurred in feminine and masculine tasks: women replaced men who had died or who were in hiding to avoid being recruited into subversive forces or into the army. But it was also women who went to the military bases to claim missing persons. "Protecting the men," or demonstrating their courage and physical and moral strength, was relatively unusual for these women and their testimonies overall reflect their consciousness of their contribution to what they call "pacification work" and their role in the defense of their communities. These women claim recognition for the importance of their role, not as women, but as individuals who took on responsibilities in the counter subversive operations. It seems to them that they demonstrated as much courage as the men, and showed themselves capable of taking on as much, or more, responsibility because they sought to "protect" the men from the army and subversive groups. Yet the idea of protecting one's kin and community, defending one's territory or demonstrating courage are generally characteristics associated with masculinity. These qualities could however be attributed to women having actively participated in the defense of their communities. We would have expected to see these women demanding legitimacy through the display of qualities traditionally perceived as being essentially feminine (and therefore opposed to allegedly masculine violence), such as the protection of human life or fighting for peace. It is troubling however to see that women who participated in self-defense activities instead mobilized the same type of discourse as that was constructed by the men. Thus the women did not simply replace men in roles they could no longer assume, they in fact, to a certain extent, "became" men.

This gender inversion, although not permanent, is nonetheless behind many of the important shifts in social sex relations with the communities affected by the conflict. It is in fact relatively rare in this context to see the feminine dominate over the masculine in terms of power and influence. This is, however, exactly what happened in certain communities during the conflict. The significance of this phenomenon was underlined in the general conclusions of the CVR:

> Finally, the CVR notes that in spite of its force, the violence has not been able to destroy the population's ability to respond. In many instances, faced with the destruction of traditional social networks and the massive assassination of leaders, women have taken on new responsibilities and have challenged the country to recognize the loss of thousands of their children in massacres and kidnappings. Young women leaders are rebuilding many of the most affected communities and we have thus realized that many of them have been able to resist violence through self defense [...].[19]

Women in men's roles, men in women's roles: the general mobilization of civil society that was required by the SDCs profoundly changed the social and sexual division of labor in the rural communities affected by the conflict. Narda Henríquez thus underlines the specific role of women in the communities of the valleys of the Apurimac and Ene rivers, who were responsible for physically punishing men who had failed in their duties as *ronderos*.[20] Although some traditional practices occasionally involve women exerting physical violence over men, it is incontestable that the women of these rural communities had access to new spaces of action. It would be erroneous to think that women were opposed to armed violence; they demonstrate a certain adhesion to these violent practices that they justify by the defense of their integrity, their family, and their community. In the words of I.: "We participated in several battles. Once during one of them I managed to grab one of the guys weapons and I shot him in the head so that the others would be scared and run away. I'd never made someone's head explode before, I didn't know what to do, but well, you learn. We had to learn to defend ourselves against our enemies."[21]

The different forms of engagement by women in the SDC's activities allow us to better understand the issues at stake in demobilizing and reinserting actors who were involved in armed self-defense organizations during the conflict. Firstly, we can see that armed mobilization goes well beyond participation in strictly military activities and affects the whole social organization at the local level. Moreover, demobilization and reinsertion of *ronderos* is heavily dependent on the reconstruction of the social fabric through a return to traditional activities. But what happens when women are no longer where they are expected to be? Given that the participation of women in the SDCs is today entirely absent from the narratives built around the conflict, we may wonder what purpose this invisibility serves, and whether, in investigating the difficulties around the reinsertion of female combatants, it might help bring light to the flaws of the pacification process in the rural areas affected by the armed conflict in Peru.

A Normalization Process Disrupted by Persistent Violence

The Problem of the Demobilization of the Self-defense Committees

A number of researchers, particularly anthropologists and historians, such as Carlos Iván Degregori,[22] José Coronel,[23] or Ponciano del Pino[24] have studied the role played by the self-defense committees in the countersubversive struggle and in the various changes such organizations have provoked both at the level of the micropolitical locality but also within social relations. Few however, have really dealt with the question of the military demobilization of the SDCs, which continue to function, despite the fact that in most of the regions they were formed in, they no longer have any reason to exist. The retreat of armed rebel groups, which are today essentially active in the lower Amazon area around the drug-trafficking industry, freed most of the area from the threat of insurrection, and the state has taken their place and reinvested in infrastructure in these areas.

In spite of this, the status of SDCs has been in suspense for some time, and they remain active throughout the territory. Although armed activities decreased in intensity from the mid-1990s, it was not possible for the then government, represented by Alberto Fujimori, to demobilize the commandos that had actively collaborated with them in the countersubversive struggle. The SDCs were the subject of law no. 26479, promulgated in 1995, which exonerated all members of security, military, or civilian forces from any civil or criminal responsibility in investigations, judicial proceedings, or convictions for human rights violations. A few weeks later, law no. 26492 extended this amnesty to public servants in the military, members of the police, and civilians.[25] The members of the SDCs have never been investigated, even though some of the commandos were responsible for criminal acts. Moreover, the SDCs continue to operate under a legal status that was accorded to them at the height of the conflict. It is actually really difficult to obtain an accurate number of SDC's presently active on Peruvian territory. Nevertheless, journalistic sources and unofficial information from the joint commander of the Peruvian armed forces enable us to believe that around 500,000 people are involved in such organizations[26] in 22 of the 24 regions in Peru. This is an impressive number; even as the conflict decreased in intensity, the number of people engaged in the SDC's has paradoxically increased,[27] and collaboration between the armed forces and the SDCs has been strengthened, which leads to the multiplication and progressive institutionalization of the latter. Since 1998 the SDC members who were killed or wounded in the course of their activities have been officially awarded pensions (for themselves and their families), giving them the status of "veterans." This is important in the power relations that emerge between rural communities in the transition toward peace, because it allows (among other things) former *ronderos* to continue to claim their contribution to what they call "the defense of the fatherland." This enables them to conserve a certain autonomy vis-à-vis other types of power within the community.

The demobilization of the SDCs has thus never been the object of formal policy. On the contrary, the longevity of the militarization of rural areas is encouraged by the collaboration between the SDCs and the armed forces. Generally an agreement is reached between the community leaders and the police in the area to conduct a weekly inventory and revision of weaponry. Furthermore, the SDCs that procured their artillery themselves were able to keep their weapons, which thus continue to circulate freely. The armed collaboration between state and SDCs notably takes place in the struggle against drug trafficking. On March 2011, armed forces deployed in the Apurimac and Ene Rivers Valley have handed in to SDCs 80 rifles and 18,000 cartridges in order to gain their contribution in the "pacification operations" in course in the zone.[28]

In a country where social relations are characterized by strong discrimination against indigenous and rural populations, this association has much more than simple military significance: it is testimony to the recognition of generally marginalized sectors of society by a state controlled by a white urban elite. Participating in self-defense has thus become a means of accessing a form of citizenship that has long been out of reach. By taking on a warrior identity and collaborating with the army in the deployment of counter-subversive activities, peasants have hoped to obtain the citizenship that they have been historically excluded from. By becoming a *rondero,* they open the door to a national *imaginaire* to which they have traditionally not had access. Being a *rondero* thus becomes an important aspect of identity that is added to other cultural, ethnic, and economic dimensions. This comes across in some of the interviews conducted with *ronderos* by members of the CVR: "Of course weapons became a part of our identity: some say 'take away our weapons would be like taking away our identity card,' that's what they said."[29] This is, however, an identity that is exclusively reserved for men; masculinity thus indirectly becomes a condition for one's inclusion in the nation.

It was only with the beginning of the investigations carried out by the Truth and Reconciliation Commission that a debate on the future of the SDCs was launched. The Commission considered that the state should attempt to reclaim the monopoly of the counter-subversive struggle and the monopoly on legitimate violence more generally. It should therefore begin dismantling the SDCs. However, the means provided by the state to ensure security in these zones affected by political violence remain insufficient, and the militarization of social relations within the communities that were (or are) organized around self-defense persists.

Therefore, despite the fact that the CVR does recognize their contribution to self-defense activities, and that it openly regrets "the masculine and militarized authoritarianism" that characterizes these activities, the various programs put in place for women since 2000, as part of the transitional justice process, persistently fail to take into account the possible engagement of these women in military conflict. Alongside this, we observe a certain continuity of the violence in the domestic sphere: an increase in domestic violence is indeed a constant feature of the rural communities affected by the conflict. There is a link between the failure of demobilization of the SDCs and the expression of this violence, which although it existed prior to the conflict is today taking on new forms that are characteristic of problems posed by the militarization of Andean society.

Domestic Violence as a Transposition of the Warrior Habitus

The idea of dysfunctional social sex relations within the communities affected by political violence was inspired by an assessment of violent practices within the private sphere. Of course, domestic violence existed prior to the conflict, but it has taken on new dimensions in postconflict society. As Elisabeth Rhen and Ellen Johnson argue, domestic violence tends to be intensified by the return of peace.[30] This phenomenon is verified in the case of Peru and has attracted the attention of NGOs working in these regions. Indeed, in practice the domestic violence that existed prior to the conflict played a role in social control, it was generally carried out in public according to codified rituals reserved for specific individuals (most often the father of the family). Domestic violence as it exists in postconflict Andean communities, however, breaks all of these rules. Isabel Coral explains this in the introduction to a documentary on the subject in 2005:

> Intra-family violence is not historically foreign to Andean society, and to rural society in general [...]. However, I think that a cause and effect relationship developed between the physical abuse and a particular reason [...]. Political violence exacerbates the presence of family violence, enhances it and normalizes it [...]. But the role of the aggressor also spreads to other members of the family, the sons, the son-in-laws, men in general, and it moves out of the space of the nuclear family to incorporate the extended family, opposing some against others even within family connections. And it's important to emphasize that there is no longer a reason for this violence to be used.[31]

The testimonies from the communities in the Ayacucho region speak for themselves:

> He'd threaten me with the gun he'd bought, but only when it was the two of us, without the children seeing.
> He really beat me too much, I still have the marks on my face. He'd say 'I'm going to kill you, I'm going to kill you bitch!' [...] He threatened me and took all my money and said 'dirty whore I'll make you whelp another kid.'
> Well I was crying a lot and he was insulting me and even threatening me, he came with a knife to kill me [...]. Once he raped me violently telling me I was his wife, and on that pretext he nearly managed to hang me [...] so I turned around suddenly and I grabbed away the knife he'd used to force me.[32]

These stories are representative of the daily lives of many women living in these communities overturned by political violence. It is clear that although violence might be tolerated or even institutionalized within daily practices, it attains proportions here that have nothing to do with "tradition." The causes of the increase in this violence are many. The first elements of explanation might come from the trauma caused by the political violence and the deterioration of the mental health of the inhabitants of these rural communities. The attitudes of these men, who have become out-of-control, not only for their wives but also for the rest of the community, bears a striking resemblance to the four American soldiers who all assassinated their wives in the six weeks following their return to their base at Fort Bragg in North Carolina in 2002.³³ It is also necessary to take the problems of alcoholism into account. These problems stem from the fact that during the conflict, members of many rural communities developed the habit of coming together in one house in the evening to drink until morning, in order to overcome the fear of an attack during the night.³⁴ Finally, we can also add the problems linked to situations of extreme poverty and social decomposition, which have been heightened by the conflict but also by the draconian measures taken by the Fujimori government during the 1990s.

Family violence has developed in a situation of generalized chaos in the wake of the conflict and has curbed the reconstruction of the social fabric. Is it possible that this type of violence is the expression of an unrecognized suffering? A reaction to the loss of masculine identity, which is challenged by the conflict—or inversely—by the decrease in its intensity? Fenneke Reysoo, in asking whether conflict situations can be used to analyze gender relations, focuses on men who have returned to positions they had abandoned to women during the conflict.³⁵ This perspective confirms the idea, generally accepted in studies of gender, that the social rupture that was caused by the conflict opened new spaces of action for women that only represented a moderate opportunity, because they were only justified by the "exceptional" context. With the end of the conflict, this "exceptional situation" disappeared. Women were generally encouraged to return to their former roles in the private sphere, abandoning the positions and responsibilities reserved for men in peacetime. It is important to stress however that it is not because the women give up their places to the men that the latter are necessarily able to fill them.

The armed conflict, by forcing them to flee or to hide, dispossessed men of both their material goods and their virility. No longer able to play their usual roles in the family sphere, they had difficulties in coming to terms with their virility. When all able-bodied men in the community were called upon to form the self-defense unit, little by little the patrols were run by young men and adolescents who had grown up during the conflict, and for whom participation represented the passage to manhood. Joining the SDC may thus be associated with a rite of passage that must find a way of perpetuating itself in postconflict society. Ponciano del Pino has thus demonstrated the heroic sheen of the *rondero* identity, even to the point that they are considered gods incarnate, meant that in some instances they had unlimited power over the social, political, and economic organization of the communities they were charged with "defending."³⁶ This divine aura of the *ronderos* is also visible in many of the testimonies collected by the CVR ("they were like gods," "they acted like kings"³⁷). Self-defense thus came to replace the traditional functions of men in the communities and became a new rite of passage to adulthood based on the affirmation of gender identity. These processes, which illustrate the extreme militarization of everyday life in the communities affected by political violence, transformed male gender identity until it was limited to self-defense activities. Once the war was over, these men, who had been engaged for nearly 15 years in armed counter-subversive struggle, saw themselves brutally dispossessed of their identity as fighters, which had been the only guarantee of their virility and their place in social organization. Whether or not they had worked full-time as *ronderos*, the men who had grown up during the conflict found themselves in post-conflict society without weapons and without an enemy—elements that were both fundamental to their status within their communities.

The women were thus surrounded either by men who had lost everything because they had fled or by men who had come to terms with their identity, and even their existence, through violence. We could thus hypothesize that after the conflict, the women became scapegoats for their companions: either by taking on the weight of the frustrations that were not addressed sufficiently through public policy or by being implicitly identified as the "new enemy" against which men had to fight. This second scenario enabled men to maintain a certain continuity of identity through the daily practice of violence and the use of weapons, and it therefore appeared in the domestic violence practices that followed the end of the conflict. This figure of the "new enemy" takes on its full force in light of the abuses described by the women who are victims of domestic violence. Although their status as former soldiers is not recognized, either in civil society or by their male fellow citizens, women are still able to mobilize the connections that they built during the conflicts. They rely notably on local NGOs, who are more inclined to teach them "empowerment" than to recognize their direct or indirect participation in armed violence. This is the case for C. who, while she regrets that there is little consideration of women's contribution to the counter-subversive struggle, recognizes that she gained a certain degree of autonomy through the collective actions conducted by the women of her community:

> I remember at the time, despite the fact that I was the secretary of the self-defense committee and then the leader of a commando unit, my life as a woman was frustrated, because despite my responsibilities I was a victim of family violence—even when I moved here to San Miguel—up until 2001. Then I said "that's enough, no more domestic violence ever," but it was already pretty late because, no, as a woman it makes you completely sick [she cries]. My friends told me, "you put up with this violence for so long, you don't deserve it, and you do good things for the community, but sometimes you just have to think about yourself," and I went to all those meetings petrified with fear, thinking to myself "please let it be ok when I go home, don't let him beat me." Well it was never good, I was always afraid, I was always abused. Sometimes my friends walked me home, one day my friend was with me and she said "your husband won't do anything to me" and he beat both of us to a pulp. He hit me all the time, he was jealous.[38]

The resistance of these women to domestic violence doe not seem to be sufficient, however, to curb the phenomenon, which has become widespread in the wake of the conflict. Domestic violence is thus no longer only the expression of the distress in which former soldiers find themselves, but also the desire to deny the roles played by their wives during the counter-subversive struggle. Here the continuum of violence is as much based on the links between masculine identity and war activities, as between these activities and citizenship.

Continued Violence as a Symptom of a Crisis in Citizenship

We mentioned above the link between the participation in the SDCs and the feeling of gaining access to a form of citizenship long considered out of reach for these communities. Having the feeling of contributing to the "war effort," the members of the SDCs were able to identify with a nation from which they had been historically excluded. Contemporary Peruvian society is still having great trouble overcoming the cleavages that resulted from the social organization during the colonial period, which was based on a strict social hierarchy according to ethnicity. This led to the failure of the national project, which was not able to include its indigenous populations, of whom a proportion did not speak Spanish. It was only with the 1979 Constitution that, for the first time, the right to vote was given to the illiterate, who had been excluded from the very first days of the young Peruvian Republic. Moreover, Peru has never known an "indigenous resurgence," of the kind visible in neighboring Ecuador or Bolivia. Although the 1993 Constitution includes specific recognition of the multicultural character of the nation, which has led to a certain number of social, cultural, or education policies, such as the adoption of Quechua as the official second language, there is no question of the emergence of identity-based movements like in other countries in the region.

If we look at the history of rural Peru, and specifically at the consequences of Velasco's agrarian reform in 1969 this is understandable. In fact, for reasons due to the historicity of the country, the rural populations from the Andean areas consider themselves above all peasants and not members of an indigenous community. Their lack of interest in identity claims is also explained by the fact that when these movements were gaining momentum in Latin America, the armed conflict was still raging in Peru. Thus social movements, already limited under the Fujimori government developed above all around issues directly linked to the conflict (like forced disappearances, massive internal displacement, or arbitrary imprisonment). The conflict, in absorbing all social claims, thus acted as a filter for identity movements. But it also channeled ethnic claims by allowing people of indigenous origin to participate in the counter-subversive struggle alongside the state.

We have seen that the SDCs developed particularly in rural communities affected by the political violence, and which were the scenes of confrontation between subversive groups and coercive state forces. These were generally communities situated in the high plateaux of the Andes in the center and the south of the country but also in the villages founded by "colonizers," who were often farmers from Andean communities who had come to live on the edges of the Amazon in search of fertile land. In these zones in particular, the "colonizers" had to live alongside the indigenous people of the Amazon, Ashaninka, or Yanesha, which led to significant social and ethnic conflict. It is understandable then, that for some communities, collaboration with the army represented an opportunity to resolve old grievances with the indigenous people of the Amazon, not only on an economic level—as might be the case for example in terms of the possession and exploitation of land—but also on a cultural level. If the participation in self-defense represented the rural and peasant populations' contribution to the state's counter-subversive struggle, it is also a symbol of access to a certain social mobility. Confrontations between the SDCs and the indigenous Amazon populations, are also the expression of what might be called "cultural revenge" on the part of sections of society that have historically been victims of discrimination

However, I wish to make the hypothesis here that the domestic violence that developed in the postconflict context responds to the same dynamic. Marisol de la Cadena shows how ethnicity can influence the construction of gender identities.[39] She draws her conclusions from the observation of socials relations with an Andean community, taking into account gender identities as well as ethnic belonging. She shows that gender represents a variable that is as important as the ethnic component in defining the identity of each individual member of the community and their status within this group. Women in general are more readily identified as belonging to indigenous populations because of their sex, thus becoming "more Indian" than the men.[40] The violence that is turned against women in the rural communities organized around an SDC could thus be interpreted as a practice to guarantee the status of the members of the committee within the community. Political violence is thus converted into interpersonal violence, not only with the goal of reproducing masculine identity but also of preventing the older fighters from losing the social mobility they won thorough their participation in the counter-subversive struggle.

The negation of the role women played in the SDCs is thus a response to men's need to conserve the social and political power that they have acquired. This power is the guarantee of their identity as former combatants, and it allows them to compensate for incommensurable economic losses provoked by the conflict, as well as compensating for psychological trauma incurred by 20 years of political violence. The anthropologist Kimberley Theidon emphasizes the importance of what she calls the *ronderos'* "hypermasculinity," which allows them to fight against the limitations imposed by their ethnicity.[41] She thus discusses the *ronderos* of the Ccarhuahuràn in the Ayacucho region who fly the flag in the central square on national holiday. When she asked one of the small boys watching the scene about the purpose of this ceremony, he replied that it was to show the "terrorists," who might come and attack the village, that "Peruvians live here." When the author feigned surprise at the absence of women in the flag raising ceremony, the boy retorted, "Women are less Peruvian because they aren't armed."[42]

The observations conducted by Theidon allow us to clearly observe the links between bearing arms, exercising violence and the maintenance of a social status conceived in terms of inclusion in the nation. The absence of women in these ceremonies commemorating "heroic" acts can be seen in any of the communities organized around self-defense during the conflict. They are not invited to participate in the parades in which the *ronderos* willingly engage. The women have consequently made the choice to stand as the privileged interlocutors between their communities and the civil society organizations, in order to continue having a role in the public sphere. It is thus as members of mothers' clubs, and not as *ronderas*, that women have an access to a certain public recognition, which allows them to accomplish a political career—even if they deny this. I. does not hide her ambitions, despite her explicit aversion to politics:

> Me, no I don't like politics, I think its rubbish. From what I see, it's not healthy, it's not a good thing [...]. Me I stay out of politics. It's dirty, I see that, I analyze that and I don't go there! [...] Politicians, they just want to use us, us women we aren't conscious enough of that [...]. There isn't enough awareness among women, they sell their vote for a kilo of sugar... but me I see that I can get to the local government, except that they change their vote at the last minute so it's difficult.[43]

As for C. she explained how the intervention of the NGOs had facilitated women's access to training that enabled them to legitimately express their opinions within the communities:

> [W]hen you've suffered like we have suffered, no, and we see it from the inside not the outside, we see the reality in which we live. Me, firstly I wanted to be *regidora* [responsible for overseeing administration of public affairs], and to begin some projects for women, but not only women, young people too, they sometimes get raped too, by their parents, their neighbors, I wanted to fight against that. That's our vocation, as leaders of this time [of political violence]. Today the *regidoras* or delegates who go into political life, they forget everything, they forget where they came from.
>
> That's why I stay in this organization, why I keep fighting, keep talking to people. Last year the Mayor of San Miguel said to me "you, you know what the other women need, so I'll give you a position at the Town Hall for that kind of project." And so last year he gave

me this little job, in the framework of the projects on social development, and we go to training sessions to workshops, sometimes the NGOs give you extra tips and we make do with that, or sometimes we ask for particular training and that they pay our bus ticket too. It's important to have their economic support, even if its 50 soles [€12.50 a month], to continue with the organization.[44]

Conclusion

Even though they participated actively in the work of the self-defense committees, these women were excluded from them after the conflict, both by members of the CAD and by members of civil society organizations who concentrated above all on their identities as victims. Their contribution to the counter-subversive struggle goes unrecognized, while the reorganization of rural communities reflects a continuum of violence illustrated by the cases of domestic abuse. Proposing an analysis of the trajectories of the women in the SDCs but also interrogating the social changes in social sex relations resulting from the militarization of daily life, thus appears to be a new angle of analysis in the resolution of armed conflict and the problems linked to demobilization and reinsertion of former combatants.

Although their contribution to the counter-subversive struggle is not recognized in the collective memory of the conflict, women have nonetheless learned a certain lesson from their participation in these SDCs. Paradoxically, and because they have succeeded better than men in dialoging with the representatives of civil society, female former SDCs combatants achieve better reinsertion than men in the communities most affected by political violence. While men have established a link with the state that can only be built on their collaboration with the army in security tasks, women have the benefit of a better image within international organizations and other associations interested in development. However, this radicalization of gender identities does not allow for the realities of former civilian fighters in the conflict to be taken into account. In ignoring the role played by women in the counter-subversive struggle, it remains blind to the effects that their participation in these activities might have on the functioning of the private sphere, which represents an important issue for peace keeping. The private sphere should thus be understood as the reflection of two other levels of observation: the community sphere and the public sphere. The micro conflicts in the private sphere might help to interpret and analyze the conflicts that develop at the national level. The invisibilization of women in the SDCs does not simply conform to an identity strategy on the part of certain sectors of society, but it also—in underlining the divisions at work within families—reflects the impossibility of establishing a national consensus around peacekeeping in Peru. Translated by Katharine Throssel.

Notes

1. Comisión de la Verdad y Reconciliación, *Informe Final* VIII (2003).
2. Urban patrols also existed; collective organizations of members of a particular neighborhood, carrying out surveillance activities. Although this is a very interesting phenomenon, it will not be dealt with here because it is quite different from the patrols in rural areas.
3. L. Taylor, "La estrategía contrainsurgente, el PCP SL y la guerra civil en el Perú 1980–1996," *Debate agrario* 26 (1997): 83.
4. J. Pérez Mundaca, *Rondas campesinas. Poder violencia y autodefensa en Cajmarca Central*, working paper, no 78, Talleres no 6, Lima, IEP (Instituto de Estudios Peruanos), 8.
5. Comisión de la Verdad y Reconciliación, "Los comités de autodefensa," *Informe final* II (2003).
6. J. Coronel, "Violencia política y respuestas campesinas en Huanta," in Carlos Iván Degregori et al. (ed.), *Las rondas campesinas y la derrota de Sendero Luminoso*, (Lima: IEP, 1996), 51.
7. Comisión de la Verdad y Reconciliación, *Informe final*.
8. A. Olano, "Las rondas campesinas del Perú. Una brieve historia," *Oasis* 6 (2000): 165.
9. P. Del Pino, "Tiempos de guerra y de dioses. Ronderos, evangélicos y senderistas en el valle río Apurímac," *in* Degregori et al., *Las rondas campesinas*, 156
10. G. Caballero, "Invertirán US 150 milloners en el desarrollo del VRAE," *El Comercio*, February 21, 2007, http://www.elcomercio.com.pe/EdicionImpresa/Html/2007-02-21/ImEcPolitica0675302.html.
11. Interview conducted by Camille Boutron in March 2007 in Huanta in the Ayacucho region.
12. Interview conducted by Camille Boutron in March 2007 in Tambo, in the Ayacucho region.
13. Interview conducted by Camille Boutron in February 2007 in Musa district, in central Lima.
14. Interview conducted by Camille Boutron in March 2007 in Tambo, in the Ayacucho region.
15. Regional Federation of Mothers' Clubs (*Federación de Clubes de Madres de Ayacucho*)
16. I. Coral, "Mujeres en la guerra: impacto y respuestas," in Steve J. Stern (ed.), *Los senderos insólitos del Perú,* (Lima: IEP, 1999), 348.
17. L. Hurtado, "Después del municipio y qué? Las regidoras de Huanta. Un estudio de caso sobre las mujeres en los gobiernos locales," in Ludwing Hubert (ed.), *Ayacucho. Centralismo y desenctralización* (Lima: IEP, 2003), 161.
18. Interview conducted by Camille Boutron in March 2007 in Miskibamaba, in the Ayacucho region.
19. Comisión de la Verdad y Reconciliación, Volume VII, General Conclusion, point 161.
20. N. Heríquez Avín, *Cuestiones de género y poder en el conflicto armado en el Perú* (Lima: CONCYTEC, 2006), 62.
21. Interview conducted by Camille Boutron in March 2007 in Tambo, in the Ayacucho region.
22. Degregori Carlos Iván, "Cosechando tempestades: las rondas campesinas y la derrota de Sendero Luminoso en Ayacucho," *in* Degregori et al., *Las rondas campesinas y la derrota de Sendero Luminos*, 189–226.
23. Coronel, "Violencia política y respuestas campesinas en Huanta."
24. Del Pino, "Los campesinos en la guerra o como la gente empezó a hacerse macho," in Carlos Iván Degregori, Javer Escobal & Benjamín Marticorena (eds.), *Perú el problema agrario en debate-SEPIA IV* (Lima: Seminario Permanente de Investigación Agraria, 1992), 487–508.
25. Even though these laws were declared unconstitutional in 2002, the debate on the amnesty of members of the military charged by the Peruvian courts with human rights violations (some 600 people between 2007 and 2009) continues to rage, and it regularly resurfaces in politics.
26. Gastelmundi René, "Guerra avisada: los ronderos y licenciados del ejército detrás de los conflictos sociales," *Diario 16*, June 28, 2011, http://diario16.pe/columnista/21/rene-gastelumendi/890/guerra-avisada-los-ronderos-y-licenciados-del-ejaercito-detraas-de-los-conflictos-sociales
27. Instituto Nacional de Estadistica e informatica, Censos Nacionales XI de Población y VI de Vivienda, "Perú: población censada, urbana y rural y tasa de crecimiento en los censos nacionales 1947–2007" (Lima: PNUD-UNFPA, 2007), 19.
28. Hidalgo María Elena, "Comando Conunto entrega armas a comités de autodefensa en el VRAE", *La República*, March 21, 2011, http://www.larepublica.pe/21-03-2011/comando-conjunto-entrega-armas-comites-de-autodefensa-en-el-vrae
29. Comisión de la Verdad y Reconciliación, Volume II, Chapter One, Section Two, "1.5 Los comités de autodefensa."

30. E. Rehn and E. Johnson Sirleaf, *Women, War, Peace. The Independent Experts' Assessment* (New York: Unifem, 2002), 19.
31. Ceprodep (*Centre de promotion et de développement des populations*), *Mujeres en la guerra*, directed by Felipe Degregori, Lima: CEPRODEP, 2005, 30 min.
32. Ibid.
33. Rhen and Shirleaf, *Women, War, Peace*, 16.
34. K. Theidon, *Entre projímos. El conflicto armado interno y la política de la reconciliación en el Perú* (Lima: IEP, 2004), 93.
35. F. Reysoo, "Situations de conflit armés comme analyseurs des rapports de genre," in *Hommes armés, femmes aguerries. Rapports de genre en situations de conflit armé* (Genève: IUED, 2001), 17.
36. De Pino, "Los campesinos en la guerra," 119.
37. Comisión de la Verdad y Reconciliación, *Informe final*, 2003, Volume II, Chapter One, Section Two, 1.5 "Los comités de autodefensa."
38. Interview conducted by Camille Boutron in March 2007 in San Miguel, in the Ayacucho region.
39. M. De la Cadena, "Las mujeres son más indias: etnicidad y género en una comunidad de Cuzco," *Revista Andina* 17 (1991): 216–249.
40. Ibid.
41. K. Theidon, "Disarming the Subject. Remembering War and Imagining Citizenship in Peru," *Cultural Critique* 54 (2003): 80.
42. Ibid., 81.
43. Interview conducted by Camille Boutron in March 2007 in Tambo, in the Ayacucho region.
44. Interview conducted by Camille Boutron in March 2007 in San Miguel, in the Ayacucho region.

CHAPTER FOUR

Paramilitary Demobilization and the Return of Violence in Colombia

SOPHIE DAVIAUD

> **Abstract**
>
> This chapter deals with the demobilization process of the Colombian paramilitary groups, begun in 2003 by the government of Alvaro Uribe Vélez and ending in early 2006 with the disarmament of more than 31,000 fighters. After describing the short term effects of the process—a general decrease in the level of violence and a reduction in the number of human rights violations—the author seeks to explain the difficulties that are beginning to appear and undermine the long-term process. Various hypotheses are considered: the "warrior habitus" of the paramilitaries, which renders them incapable of other than war-like activity and a "brutalization" of Colombian society. The author believes that it is the permanent presence of narco traffic networks in Colombia that explains the creation of new armed groups and the restructuring of old ones; furthermore, that the failure of the DDR process is evidence of the infiltration of Colombian society and its political system by paramilitaries.

From his first term in office in August 2002, Colombian president Álvaro Uribe Vélez set about negotiating with paramilitary groups instead of following in the footsteps of most of his predecessors, who negotiated with the guerrillas. In many respects, this negotiation process symbolizes a change in the country's history. It was the first attempt to dialogue with a far-right, illegal armed group in the hope of demobilizing, disarming, and reintegrating (DDR) all paramilitary groups on national ground. A remarkably high number of combatants were directly concerned: while negotiations with five groups of guerilleros[1] between 1989 and 1994 facilitated the reincorporation of approximately 4,000 combatants into civil society, Colombian paramilitaries numbered over 31,000. These groups were defined by their cruelty toward civil populations and their responsibility for several human rights violations in Colombia (arbitrary executions, disappearances, massacres, torture, and forced migration). According to the nonprofit organization Cinep's database, 14,000 people were victims of paramilitary activity between 1988 and 2003,[2] and paramilitaries were responsible for over 80 percent of all human rights violations between 1990 and 2000. This was a relatively fast and dramatic process and the agreement marking the beginning of official negotiations was signed on July 15, 2003, in Santa Fe de Ralito.[3] The government managed to have a "justice and peace" law adopted in July 2005, which detailed the legal framework for the demobilization process and established a national commission for compensation and reconciliation in Colombia. At the beginning of 2006, Álvaro Uribe Vélez could boast of having had the large majority of paramilitary fighters brought to justice and over 31,000 fighters demobilized.

However, the medium-term results of the DDR process with paramilitary groups seemed far from certain. New illegal armed groups were formed (in 2009 they numbered over 10,000 men), new centers of violence sprung up, and reintegration programs had limited success.

How can you get to grips with this phenomenon? How do you explain why phase R of the process seemed seriously compromised in Colombia? Beyond the problems imposed by the return of ex-fighters to civil society, are wartime structures and networks still in place after demobilization? Can we speak of the historian George L. Mosse's[4] "bullying" or even "cultural demobilization"?[5] We would like to present various hypotheses while highlighting that paramilitary structures' hold over society remains in place. The Colombian DDR process is at a dead end due to the paramilitary's influence over the political system and society itself.

A Seemingly Successful DDR Process

Undeniable Short-term Results

We should firstly place the paramilitary demobilization policy within the general framework of Álvaro Uribe Vélez's democratic security policy, which took effect in 2003. The policy was put in place at a time when the number of illegal armed groups had recently grown and posed a real threat to the stability and legitimacy of the Colombian state. President Andrés Pastrana Arango (1998–2002) failed in his negotiations and did not obtain any significant political commitment while the guerrillas built on their military equipment and carried out attacks all over the Colombian territory. During this time paramilitary groups grew at an incredible rate, and in 1997, the *Autodefensas unidas de Colombia* (AUC) was founded to group all the factions on the national territory together in the same structure. President Uribe presented himself as a supporter of hard-hitting speech when it came to the Fuerzas Armadas Revolucionarias de Colombia (FARC), improving military strategy and reestablishing security; his "democratic security policy" presents this very synthesis. The main idea was to reestablish order and protect the civil population from the various armed groups but within a legal framework that also aimed to strengthen the state of law.[6] The strategy involved strengthening capacities in terms of the Colombian armies' human resources and equipment to be able to confront the guerrilla forces on their territory and allow the state to guarantee its nationwide presence.[7] The long-term objective was to force rebels to negotiate by inflicting military fatalities on them.

The DDR with paramilitary groups therefore belonged in a context of a perennial armed conflict as the two main guerrilla factions remain active. It was seen as a means to facilitate the transition from war to peace, reestablish security, and reduce the level of violence and violation of human rights. Pragmatism and a progressive character defined the government's favorite negotiation method. Unlike the negotiations held previously in Colombia with guerrilla groups, it was not part of a global peace agreement setting up a number of institutional measures enabling the groups to make a new start politically.[8]

President Álvaro Uribe Vélez announced that he was ready to negotiate with illegal armed groups as long as they agreed to declare a ceasefire. On November 29, 2002, three months after taking office, the AUC's political and military leaders released a statement declaring a ceasefire from December 1 and imposed a number of conditions to begin negotiations with the government. On December 4, 2002, 29 fronts of the Central Bolivar Bloc (BCB) agreed to the ceasefire. In January 2003 the government published Decree 128 granting legal and economic benefits to demobilized combatants. These benefits could only be awarded to those who could be granted amnesty for their crimes and not to paramilitaries who had committed crimes against humanity (law 782, article 50). On July 15, 2003, the government and paramilitary groups signed the Santa Fe de Ralito agreement that marked the beginning of official negotiations and established the mission of the OEA to support the Misión de Apoyo al Proceso de Paz en Colombia de la Organización de los Estados Americanos [The Organization of American States' Mission to Support the Peace Process in Colombia] (MAPP-OEA). The paramilitaries were thus committed to progressively demobilizing all their members (see note 3). The government was committed to "putting all necessary measures in place to reintegrate ex-fighters to civil society." Natalia Springer highlights the fact that the government had made almost no concrete commitments except for very precise technical issues such as the establishment of reinsertion measures and the guarantee that army soldiers would continue surveillance on areas with a high concentration of fighters; it was defined as an "agreement without content" meaning with no precise agenda: "The Santa Fe de Ralito agreement is a programme for the concentration of forces and the demobilisation of the AUC without further negotiations or demands. It's a negotiation agreement that lacks content."[9]

On May 13, 2004, the government and paramilitary groups signed a second agreement in Santa Fe de Ralito after which the government created a 370 km^2 concentration zone in Tierra Alta, in the Cordoba region, for the ten paramilitary leaders involved in negotiations. This agreement was lacking in as much content as the last and was more like a code of conduct. The zone's sole reason for being was to ensure the ceasefire was kept and facilitate the demobilization of the paramilitaries.

The peace process was therefore relatively fast: it lasted less than four years. At the end, 31,671 paramilitary group members were demobilized including approximately 18,000 fighters according to government estimates. During the process, 38 demobilization acts, starting with the demobilization of the Nutibara bloc in Medellin on November 25, 2003, and ending with that of the Elmer Cardenas bloc on August 15, 2006, took place. The organizations with the highest number of fighters were the Central Bolivar bloc with 6,348 men; the northern bloc with 4,760 men; the Mineros bloc with 2,780 men; and the Héroes de Granada bloc with 2,033 paramilitaries. On top of the number of collective demobilizations were 2,538 individual ones between 2003 and 2006. Only a few groups refused to demobilize including the Cacique Pinpintá bloc in the Caldas and Risaralda region, the Casanare peasant self-defense groups and a structure in the Cundinamarca region.

The demobilization process had two main results. It contributed to decreasing the overall rate of violence and human right violations. The number of murders is a good way of illustrating paramilitary groups' involvement in violence. Paramilitary groups used murder as a means to establish authority over areas previously dominated by guerrillas. Between 1993–1997 and 1998–2002, murder rates in areas in which paramilitary groups were present rose from 29,800 per year to 56,666. Between 2003 and 2007, rates dropped by 70 percent to an average of 17,050 per year. This reduction in murders in areas in which self-defense groups were present had an effect on the overall murder rate in Colombia. During the 1990s there were over 80,000 murders per year while the number dropped to 17,479 in 2006. The demobilization process also led to a decrease in human rights violations. The general security conditions of the Colombian people improved and this was the main argument for President Uribe's landslide victory at his 2006 reelection. The state was present in all Colombian municipalities: the roads were safer (especially major roads). Most indicators of violence dropped, partly due to the demobilization of paramilitary groups that had spread their influence over the area by terrorizing civilians. Massacres, which had already begun decreasing in numbers before demobilization, continued decreasing; over 1,400 massacres were recorded in 2000, the most critical year. From 2001 the number of massacres began to drop due both to the paramilitaries who came to move the guerrillas from most of their areas of influence and to the paramilitary groups' decision to use more discreet methods than massacre. The reduction is of course more significant since the demobilization process, with 26 massacres recorded in 2007.[10] As for forced migration, the long-term trend is toward an increase in the number of people forced to migrate through violence. There were over 44,547 people forced to migrate in 1998 compared to 261,987 in 2007. Forced migration increased significantly until 2002, dropped in 2003–2004, rose again between 2005 and 2007 then dropped in 2008. On the whole, the number of assassinations (mayors, head teachers, trade unionists, journalists, town councillors, natives, etc.) dropped. Although figures for kidnapping should be handled with caution, there does seem to be a decrease in numbers from 2007. According to the international Red Cross, there were 379 disappearances in 2007 (the number of kidnaps between 1996 and 2004 was approximately 448 on average per year according to the *Comision colombiana de juristas*).

The Main Limitations: Rearmament and Reintegration Program Issues

Even if the demobilization process seemed to have been a success, the outlook in the medium-term seemed fairly uncertain with more and more new armed groups of different types bursting onto the scene. From the beginning of 2006, the media, international organizations, and national nonprofit organizations began to worry about the appearance of emerging groups. *Los Aguilas Negras, Los Machos, Los Rastrojos,* and *Nueva Generación* are now well-known names. The existence of these groups seems to be based on three factors: the continuation of criminal activity by paramilitaries who were meant to be demobilized, the presence of paramilitaries who have not been demobilized and the formation of new paramilitary groups involved in drug trafficking and other criminal activity. OEA's mission to support the peace process periodically focused on reports about the reorganization of demobilized members in criminal gangs, the existence of fighters who have not been demobilized and the emergence of new armed groups in areas that were previously occupied by demobilized groups, with a marked increase from the first reports in 2005 to the last at the time of writing (12th quarterly report in February 2009[11]).

> After highlighting the presence of non-demobilised groups and rearmed structures in areas such as Cordoba, Uraba, Narino, southern Cesar and Meta in our quarterly reports, the Mission is concerned that these factions still exist and are even growing despite activity implemented by public forces. This is proof of the groups' resistance and of their resources which provide constant recruitment and continue local corruption.[12]

CNRR's report, which goes over some of OEA's typology, identifies three types of group[13]: the dissidents who belonged to paramilitary groups and have not been demobilized, the rearmed who took part in the negotiation process but are actually still involved in various criminal activity, and emerging groups formed following the paramilitary demobilization. There are variations in the numbers of emerging groups in the country and their geographical spread. Nuevo Arco Iris corporation's armed conflict watchdog stated that there are emerging gangs in 246 municipalities and 27 regions of the country (December 2008, *Bandas criminales, seguridad democrâtica y corruption*). MAPP-OEA identified 28 regions affected in 153 municipalities in its 12th report. According to sources, the number of group members fluctuates between 3,000 (national police figures) and 10,000 (figures provided by various nonprofit organizations including *Corporation Nuevo Arco Iris*). CNRR highlighted the existence of 34 groups in 22 regions and in 20 percent of Colombian municipalities. In geographical terms, they are located in demobilized paramilitary group influence zones. There were four main areas: the north (the Caribbean) where the AUC northern bloc was; the regions of Antioquia, Cordoba, south Bolivar, and Magdalena Medio; the Oriental Plains (Meta, Vichada, y Guaviare); and the Pacific region in Choco, Cauca, Valle, Narino, and some of Putumayo. There are two ways of interpreting the groups' activity and their objectives: the analysts see it as a continuation of paramilitary groups while the government sees it as criminal gangs involved in drug trafficking. One thing is certain: it still seems premature to see these groups as the beginning of a new generation of paramilitaries acting as a unit throughout the country and adopting the same modus operandi as the former paramilitaries. However, their activities do not just involve drug trafficking and organized crime; they are also attacking civilians and are a threat to the peace and reinsertion process. The *Comision colombiana de juristas* (CCJ) stated in a report published in September 2008 ("Neoparamilitarism and New Massacres") that these groups' actions are directed against members of social organizations and civilians. MAPP-OEA highlights that some of these groups threatened left-wing sectors, social organizations, and the Church. For example, several of those who organized the national protest against state crimes and crimes against humanity on March 6, 2008, were threatened, and some promoters were assassinated. There has been an increase in massacres committed by emerging groups according to the CCJ, such as the massacres in Puerto Libertador (Cordoba), which claimed seven lives, San Juan de César (Guajira), where four died, and Pizarro (Choco), where nine were killed. Some of these massacres led to the population migrating such as that of Istmina (69 people migrated). The overall decline of the murder rate is beginning to reverse in areas where there is a concentration of groups. Cordoba is one of the most affected areas in terms of increased murders (over half of its municipalities have seen murder rates double since 2007). The main reason for this increase seems to be disputes between illegal armed groups. Antioquia also saw its murder rate rise significantly after paramilitary demobilization. This trend began to reverse in 62 of the 125 municipalities during the first semester of 2008. This number represents a 9 percent increase for the whole region.[14] This increase in violence is linked to territorial clashes between rival armed groups such as Daniel Rendon Herrera's faction (alias *Don Mario*) that claims influence from Uraba to the east via Medellin and the *Oficina de Envigado* and its armed branch *Los Paisas* wanting to make its presence felt from Medellin to the south of Cordoba up to Barrancabermeja (Santander). Civil society faces three threats: the presence of an illegal armed structure, the response of the illegal armed factions to the state's actions against them, and the disputes between drug-traffic related armed groups.

The presence of illegal armed groups in demobilized paramilitary influence zones has direct repercussions on civil society. It limits their movement, exerts social control, and establishes an illegal economy based on extortion. Those who resist the armed factions are usually threatened and sometime murdered. The illegal armed groups try to disrupt the institutions' day-to-day running when faced with pressure from public forces. Several members of the public forces have recently been assassinated along with members of the legal system. Public order has been particularly disrupted in Narino.

This decline in security conditions linked with the presence of armed groups has become an obstacle to victims of the justice and peace process during ex-paramilitary court hearings. According to MAPP-OEA, victims living in areas where emerging groups are present prefer not to participate through fear of the consequences. During the trial of Jorge 40 (a paramilitary northern bloc fighter) in Montena, only 10 people had the courage to testify while there has been over 3,000 victims. There have already been approximately 20 assassinations because the victims have taken part or planned to take part in trials. The demobilized population is also a potential target. According to OEA figures, 1,658 ex-fighters have been assassinated since the beginning of the demobilization process, the most affected areas being Antioquia, Cesar, Cordoba, and Magdalena, especially in urban areas. Several ex-fighters have been murdered because they refused to take up arms again. The increase in rearmament highlights the risk of violence returning.

Reintegration programs for demobilized members have become crucial in Colombia as rearmed groups put demobilized members under intense pressure. Yet we must acknowledge that up to now public policies have proved themselves to be lacking and incapable of suppressing rearmament. For over two years (2005 to the end of 2007), these policies were defined by their sheer improvisation and informality with the concentration of troops and demobilization as their main priorities. From 2005 a program that had been handling individual demobilizations for the Ministry of Home Affairs (PRVC) for three years began to also handle collective demobilizations. The approach was extremely focused, regions were barely involved, financial support was delayed and few insertion projects actually took place. Only a support policy was deployed: ex-fighters received financial support for an 18-month period (with 40 percent coverage of demobilized members). There was no difference in the programs and all the ex-fighters were treated the same way no matter their rank. Consequently a group of middle-ranking fighters began to rearm. At the end of 2007 the government adopted a new strategy by establishing the *Alta Consejeria para la reintegracion* (High Commission of Reintegration) directed by entrepreneur Frank Pearl. He decided to extend humanitarian aid to ex-fighters by six months. He announced that the idea of reinsertion was no longer valid and replaced it with reintegration and its long-term connotations. Pearl set up 37 local aid management centers (CROS: *Centros de referencia y oportunidades*) to better benefit the regions where the demobilized mainly live with the support of a centralized national center from which the programs were designed. The ACR planned to launch a reintegration strategy based on community, which implied the simultaneous involvement of two main players: the demobilized and the community.

Over three years after these public policies began, what are the results? First, Colombia launched a process to demobilize ex-paramilitary combatants but no reintegration process.[15] Out of 31,651 demobilized paramilitaries, the ACR managed to have 23,081 of them involved in reintegration programs[16]; 1,658 were assassinated, and 7,000 have had no involvement whatsoever. However, OEA's 12th report states that demobilized groups are continuing their illegal activity despite being involved in some regions' reintegration programs (Bajo Cauca, Cordoba, Santander, and Norte de Santander). Also, despite the government's policy of reintegration to civil society, the programs do not address things like the participation of demobilized members in politics and institutional reforms or economic reforms to be adopted. They lack an all-encompassing approach and limit themselves to providing financial support equivalent to minimum wage for two years, access to health care, and very basic training. There are too few health, education, and employment programs, and they only cover a small proportion of the demobilized population. There is only 65 percent coverage in the health sector, 18 percent in psychosocial support, and 33 percent in employment-based training programs. Although the government states that 57 percent of ex-fighters have found a job, 68 percent of them have a job in the informal sector. By the end of 2006 there were only 26 active projects with just 2.9 percent of ex-fighters' involvement compared to 41 at the beginning of 2008. We should highlight the involvement of some private sectors such as *la Fundacion Argos, Globalcontex, la Constructora Bolivar,* and *la Fundacion Carvajal.* The ACR announced they had signed 24 agreements with the private sector in 2009 but most of the companies are still reluctant to get involved. MAPP-OEA's most recent report states that demobilized members are always citing the lack of opportunity in finding work.[17] There is still a wide gap between local and national level, with the local level still having little involvement in program development and establishment. Most of the various municipalities' local administrations and social and economic players do not have any relationship with the programs and do not have a well-defined role in terms of politics, the economy, and institutions. While CROS carries out all the programs locally and aims to reach the demobilized population directly, these centers report to central government and do not leave any room for local players to get involved. The process is thus seen as alien and imposed by the national government. It addresses ex-fighters alone and has not managed to bring ex-fighters, victims, individuals who have migrated, and members of the community together. If anything, the gap between these players is getting wider and wider due mostly to reintegration programs being for ex-fighters alone. Most of the interviews that we held in August 2007 in Colombia with victims of the paramilitaries showed that resentment was rife because of the gap between support provided to the "butchers" and the lack of state compensation to victims. A., from the association for victims *Madres de la Candelaria de Medellin*, said: "All the money is going to paramilitaries who cut their victims up into little pieces." The victims get nothing out of this process.[18] The administrative compensation program only began setting up in the first half of 2009. The time difference is seen as a reward for crimes committed.

The main difficulty with current programs is the depoliticization of former AUC members, which tends to put them to one side, as though the state does not wish to address their relationship with the state and the rest of society. This is certainly proof of guilt and trauma due to these members' past infiltration of the political system. The long-term challenge however is the establishment of a political process to overhaul the social contract.

Possible Explanations: Continuation of Former Networks, Narco-paramilitary Influence over Society and Politics

We will offer several explanations for rearmament and reintegration program failings. Are paramilitaries capable of anything but war given their warrior habitus? As for Colombian society, has it been "bullied," in George L. Mosse's sense of the word, after living with violence for many years and unable to see a future in "cultural demobilization"? With the battle waging on, we have good reason to think so.

It seems difficult to believe that paramilitaries are violent to the core. There is nothing special about paramilitaries: there are differences in terms of status, responsibility, offences, intellectual authority in crime, and in the feeling of guilt. Scientific research on demobilized paramilitaries is hard to come by in Colombia. In 2006 the anthropologists Kimberly Theidon and Paola Andrea Betancourt carried out research on FARC demobilized individuals and collectives and paramilitaries in Colombian cities. Out of 112 interviews, 90 percent of those questioned were low-level fighters or leaders of small groups (10–15 men). Their research found that on the whole demobilized paramilitaries wanted to make a fresh start but the wartime context hindered this transition: "Our research shows that demobilised members really want to abandon the war [...]. The irony is that they are 'transitional' subjects and unfortunately the social context is not yet at that stage."[19]

The successful local reinsertion programs, especially that of Medellin Town Hall, show that a large number of ex-fighters managed to reinsert themselves into the community in the long-term. Some say that they managed to break all ties with their previous life largely thanks to the training course financed by the *Paz y Reconciliacion* program. This is what happened to C. A. C. who had been involved in the program for over two years after being in paramilitary groups (including Medellin's Metro bloc) for 15 years. He is now a math teacher, and he confesses to being skeptical about the DDR process during 2003 collective demobilization. His doubt came from his inability to do anything but fight and his desocialization: "I didn't know how to do anything else... self-defense groups had become my real family. I distanced myself from my other family so they wouldn't have any problems at home. I was holed up in the same area with the same future ahead of me."[20] He confessed to having taken up arms several times since for the same reason.

Originally from the poor part of Medellin, Aranjuez, C. soon joined gangs of young hired killers working for drug traffickers and controlled by Pablo Escobar. He was attracted by easy money and the fact that a lot of his friends were in gangs: "We all bet on that. That's where the money was. It was easy. We didn't need to make a lot of effort."[21] When Pablo Escobar died, self-defense groups began to take over areas that the drug traffickers had left empty. C. then decided to join one of these groups: "We didn't know how to do anything else. We were potential warriors. We were given weapons and we said OK."[22] He was paralyzed and found refuge in a halfway house for two years after being wounded in the spine during an ambush with guerrilla militia in 1998. He rejoined the self-defense groups as a spy when he regained the use of his hands. He spent a year in prison after being arrested by the police in 2000 and went back to the self-defense groups upon release: "I picked up where I'd left off with my friends. I didn't know how to do anything else. It was my world." After being demobilized, he began taking part in the *Paz y Reconciliación* program, which helped him go back to university. He qualified in 2008, and the program took him on as a math teacher. C. seems happy with his journey from "weapons to books" and the recognition and status he has managed to achieve. He has completely changed his life, left his nieghborhood, and made up with his family. Nevertheless, he admits that the process is not easy as the war is still waging, and there are lots of temptations: "Demobilization has to come from the heart. It needs to be decisive. It's a difficult journey as they always come knocking at your door." Carlos seems to have managed to see the positive in his past life as a paramilitary: "We were good at being bad so we must be great at being good. We were once part of the problem. Now we are part of the solution."[23]

Other demobilized paramilitaries from the Medellin program also spoke of their doubts, fear, and difficulties in their new life. J. C. G. N. says he saw the process as an opportunity: "We were given money and the chance to study."[24] Originally from the poor part of Manrique, he also started out in gangs working for drug traffickers before joining the Metro bloc. After spending four years in prison, he decided to take up arms and join Putumayo's self-defense groups. He has fond memories of this time: "There was a great camaraderie. 'Paraco' life is crazy. We all smoked and partied."[25] J. C. also speaks of the atrocious paramilitary techniques such as how they would use a chainsaw to chop up victims' bodies and then throw them into large pits (*picaban a las personas*). Although he says that some people were happy to do such things, he says he was never attracted by such cruelty: "That was never me." When he speaks of his current situation, he does not seem attracted by the violence anymore but rather "lost." He was fired from his first job because of his cocaine addiction, which he says he has now conquered, and wants to go to university. Unlike C. , he has not achieved recognition or status, and this makes him more vulnerable. On several occasions his fear is evident, and he cries when showing photos of his children he is scared of losing. "I'm still afraid of paying my own debts. I don't feel safe in the city. I'm frightened they will come and kill me."[26]

Several testimonials show that most ex-fighters wish to break their ties with violence even if they still live in violent surroundings. If they are kept from temptation, some of them are capable of doing something other than war. The quality of the reintegration programs is therefore essential.

Is the answer to be found in a "bullied" Colombian society? Even if people's experience of violence has produced long-lasting trauma and widespread fear, it has not entailed, with the exception of certain groups, a culture of war that would lead to friend/enemy division. The growth of drug trafficking has meant the country is in a generalized violent situation that affects armed battle, the institutional crisis, and the chaotic social fabric. Those involved in the drug economy are so varied and relationships between them so complex that the settling of these two opposed camps' differences is not going to happen in the near future. It also seems that the population shows a desire for peace at any given opportunity. Rejecting violence and focusing on peace has symbolized Colombian social mobilization since the end of the 1980s. The position on speech owes much to the idea of a civil society and, as Daniel Pécaut puts it, "War has left its mark on Colombian society: it defines itself in relation to the issue of peace."[27]

Pro-peace mobilizations relied on political speculation, a drop in violence, and negotiations with rebel groups. The first national initiatives took place at the end of the 1980s following a wave of massacres and political assassinations by paramilitary groups. According to Carlos Fernandez, Mauricio Garcia Duran, and Fernando Sarmiento, there are three major periods in terms of pro-peace movements: civil society's first pro-peace activities (1987–1992), the organization of the movement and active mobilization (1993–1999), national mobilization crisis, and increased local activities in civil society (2000–2005).[28] On October 26, 1997, during the presidential elections and as part of a Citizen Mandate for Peace supported by several civil society organizations, over 10 million Colombians attached a certificate in favor of peace to their normal ballot paper demanding pacifist solutions to armed conflict, respect of international human rights, and for all armed groups to call a ceasefire. This was certainly the first time that violence had been publicly rejected on such a large scale. More recently, during the second term of Álvaro Uribe Vélez, there was a new wave of national mobilizations against violence. The protest against the FARC on February 4, 2008, is something that was unheard of in this context and brought 12 million people from all over the country together. On March 6, a protest for victims of state and paramilitary crime brought approximately 500,000 to Bogota. Colombia has never stopped expressing its rejection of violence despite armed players' terror tactics, and this is one of Colombia's main assets for the future, as Daniel Pécaut agrees: "Circumstance permitting, we must continue to privilege a society based on tolerance and common sense, otherwise known as civility and Colombia's most important asset to escape its current situation."[29]

How can we get to grips with rearmament and the return of violence? The most plausible way would be to go down the utilitarian analysis road. In the case of Colombia, analyses pointing to economic reasons for violence are very convincing.[30] If violence initially hides a social and political dimension, the increase in violence that occurred in the mid-1980s and onwards cannot be addressed without considering the resources supporting the conflict, mainly the changes caused by the economy of drug trafficking. The drug economy therefore plays an essential part in the transformation of violence; it contributes to strengthening certain armed players and helping new players start up. From a conflict point of view, drug trafficking makes guerrilla groups stronger. After a period of crisis and division that poses a serious threat to the various movements, the guerrillas go through a real transformation. Drug trafficking also contributes to the blossoming of a new armed actor: paramilitarism.

We do not wish to go over the birth and evolution of Colombian paramilitary groups in greater detail. We must however underline that these groups have been closely connected to drug traffickers and drug trafficking resources from the outset. Yes, the first private armed groups go back to the nineteenth century and more recently the mid-twentieth century, *chulavitas*[31] and *pâjaros*,[32] then there are the self-defense groups that were legalized in 1965 as part of the Cold War containment strategy.[33] But the paramilitarism that was born in the 1980s is in a league of its own. It is neither self-defense nor state-owned but stems from the growth of private armed groups in illegal industries (drug trafficking and emerald trade). Analysts agree that the appearance of this type of paramilitary group in Colombia is related to the peace process failures of President Betancur. FARC's growth and the reformation of the *Ejército de Liberación Nacional* (ELN) and *Ejército popular de liberacion* (EPL) gave large landowners the impression that guerrillas were the only ones to benefit from the peace process. The Patriotic Union's (UP) relative election breakthrough[34] after the first mayoral election by universal suffrage in 1985 could but add to this impression. It would seem that two groups are to blame for the birth of the paramilitary phenomenon:

> If you are interested in where self-defence groups sprang from, we can confirm that the State is as much to blame as the guerrilla forces for the birth of this illegitimate creature. The former because of its weakness and lack of public order which allowed private solutions to take hold. The latter because of the deterioration of its methods and its political objectives that destroyed regional civil communities to the point that the right-wing movement was their only solution.[35]

In some regions, those that had prospered from drug trafficking began to buy the land that former owners, who were tired of guerrilla extortion, were happy to sell. Supporting the paramilitary economically was the only way to limit territorial guerrilla expansion when the state proved itself incapable of containing the problem. The first rural self-defense groups were thus formed by owners, police, and army members. The first death squad to become known to the public was the MAS (*Muerte a secuestradores*: death to kidnappers), an organization founded by the Medellin cartel in 1982 after M-19 guerrillas kidnapped one of the daughter of the cartel's important member. Founded by the mafia, it also attracted the military and police who launched a campaign of intimidation against the left-wing movement, trade unionists, political figureheads, and alleged guerrilleros. Carlos Medina Gallego showed how much the case in Puerto Boyaca[36] (region in Cundinamarca, between Boyaca's emerald production area and the Antioqueño colonization) brought together the main features of the paramilitary. The FARC reigned terror in this area among mid- to large-property owners while local property owners and drug traffickers financed armed squadrons to hunt down guerrillas. Drug traffickers played a crucial role in consolidating a defense network in areas highly affected by guerrillas. Once the paramilitary groups became illegal (1989), the Castaño brothers (Fidel and Carlos), who were famous for their involvement in drug trafficking, devoted themselves to a new form of anti-insurrectional activity in the banana-growing region of northwest Antioquia. They appointed former policemen and soldiers to the group that was to become AUC in 1996. Paramilitary groups' ties to drug trafficking, which were strong from the beginning, only got stronger. During interviews on Colombian TV in 2000, Carlos Castaño admitted that drug trafficking financed 70 percent of the AUC. From 2002 the drug traffickers steered the movement or took complete control of its management.

However, one of the biggest failings in the negotiations between the Uribe government and the paramilitaries was not addressing the topic of drug trafficking. Nathalia Springer rightly highlights that it was strange to think that, if the aim was to end paramilitarism, only dealing with leaders and demobilizing them would bring an end to the movement: "It is odd that the Ralito II text avoids any mention of such crucial topics as the dismantling of financial structures, territorial concentration and the responsibility of these groups in perpetrating such atrocious acts for which they cannot be granted amnesty."[37]

In order to bring down drug trafficking organizations in Colombia, drug trafficking would have had to be one of the main topics during negotiations and agreements between the government and paramilitary would have had to entail as much commitment from the state as from the demobilizing groups. A recent publication about public policies' failings in the war against drug trafficking in Colombia also says: "We've lost a great chance to award legal benefits to paramilitary leaders linked to drug trafficking and demand that they dismantle their labs, eradicate crops, supply information about drug trafficking routes etc. If we had made the most of this opportunity then drug trafficking would have been hit hard."[38]

The government presumably preferred to achieve fast demobilization to make the process legitimate and did not want it to look like they were negotiating with drug traffickers. In fact, those known solely as drug traffickers were on the side of paramilitaries from the start of negotiations. In September 2004 the *Semana* review published a special report about the *narcos de Ralito* and mentioned the names of eight drug traffickers who had become paramilitary fighters.[39] While the first legal projects framing the demobilization process made no mention of extradition, the Uribe government felt compelled to announce in a statement in April 2004 that they would not hesitate to extradite paramilitary leaders who did not respect the rules of the negotiation process. Since then the subject of drug trafficking has only been dealt with from a criminalization point of view and never politically. In May 2008, the government decided to extradite 14 paramilitary leaders to the United States (including Salvatore Mancuso, Rodrigo Tovar Pupo alias "Jorge 40," and Diego Fernando Murillo alias "Don Berna") as they had not told the whole truth about the human rights violations that they had committed (as per the Justice and Peace law), they had been involved in illegal activity from their prison, and they had not respected the victim compensation conditions of the demobilization process.

The emergence of new armed groups from the start of 2006 logically highlighted the spread of Colombia's drug trafficking network. The network brought violence once again to the fore and the groups were based in demobilized paramilitary influence zones, which became drug zones.[40] In the case of Colombia, the main leaders, mid-level combatants, and most soldiers were demobilized without the network feeding drug trafficking resources being dispersed. No study of paramilitaries who have decided to take up arms has been made (to our knowledge) for obvious reasons: they do not want to talk. On the other hand, MAPP-OEA's 12th report provides the preliminary findings of an investigation into reasons for taking up arms again (with ex-fighters who have been captured). One of the main reasons is the "influence of illegal contexts."[41] Approximately 48 percent of those questioned confirm that demobilized paramilitaries, delinquent groups, guerrillas, and new emerging groups controlled public order in the area they lived in before being captured.

In the end, generally speaking, the failure of Colombia's DDR process shows the influence of paramilitarism over society and politics. The current DDR process has avoided the social and political aspects of the paramilitary. It has focused on the main leaders (or "warlords" as Gustavo Duncan calls them)[42] and set the social and political structures supporting the paramilitary to one side. This has resulted in what Duncan calls a "structural fault" with the process: "We mistakenly thought that the leaders' interest in resolving the question of extradition and expropriation of their property would be enough to end private army domination. But the warlords' roots are tied to a number of social issues: society's organisation around drug trafficking and armed units which spreads their role regulating illegal trade to all aspects of social life. [...] The conditions for reorganising private armies and the risks of their return will always exist."[43]

The DDR process with paramilitaries was a double-edged sword. It provided up to date information about the extent of paramilitary groups' involvement in the Colombian political system. This, along with drug trafficking, helped anti-guerrilla militia to expand significantly. Paramilitaries' revelations highlighted the extent to which they depended on powerful political, social, and economic networks. The "para-political scandal" of Colombia began in May 2006 when Clara Lopez Obregon, a member of the Polo democratico alternativo[44] party, asked the Supreme Court to begin studying the statement Salvatore Mancuso (ex-paramilitary leader of the northern bloc of paramilitary groups) made in March 2002 in which he spoke of paramilitary victory in the legislative elections estimating that over 35 percent of the elected candidates shared their ideas. The investigation found the following:

- The court seized information from the personal computer of Jorge 40 (the no. 2 of the northern bloc). This information proved that Jorge 40 was connected to some politicians on the Atlantic coast who would spread paramilitary power.
- The signing of a secret pact (Ralito Pact) between the self-defense chief of staff, seven MPs, four deputies, two governors, and five mayors belonging to a coalition supporting the president, drawn up on July 23, 2001, in Santa Fé de Ralito whose aim was to "re-establish the country." At the same time the government and paramilitaries

were involved in the peace process with the latter preparing to sign a ceasefire.⁴⁵ This was not the only pact and the existence of other verbal and written agreements shows that para-politics existed before and after the 2002 legislative elections not just to "befriend" candidates but also to use government power. *Verdad abierta*'s 2008 report about para-politics mentions the signing of secret pacts between paramilitaries and local politicians in several other regions: Pacts of Chivolo (2000), Pivijai (2001), Uraba, Magdalena Medio, and Caldas.⁴⁶

- The former director of the Department for Administration and Security (DAS), Jorge Noguera Cotes, was accused then arrested for allowing paramilitaries to access the department. He was one of President Uribe's campaign leaders in the Magdalena Medio region.
- The Minister of Justice demanded the capture of Hernando Molina Araújo, governor of Cesar, accused of being friends with Jorge 40.

The Supreme Court began its investigations in June 2006 and ever since then the names of new political leaders with links to the paramilitary are announced on a daily basis. Currently they number 34 out of the 102 senators elected in 2006 (33 percent) and 25 of the 168 deputies (15 percent). These figures show that narco-paramilitarism has taken over where drug traffic infiltration left off. When Pablo Escobar was elected deputy in 1982, he won under 1 percent of the Senate's votes. When it was discovered that the Cali cartel had infiltrated the 1994 elections, 8 percent were prisoners. This increase shows that drug traffickers managed to refine their infiltration techniques. As well as 59 deputies, 253 civil servants (either elected or members of armed forces) also stood trial for links to paramilitaries. Current investigations show that this was not limited to the north coast of Colombia (especially Cordoba where it was a known fact); no place on the national territory was spared. We should state that almost 75 percent of the senators and deputies currently accused of having links with paramilitaries belong to movements or official parties and many of them are President Uribe's confidants. Uribe has seen many of his allies fall: his minister of Foreign Affairs, María Consuelo Araújo, was forced to resign after his brother was imprisoned and his father accused; the former director of the DAS, Jorge Noguera Cotes, was arrested; the president of the main party of his coalition was investigated along with Nancy Patricia Gutiérrez Castañeda, president of the Senate. In April 2008, his cousin and former senator Mario Uribe Escobar was arrested by the Supreme Court after trying to escape to Costa Rica. President Uribe's strategy was to express his solidarity with the politicians under investigation and partly delegitimize legal proceedings. In mid-2007, when the Supreme Court ruled that paramilitarism was not a political offence (and therefore an offence for which amnesty could not be granted), Uribe accused the Court of being "ideologically in favor of guerrillas and an obstacle to peace."⁴⁷ When the same Court requested that the Constitutional Court revise the legislative act passing reelection, the president accused the Court of lending itself to the "power of terrorism" and "exercising selective justice."[48] The head of state seems ready to do anything to hinder justice being done.

Besides paramilitary influence over the political system, statements from paramilitaries have also shown links with the economy. The multinational Chiquita Brands admitted to having made payments to paramilitaries and guerrillas and were fined $25 million. In April 2009, during a hearing in Washington, ex-paramilitary leader Salvatore Mancuso Gómez gave the names of several national and international companies that had paid paramilitaries: the drink company Postobon (monthly tax of 10 million pesos), Bavaria (1,000 pesos per case of beer), Proleche, Cicolac; transport companies Copetran and Brasilia.[49] There is a possibility that most of the companies on Colombian soil have been involved in this type of financing.

To conclude, the DDR process with paramilitary groups that took place during a period of partial transition in Colombia has not ended paramilitarism. There was a short-term reduction in violence as the murder rate began to rise again in 2007 in certain areas in particular. Instead of making private armies extinct, the DDR process gave rise to a new type of private structure to dominate local societies whose growth is still uncertain. The main reason is that the leading reinsertion programs did not deal with the social and political reasons for the paramilitarism, drug trafficking being top of the list. As long as drug trafficking exists, there will always be a demand for armed protection and in this regard Colombia has certainly not learnt enough from other countries (Salvador, Guatemala, Nicaragua, and Ethiopia). These countries showed us that extensive political, institutional, and economic reforms are essential to the process' success. Despite the number of revelations about links between politicians and paramilitary groups, Colombians still vote for the political parties most involved in parapolitics and support President Uribe.[50] The timid political reform passed in May 2009 hardly inspires optimism. The reform is supposed to sanction political parties whose members are allied with illegal armed groups, but it gives no details of the sanction for this type of conduct and the planned bans will only come into effect in 2010.[51] That being said, there is no way Colombia can escape a political process to redefine the social contract in the long term. Translated by Société ATENAO, Aix-en-Provence.

Notes

1. M-19 guerillas from the PRT (Partido Tevolucionario de los Trabajadores), EPL (Ejército Popular de Liberacion), MAQL (Movimiento Armado Quintm Lame), and the CRS (Corriente de Renovacion Socialista).
2. Cinep, *Deuda con la humanidad, paramilitarismo de Estado, 1988–2003* (Bogota: Banco de datos Cinep, 2004).
3. Based on this agreement paramilitaries agreed to "progressively demobilise all their members. The first demobilisations will take place before the end of the year and the last before December 31st 2005."

4. G. L. Mosse, *De la Grande Guerre au totalitarisme. La brutalisation des sociétés européennes* (Paris: Hachette, 1999).
5. An expression coined by John Horne, *"Démobilisations culturelles après la Grande Guerre"*, in *14-18, Aujourd'hui, Today, Heute* (Paris: Éditions Noésis, 1998), pp. 45–53. Cultural demobilization describes an evolution which occurs at both a group and individual level and whose main components include the move away from violence, the rise of the pacifist ideal, and the rehabilitation of the enemy.
6. The National Development Plan 2002–2006 defined security as "the exercise of an effective authority which conforms to rules, contains and dissuades violent people and is committed to the respect of human rights, political pluralism and citizen participation."
7. The security policy translated into the investment of an enormous amount of resources and a series of initiatives to increase the government's capacity to maintain order. In material terms, security expenditure rose from 4.4 percent of the GDP in 2000 to 5.1 percent in 2002 and has remained relatively stable since then. Public force rose from 295,000 men in 2002 to almost 375,000 in 2006.
8. In the case of the M-19, the peace agreement signed with the government in March 1990 led to legislative initiatives, a specific reinsertion program, and the recognition of AD M-19 as a legal political party. Peace negotiations with the EPL, PRT, and MQL were directly linked to the Constitutional Convention's process. The various peace agreements allowed ex-guerrillas to take part in the Convention and new political movements to be formed.
9. N. Springer, *Desactivar la guerra. Alternativas audaces para consolidar la paz* (Bogota, Aguilar, 2005), 316–317.
10. Programa presidencial de derechos humanos y derecho internacional humanitario, Vicepresidencia de la Republica, *Situation de derechos humanos y de derechos international humanitario*, 2007, 6.
11. MAPP-OEA, *Décimosegundo informe trimestral del secretario general al Consejo Permanente sobre la mision de apoyo*, Bogota, February 2009.
12. Ibid., 2.
13. CNRR, *Area de desmovilizacion, desarme y reinsercion, Disidentes, rearmados y emergentes? Bandas criminales o tercera generacion paramilitar?*, Bogota, August 2007.
14. MAPP-OEA, *Décimosegundo informe trimestral*, 8.
15. Results found by *Fundacion Seguridad y Democracia*, "La reinsercion paramilitar, un balance," *Coyuntura de seguridad*, (March 14, 2008): 14–20.
16. According to ACR, a demobilized member is considered active if he has taken part in at least one ACR activity in the last three months.
17. MAPP-OEA, *Décimoprimer informe trimestral del secretario general al Consejo Permanente sobre la mision de apoyo*, Bogota, March 2008.
18. Interviews with members of the *Madres de la Candelaria de Medellin* association, August 17, 2007, as part of a mission financed by ACI Prosodie "Grammaires internationales de la réconciliation" led by Sandrine Lefranc (ISP/CNRS).
19. K. Theidon and P. A. Betancourt, *"Transiciones conflictivas: combatientes desmovilizados en Colombia,"* *Analisis político*, 58 (September–December 2006): 102.
20. Interview with C. C., in Medellin in March 2009 by Marcela Barrios as research into the reinsertion of paramilitaries in Medellin.
21. Ibid.
22. Ibid.
23. Ibid.
24. Interview with J. C. G. N. by Marcela Barrios, Medellin in March 2009.
25. Ibid.
26. Ibid.
27. D. Pécaut, *Les FARC, une guérilla sans fins?* (Paris: Éditions Lignes de repères, 2008), 162.
28. C. Fernández, M. Garcia Duran, and F. Sarmiento, "Movilizaciones por la paz en Colombia, 1978–2002," *Controversia* (February 2004): 17–23.
29. Pécaut, *Les Farc, une guérilla sans fins?*
30. We are referring to the works of Camilo Echandía, especially *El conflicto armado y las manifestaciones de violencia en las regiones de Colombia* (Bogota: Presidencia de la Republica de Colombia, Oficina del Alto Comisionado para la Paz, 1999).
31. An armed group of conservatives from the Boyaca region.

32. "Birds" is the name given to murderers who spread terror on behalf of the conservatives of the Cauca area.
33. Decree 3398 of 1965 became Law 48 in 1968 and allows military commandants to provide civilians with weapons for private use (article 33) and the government to get civilians involved in armed activities. The Supreme Court of Justice declared these articles to be anti-constitutional on May 25, 1989.
34. The Patriotic Union (UP) was founded in 1985 in Colombia following the demobilization of part of the FARC and their reappearance as a political party.
35. W. Ramfrez Tobón, "Las Autodefensas, un tema difícil," *Coyuntura política* (October 15, 1999).
36. C. Medina Gallego, *Autodefensas, paramilitares y narcotrafico en Colombia* (Bogota: Editorial Documentos Periodisticos, 1990). The author gives a very detailed account of these groups' reasons for action to understand how they spread to other areas of Colombia, such as Puerto Berrio, Puerto Nare, Puerto Triunfo, Yacopi, Cimitarra, Puerto Salgar, and la Dorada.
37. Springer, *Desactivar la guerra*, 321.
38. Fundación Seguridad y Democracia, Alfredo Rangel (ed.), *La batalla perdida contra las drogas: legalizar es la opcion?* (Bogota: Intermedio, 2008), 18.
39. Francisco Javier Zuluaga Lindo (alias Gordo Lindo), Ramiro Vanoy Murillo (alias Cuco Vanoy), Victor and Miguel Angel Mejia Munera (alias Los Mellizos), Diego Fernando Murillo Bejarano (alias Bon Berna), Juan Carlos Sierra Ramirez (alias el Tuso), and Guillermo Pérez Alzate (alias Pablo Sevillano). They were all subject to demands for extradition to the United States for drug trafficking.
40. We are referring to different MAPP-OEA reports quoted in our text and specifically information relating to the influence zones.
41. MAPP-OEA, *Décimosegundo informe trimestral del secretario general al Consejo Permanente sobre la misión de apoyo*, Bogotá, February 2009, OEA/Ser.G CP/doc. 4365/09 corr. 1. Available at: http://www.acnur.org/secciones/index.php?viewCat=1412
42. G. Duncan, *Los senores de la guerra. De paramilitares, mafiosos y autodefensas en Colombia* (Bogota: Planeta, 2007), 1.
43. Ibid., 2.
44. Left-wing party founded at the end of the 1990s.
45. Senator Miguel de la Espriella, who also signed it, revealed the existence of this document in January 2007.
46. A. Verdad, C. Lopez, and O. Sevillano, *Balance político de la parapolítica* (Bogota: Verdad abierta, 2008), 6–8.
47. Ibid., 16.
48. "Corte Constitucional no revisara falloque dio via libre a la reeleccion del presidente Uribe," *El Tiempo*, March 7, 2008.
49. "Mancuso revela sus socios narcos y salpica a Moreno," *Semana*, April 29, 2009.
50. Lopez and Sevillano, *Balance político de la parapolítica*, 23–25. The report highlights that out of the five Uribe-supporting parties that were most compromised by the para-politics scandal, four were strengthened and continued during the 2006–2007 elections.
51. "Paso la reforma politiquera," *Semana*, May 12, 2009.

PART 2
Process of Reintegration, Cultural Demobilization?

CHAPTER FIVE

A Veteran's Challenge: From the Test of War to the American Dream[1]

BÉATRICE RICHARD

Abstract

What is it like for a war veteran to return to a peaceful and prosperous civilian society? This question is particularly relevant in Canada. Far from the massive operational theatres of both world wars, Canadians experienced these events in a schizophrenic mode: some were caught in the turmoil of the front lines, others remained unharmed on a relatively secure home front. The resulting cultural clash between veterans and civilians was inevitable. How did the veterans experience their return? What were the outward signs of their crises? Veterans told us that after signing their discharge they were asked to abandon their warrior habitus on the spot and pursue the American Dream. It was assumed that the emerging welfare state would create a peaceful and well-ordered life for veterans. However, it neglected to take into account the symbolic dimensions of "civilianization." At best, the community commemorated its heroes' ultimate sacrifice, but paid little attention to those who had survived, taking it for granted that they were back to "normal." Thus, because the community offered no "re-aggregating" rituals, which might have helped veterans evacuate the hubris imbued in them by the nation at war, returning soldiers were left to find their own way of repressing their "dark side" and coming to terms with the loss of their brothers-in-arms. Some managed better than others. But does one ever come back from war?

The current involvement of Canada in Afghanistan brings again to the forefront a problem probably as old as war itself: the readaptation of combatants to civilian life.[2] In March 2007, *MacLean's* magazine devoted its cover to the "homecoming" of Canadian soldiers. It featured the moving picture of a handsome young man in combat uniform, standing upright, leaning on a cane and... on his one remaining foot. At the bottom of the page, a legend stated laconically: "Cpl. Michael Barnewall lost his right foot to a land mine."[3] In the inside pages, a story with an evocative title, "The War at Home," discussed the rehabilitation of soldiers who were injured or maimed in Afghanistan. The reader was introduced to well-cared for and optimistic-looking men despite their uncertain future,[4] with a generous support program as backdrop.[5] This is a good illustration of Canada's policy toward its troops, which involves mobilizing the community to welcome them back and to help them reintegrate into civilian life as painlessly as possible. Such a noble goal is not typical of the post–September 11 period: it is rather linked to a rehabilitation system closely connected with the genesis of the modern Canadian state, which was cited as an example as early as 1943.[6] But is this ideal model fulfilling its promises? Although it is still too early to pronounce on the fate of Michael Barnewall and his peers, it is not so for Canadian veterans of the Second World War, whose demobilization has been scrutinized in several studies. An often mixed portrait emerges from this literature; while demobilization took place without any apparent disorder, it often turned into a crisis in the privacy of the British dominion's homes...[7] This picture in halftones is hardly surprising in a country that paradoxically both suffered and profited from the war. It nevertheless leaves whole the following riddle: although they benefited from one of the most generous rehabilitation schemes, and lived rather successful lives, Canadian combat veterans[8] seem to have never entirely come out from the war. This is in any case what comes out from a series of interviews conducted with 28 such veterans.[9]

This issue brings us back to the broader question of the cultural demobilization of the warrior, which has already been approached from the angles of identity reconstruction, "moral economy of thanking," "return to normalcy," and "tales of return."[10] Many such aspects have resurfaced during our inquiry. All respondents reported having been rather successful in achieving their social and professional reintegration, although a few had to resort to psychotherapy from time to time. In this, their stories mirror Joanna Bourke's observations about the combat veterans' potential for resilience, a phenomenon still largely underestimated in the literature.[11] That does not however mean that the dissipation of the war culture had not been a challenge for Canadian veterans, much to the contrary. Their testimony indeed reflected an ambiguous process of cultural demobilization, for the veterans' discourse was paradoxical in this respect. Although the rehabilitation program was generous for the time, it was not very present in their reminiscences, except to complain about its dehumanizing character. The memories of sometimes ferocious combats were still haunting veterans, more than 50 years later—bringing tears to the eyes of some of them—but did not elicit any regrets.[12] It was especially the interpersonal and social aspects of the "civilianization" that was at the center of their preoccupations: respondents stressed almost unanimously how unreceptive the community had been to their experience of the war as they "lived" it, as opposed to the way the war was "commemorated." Perhaps their suffering laid precisely there, in the negation of their experience; in the community void, typical of the welfare state, which had marked their return. This is the path we would like to further explore here.

When studying more closely the system of demobilization-rehabilitation-reintegration established by the Canadian state, one realizes that although it had generous objectives, it could not fulfill on its own all of the veterans' needs or expectations. The formula was simple: the combatant was asked, upon his return from the front, to wipe out his "warrior's habitus" in pursuit of the American dream. In a climate of the relative economic prosperity, the emerging welfare state was showing him the way toward clean and peaceful suburbs through diverse reinsertion measures. In this perspective, giving up arms and the right to kill—to be demobilized—should have amounted for each individual to no more than a signature at the bottom of a form.

However, some of the veterans' testimonies reveal the limitations of this model. In many cases, the individual remained prisoner of a warrior's identity, born on the battlefield; a phenomenon reinforced by a tacit "code of silence" between combat veterans and civilians.[13] The "homecomers" were trying to forget the violence of battle, while their families and friends preferred to ignore it—some even simply refusing to believe it.[14] In other words, if he wanted to be readmitted in civil society when he returned, the demobilized had to repress the warrior's "dark side."[15] Renouncing to this aspect of his personality and past experience also meant the mourning of his military family, the combat unit, the regiment. Even if the community did hold welcome and, later, commemoration ceremonies, we will see that Canadian veterans did not find this type of events fulfilling, often describing them as superficial, which resulted in a long-lasting mutual incomprehension between the civilians and the demobilized.[16]

As in the case of France after 1918, we can observe here that the prominent voice given to institutions was not sufficient to ensure the success of the rite of passage to civilian life. We will see how, to paraphrase Bruno Cabanes, although speeches and ceremonies reaffirmed the place of veterans and civilians in the "post war moral economy of thanking," they did not have a cathartic effect.[17] In this particular case, the community founds itself lacking effective "re-aggregating" rituals capable of solemnly releasing the combatants from the hubris from which they had been invested, and to literally allow them to be born again to civilian life. This is perhaps where the core of the problem lies.

Historical and Geographical Context

The historical and geographical singularity of Canada's military experience must be stressed from the start, for it has contributed to further deepen the inevitable psychological gap between the front and home, as well as between combat veterans and civilians. Since the twentieth century, Canadians have had a schizophrenic experience of armed conflicts. As a result of their remoteness from the great theaters of operations, they consider that they "are not a military people."[18] This is even when, by 1945, one Canadian in ten had already worn the uniform in either World Wars.[19] Furthermore, for complex historical reasons, among which its colonial status until 1931 and the absence of a real enemy on its borders,[20] Canada has always maintained a defense system with a "variable geometry." It was essentially based on a small nucleus of military regulars. They were British until 1870, doubled with a contingent of reservists with little training, in theory volunteers, but who could potentially be conscripted. This organization was well-adapted to the defense of a national territory that was immense but under little threat, as it allowed the quick mobilization of troops in time of crisis, as it happened in 1914 and 1939.[21] From a core of 3,000 regulars on the eve of each world conflict, the Canadian armed forces grew to reach 600,000 men in 1914–1918, and more than one million in 1939–1945, most of whom had never held a rifle before. In such specific contexts, the soldiers "factory" had to work at full steam: it was a matter of transforming the citizen into a professional soldier within a few months, an objective that also required a baptism of fire for each soldier to be fully achieved. As the war ended, following the inverse process was necessary: giving back to the soldier his citizen status, and returning him to both his family and his community. This meant stripping the "homecomer" of his uniform and of the status of "lawful bearer of arms" that came with it.[22]

Genesis of the Veterans Charter

After the Great War, the process of demobilization resulted in failure: the Canadian government had waited as late as November 1918 to set up a repatriation committee. It therefore proved necessary to reintegrate in earnest some 423,000 men amongst a civilian population of 8 million.[23] The consequences were sometimes dramatic. Without planning and adequate measures, many veterans lived thereafter in a precarious state, if not indigence, a phenomenon that was made worse by the 1929 Depression.[24] Some even became active participants in the harsh social conflicts that marked the postwar era, including the Winnipeg general strike of 1919 in which they distinguished themselves both in the union ranks and in the bosses' camp. During the 1930s, strong militant associations of veterans were created, which forced the government to improve the far-from-generous program that already existed.[25] During the Second World War, however, quite a different scenario unfolded. The authorities had obviously learned lessons from the previous experience since the minister of Pensions and National Health suggested, as early as October 30, 1939, to create a committee that would oversee the development of a demobilization and rehabilitation policy. Two days later, prime minister William Lyon Mackenzie King replied with an unambiguous message: "We cannot begin upon it too soon."[26] The first Canadian contingent had not even yet sailed for England at the time.[27] Halfway through the war, soldiers repatriated for health reasons already benefited from support measures. At the close of the 1944 session, the Parliament unveiled a program offering multiple benefits: the Veterans Charter.

The National Stakes of Demilitarization

With this document, the Federal government was making the solemn commitment to offer veterans "opportunity and security"; whether through preferential measures, loans, allocations, or various insurance benefits, they would in principle be looked after for as long as necessary before they return to a normal life. In this respect, the symbolic role of the Charter was clear—it was meant to officially recognize service rendered to the nation—but it nevertheless expressed complex political stakes. Its implementation, especially because it was accompanied by an embryo of social legislation, proved to be consubstantial with the emergence of the welfare state in Canada.[28] In other words, the Canadian way of "civilianization" was embedded in the elaboration of a national system aimed at regulating socioeconomic relations.

This process contributed, among other things, to redefine the collective identity, especially among Anglo-Canadians: as the colonial link with the British Empire weakened, a growing use of terms such as "citizen," "people," "national" to legitimize the new pan-Canadian state interventionism could be observed.[29] From this crucible emerged a new citizenship: Canadian, stripped from any ethnic connotation, which gave those who enjoyed it universal rights to well-being and to a providential mission. By putting the Keynesian scheme at the service of a mobilizing national project, the government of the day was laying the foundations of a new social and political contract. The "demilitarization" of veterans was very much party to this process. Men had fallen in action to secure a better world; back home, society had a duty to fulfill this destiny. Such was the founding pact of modern Canada. Such was also the meaning of the statement made by Prime Minister Mackenzie King at the end of the war: "To be worthy of Canada's wartime achievements, to be worthy, above all, *of the sacrifice of human life*; let us resolve to work together to make Canada a land of ever widening opportunities, for all our people, regardless of origin, of class or of region, the best land on earth in which to work and to live."[30]

The Demobilization Machinery

The realization of such a better world obviously involved the reconditioning of military men into fully functioning civilians. The Veterans Charter codified this process through what was literally called "the machinery." This concept was informed by a mechanistic conception of the process of civilianization, as revealed by the use of expressions such as the "demobilization machinery of the armed forces" and "the machinery of re-establishment." Ever present in official documents, they suggest that the return to civilian life involves an appropriate mechanism...[31]

The system literally models the transformation industry. We will only highlight the main stages of the process, as detailed analysis of almost each of the steps has already been published.[32] Notwithstanding which branch was involved, Navy, Army, or Air Force, the reverse path of the combatant is in essence the same. The "machinery" gets into full gear from the moment the serviceman lands in Canada and goes through the transit center, where he will sign his discharge papers, and be subjected to a medical examination as well as an interview with a resettlement officer. He will also be offered the possibility to take part in information sessions on the different aspects of the rehabilitation program. In possession of all the necessary certificates, ration, and travel coupons, as well as 30-day's paid leave, the veteran will then have to set on the transition path to "civvy" street, from where he will opt to either return to school, undergo professional training, or directly reenter the job market. The less fortunate will benefit from the support of unemployment insurance until they reach the ultimate goal: finding a job, a home, and a heart. In that regard, the Canadian rehabilitation "machinery" can be interpreted as the bureaucratic version of the achievement of the "American dream" that epitomized the 1950s: owning a home in the suburbs—indeed by 1960, a third of Canadians will have reached this ideal.[33]

The reprocessing of the soldier into a civilian seems thus to focus on the purely material aspects of the issue. Everything happens as if soldiering was an expertise that could be replaced without too much problem for another, or something someone could shed as a simple uniform. It however remains to be seen whether this model satisfied those who were subjected to it.

The Demobilization Experience

In material terms, the support of the state appears to have been appreciated by all the veterans interviewed, even those claiming they did not have to rely on it. For instance, P. D. benefited from the professional reorientation system. After learning the trade of cabinetmaker, he was recruited to work in a factory and then easily won promotions, notably thanks to the veterans' network: "The guy who hired me, he was also a veteran. So, he gave me a good job. I moved even further up later."[34]

However demobilization also left regrets. So it was for P. T., who had to renounce staying in the army, his first choice; the war had represented for him the four "very best years" of his life, despite nine difficult months of captivity in Germany. After a brief professional training, he became a haberdashery salesman for the rest of his days.[35] A. F. did not appreciate to see men treated as cattle: "We were almost all discharged at the same time...just like a flock of sheep." At that point, he also became aware of the fact he was no longer suited to civilian life after serving for five years: "In the Army, you don't have any problem, in a way. You're fed every day. You're dressed, this sort of things [...] But as a civilian, you needed to find clothes, food, and logging for yourself. So, all those responsibilities weighted on your shoulders."[36] That did not stop him from managing to find his own job, first as a brewery worker, then later as a taxi driver.

Despite those few glitches, most of the veterans seem to have found their way in the bureaucratic maze they were drawn into. Did they for all that agree to participate in the "American dream" that was presented to them? Not entirely, because the scars of combat erected a barrier between "them" and the "others,"[37] a fact that contradicts the message of a mass culture quick to romanticize the reunion between the war hero and his entourage. Indeed, the scientific literature depicts a reality that is a lot less rosy: men confronted with family issues, disconnected and depressed, unable of assuming a new destiny, broken and alcoholic, prisoners of unbearable images.[38] Even if those extreme cases are not the majority, rare were those who were completely spared by physical or psychological ills.[39] Such sufferings, because perhaps too diffuse, do not seem to have been either named or supported either by the medical profession or the community.

Reflecting this occultation, Figure 1 in Soby's report does not show any hospital, when 55,000 Canadian servicemen came back from the war afflicted by various traumas.[40] More detailed illustrations of the discharge process simply refer to a routine medical examination.[41] Our interview sample suggests however that the real number of people in bad shape was much greater than the published data. Almost all the veterans interviewed recognize that they have experienced a range of mild but permanent physical and psychological ailments stemming from their ordeal on the battlefield and/or in the prisoners of war camps. Most claim that these illnesses were not fully recognized or taken care of. Such is the case of A. F., whose chronic stomach aches induced by captivity were never recognized by the medical authorities: "[When I got back] I was weighing 90 pounds (45 kg), and then I was told when I was discharged that I was in perfect health!"

Failure to recognize combat-related psychiatric injuries was also frequent. Jean M., a Dieppe veteran, returned to Canada with amnesia and posttraumatic stress that, according to him, were neither recognized, treated, or compensated, and that continued to haunt him.[42] It is now established that almost half the veterans taken prisoners after the

Dieppe raid (48 percent) were suffering from posttraumatic stress disorders (PTSD) in 1946, when only 5 percent of them qualified to receive compensatory pensions. According to historian Terry Copp, this situation reflects a prejudice deeply rooted in the medical culture of the time, which considered trauma caused by combat stress as a form of neurosis. Such a diagnostic provided ground for neuropsychiatrists to argue that awarding a pension would encourage patients' dependency as well as their manipulating tendencies. It is no surprise that the response given to such distress, when recognized, was purely instrumental: screening tests, for instance, or use of electroshocks. Needless to say, such approaches resulted in failure.[43] Those who remained undiagnosed had to contend alone with their torments.

Rebuilding an Identity and Adhering to a New Set of Norms

Beyond such illnesses, whether recognized or not, veterans shared a common indescribable malaise that could not be reduced to strict medical parameters, and that we could call "the existential crisis of the demobilized." They were "civilianized" on the outside, yet their mind was still prisoner of their own battlefield demons. A. F. described this state in the following terms: "The memory of the war, then of prisoners of war, then the army, for me that has never gone. For me that will never be gone." As Charly Forbes, another veteran, explains, the warrior habitus cannot be eliminated at the snap of fingers; it is a legacy that has weighed on his closest relationships: "I do feel deep down that my war years have distorted my values," he writes in his memoirs. "As a natural leader, I demanded from my wife the same sacrifices required from men on the battlefield, the way to success."[44] L. G., from the Canadian Royal Air Force, considers that fellow soldiers returned from the war "children-like," their incapability of assuming the responsibilities of civilian life often resulting in marital problems. He himself divorced "not because the lady wasn't nice, but because I was lacking in maturity."[45] According to him, this disconnect was made worse by the generational gap, as available girls were often younger. He reports: "When we came back, we all married girls who were six years younger than us. The adaptation wasn't easy. Because they did not understand what we had gone through."[46]

This erratic return to intimacy went together with a crisis linked to the rebuilding of a personal identity, a phenomenon that is apparently common to veterans of twentieth century wars, but that researchers are only starting to explore.[47] The demobilized, however, have been addressing this issue for a long time, through stories or novels. Among the witnesses who have, in our view, most accurately described this phenomenon, James Jones, an American veteran from Guadalcanal and the author of the famous novel *The Thin Red Line* (1962) deserves a mention. In a text written in 1975, he explains that beyond a certain state the fury of combats and the scene of massacred comrades lead soldiers to see themselves as men already dead, even if their own body has been spared. This is what the novelist calls "the evolution of a soldier." Once this stage is reached, responsibilities for tomorrow vanish to make way for the enjoyment of the moment. As this is all that ultimately matters, the implications of deeds no longer weigh much on their conscience since they consider themselves as sort of living deads, hence a perverse feeling of freedom. No one who has experienced combat escapes this phenomenon and some remain so much involved in it that they come to regret returning home, as it ended this climate of pathological exaltation. He writes:

> Some men like to live like that all the time. Some are actually sorry to come home and see it end. Even those of us who hated it found it exciting sometimes. That is what the civilian never understand about their returned soldiers, in any war, Vietnam as well. They cannot understand how we could hate it, and still like it; and they do not realize they have a lot of dead men around them, dead men who are walking around and breathing. Some men find it hard to come back from their evolution of a soldier. Some never come back at all, not completely. That's where the de-evolution of a soldier comes in. Sometimes it takes at least as long to accomplish as its reverse process did.[48]

Such accounts show that the process of reinsertion for the veteran, no matter how perfect its inner workings may have been, could only deal with the rational and institutionalized dimension of the veteran's experience—as a professional soldier—and ignored the more archetypal dimension of the warrior within. In this respect, a parallel could be made between the evolution of the soldier and the warrior's possession by "evil spirits" of war as described in the study of so-called "traditional" societies, a point on which we will come back later. If a signature at the bottom of a discharge paper seemed for a time sufficient to deactivate the "soldier" function in Canadian veterans, such was not at all the case for the "warrior" function, which everyone seemed to have confused with the first and which indeed eluded bureaucratic mind. This situation makes more sense when we consider that as of September 30, 1945, day zero of the troops' repatriation, the government had planned to demobilize soldiers at a pace of 38,500 servicemen a month, in other words nearly half a million men (462,000) within a year.[49]

Personal War Storytelling

Another source of anguish associated with the foregoing was the transmission of the narrative of war. Upon their return, veterans mainly looked forward to turning the page, or at least this is what they pretend. Apart from the most affected among them, they were more concerned with rebuilding their lives—by finding a job, setting up a business, getting married, and starting a family... buying a house—than rehashing the past. "This wasn't [telling about the war] what occupied my mind then. It was making a living and being independent," is a type of comment frequently made.[50] In the same breath, veterans admit that a barrier was erected almost instantly between them and others, encouraging them to repress their memories. P. J. gives a good summary of his peers' perception in this respect[51]: "We heard about it so little! It was like unspoken of! [...] Even at home. It was more or less hidden." Both the fear of reviving the trauma on one side and to hear the unspeakable on the other seems to have sealed a pact of silence between insiders and outsiders. Sometimes, the trauma of combat had left wounds so obvious that both friends and family did not dare ask questions: "At the age of 23, I was in theory responsible for 125 men, says A. A. And then, what had marked me most—I've had dreams about it for years—was the responsibility to say, to make [my men] do things that were going to get them killed."[52] Moreover, verbalizing this kind of experience is most often impossible: "Yes, people were interested [in my war experience]. But knowing that it affected me, on account of the nightmares I had, being polite, they avoided making me speak about it. But [at the same time] they wanted so much to show me they cared that they made me speak anyway! So [...] when you speak to someone and you sense a sympathetic ear, you're inclined to go further. Then, against your better judgment, you forget, then you say more than you wanted to say. [...] Then, it hurts."[53]

The worry not to be believed, or to be misunderstood, often comes back in the comments. Some have fought isolation by going to veterans associations. A. L. claims that he only found a listening ear at the Legion[54]: "There, it was good. But with civilians, no way! [...] Even when you want to tell something to a civilian who has never been [to war]... First of all, he doesn't believe you [...], then second, he's going to say: 'You weren't forced to go.'"[55]

Among themselves, veterans have their codes, their common references, and do not need to explain or justify themselves; they can understand a hint and they form a brotherhood of insiders: "When there were civilians around we'd shut our mouth," explains P. D. "[...] Because, those people, them they found that horrible."[56] Especially as, stresses M. S., civilians were asking them annoying questions: "[They were asking us] if we lacked food or water, if... if we were not able to wash. Things excessively insignificant, you see?" The war experience as such? "They weren't interested, no. They just weren't interested!" It is difficult not to compare such testimonies with that more recent of Lieutenant-General Roméo Dallaire describing the impact of the Rwandan genocide on his unit: "Our experience in the previous months had separated me and my small band of warriors from the world and, in some senses, had made us all into prisoners of memories too personal to share and to difficult to express."[57]

Heroes Nevertheless

At first glance, the homecoming does not appear to have been very successful: veterans and their families apparently lived in a mutual misunderstanding that persisted and became source of bitterness and mutual regrets, even some very deep personal crisis—as previously mentioned, some experienced serious marital problems. Worst still, the veterans seem to have been left struggling with memories so full of atrocities that they could not be shared. However, on the whole, what they say is consistent with a more nuanced picture of their "exit from the war." Some even managed to carve out a place as a hero in the family memory, through stories that were sufficiently sanitized and positive to be understood by noninitiates, most of the time their children or grandchildren. Such is the case of B. R., who was a corpsman on some of the worst battlefields in Sicily, Italy, Holland, and Germany: "My children, when they came of age, learned that their father had been a soldier. [...] They were appreciative. 'My father was a hero.'" G. J., a Leading Seaman on HMS Nabob, the first Canadian manned aircraft carrier, agrees: "Them [the children] know about it [...] They know that the Old Man was there [in the war]. The Old Man his war story, that was important to him. [...] 'Tis important for them [the children] too. It's important, they're proud..."

For many, like B. R., the test of war was even positive: "I was a completely changed man. Oh! I was no longer the same man, in all respects. I no longer saw things with the same eye. No. I had matured. I was less of an adventurer. More aware of the value of life. And again, it gave me what it takes to be the father of a family. [...] What it has brought me in terms of experience, no university can teach you [...] No, you have to live through it! [...] There isn't a single experience in the whole world that can show you...human value."

Others seem to have favored nonverbal-communication strategies, such as gestures, postures, mimics, innuendoes, etc. Y. G.'s account is significant in this respect: "The day after I arrived back home, I was the first to get up. [...] I still picture my father's rocking chair near the stove. It was empty. It was his spot. It was sacred. Nobody would have dared to sit in it. Some embers remained in the stove. I put some tea to heat. While waiting, I sat in my father's chair, with my feet leaning on the stove. When my mother came downstairs, I was in that position with my eyes closed. She warned everyone: "Do not make any noise, he is sleeping." She said nothing. Neither did my father. I think they felt compassion for me. [...] How many times have I seen my mother cry when thinking about all this? [...] She also had gone through hell in Canada. [...] Me, I knew all what it involved [the war]. I was a lot more serene."[58]

This type of scene has a recasting dimension that allows to apprehend the readaptation of the combatant no longer solely as a process of personal and social "reconstruction" for an individual who was damaged or destroyed, but rather as the last stage of a "rite of passage," in the sense in which Franco-Dutch ethnologist Arnold van Gennep understood it as early as 1909. There are three fundamental and universal sequences allowing for the "passage" of individuals or groups from a state (or a status) to another, while reaffirming the unity and unanimity of a group around common symbols and references:

- Preliminary phase, or so-called separation—in this instance the departure of the combatant;
- Liminality, or phase of latency, when the individual find himself in a sort of symbolic and initiatic no man's lands—here the war;
- Postliminality, or phase of "reaggregation," finally, during which the person acquires a new status and achieves his or her metamorphosis.[59]

The previous testimony shows how war is a test for all family members it separates; at the same time, it transforms the family order by investing the son with the authority to replace his father. The test of battle has transformed him into a man to whom respect is due. Therefore the rite of passage, such as described above, seems to have come to a conclusion. This type of example should encourage us to address the issue of returning veterans no longer solely through its spectacular, if not pathological aspects, but also in its more discrete, if not unconscious expressions. In this respect, ethno-psychiatrist Tobie Nathan proposes a relevant conception of trauma as a process of transformation through suffering, which generates forces and difficulties.[60] This perspective would allow the rehabilitation of the warrior to move away from a logic of trauma and to focus on its initiatic and structuring dimension. Such an approach implicitly assumes that the community participates actively in the phase of the veteran's reaggregation. But that is not the case in Canadian society.

Gaining Moral Recognition

It is necessary to stress that even if some have been hit hard psychologically, almost all men surveyed draws an immense pride in their combat experience. "If it were to be done again? I would do it immediately, with no hesitation," is in the substance of their common reflection. While the narrative of the return appears most of the time tinted with frustration, absolutely none of the veterans interviewed said they regretted their serving time. Even P. D. who was taken prisoner in Hong Kong and languished for five years in Japanese prison camps, finds a way to affirm, with a philosophical spin: "You know, after all, this wasn't so hard. You know...Look at me today, I [am] fairly well. [...] When we think about it, it didn't kill me. I'm not dead...I'm not an infirm, I'm not this, I'm not that..."[61]

A feeling of superiority sometimes transpires from this kind of discourse. What P. D. has to say is revealing in this respect: "It's stupid, hey? A soldier...it was the most beautiful story [...] It was glory for us. It was a separate life [...] Me, I didn't regret because I learned a lot [...] I'd never have learned that in books, what I've learned there. [...] I can't explain: I was blossoming inside. It was something else. Leaving so young, then to go and see all that, there...[...] When we came back to Canada, we knew more than all Canadians, here. [...] Us, we knew what war was about [...] We were like, I would say, ready for anything, like you know. In life..."[62]

Such a positive state of mind nevertheless was confronted to a reality that many of them deplored: the lack of understanding, and the lack of social thanking, for their combat experience. Although commemorative ceremonies were important rituals in their eyes, they could not help but notice their limited collective resonance. "We have seven grandchildren, not one of them understands; none of them know the story," complains P. L.'s spouse.[63] In 1995, H. A. described in these words a situation, which we had the opportunity to witness 12 years later during a commemorative ceremony for the Dieppe raid in Longueil (Quebec): "There are some people forming a crowd. Those who are there, they're family or friends of the veterans, or who-ever-else who are there for a reason. Them, they applaud during the ceremony. But on the other side of the road you have...how to say that?...observers and passersby, whatever. That's not meaningful to them at all. They have no idea anyway. But that's sad..."[64]

In other words, even if the state has put in place the elements of a "moral economy of thanking," it has only been working in close circuit, in the confidential circle of veterans and those close to them.

The reintegration "mechanism" did bear its fruits, most respondents believing they have succeeded in life, to the point where one wonders if the experience of war has fundamentally changed the fate of some. Nevertheless, moral—and sometimes physical—scars remain visible: the "retransformation" of the Canadian combatant into a civilian seems to be an unfinished business. A part of himself remains cut off from the community and its common memory, a part that seems never to have been looked after. But which one? As we have just seen, only two actors provided support to the Canadian veterans of 1939–1945: the state—through a process of social regularization and normalization—and those close to them—on an individual and ad hoc basis, as the case of Y. G. has shown. Between these two levels, we see a void within the community space, with the possible exception of sporadic and superficial celebrations marking the return of the first soldiers.[65] In this respect, the management of individual destinies by the state seems to have overridden the collective rituals whose function in the so-called traditional societies is to help the individual to cross the great trials of life—including war—and give them meaning.[66] However, studies seem to demonstrate the beneficial effect of such "community interventionism" on veterans.

It was particularly noticed that participation in rituals of reintegration had improved the mental health of Native American veterans from the Vietnam War.[67] On the whole, this specific population presented a significantly elevated rate of PTSD, but those of its members who were subject to honorific or purifying ceremonies seemed to have overcome problems better than others. The tribes concerned organized return ceremonies to purge the warrior from the trauma of battle.[68] These rituals were intended to restore harmony in the warrior as much as within his community. It was feared that unless the veterans were purged from the trauma of battle, they would bring back the memory of conflict to the tribe, hence causing disorder.[69] This was a way for the close community to help the warrior discharge himself from his hubris, de facto acknowledging its existence. It contributed so to speak to the deevolution of the warrior, which has been mentioned previously. A similar phenomenon has been observed more recently among veterans of the civil war in Mozambique (1976–1992). At the end of this bloody conflict, local communities took charge of the reintegration of their veterans by subjecting them to a series of "cleansing" rituals, which were either individual and involved a healer, or collective, and involved the entire village. There again, the objective was to ensure that the veteran did not pose a threat either to himself or to the society that was welcoming him back. To that end, the veteran was asked to mimic the war to the villagers. This process allowed the homecomer to tacitly share the reality of the "war he lived" with the community, which in turn was led to consider him again "like the others."[70] In contrast to the Native American and Mozambican experience, the reinstatement of the Canadian veterans seems to have taken place in a moral and social isolation. We have seen how, in the best cases, some had attempted a strategy of covered-words with their entourage. Patronizing veterans associations allowed others to share without having to verbalize. The community dimension of reintegration was therefore entirely left to individual initiative, with the limitations outlined by our interviewees.

Conclusion

Can bureaucratic management suffice to heal rifts between the community and those who represent it on "planet war"? The example of the Canadian veterans of the Second World War demonstrates how the homecomer, even from a very distant front, brings back the experience of being under fire with him; whether he and his entourage like it or not, it will be part of their shared postwar experience. Armed actors of the conflict have the feeling to have been part of history in the making, and therefore to have lived a very rich and condensed time that mobilized their entire being, while those who remained on the home front have experienced the conflict from far, without facing such tests or comparable questioning. From this gap emerges a paradox: the return to peace that was so much longed for confronts veterans to a time and experience, that of their relatives, which often appears absurd and inconsistent to them. In this sense, the content of the "American dream" of the 1950s initially seemed to meet the homecomers' expectations, but it could not possibly fulfill them all. By signing his discharge, the soldier was invited to instantly give up his "warrior's habitus" for a suburban ideal that was light years away from what he had just experienced. Likewise, the civilian felt alien to this hero covered in glory and medals, but ill suited to daily life. In other words, the process of ending the war entailed a remaking of the social unity between demobilized and civilians, which proved impossible since the two parties were unable to share a truly cathartic experience. As the process of "civilianization" was taking place exclusively between the state and the individual, without structured community mediation, it remained empty of meaning for the veteran. If Canada was able to develop effective mechanisms for the demobilization of the bodies, they proved unable to demobilize the souls, to help warriors "de-evoluate." And besides, was it really the role of the state? Once they were provided material support, the work that remained to be done with the veterans who remained under the spell of Ares was more a matter of exorcism than demobilization, as the Amerindian and Mozambican cases illustrate so well. However the state mechanisms of social regulation were already in place: by replacing the traditional ties of solidarity,[71] did they not further remove responsibility from the community?

In any case, the lack of ritual around the coming back from the war did not allow the "homecomers" to be solemnly discharged from the "hubris" the Nation at war had invested them. In that sense, the way the state accompanied the veterans of 1945 in their demobilization proved necessary but insufficient. Ever since that time, the various Canadian missions have steadily generated "homecomers" who have been facing similar problems. The support given to veterans has continually improved and the phenomenon of combat-induced PTSD has become better known and recognized. The premature death by suicide of a Canadian female soldier during her second deployment in Afghanistan has recently revived the question. In response, the Department of National Defense is working to double the number of mental health professionals assigned to the treatment of affected members.[72] Will this individual approach be sufficient to heal wounds, which, as we have seen, are likely to spread to the social fabric? Past experience suggests that it will not. Translated by Louise Côté and Pascal Venier.

Appendix 1

Questionnaire "The demobilization"

1. If you were taken prisoner, in what circumstances were you then freed?
2. In what circumstances were you demobilized?
3. How were you received when you returned by your family, by your entourage?

4. After years of absence, how did you perceive your home environment?
5. Did you find a job?
6. Did you find it difficult to live "as before"?
7. Did you feel you had changed? Aged?
8. After you return, were you talking about your war experiences with your family? In your community? Did people listen to you?
9. Do you think history books speak enough about you (the combatants)?
10. Do you feel that younger generations are aware of what you have experienced?
11. Do you think that what you have lived has been useful in some ways?
12. With hindsight, do you regret having joined up?

These questions reflect the overall structure of the interviews. However:

1. Some of the questions listed here could have been already answered by the interviewees before they were formally asked. To avoid a questionnaire that would be too rigid, even redundant, we have given ourselves the possibility to skip questions already implicitly answered by the interviewee.
2. We reserved the right to ask subsidiary questions—not included in this survey—to clarify some of the information arising in the course of the interview, as relevant in the context of our project.

Appendix 2

Interviews

1. M. J. A. Fusiliers Mont-Royal, Dieppe, German POW camps, February 3, 1995, Laval, (Quebec).
2. A. A., Régiment de Maisonneuve, Normandy, North of France, October 18, 1995, Chomedey-Laval (Quebec).
3. R. B., Fusiliers Mont-Royal, Normandy, North of France, Belgium, and Netherlands, April 30, 1995, Lavaltrie (Quebec).
4. C. B., First Service Special Force (Airborne forces), liberation of France, Belgium, and the Netherlands, September 21, 1995, Brossard (Quebec).
5. P. D., Royal Rifles, prisoner of war in Hong Kong, August 8, 1995, Saint-Jérôme (Quebec).
6. P. D., Fusiliers Mont-Royal, Dieppe raid, February 28, 1995, Lachine (Quebec).

7. P. D., Fusiliers Mont-Royal, Dieppe raid, German prisoners camps, February 16, 1995, Sainte-Sophie (Quebec).
8. H. J. D., Fusiliers Mont-Royal, Dieppe raid, 1942, German prisoners' camps, March 2, 1995, Saint-Jean-sur-le Richelieu (Quebec).
9. G. G., Fusiliers Mont-Royal, Normandy, liberation of France, Belgium, and the Netherlands, September 28, 1995, Longueuil, 1995 (Quebec).
10. L. G., Royal Canadian Air Force, Africa, Sicily, Italy, Balkans, Germany, October 3, 1995, Saint-Bruno (Quebec).
11. G. J., Leading Seaman, HMS Nabob, Battle of the Atlantic, May 8, 1995, Lafontaine (Quebec).
12. A. L., Royal Canadian Air Force, 438 (Wild Cats) squadron, bombing on Germany, September 28, 1995, Saint-Hubert (Quebec).
13. Dr A. P., Military doctor in England and Europe..
14. J. G. P., Royal 22e Régiment, Sicily, Italy, Belgium, Netherlands, September 1, 1995, Saint-Bruno (Quebec).
15. M. S., First Horse Field Artillery, Normandy, liberation of France, Belgium, and the Netherlands, October 3, 1995, Lanoraie (Quebec).
16. P. T., Fusiliers Mont-Royal, Normandy, liberation of France, October 10, 1995, Montréal (Quebec).
17. A. F., Fusiliers Mont-Royal, Dieppe raid, 1942, German prisoners' camps, February 7, 1995, Laval (Quebec).
18. R. G., Fusiliers Mont-Royal, Dieppe raid, 1942, German prisoners' camps, February 28, 1995, Outremont (Quebec).
19. M. J., Fusiliers Mont-Royal, Dieppe raid, 1942, German prisoners' camps, March 10, 1995, Sainte-Anne-des-Plaines (Quebec).
20. P. J., Fusiliers Mont-Royal, Dieppe raid, 1942, German prisoners' camps, no date, Quebec (Quebec).
21. P. L., Royal 22e Régiment, Sicily, Italy, British secret service, special operation in Europe, March 28, 1995, Île-des-Sœurs (Quebec).
22. A. L., Fusiliers Mont-Royal, Dieppe raid, 1942, German prisoners' camps, February 21, 1995, Montréal (Quebec).
23. J.-P. L., Fusiliers Mont-Royal, Dieppe raid, 1942, German prisoners' camps, March 2, 1995, Beaconsfield (Quebec).
24. J. M., Signals corps, Dieppe raid, 1942, German prisoners camps, March 21, 1995, Magog (Quebec).
25. R. M., Fusiliers Mont-Royal, Second Canadian Armored Brigade Workshop, Normandy, liberation of France, Belgium and the Netherlands, March 4, 1995, Montreal (Quebec).
26. A. M., Fusiliers Mont-Royal, Dieppe raid, 1942, German prisoners' camps, no date, Maskinongé (Quebec).
27. J. P., Fusiliers Mont-Royal, Dieppe raid, 1942, German prisoners' camps, February 15, 1995, Laval (Quebec).
28. B. R., 7th Light ambulances unit, Sicily, Belgium, Netherlands, Germany, March 10, 1995, Rosemère (Quebec).

Notes

1. The author wishes to thank historians Louise Côté and Pascal Venier for translating this article, which was originally untitled "De l'enfer au paradis. Le vétéran canadien de 1939–1945 est-il soluble dans le rêve américain?"
2. It must be remembered that, since 2003, some 2,500 members of the Canadian Forces are permanently deployed to take part in operations in Afghanistan as part of the International Security Assistance Force (ISAF) led by NATO (Canadian Forces Operations in Afghanistan. Canada. BG-07.009, May 15, 2007).
3. Michael Friscolanti, "The War at Home," *Maclean's* (March 26, 2007).
4. Since May 2007, injured soldiers have three years to recover completely, failing which they receive a discharge on medical ground. Corporal Barnewall says he wishes to remain in the ranks of the army irrespective of his handicap, while one of his colleagues just as seriously injured dreams of returning to Kandahar.
5. Friscolanti, "The War at Home," 17–25.
6. A. Soby, *A Study on Demobilization and Rehabilitation of the Canadian Armed Forces in the Second World War, 1939–1945*, report no. 97, Historical Section (G. S.), Army Headquarters, May 1960, 60–68.
7. M. Fahrni, "The Romance of Reunion: Montreal War Veterans Return to Family Life, 1944–1949," *Journal of the CHA/Revue de la SHC*, New Series 9 (1998): 187–298.
8. We use the term "veteran" in its strict sense. It is important to clarify this point for the industrial armies of the Second World War have rarely mobilized more than 10 percent of their effectives in combat positions. See P. Fussell, *Wartime. Understanding and Behavior in the Second World War* (New York/Oxford: Oxford University Press, 1989), 283.
9. The interviews have been deposited with the archives of the Directorate of History and Heritage (DHH) at the Department of National Defence, in Ottawa. B. Richard, "Entrevues avec les membres des Fusiliers Mont-Royal et quelques autres," Fonds Béatrice Richard, série 1, 96/11, 1995–1996.
10. B. Cabanes, "Le retour du soldat au XXe siècle. Perspectives de recherche," *Revue historique des armées* 245 (2006): 4–15.
11. J. Bourke, "Going Home: The Personal Adjustment of British and American Servicemen after the War," in R. Bessel and D. Schumann (eds.), *Life after Death: Approaches to a Cultural and Social History of Europe during the 1940s and the 1950s,* (Cambridge: Cambridge University Press, 2003), 149–160. Quoted in B. Cabanes, "Le retour du soldat au XXe siècle."
12. The majority of the veterans interviewed had taken part in the Dieppe raid of 1942, which turned out to be a real slaughter.
13. This aspect is explored in Raphaëlle Blanche's paper, "Clémentine et bifteck ou le retour d'un appelé d'Algérie dans sa famille," in B. Cabanes and G. Picketty (eds.), *Retour à l'intime au sortir de la guerre* (Paris: Tallandier, 2009).
14. A Quebec novel, *La famille Plouffe*, ends on a true piece of anthology in this respect. While the return of the young son is being celebrated, one of the brothers reveals to their mother the content of his letters from the front, which had been kept secret during the entire war. In one of his letters, the young veteran explains in details how, after having himself narrowly escaped death, he had killed two Germans. The mother's reaction: "This is unbelievable: Guillaume killing men!" See R. Lemelin, *La famille Plouffe* (Montréal: Cercle du livre de France, 1968), 400.
15. The term "warrior" as used here refers to the ontological dimension of the combatant, defined through the act of war, by opposition to the instrumental dimension of the "soldier," a combatant at the service of the state and/or the nation.
16. Bruno Cabanes identifies a similar misunderstanding between the demobilized of 1918 and the population "at home," both having incompatible visions of the war: "Civilians seem prisoners of heroic representations of the war and of an obsession with showing themselves up to the soldiers sacrifice in their gestures of thanking. Meanwhile the veterans are exasperated with their incomprehension of life on the front." *La victoire endeuillée: la sortie de guerre des soldats français, 1918–1920* (Paris: Seuil, 2004), 494.
17. Ibid.
18. G. F. G. Stanley, *Canada's Soldiers. The Military History of an Unmilitary People* (Toronto: Macmillan, 1960), 1.

19. In 1942, there were 11 million inhabitants in Canada, and it is estimated that 1.5 million Canadians have served during the two World Wars.
20. In 1871, the treaty of Washington between the United States and the United Kingdom fixed the U. S.-Canadian border on the 49th parallel.
21. For a synthesis on Canadian military history, see D. Morton, *A Military History of Canada: From Champlain to Kosovo*, 4th ed. (Toronto: McClelland and Stewart, 1999).
22. The expression is John Keegan's. See J. Keegan, *A History of Warfare* (Toronto: Key Porter Books, 1993), 4.
23. A. Soby, *A Study on Demobilization and Rehabilitation*, 2–3.
24. D. Morton, "The Canadian Heritage From The Veterans' Heritage From The Great War," in P. Neary and J. L. Granatstein (eds.), *The Veteran Charter and Post-World War II Canada*, (Montreal: McGill-Queen's University Press, 1998), 15–31. This collection of articles approaches the system for demobilizing and rehabilitating Canadian veterans during the Second World War from different angles: the Great War legacy, repatriating, qualifying for compensations, returning to studies, psychiatric problems, measures of assistance to handicapped veterans as well as returning home.
25. Morton, "The Canadian Heritage from The Veterans' Heritage From The Great War."
26. Public Archives of Canada, Mackenzie Papers, file—527—10 vol. 1.
27. On December 10, 1939, 7,449 men from the 1st Infantry Division embarked at Halifax.
28. See J. Struthers, "Family Allowances, Old Age Security, and the Construction of Entitlement in the Canadian Welfare State, 1943–1951," in Neary and Granatstein, *The Veteran Charter*, 179–204.
29. G. Bourque and J. Duchastel (with V. Armony), *L'identité fragmentée. Nation et citoyenneté dans les débats constitutionnels canadiens, 1941–1992* (Montréal: Fides, 1996), 46–58.
30. "Opening Address by Prime Minister," *Dominion-Provincial Conference on Reconstruction*, House of Commons, August 6, 1945, Ottawa, Edmond Cloutier, 2.
31. In this respect, a picture destined to repatriated soldiers speaks for itself. A reproduction is available on line in Soby, *A Study on Demobilization* http://www.cmp-cpm.forces.gc.ca/dhh-dhp/his/rep-rap/doc/ahqr-rqga/ahq097.pdf (accessed on February 12, 2012), 101.
32. See the studies brought together in Neary and Granatstein, *The Veteran Charter*.
33. D. Owram, "Canadian Domesticity in The Postwar Era," in Neary and Granatstein, *The Veteran Charter*, 213.
34. Member of Fusiliers Mont-Royal, Dieppe raid, 1942.
35. P. T., Fusiliers Mont-Royal, battle of Normandy, 1944.
36. A. F., president of the Dieppe Veterans and Prisoners of War Association, Fusiliers Mont-Royal Regiment, Dieppe raid, August 19, 1942.
37. M. Fahrni's study "The Romance of Reunion: Montreal War Veterans Return to Family Life, 1944–1949," based on detailed archival research, attests of this phenomenon. It emphasizes family conflicts after the return, which could sometimes be dramatic. They opposed veterans and either their spouse or other family members and were often caused by the deep gap between their respective experiences.
38. Ibid.; T. Copp, "From Neurasthenia to Post-traumatic Stress Disorder: Canadian Veterans and The Problem of Persistent Emotional Disabilities," in *The Veteran Charter*, 149.
39. Is it necessary to call attention to the extreme brutality of the Second World War battles? The sanitized image of military operations showed in films and documentaries is an obstacle to a correct appreciation of their impact upon the soldiers. Paul Fussell has argued that "the real war will never get in the books" in *Wartime: Understanding and Behavior in the Second World War*, 267–297. He notably quotes an Okinawa veteran, particularly disgusted by the anonymity in which such series of massacres were taking place: "It was common...throughout the campaign for replacements to get hit before we ever knew their names. They came up confused, frightened, and hopeful, got wounded or killed, and went right back to the rear on the route by which they had come, shocked, bleeding or stiff. They were forlorn figures coming up to the meat grinder and going right back out of it like homeless waifs, unknown and faceless to us, like unread books on a shelf." (66).
40. Soby, *A Study on Demobilization and Rehabilitation*, http://www.cmp-cpm.forces.gc.ca/dhh-dhp/his/rep-rap/doc/ahqr-rqga/ahq097.pdf (February 12, 2012), 101.
41. Ibid., respectively 102, 103 and 104.
42. Member of the Signals Corps, Dieppe raid of 1942.

43. Copp, "From Neurasthenia to Post-traumatic Stress Disorder," 155–156.
44. "Je sens bien dans le fond de mon âme que mes années de guerre ont faussé mes valeurs. Chef naturel, j'exigerai de ma femme les mêmes sacrifices demandés à des hommes sur le champ de bataille, la voie du succès." C. Forbes, *Fantassin, pour mon pays, la gloire et... des prunes* (Sillery: Septentrion, 1994), 195.
45. L. G., Royal Canadian Air Force, seconded to the Royal Air Force, Africa, Sicily, Italy, Balkans, Germany, October 3, 1995, Saint-Bruno.
46. Ibid.
47. See Cabanes and Piketty, *Retour à l'intime au sortir de la guerre*.
48. J. Jones, "From The Thin Red Line" in P. Fussell (ed.), *The Norton Book of the Modern War*, (London, New York: W. W. Norton, 1991), 341–342.
49. AHC, Memorandum for Cabinet War Committee, April 19, 1945, Report no. 97.
50. A. F., Fusiliers Mont-Royal, Dieppe raid, 1942.
51. P. J., Fusiliers Mont-Royal, Dieppe raid, 1942.
52. A. A., Régiment de Maisonneuve, battle of Normandy, North of France.
53. J. M., Fusiliers Mont-Royal, Dieppe raid, 1942.
54. A veteran association founded in the 1930s.
55. A. L., Fusiliers Mont-Royal, Dieppe raid, 1942.
56. Member of Fusiliers Mont-Royal, Dieppe raid, 1942.
57. Lieutenant-General (ret) R. Dallaire, *Shake Hands with the Devil: The Failure of Humanity in Rwanda* (Toronto: Random House, 2003), 592.
58. Y. G., Régiment de la Chaudière, Normandy landing, June 1944, and campaign in Europe.
59. A. van Gennep, *Les rites de passage. Étude systématique des rites* (Paris: Picard, [1909] 1981). See also, T. Goguel d'Allondans, *Rites de passage, rites d'initiation: lecture d'Arnold van Gennep* (Laval: Université Laval, 2002).
60. T. Nathan, "La migration des âmes," *Nouvelle Revue d'ethnopsychiatrie* 11 (1988): 25–42.
61. P. D., Royal Rifles, Hong Kong, December 1941.
62. Ibid.
63. P. L., Royal 22e Régiment, Sicily, Italy, British secret services, special operations in Europe.
64. H. A., Fusiliers Mont-Royal, Dieppe raid, 1942.
65. Veterans coming back long after the blares of Liberation, complained in their accounts about the climate of collective indifference in which they came back.
66. The "rites of passage" have not so much completely disappeared in our Western societies; they have a tendency to resurface in a wild and spontaneous manner, particularly among young adults, through extreme sports or any other activity that involves an "endangerment" whether it be real or symbolic. However, as David Le Breton remarked, such ritual need to be set in the context of individual practices, which even if they are covered by the media, take the form of an "obstinate and solitary quest for meaning." D. Le Breton, "Jeux symboliques avec la mort," *Religiologiques* 16 (Fall 1997): 55–65.
67. T. Holm, "Culture, Ceremonialism, and Stress: American Indian Veterans and The Vietnam War," *Armed Forces & Society* 12 no. 2 (1986): 237–251.
68. These very ancient rituals had incidentally been reactivated in the aftermath of the Second World War.
69. Holm, "Culture, Ceremonialism, and Stress," 243.
70. P. Granjo, "The Homecomer: Postwar Cleansing Rituals in Mozambique," *Armed Forces & Society* 33, no. 3 (2007): 382–395.
71. The industrialization and urbanization of Canadian society from the mid-nineteenth century onwards had started to erode those links. The support provided by the state following a rationalist and technocratic model must not be understood as one of the causes for the difficulties inherent to the return but because of deeper social transformations.
72. P. Bergeron, "Une militaire canadienne retrouvée sans vie dans sa chambre," *Le Soleil*, April 24, 2009, http://www.cyberpresse.ca/le-soleil/actualites/politique/200904/24/01-850014-une-militaire-canadienne-retrouvee-sans-vie-dans-sa-chambre-a-kandahar.php (accessed on April 2011).

CHAPTER SIX

The Position of Former Combatants, French Authorities, and Public Opinion Vis-à-Vis German Prisoners of War (1944–1949)

FABIEN THÉOFILAKIS

> **Abstract**
>
> This chapter offers an analysis of the "cultural demobilization" of French veterans. The complex relationship between French veterans and German prisoners of war (POWs) and with French society as a whole reflects the difficult process of reintegrating veterans that began in 1945 and lasted until the departure of the last POW in 1949. The chapter discusses the impact on this process of how the enemy was viewed, the role of political structures, and the importance of the international context—at three points in time. From 1944 until October 1945, a rationale of surveillance toward an enemy universally despised justified the participation of veterans—in recognition of their sacrifice—in the administration of POWs. As time went on however and the war receded into the past, POWs began to take on a more human and positive image as workers for France, which frustrated veterans' attempts to remain the focal point of the country's reconstruction. In 1947, there was a turning point in the relationship of French society with both POWs and veterans. Official projects aimed at the integration of the soon-to-be-liberated POWs, now accepted by public opinion, aroused conflicting reactions on the part of veterans and foreshadowed their marginalization by French society in the 1950s.

In 1945, shortly after his return to France from Dachau, Robert Antelme denounced the treatment of German war prisoners and advised his fellow deportees to be cautious: "It would be untrue to say we feel indifference towards them, but it would be nonsense to think we feel some sort of temptation to take revenge on them, ridiculous to believe that we 'more than others' might harbor such a temptation. We're left with a kind of stupor within, that can't be translated into any sort of act."[1] Thus a study of how former French prisoners of war, deportees, and resistance fighters positioned themselves toward German war prisoners after 1945 demands a nuanced analysis of relations between two groups of former combatants that the lottery of arms made alternate winners and losers of the wars they fought against each other. This unique interchange of experiences of war, occupation, captivity, and deportation enables us to approach certain issues at the heart of transitions from war to peace: how did the cultural demobilization of French ex-combatants take place after these experiences? In what way does the existence of a democratic framework seeking legitimacy impose modes of pacification that proscribe recourse to violence? What influence does the confrontation with enemy war prisoners in peacetime have on reintegration into postwar society?

The question of French ex-combatants' reactions in face of German war prisoners just after the war and how attitudes toward violence and the enemy evolved during peacetime also allows us to put the after-war period into the broader historic perspective of the Thirty Years' War[2] and to take another look at the false resemblances between the two immediate after-war periods. Indeed, 1914–1918 remained present for the new generation of soldiers, most of them having lived through the First World War and inherited the image of the German as a hereditary enemy. But this original face-to-face has meaning, only if, alongside the former combatants, we bring into play—through the rather delicate notion of "public opinion"—two other groups of actors by nature unequal: official authorities, both national and local, and French society.

I will focus here, in a possible first interpretation,[3] on three dimensions at the core of France's transition from war to peace between 1945 and 1949 that, paradoxically, this category-specific end of war illustrates particularly well. It will thus be analyzed first as a cultural demobilization[4] in terms of changes in the representations of the enemy, studied on the basis of the interrelations between former combatants, French opinion, and the authorities; then in terms of structures, with the installation by the Republican state of authorities that tended toward exclusive management of their German captives; finally, in terms of the recovery of rank and power, international contexts that directly influenced national representations of how these prisoners should be managed.

This analysis however has its limits, besides my own of not being a specialist in deportation, resistance, or former combatants. First of all, there is the problem of categories. In the documents consulted, although it was sometimes difficult to distinguish between prisoners of war, political deportees, even resistance fighters who remained in France, it should be emphasized that they all had very different experiences of war, contacts with the enemy, and the Vichy regime. Obviously, it would be difficult to place under a single category the ex-combatant of the First World War, the soldier taken prisoner under the Third Reich from 1940 to 1945 (on the condition that he did not take advantage of the collaboration policy to be repatriated before), and the resistance fighter, inside the country or in unoccupied France, deported or not. It is all the more difficult to lump them together as these various experiences were differentiated in the perception of the French people of the Liberation: unlike the preceding conflict, it was no longer the French prisoners of war who were seen as winners—the real heroes were the *résistants* and political deportees. Why then, through a misuse of language, were they all called "former combatants"? It was not only to underscore the authorities' determination, as of 1944, but to celebrate a France united in the Resistance.[5] During the war, these groups shared more or less the same negative representation of Germans, a "same hostility towards the German occupant."[6] One of the issues this study concerns itself with is precisely that of taking into consideration various cultural changes in time and space that help explain discrepancies in the evolution of relations between these three categories—prisoners of war, deportees, and *résistants*—and German war prisoners.

The sources consulted were another difficulty. Searching for indexation material was a laborious process because of the actors involved and an archival classification in which "German war prisoners" was not a priority. The corpus is based unequally on four large collections: local archives of about ten departments[7] mainly providing reports to prefects, but personal letters as well; the more centralized archives of the main ministries concerned with relations between former combatants and German war prisoners, such as the ministries of Labor, Finance, Agriculture, and the Ministry of Deported and Refugee Prisoners; the archives of the International Committee of the Red Cross in Geneva, and lastly the press. The journal of Communist allegiance *Le patriote résistant,* voice of the *Fédération nationale des déportés et internés résistants et patriotes* (FNDIRP), and the more politically centered journal *Le PG,* voice of the *Fédération nationale des PG* (FNPG, National Federation of Prisoners Of War [POWs]), were searched for 1945/46–1949. These archives—private and public, individual and collective—have been retained for the sake of taking into account local experiences of occupation as perceived by German war prisoners, even if this chapter is not always able to include them for lack of space. From reports by the authorities to motions of associations, these documents reflect the subjective evaluation of what, in the opinion of the actors of the times, the "normal" treatment of German war prisoners should be, and as a result, oblige the researcher to study not only public opinion but also how it is "fabricated."[8]

The German POW Is the Enemy!
(Late 1944–September/October 1945)

Former Combatants and Public Opinion: The Heroic Avant-garde

The first period extends from the end of 1944 to September–October 1945. As soon as the territory was liberated prisoners were taken. Liberation marked the end of fighting and the taking over by resistance elements but not the end of the war. This period was marked by a very strong and unified cultural mobilization, both because the war effort was not yet over and there remained enemies to be beaten, and because, beginning in May 1945, the return of French POWs and deportees reinforced the negative image of the German. In this context, the group consisting of *résistants*, prisoners of war, and deportees enjoyed considerable moral authority on the whole of French society.

Both the archives and the press adopted this group's points of view and positioning vis-à-vis the enemy. As of September 1944, the recently liberated population of Marseille wanted to see "enemy prisoners of war (...) treated like ours" in Germany.[9] In February 1945, one woman denounced conferences held by French former prisoners of war repatriated before the arrival of German POWs for "inciting the opinion of the population against these prisoners of war," as the population then used "this hate propaganda."[10] In the weeks following the liberation, several security service reports emphasized the similarity in the reactions of *résistants*, French prisoners of war, deportees, and overall opinion: six months after the liberation, the Municipal Council of Bouscat in Gironde, acting as the "interpreter of prisoners and deportees as well as that of the whole of the population,"[11] denounced the food supplies given to German war prisoners. The German prisoner of war was a dual symbol of victory: victory over Nazi Germany in the first place and, consequently, of France belonging to the winning camp. The head of the provisional government of the French Republic made a point of this in his radio speech on February 6, 1945, celebrating the fact that "out of 825,000 Germans made prisoner by the Allies since June 6, 1944 [and the beginning of the campaign in France], 210,000 were taken prisoner by the French—120,000 by the First Army, over 50,000 by the single Second Armoured Division operating with one or another of the American armies, and 40,000 by our interior forces."[12]

This concordance on the representations of the German war prisoner can, to a great extent, be explained by the two ideological functions assumed at the end of the war by deportees and *résistants* on one hand, and French prisoners of war on the other. *Résistants* gave France its heroes, those who chose action to defend their country against the occupant and collaborators. For the majority of them, the combat was for Republican values and was eminently political. In their eyes, liberation was to be pursued through purges, through rebuilding the Republic and leading a harsh policy toward Germany. Prisoners of war and deportees gave France its martyrs in the Greek sense of "witnesses," those who bore the stigmata of Nazi barbarism, who embodied the suffering of France and the sacrifices of its sons. While their status was minimal on Liberation day, they, by their number and networks, constituted an efficient and lasting pressure group afterwards. With the heroization of some and the return home of others, there was a renewal of cultural mobilization against German prisoners of war. For example, at the end of May 1945 in Nancy, as people were exiting a conference given by Henri Teitgen on his deportation in Buchenwald, a column of German POWs passed by: several persons "rushed on the prisoners and struck many of them."[13]

The privileged position of the two groups was based on a radical opposition with the enemy: yesterday's victorious soldier, today's defeated prisoner. The end of the war gave their sacrifice a positive value, but paradoxically, imposed on them moral rights and duties toward German prisoners, which delayed their own cultural demobilization.

The French Authorities' Attitude toward German POWs: The Rationale of Surveillance

The central authorities, eager to extend engagement in resistance to the whole of the nation,[14] also took up the social and historical image of German war prisoners held by former combatants. In this first phase, French authorities, prisoners of war, and deportees shared the conviction that the German prisoner of war "should not be an intimate part of French life."[15] To this end, the authorities imposed regulations concerning the use of captives for economic purposes. In a diplomatic note in the summer of 1945, the prefect of the Bas-Rhin reminded mayors that war prisoners must be "interned after work or on days of rest in a single place (...) kept by armed men (...) led back in the evening at a fixed time, and after roll call (...) locked up under careful guard until the next morning."[16] They were to wear their military uniform or civilian wear bearing the initials PG *(prisonnier de guerre)*. They were not allowed out on Sundays and holidays except under escort. Access to public places was forbidden.[17] These prescriptions, present in all the departments, reflect what Michel Foucault called a disciplinary rationale. Focusing on "individual bodies to keep watch on (...) and possibly punish,"[18] bodies that "must be made both useful and docile," this rationale aims at a continuation outside the camp of the order reigning inside it. It seeks to regulate everything: spatial separation, separation of clothing, social separation. It is almost a police rationale, apprehending the German only as an enemy body and drawing a line between "them" and "us."

Did Former Combatants Second the French Authorities in the Management of German War Prisoners?

Under the rationale of surveillance, former combatants positioned themselves as supporters of the authorities in the daily supervision of captives, whose numbers increased along with liberation: 35,500 in January 1945, 115,000 in May, 719,840—the maximum number—in November. Numerous protests, particularly concerning food, were sent to prefects informing them of excesses to be curbed. The local Comité de Libération of Valenciennes, marked by the German occupation that had gone on until September 1944, wrote that "members of the Resistance cannot accept that we fatten up those *boches* who destroyed our land, when our comrades worked under the threat of brutal thrashing and were given water for soup and all of 100 grams of bread for the day's food."[19] But other aspects of captivity were concerned as well. Thus in the Haut-Rhin, annexed by Nazi Germany, which had put in place its own administration, the Benfeld Committee for defense against Nazism denounced the fact that war prisoners went out "in bourgeois dress (...) with no distinctive mark of being a war prisoner."[20] The last broad area of intervention was the employment of war prisoners as labor. Those who intervened—either in favor of putting them to work for the benefit of reconstruction or, on the contrary, refusing to do so to avoid competition with French workers—thought of their actions as patriotic and in the right. The intervention of former combatants who, thanks to their war experiences as prisoners or *résistants*, considered themselves bearers of some of the legitimate violence, was at the source of the majority of reports to the local police for breach of discipline.

The authorities' reaction was ambiguous. On one hand, they recognized the moral authority of former combatants; for example by inviting the president of the Calais former deportees to a conference on mine disposal.[21] In answer to the population's expectations,[22] they tried to use the continuing mobilization of French war prisoners and former deportees to compensate for their own military demobilization by giving them priority for employment as guardians.[23] Was this a way of sharing state violence, an attempt to keep control over financial repayment, or an accompaniment policy? Reticence was greater on employment issues, where there was a growing tension between local or rebellious administrations—more inclined to seek out former combatants—and national administrations, which intented on keeping control over this key sector. The case of the police superintendent of the Republic of Savoie, who, in July 1945, ordered the creation of a commission, made up of two French war prisoners or political deportees, in charge of helping mayors in the supervision of the work of POWs, was certainly unique at the time. It can doubtlessly be explained by that department's war experience[24]—first occupied by the Italians between 1942–1943 and then by the Germans, who fought against the Resistance until March–April 1945.

With the return of deportees from Germany between April and the summer of 1945, the authorities were faced with an economic problem, one that bore a dimension of symbolic recognition that was a legacy of the war. Many repatriated farmers asked the authorities for POWs' labor. Having made enormous sacrifices, they expected reparation from the state in the form of preferential, less expensive war prisoners. Thus began the debate on compensation.[25] Total exoneration initially concerned farmers who had lost a limb.[26] In May 1945 the Ministry of Prisoners, Deportees and Refugees proposed exoneration for repatriated war victims. The

Ministry of Labor accepted but limited the provision to one month[27] in order to avoid upsetting the equilibrium of the work market. In the period of exaltation of the *"France résistante,"* the Ministry of Prisoners, Deportees and Refugees was able to extend the provision to three months.[28] Faced with the pressure from associations, the Ministry then demanded in August 1945, a six-months exoneration for those who had "worked five years on German farms for ridiculously low pay."[29] These tensions at the highest level of the state did not end with the return of the French from Germany. On the contrary, they show that fair symbolic and material recognition of former combatants was an important postwar issue both for particular groups of individuals and for the whole society.

In this immediate postwar context, whether former combatants would maintain their moral superiority thanks to institutional recognition reflected an issue of fundamental importance to the whole of French society: if they did, would it be a first step toward institutional normality and political pacification, or would the aim of such recognition only be to maintain the special status of former combatants? The change in the image of the German war prisoner beginning in the summer of 1945 brings a few possible answers.

Postwar Dynamics Become Increasingly Discordant (end 1945–1947)

A number of political and social factors destabilized the resistant dynamic, modifying the configuration of concordant ends of war.

Factors of Change and the Development of a Security Rationale

The unconditional surrender of Nazi Germany and the end of French repatriation[30] lessened the emotional charge of the figure of the German war prisoner. The need for manpower indispensable for reconstruction led to the employment of war prisoners in all economic sectors. Millions of French people no longer mingled with abstract occupiers or *"boches"* but with flesh-and-blood German workers, employed in work detachments and then, beginning in September 1945, with private individuals, like the 1,184 German war prisoners distributed over 260 communes of Ille-et-Vilaine in 1947.[31] Thus in many layers of society a new image of the German war prisoner began to develop. Even if material difficulties were a constant reminder of the extent of destruction and helped maintain hatred of the *"boche,"* they also resulted in an economic rationale making the German war prisoner a productive force to be well taken care so as to obtain the most of it. Thus in the eyes of the authorities, the former enemy became a builder to be mobilized at all costs, as required by their transition credo: "Make those who reduced the country to ruins rebuild it / Make those who wanted to destroy your cities beautify them / Put your enemy prisoners to work."[32]

This new presence modified the relations between POWs and local populations, as illustrated by the archives of the labor department of the Bas-Rhin.[33] Indeed, the rise in the number of offences involving escape attempts—from 21 in 1945 to 286 in 1946—which corresponds to the increase in the number of POWs employed in the department, shows that the authorities were pursuing a policy of surveillance. But it does not explain the increase in 1947 of requests to house German war prisoners—whereas this had already been possible for a year and manpower needs had not suddenly increased—nor the increase in cases of clandestine correspondence, both of which reflect changes in the way Alsatian farmers viewed prisoners of war: it became acceptable to house a German, the worker taking priority over the enemy. The local population dared to make these requests without fear of being called a "bad French" in a department that the administration could have suspected of not being sufficiently patriotic. Besides economic motivations, confidence played a role in effacing not only the figure of the enemy, but also that of the Nazi and occupier.

This large-scale cultural demobilization deactivated the disciplinary rationale, since authorities and local populations no longer shared the same image of the German. Everyday living together ended up in what can be called a security rationale,[34] illustrated by what happened to Jacques, a Hurtigheim farmer who was supposed to accompany his prisoner back to the communal premises after 12 P.M.[35] As usual, he only watched him go, until April 28, 1946, when his prisoner escaped. Jacques recognized that he was supposed to take his prisoner back, but he added "no one had ever done that until now." One of the guardians confirmed his statement: "employers don't at all conform to the rule applicable to prisoners of war (...)." When informed, the mayor barely reacted and tolerated prisoners wearing unmarked clothing. As for the guardians, one of them left, leaving the commando without supervision for two days. This new behavior was part of a security rationale whose aim was not to discipline bodies, but to find an overall equilibrium in this reality where prisoners played an important role. It let the actors organize themselves. In the end, putting the German war prisoner to work and making him an actor in the life of the village resulted in humanizing him.[36]

There was a turning point on the political level, with the installation of legal authorities and institutions to the detriment of local powers, such as the Comités de Défense Locale (CDLs, Local Defense Committee) inherited from the Liberation, or militias, a legacy of Resistance power.[37] The inability of Resistance movements to preserve their union outside classical partisan structures marked the end of their radical reform project, confirmed by their electoral failures between April and October 1945.

The international situation also contributed to changing the priorities of ministries concerned by the management of German war prisoners and their balance of power with former combatants and their local supporters. Following the warnings of the International Committee of the

Red Cross, which in the autumn of 1945 foresaw the death of 200,000 captives if nothing was done to improve the situation of war prisoners in France, the United States stopped its transfer of POWs to France.[38] In fact, by the March 1945 agreement, the French authorities obtained the cession of 1.75 million German war prisoners to reconstruct the country. However, American public opinion—much less mobilized culturally by a negative figure of the German—and the main French newspapers as well, were at the source of a national press campaign on the theme "Don't imitate them—a prisoner, even a German, is a human being."[39] Important Resistance figures, like Robert Antelme, and the Catholic milieus did not hesitate to intervene. Their words reflected a broader change in opinion,[40] whose main argument did not concern the German war prisoner as a person, but rather the honor of France and respect for the values it had fought for. In a way, it chipped away at the patriotic monopoly of former combatants, since one could be a good French and defend the *boche*.

The Reaction of Former Combatants to the "Humanization" of the German POW in French Society

What was the institutional reaction of former combatants, inasmuch as can be judged from the archives consulted? It crystallized around the figure of the German war prisoner as an enemy in an effort to sustain a weakening cultural mobilization and thus preserve its influence. Although in November 1945 the National Federation of War Prisoners denounced the "inhuman procedures used in certain places[41]" against German war prisoners, the Federation also defined rules of treatment designed to limit contact with the population, refusing to abandon the rationale of supervision.

In reaction to the diffuse humanization of German POWs in French society, many individuals and associations took a long-term view of the two after-war periods and defended the vigilance of former combatants who, having resisted Nazism, were the only persons capable of seeing the hereditary and eternally evil enemy under the mask of the new German. In June 1946, the *Fédération Nationale des Déportés et Internés Politiques* (FNDIP) interpellated the prefect of Savoie about the "great feeling of bitterness" that comrades felt in the face of the privileged treatments of German war prisoners: "We understand (...) that it is difficult to avoid fraternizing. But other than the fact that there is something indecent about it, it is also extremely unwise (...). The German mentality is absolutely incomprehensible to our Latin soul."[42] Calling on the vigilance of the French with their "short memory," they also sought to maintain their role as national martyrs of Nazi barbarism, which they, at least, would not forget. Thus Officer L., who spent his captivity in German hospitals and whose brother had still not returned at the end of October 1945 when he sent his letter to the ICRC, had not "forgotten the memory of what 90% of the Germans were: arrogant when power was behind them, cowards when they had nothing but their own hands and brains to defend themselves, obsequious, mechanized brutes. They're not in a hurry to change, let them pay now, each one in turn."[43] With the exception of some very precise areas, the treatment of SS prisoners,[44] prisoners in American hands, and the question of food, these complaints do not seem to have met with real or lasting echoes in the opinion. This difference in perception is easily recognizable in certain headlines of local newspapers still heavily marked by the spirit of the Resistance, such as *Sud-Ouest,* which did not relay the campaign denouncing the lot of German war prisoners present in the national press. It was difficult to condemn the "inhuman" conditions of captivity without de facto undoing the sacred aura of the Resistance's cause.

In reaction to the failure of the political project and the lassitude of public opinion faced with the mobilization inherited from the Black Years, a new theme was added to the figure of the German war prisoner: denunciation of the attitude of bad French toward the German POWs. To my mind, this new *topos* reveals to what extent the German war prisoner remained an abstraction, timeless and therefore unchangeable, in the institutional discourse of former combatants. It also reveals that underneath it all, this discourse was not aimed at the German POW. As we read in *Le Dauphiné Libéré* of August 29, 1946, in an article denouncing the presence of a German war prisoner at a ball in Aix-les-Bains, "obviously, we can't reproach him with anything. It would have been wrong for him to have rejected the kindness of the Coutant family, it is they who are to be blamed," and the article demands "harsh sanctions."[45] The POW thus became the crystallization figure enabling the former combatant, while weakened by the change in configuration, to preserve his position as an essential actor by creating discourse around the "scandal" of the treatment of POWs and these difficult after-war times.

Faced with this humanization, movements of former combatants reacted violently, denouncing "fraternizing" with the enemy. In Verquigneul in the Pas-de-Calais region, where war prisoners made a bit too merry instead of working, in April 1946, members of the liberation committee considered it "their duty as Frenchmen" to demand an end to these "acts of collaboration."[46] In July in the Bouches-du-Rhône, the Association of War Prisoners asked the military authorities to crack down on POWs involved in black market activities.[47] Such interventions were new more in content than in number.

The legacy of sacrifice for France and enmity toward German war prisoners was gradually taken up again in a new discourse denouncing the too numerous evasions and incomplete purification of the social corps. Though the target was the German war prisoner, what was really being blamed was an end of war over too soon to definitively destroy anti-France and rebuild the Republic. If prisoners of war were escaping in large numbers, it was due to escape chains composed of vengeful Vichyists and foreign gangs. If war widows and war orphans had not enough to eat, it was because ex-collaborators preferred dealing with the enemy. If the Germans liked to go out, it was because women continued to practice horizontal collaboration. By bringing back the political weaknesses inherited from the occupation, this reading of the present through the prism of the "Franco-French war" sought a cultural remobilization, the only way to justify its renewed social utility and remind the French people of their duty of recognition toward the primary victims of Nazism.

The Authorities Distance Themselves from Institutions of Former Combatants

The official reaction was ambivalent. It reflected their transition from a surveillance to a security rationale, but at the same time made room for the intervention of individual personalities and the specificity of local situations. True, the Savoie military authorities required the deportees association to report all offences, given the high degree of complicity between employers.[48] However, it also seems that both national, then local authorities increasingly distanced themselves from the demands of former combatants. In September 1945, the National Federation of War Prisoners passed a resolution requesting the government to allow the representation of its departmental associations in the organizations in charge of distributing POW labor. At the same time, it requested that its associations be authorized to demand the withdrawal of POW labor and that the presidents of their local sections be accredited, along with prefects and local mayors, to report all potential offences.[49] Departmental committees for labor were then set up, like that of the Eure-et-Loir. In September, at the request of the departmental commission of war prisoners, the prefect decided to create a supervisory committee for the employment of German POWs in which the departmental commission would be represented.[50] The minister of Labor, however, not having been consulted, refused to give his agreement,[51] which was the end of the commission. Nonetheless, departmental commissions were set up by the Ministry of Labor, but without representatives from the milieu of former combatants, or so it would seem.

The same evolution took place on the issue of the compensatory indemnity. While the Ministry of Former Combatants under Laurent Casanova requested an extension of exoneration,[52] the Ministry of Labor under Ambroise Croizat unilaterally decided on an end to all exonerations as of January 1, 1946, despite the opposition of the Ministry of Agriculture[53] under Tanguy-Prigent and federations of prisoners and deportees. Its decision was mainly due to economic considerations: to avoid competition with French workers, to implement a rational management of manpower, and get some cash into the state treasury. An international dimension was also present, since by increasing the cost of POW labor, the Ministry hoped to improve the conditions of war prisoners and avoid France being accused of "death camps." Above all, the symbolic justification given by the Ministry opened the way to institutional normalization that would deal with the issue of recognition in a different way. Indeed, it considered that "the reparation represented by the work of German war prisoners was in repayment of a debt owed to the whole Nation," which also had its victims, and for that reason its benefits cannot "be reserved for only part of the population."[54] It refused the interpretation of the measure as "a waning of the government's concern" for victims of the war,[55] but by insisting on equal treatment, avoided the possibility of competition among victims.[56] These growing discordances doubtlessly explain the reaction of some former combatants, like the customs officer who felt that the "[French] prisoners of war are becoming an annoyance in the country. There are too many of us and we know it."[57] The last phase reinforced this discrepancy.

Did French Prisoners of War and Deportees Remain Résistants? (1947–1949/50)

The Cold War rationale and the reassessment of US policy toward Germany forced the French authorities to free their prisoners earlier than planned. To answer the American request to repatriate German POWs transferred from the United States to France, the French authorities offered POWs a transformation of status into free civilian workers (TCL, *Travailleurs Civils Libres*). This new context favored, beginning in mid-1947, the emergence of a final configuration between authorities, the opinion, and former combatants.

The French Authorities Organize German Immigration

The fact that the French authorities were now proposing what they had envisaged in August 1945 and immediately rejected, judging it to be "premature,"[58] shows that they were abandoning the rationale of security. They no longer hesitated to offer their former enemies the same advantages as those given to immigrant workers, including the right to bring over their family. From then on, ahead of French society in terms of relations with the Germans, they planned a German immigration also first envisaged in 1945. In March, when the High Committee for Population defined France's immigration policy in anticipation of the Liberation, it made a distinction between a temporary, quantitative influx aimed at satisfying manpower needs and a permanent qualitative immigration to compensate for the demographic deficit. Germany was then ranked next to last in the list; at the end of their contract, German prisoners, the future quantitative manpower, would be "automatically repatriated and *immediately evacuated from French territory.*"[59]

In 1947–1948 the authorities were therefore reversing their position. Not only would massive immigration be encouraged but Germans would be encouraged to settle definitively, if possible. Three years after the end of the war, the authorities were promoting a third, population rationale,[60] also giving prisoners of war, once free, the right to become French.

Reactions of French Society to the Transformation of German War Prisoners

Whereas reactions to previous projects had been extremely hostile, the gradual announcement of transformation operations does not seem to have aroused lasting negative opinion. Although the unions at first rejected the "option" for reasons of competition, the labor shortage[61] and the attitude of the transformed prisoner of war, whose "productivity and docility" had diminished, brought about a change in their position and the *Confédération Générale du Travail* (CGT) launched a membership campaign among these new comrades. Stating in the first issue of *CGT Information. Mitteilungsblatt für die in der GGT organisierten deutschen Berufstätigen in Frankrech,*[62] that "the duty of unions is to ensure the defense of salary and working conditions (...) without racial or national distinction," in his editorial, Julien Racamond, secretary of the CGT, described the transition from German prisoner of war to worker, from enemy to comrade, from German subjected to Nazism to democrat in the process of reeducation. The dual updating based on the discourse of anti-fascist struggle and workers internationalism enabled him to speak of "the difficult years of the war and occupation" in France and the responsibility of the "German people" to propose a way out of the obsolete fixation on the enemy figure: transformation under the CGT would allow the German working class to "unite its forces (...) with the working masses of the world." Nearly 137,000 prisoners of war were transformed into TCLs, far beyond official expectations. Furthermore, the archives of the ICRC show that there were very few conflicts between TCLs and the French population.

From Opposition to Marginalization of Former Combatants

In 1946, as rumors of transformation increased, former combatants reacted in unison with the population: in Pas-de-Calais, "resistant movements cannot accept that such a proposition can be considered hardly two years after the liberation."[63] A year later, contrary to French opinion, they continued to refuse transformation because it meant the disappearance of the mobilizing figure of the German war prisoner, and with it, one of the last arguments supporting their special legitimacy in French society. The elected representative of the Yonne region, relaying to the Ministry of Labor the protests of his department's association of war prisoners, stressed that such an operation "can only be considered an insult to the memory of our heroes and an encouragement to the militia and to traitors who escape daily."[64]

Doubtless, this last remark explains why opposition on the part of the various local associations of former combatants focused on three issues. Several federations criticized first of all the exchange of clothing bearing the letters "PG"—theoretically at least—for unmarked civilian clothing[65] after transformation. This was an accusation of favoritism—the Ministry of Former Combatants lacked stocks to clothe its repatriated men[66]—but it also indicated that along with the visual disappearance of the enemy figure, an argument central to their cultural mobilization would be lost. Several motions then demanded that transformed war prisoners be prohibited from membership in a union—and thus possibly become leaders of union organizations—to avoid their involvement in "the interior or exterior politics of France,"[67] already forbidden by the work code. However, the demand that they be deprived of the right to go on strike was not granted. Each time it was a matter of limiting as well as possible a dangerous assimilation with an enemy who might at any moment become a fifth column. Finally, several motions of the associations denounced the right of German war prisoners to send their families packages containing five kilos of food, while former combatants and the "*French* victims of the war,"[68] as well as their families, were suffering from hunger: thus an association of former combatants in the Seine department considered that "German war prisoners stuffed themselves enough during the occupation, while our wives were deprived and we ourselves had it hard behind barbed wire (...)" and could not "look on without anger when those responsible for our suffering were getting food for nothing."[69] Despite the authorities' explanations, which showed that these packages in no way deprived the French population, even moderate associations like the FNPG insisted that the government, which would otherwise "be breaking a 'moral contract' with the entire nation,"[70] postponed sending these packages, which had the misfortune of being managed by the "colis français" (the French Post Office).

However, the mobilization against packages shows how much, by ending the war captivity in 1947–1948, the transformation of German POWs into German civil laborers revealed the *résistant*'s dual identity crisis, in terms of an institutional, even ideological unity, which it was no longer possible to preserve, and in terms of the *résistant*'s role in society. In that sense, it is interesting to note that in the sources consulted, it was thereafter almost always the associations that denounced the transformation operation. This institutionalization went along with a widening split within the associative world and that goes beyond how the German—prisoner and/or transformed—was perceived. Whereas the article published by *Le PG* was not motivated, it expressly states, by "a feeling of hatred, resentment or base revenge," and transformed POWs were referred to as "ex-enemies,"[71] as of September 1946, *Le Patriote résistant* deployed a rhetoric of "scandal"[72]:

> (...) we want to keep even *boches* on French soil. Have we forgotten that those prisoners of war who were so docile when first captured, are those same SS, those same soldiers of the Wehrmacht who tortured and massacred us, who devastated and plundered France? (...) Are they really proposing that we who were deported and interned, that we, the *résistants*, mingle side by side in everyday life with our former SS guards or others who, thanks to their blind obedience, made possible the continuation of Hitler's regime?

The growing politicization of deportation and resistance experiences that covered up opposition to Communist attempts to recoup these memories[73] turned the question of German POWs into one of domestic policy. In doing so it provided the issue with a larger framework, that of the Cold War, which, paradoxically, by causing disunity within associations and among *résistants*, contributed to facilitating day-to-day life for the TCLs.

Conclusion

Immediately after the war, former combatants were at one with public opinion in their perception of German war prisoners and intent on aiding the new authorities in the daily management of this captivity and on embodying an image of moral justice. Three years after the end of the war, the configuration was reversed and along with it, the perception of the German, a more or less tolerated worker: the authorities led a policy of assimilation and opinion yielded. Yet former combatants could not make their peace with the enemy. When their exoneration was suppressed, followed by their POW laborers, there remained nothing but the feeling of having sacrificed themselves in vain: "Ouradour, Dachau, etc. are too soon forgotten," one former combatant of both wars deplored, a *résistant* since 1942 and besieger of the pocket of la Rochelle.[74] Doubtless because their war experience had already been taken over by the partisan rationales of the Cold War. They were already in it, so to speak, having entered before having finished with the preceding war.[75] Doubtless also because it was more difficult for them than for other groups to rid themselves of a certain image of the German, which was part of their identity as a *résistant*. Because finally a certain de-humanization of the enemy allowed them to put off reconversion into civilian life and to more or less strategically maintain a prestigious symbolic status. These interpretations, which do not exclude others, lead us back to the diversity of war experiences of these former combatants. Translated by Judith Andreyev.

Notes

1. R. Antelme, *Vengeance?* (November 1946), *Les Vivants. Cahiers publiés par des prisonniers et déportés, 1946,* (Tours: Farrago, 2005), 16–17.
2. Expression used several times by General de Gaulle, particularly in his speech of July 28, 1946 at Bar le Duc, as a way of thinking in continuity of the period of the two World Wars.
3. The subject is closely related to my thesis "Prisonniers de guerre allemands en mains françaises (1944–1949): captivité en France rapatriement en Allemagne," Universities Paris X Nanterre-Augsbourg, 2010.
4. On this concept, see J. Horne, "Kulturelle Demobilmachung 1919–1939. Ein sinnvoller historischer Begriff?" in Wolfgang Hardtwig (ed.), *Politische Kulturgeschichte der Zwischenkriegszeit 1918–1939,* (Göttingen: Vandenhoeck & Ruprecht, 2005), 129–150.
5. See the poster "Ils sont unis, ne les divisez pas!" (They're united, don't divide them!) showing a French soldier in uniform with the initials "PG" (POW) and a labor conscript in work clothes, supporting a deportee in a striped suit.
6. P. Lagrou, "La Résistance et les conceptions de l'Europe, 1945–1965. Le monde associatif international d'anciens résistants et victimes de la persécution devant la Guerre froide, le problème allemand et l'intégration européenne" in A. Fleury and R. Frank (eds.), *Le rôle des guerres dans la mémoire des Européens. Leur effet sur la conscience d'être européen,* (Berne: Peter Lang, 1997), 139.
7. Archives from the following French departments: Nord, Pas-de-Calais, Haut-Rhin, Bas-Rhin, Eure-et-Loir, Haute-Vienne, Savoie, Bouches-du-Rhône, Hérault, Gironde, Côtes-d'Armor.
8. B. Gaïti, "L'opinion publique dans l'histoire politique: impasses et bifurcations," *Le Mouvement Social* 221 (October–December 2007): 96–104.
9. Archives départementales des Bouches-du-Rhône (ADBR, Marseille), 149 W 128, September 19, 1944, on "travaux exécutés par les prisonniers allemands." Marseille was liberated on August 28, 1944.
10. Archives of the Comité International de la Croix-Rouge (ACICR), Geneva, G8 / 51 XII, 321, note n°3273, February 2, 1945, on the "requête de Laure Meine, Graffingy-Chemin en faveur de 17 PGA logés chez elle" (petition in favor of 17 POWs housed in her home).
11. AD de la Gironde (ADG, Bordeaux), SC 2183, *Courrier français,* June 26, 1945, "Une protestation de la municipalité du Bouscat concernant les rations accordées aux prisonniers de l'Axe."
12. C. de Gaulle, *Discours de Guerre (mai 1944–septembre 1945)* (Paris: Egloff, 1945), 163.
13. National archives of France (ANF, Paris), F 1a 4024, report of the *Commissariat de la République,* Nancy region, June 2, 1945. However, we do not know to what extent the return of 40,000 deportees involved a change in the image of German war prisoners among the population. A more detailed study should attempt to answer this question.
14. H. Frenay, then commissioner of the Comité Français de la Libération Nationale indicated in September 1944 that the aim of his propaganda was "the communion of sentiments between prisoners, deportees and the rest of the nation," ACICR, G25/621, note of the Comité Français de la Libération Nationale, commissariat aux prisonniers, déportés et réfugiés of January 21, 1944 on the "Politique générale du rapatriement" [general politics of repatriation].
15. *L'Historique du service des Prisonniers de guerre de l'Axe, 1943–1948,* drafted in 1948 under the direction of General Buisson of the Direction Générale des Prisonniers de Guerre de l'Axe, 149.
16. ADBR, 324 D 6, note 933/45 from the prefect to the mayors concerning "accommodations and supervision of German prisoners of war." Version of July 7, 1945, but the original version obviously dates back from June 14, 1945. This type of instruction is found in almost all the departments.
17. ADBR, 349 D 86, note de service 3016 5/FS/HF of the *état-major* (chief of staff), 10° Région Militaire on the "surveillance des prisonniers de guerre allemands affectés aux besoins civiles" (supervision of German prisoners of war assigned to civilian needs).
18. M. Foucault, , "Cours du 17 mars 1976," in *Il faut défendre la société, Course at Collège de France, 1976–1977* (Paris: Hautes Etudes/Gallimard/Seuil, 2004), 222. The mention of Foucault is not meant to suggest the assimilation of imprisonment in jail with captivity during a war. The reading of Foucault enables us to see how, at first, the management of prisoners is apprehended by the authorities according to military norms, which, through the "panoptic principle" applied in the camps, seek to fix the image of the German as an intractable enemy because he represents

an ideological and economic danger to French society. Foucaldian analysis becomes interesting heuristically in the "disciplinary rationale"/"security rationale" pair (see note 34 in this chapter) in that it makes it possible to think about how prisoners leaving camps corrupt this attempt at disciplinary control by gradually managing to impose new norms of treatment. The transformation of the very nature of captivity in civil surroundings poses the question of the relation of the prisoner with French society, which he is integrating and which he in turn contributes to changing. This evolution provides a relevant criterion for judging the dynamics of after-wars and the link between cultural representations and social relations between two populations less and less enemies to each other.

19. AD du Nord (ADN, Lille), 27 W 38361(1), report no. 2552-AG by the Renseignements Généraux, June 13, 1945, concerning the "Protestations formulées par les Comités locaux de Libération relatives aux rations alimentaires accordées aux prisonniers allemands" (Protests by local Liberation Committees regarding food rations granted to German prisoners).
20. ADBR, 1458 W 146, note from the sous-préfet d'Erstein, August 8, 1945, on the "Comité de défense contre le nazisme, groupe de Benfeld" (Defense Committee against Nazism, Benfeld group).
21. AD du Pas-de-Calais (ADPC, Arras/Damville), 1 W 9603, note NM/2979 on the "Prisonniers allemands, déminage" (German prisoners, mine clearance).
22. AD of Eure-et-Loir (ADEL, Chartres), 1 W 132, rapport no. 163 of the Commissaire special, January 12, 1945, on the "Situation morale, économique et politique de la population" (Moral, economic, and political situation of the population).
23. Service Historique de la Défense (SHD, Vincennes), Service de l'Armée de terre (SHAT), 29 R 1 (2), note of the DGPG, October 10, 1944, on the "Organisation du service des PG dans la métropole." Even if that consisted of an emergency measure and reflected the difficulties involved in planning the end of the war—or the incapacity of the officials of Free France and Germany.
24. AD of Savoie (ADS, Chambéry), 1399 W 12, decision 1169 of the Commissaire de la République, July 7, 1945, regarding "Conditions de vie, garde et surveillance des prisonniers de guerre allemands, employés aux besoins de l'agriculture" (living condition, guard, and surveillance of German war prisoners employed by farmers).
25. The amount of money paid by the private employer to the state to guarantee that prisoner labor be no less expensive than free labor.
26. AD of Hérault (ADH, Montpellier), 2 W 999, note 670 60 of the Inspection Divisionnaire du Travail of June 6, 1945, concerning "Paiement de l'indemnité compensatrice" (Payment of compensation).
27. Archives of the Ministry of Labor (AMT, Fontainebleau), 19770623/86, note 8709 MOC of the PGE (Prisonniers de Guerre Ennemis) Section, June 6, 1945, on Exonération du paiement de l'indemnité compensatrice pour les agriculteurs rapatriés employant des PGE (Exoneration of the payment of compensations for POWs farmers repatriated and employing PGE).
28. AMT, 19770623/88, note ASR 8805 of the Ministry of War Prisoners, Deportees and Refugees, July 6, 1945.
29. AMT, 19770623/86, note of August 23, 1945 of the Ministry of War Prisoners, Deportees and Refugees on the "main-d'œuvre allemande" (German manpower).
30. Except for those in Alsace-Moselle incorporated by force, the last of whom returned only in the 1950s.
31. J. Fritz, *Les prisonniers de guerre allemands en Bretagne. Rencontres et expériences entre capture, captivité et vie parmi les Français, 1944–1948/49*, Masters dissertation, Rennes 2 University, 2004, 114–121. With 33 percent POWs employed in the agricultural sector until June 1946, Brittany's rate was lower than the national average, which can partially be explained by the small size of farms and the poverty of the local peasant milieu.
32. Local Archives, Bas-Rhin (ADBR), Strasbourg, 349 D 87, brochure of the Ministry of Labor for des municipalities, s.d. (probably 3rd trimestre 1945).
33. ADBR, Saverne, 1366 W 54, "PG (hébergement, indemnités compensatrices)"; Erstein, 1458 W 146, "Main-d'œuvre: prisonniers de guerre employés comme main-d'œuvre: instructions et correspondence."
34. Defined by Michel Foucault in opposition to the disciplinary rationale, rather than individual obedience, it seeks "the security of the whole in relation to its internal danger," by seeking an equilibrium between each of the elements that make up reality. It acts as a centrifugal force that

tends to insert the prisoner in a more open environment. See M. Foucault, "Leçon du 18 janvier 1978," in *Sécurité, territoire, population. Cours au Collège de France, 1977–1978* (Paris: Hautes Etudes/Gallimard/Seuil, 2004).
35. ADBR, 324 D 9, statement of the gendarmerie no. 269, April 29, 1946 regarding the "évasion de deux PGA à Hurtigheim" (escape of two German POWs at Hurtigheim).
36. Other departments doubtless had more moderate rapprochement dynamics, such as la Haute-Vienne, where, in May 1947, the use of POWs was "contre-indiqué" (contraindicated) in Oradour-sur-Glane at the risk of "sérieux incidents" (serious incidents). AD of la Haute-Vienne (ADHV, Limoges), 993 W 204, inquiry on "Emploi de la main-d'œuvre" (Employment of manpower), May 25, 1947.
37. P. Buton, *La joie douloureuse. La libération de la France* (Paris: Complexe/IHTP-CNRS, 2004), pp. 136–149.
38. Between January 1945 and May 1946 the Americans and the British ceded nearly 765,000 German war prisoners in six transfers.
39. J. Fauvet, "Un prisonnier, même allemand, est un être humain" [A prisoner, even German, is a human being], *Le Monde*, no. 245, October 1, 1945. See also *Le Figaro, La Croix, Libération*.
40. ADHV, 986 W 532, note 3 778 of the Renseignements Généraux, October 12, 1945, on the "Traitement des PGA" (Treatment of the German POWs).
41. "5° Emploi des prisonniers allemands dans l'agriculture," *Le PG*, organe de la Fédération nationale des PG, no. 12 (November 30, 1945): 40.
42. ADS, 1362 W 110, letter from la Fédération Nationale des Déportés et Internés Patriotes, June 28, 1946, to the prefect on German POWs.
43. ADG, 87 AW 2 (1), letter from Dubourg Jean, president, Local Liberation Committee, November 1, 1945, concerning the "Surveillance des PG."
44. ADS, 1382 W 23, report 764 of the RG of Albertville, April 5, 1946, "un certain émoi à Ugine" (agitation in Ugine).
45. ADS, 1362 W 10, *Le Dauphiné libéré*, August 29, 1946, "Il est si gentil, Rodolph!" (Rodolph is so kind!).
46. ADPC, 1Z–463, letter from the president of the Comité de Libération, Verquigneul, April 2, 1946, on the supervision of German POWs.
47. ADBR, 150 W 172, note 1446 of the commanding general of the 9th RM, July 2, 1946, on the "attitude des PG de l'Axe."
48. ADS, 1362 W 110, note 2369/I from General Collignon to the prefect, July 13, 1946.
49. SHD-SHAT, 29 R 5 (2), report, September 3, 1945, of the Fédération Nationale des PG, reunion of the federal committee of August 31, 1946, regarding the treatment of war prisoners of the Axis.
50. ACICR, G 85/ 70-74, 9-15, letter from the CICR to the Ministry of Foreign Affairs, April 5, 1946, regarding camps visits.
51. ADEL, 1 W 102, note from the préfecture to the Services Généraux, November 7, 1946, on the "prisonniers de guerre de l'Axe" (war prisoners of the Axis), letter of the departmental association of the war prisoners of Eure-et-Loir.
52. AMT, 19770623/88, note PC/AB from the Direction Générale du Travail to the Ministry, February 12, 1946, on the "Indemnité compensatrice due au titre de l'emploi des prisonniers allemands dans l'agriculture."
53. AMT, 19770623/88, document of the Ministry of Agriculture to the Ministry of Labor, March 16, 1946.
54. AMT, 19770623/88, note PC/AB from the Direction Générale du Travail of the Ministry, February 12, 1946.
55. AMT, 19770623/100, answer 1022 M/ME of the Ministry of Labor to Jules Moch, January 31, 1947.
56. AMT, 19770623/86, letter no. 16623 from the Ministry of Labor to the Ministry of War Veterans, November 19, 1946, on the "Emploi des PG par des Français rapatriés" (Employment of war prisoners by French repatriated).
57. ACICR, G17/51, G17/Fr.XII, 120, letter of Louis Gueno to the CICR, October 17, 1945.
58. Ministry of Foreign Affairs, Archives of the French Occupied in Germany and Austria (MAE-AZOFAA), Colmar, AP 311-1, note 1002/D3300, August 18, 1945, on the "situation de la main-d'oeuvre en France et l'emploi des prisonniers de guerre" (situation of manpower in France and war prisoners' employment).

59. ANF, F 7 16040, note of the Direction des Conventions Administratives on the "politique d'immigration" (immigration policy), March 16, 1945. Emphasis in the original document.
60. A. Spire, *Etrangers à la carte. L'administration de l'immigration en France (1945–1975)* (Paris: Grasset, 2005).
61. ADPC, 1 Z 483, intelligence report no. 4362/4/CG of Béthune, November 20, 1946, on the "Milieux syndicaux au regard de la main-d'oeuvre allemande" (Unions' attitude toward German manpower).
62. *Bundesarchiv*, Lichterfelde, SAPMO, DY 30–190.
63. ADPC, 1 Z–463, note 4055/10/CP, October 31, 1946, on the "Transformation de 200,000 des prisonniers de guerre en travailleurs libres" (Transformation of 200,000 war prisoners into free workers).
64. AMT, 19770623/90, letter PM/PH 8679 de Prosper Môquet, representative of the Yonne to the Ministry of Labor, November 20, 1947.
65. AMAE (Paris), Z22, letter from the DGPG to the Garde des Sceaux, September 25, 1945, concerning the "naturalisation des PGA."
66. AMT, 19770623/90, note 1118 JV from the Ministry of War Veterans to the Ministry of Labor, June 21, 1947.
67. AMT, 19770623/90, letter LB/JJ 4476 from the Fédération Nationale des Prisonniers de Guerre to the DGPG, December 10, 1947, concerning the "Droit syndical des PGA transformés" (Union law for transformed POWs).
68. Emphasis in the original document.
69. AMT, 19770623/91, letter from the Association des Combattants, PG of the Seine department, section Levallois to the representative of the Seine, December 10, 1948.
70. "Une étrange décision. Les avantages d'être Allemand," *Le PG* (62) (October 12, 1948): 1.
71. Ibid.
72. "Scandale. Les PGA deviendraient sous peu travailleurs libres" (German POWs soon to become free labourers), *Le Patriote résistant* (14) (September 15, 1946): 1.
73. On this subject, see P. Lagrou, "Le martyre national" in *Mémoires patriotiques et occupation nazie. Résistants, requis et déportés en Europe occidentale, 1945–1965* (Paris: Complexe/IHTP-CNRS, 2003), 203–237.
74. ADHV, 986 W 532, letter from Palçon Henri to the prefect, June 25, 1947.
75. See Lagrou, "La Résistance et les conceptions de l'Europe."

CHAPTER SEVEN

The "Recycled" Militiaman: An Examination of the Postwar Reconversion of Four Former Members of a Serbian Armed Group

SAMUEL TANNER

> **Abstract**
>
> How do former militiamen who have participated in mass violence "recycle" once the war is over? Do they reintegrate into the postwar "normalized" day-to-day framework of social, political, and community relations? Or does the violence experienced during the war transfer into the postwar context? And if so, can we speak of a violent habitus? This chapter, an ethnographic study of the post-war reconversion of four former Serbian militiamen who took part in mass violence in the former Yugoslavia during the 1990s, underlines the need to view such conversion experiences from a dual angle: collective and individual. From the collective point of view, we find a reconfiguration of the community's social economy with a tendency toward a new order giving these former members of armed bands the status of a local elite. Individually, the vestiges of war are reflected in the difficulty these men have making sense of their personal investment in an unjustifiable past, in addition to which some also suffer from the continued presence of these war experiences within. This becomes apparent in their ambivalent relation to violence.

The "Recycled" Militiaman

How do former militiamen who have taken part in mass violence reinvent themselves once the war is over? Do they return to a "normal"[1] social, political, and community life? Is there a transfer of the experience of violence through the acquisition of registers or a habitus of violence? And if so, by what means and how do these become manifest? It should be noted that habitus refers to "a system of sustainable and transferable tendencies that, integrating all past experiences, operates at each instant like a matrix of perception, awareness and action [...]."[2] It is the product of socialization, or the assimilation of past experiences and, in the context under consideration in this chapter, of participation in mass violence. Social practices, including violence, result from a *conjuncture*, or a meeting between habitus and a given situation.

The reconversion and reinsertion of former militiamen invariably falls into a group of multidisciplinary debates concerning the fate of former combatants in the transitions from war to peace. Whether it relates to the interests of political science in the question of spoilers, of political sociology regarding the necessary reintegration of militiamen into civilian life, or the concerns of criminologists about the link between reintegration, reconversion, and crime rates in postconflict societies, the question of their role in the outcomes of war requires particular attention, even if only in the context of preventing these people from returning to the military life.

This transition from war to "peace" will be examined using an ethnography of the reintegration of four former Serbian militiamen, Radislav, Ivan, Nenan, and Janko,[3] into their community. Field investigations and the observations that were gathered demonstrated a need to address this integration from a dual perspective: the collective and the individual. From a collective perspective, one can observe a restructuring of the social dynamics within the community that tends to create a new order, eventually elevating these "veterans" to the status of local elite. From an individual perspective, the remnants of war are evidenced by the difficulty experienced in making sense of their past involvement and the challenge for some of those involved to live with this experience. This is reflected in their ambivalent relationship toward violence.

This chapter begins with a presentation of the subject matter and the four militiamen. In a second section, the focus is on the collective dimension of their reintegration into the community. This phase emphasizes the rebuilding of their identity through the assimilation of past violence into a mythical setting inspired by the Serbian nationalist tradition. As will be demonstrated, the collective dimension of reintegration needs to be understood in the light of a new economy for the local distribution of material resources. A third section examines the transition from war to peace for these men from an individual perspective. The differential and ambivalent relationship that they have with violence will also be examined. In fact their relationship with violence varies depending on whether reference is made to the violence experienced during the war (as a perpetrator of it) and the trauma it has left them with or, conversely, if the violence is experienced in a mythical way and undertaken in the name of a more global objective, such as the defense of the nation. Finally, a conclusion is drawn in which, while taking account of the limitations of our approach, we revisit some precautions of a theoretical nature that relate to the general issue of the acquisition of a habitus of violence by these men and its ultimate transposition into a postconflict context.

Four Former Militiamen: Radislav, Ivan, Nenan, and Janko

By way of introduction, some general remarks need to be made about methodological issues concerning the material forming the basis of this chapter. As mentioned already, the material is mainly derived from discussions with four people who claimed to have been active in Croatia and Bosnia-Herzegovina during the mass violence that occurred there in the 1990s. First, Radislav was a key source of information in the fieldwork, and it was through him that we were introduced to Ivan, Nenan, and Janko during the course of the two visits that we made to Serbia in the mid 2000s. An unexpected encounter when setting up the fieldwork brought us into contact with him. The third party that introduced us assured us that Radislav, who had war experience (although we did not know of what kind), would definitely be helpful for our research so naturally we made contact with him. Secondly it should be noted that this is a small sample of just four subjects who are not necessarily representative. For example, Radislav, Ivan, and Nenan were affiliated with the nationalist opposition to the Slobodan Milošević regime, namely the Serbian Renewal Movement led by Vuk Drašković, whose armed men and units only operated for a few weeks in Croatia before being disbanded by the regime of the former president.

All of these units were referred to by the generic term Serbian guards. Also, the individuals discussed in this chapter, in comparison to units such as the Chetniks led by Vojislav Šešelj, and the Tigers of Zeljko Raznjatovic, better known by his *nom de guerre* Arkan, acted on the fringes of the units that carried out most of the extermination of the civilian populations in Croatia and Bosnia-Herzegovina. Even so, these four men claimed to have been involved in the violence. As such, and as former fighters reintegrated into their community at the time of the fieldwork, their opinions enabled us to investigate the transition from war to peace for this particular type of veteran thus justifying the present analysis. Using a qualitative, ethnographic approach was particularly valid since the information available in the literature about this type of actor in the war mainly comes from legal sources and documents. Important though these are, they provide only a limited view of their postwar journey. They are not sufficient for an understanding of the way of life of such people, their social relationships, and their place in their community, nor do they take account of their opinions nor the way they view their past actions. Yet these elements are necessary for the development of a theory of the dynamics and sociological processes influencing transitions from war to peace of actors such as the militia. Hence a methodological approach that is ethnographic in nature is preferred whenever possible—although this is invariably dependent on the vagaries of fieldwork—since it permits new and more comprehensive knowledge to be obtained, enabling a more detailed analysis of phenomena that are usually approached in a too narrowly top-down way.

The four subjects have a number of things in common: they all come from the same area and, at the time under review, acted outside the legal and state chains of command; they were all volunteers and participated in the violence in whatever way they could, and they have known each other a long time. However, they are also characterized by a number of differences: they have different professional profiles ranging from health services to employee in a transport company; while Radislav has a higher education, the others do not. Also, these men are from two armed groups with different structures and goals. As mentioned above, Radislav, Ivan, and Nenan were affiliated with an armed group acting under the nebulous umbrella known as the Serbian Guard, comprising all the armed groups affiliated with the monarchist opposition. The structure of most of these armed groups was extremely unstable, and the Serbian Guard was only active as such for a few weeks in the armed conflict in Croatia.[4] Meanwhile Janko belonged, albeit marginally, to the Tigers—an armed group that was incredibly well organized and equipped. Finally, the differences are also marked when account is taken of the time and geographical horizons of their respective involvement in the violence. According to their claims, their involvement varied from just a few months in Croatia, in the case of Radislav, to nine years for Nenan in Croatia, Bosnia-Herzegovina, and Kosovo. Janko was active during the four years of war in Bosnia, while Ivan participated in the violence in Croatia and later in Bosnia-Herzegovina. Let us now take a more detailed look at their stories.

At the time of his involvement in the conflict during the fall of 1991, Radislav was a health professional. His graduate training had honed his commitment to and involvement in the major sociopolitical issues of his country—as he likes to put it. And it was precisely because of a political issue that he *voluntarily* got involved in the conflict between the Serbs and the Croats in Croatia. Initially, and outside any institutional framework—army or police—Radislav signed up to "help."

But little by little, as a consequence of circumstances and meetings, his involvement in the events that led to open conflict and the accompanying violence gradually developed and unfolded. The catalyst for his career as a militiaman was the political conflict within the Serbian nationalist arena. At this time he shared the ideas of the Serbian Renewal Movement, the main anti-Communist, nationalist opposition to Milošević who was to be beaten in the first multi-party elections held in Serbia in December 1990.[5] The primary cause of his involvement was not so much a desire for gain, or even ethnic hatred, but an expression of nationalistic "self-help" and political action in opposition to the Milošević regime.[6] Radislav then went to Knin that, at the time, was the main town of the Croatian Serbs. It was there that he was inspired by some protagonists in the events to come. Among these was Dragan Vasiljković, known as "Captain Dragan," who, in the eyes of local Serbs, was an influential figure with significant symbolic capital within the group.[7] At that time he was setting up camps to train volunteer Serbs in the region, and elsewhere, to prepare them for the defense of the autonomous Serbian region of Krajina.[8] Radislav's career[9] took a decisive turn when he joined one of these training camps. This was to have a major impact on both his perspective on current events, but also, in fine, on his behavior. It was during his stay in a camp that, accompanied by Ivan, Radislav was trained in the use of arms. This was completed by ideological training. It was here that the two men met Nenan. After a few weeks, in the fall of 1991, the three men went to Vukovar at the time when the city was subjected to the violence carried out by Serb forces.[10] Radislav permanently ended his involvement in the war when the United Nations Protection Force (UNPROFOR) arrived in Croatia in February 1992. At the time that we met him, Radislav had completely abandoned the profession he had before the conflict and had a job in the local public sector.

Ivan was a friend of Radislav—in fact the two men came from the same area and had known each other since before the collapse of Yugoslavia. Ivan did not reveal that much about his past, and while we do not know what his profession was, we do know that he practiced a martial art before the war. Clearly much older than Radislav, Ivan had a significant influence on him. He was with Radislav in Croatia in the late summer of 1991, and was involved in the same events as his friend until he left the region in February 1992. Like many others, Ivan followed the movement of Serb forces to Bosnia-Herzegovina following the arrival of UNPROFOR. He claimed to have been involved in the violence that took place in the eastern part of Bosnia from April 1992.[11] As for his work after the war, or at least his source of income, he mentioned that he lived from "small jobs here and there," which will be discussed later in this chapter.

Nenan was a former professional soldier in the Yugoslav Peoples' Army. At the time, he also shared the ideas of the Serbian Renewal Movement. Nenan deserted the army when it became known that the command of the Yugoslav Peoples' Army was being transferred from the collegial presidency of the Yugoslav federation to Yugoslavia's new strongman, Slobodan Milošević. It was then that Nenan decided to go to Knin. In addition to his presence during the events in Vukovar, Nenan claims to have been involved in the violence that took place in the region of Sarajevo[12] and Kosovo. In all, he was involved in the nine years of war that ravaged Yugoslavia. At the time of our meeting he had no steady work but travelled the roads of the Balkans (including outside of Yugoslavia), living from odd jobs and the generosity of people encountered along his way. In fact he told us that at the end of the war he withdrew to an Orthodox monastery overseas.

Lastly Janko claimed that he belonged to the Tigers, led by Arkan. He came from the same area as Radislav and Ivan. His testimony showed that he was active in eastern Bosnia–Herzegovina. This unit was set up in October 1991 and was disbanded by Arkan himself in 1996. According to some analyses, the Tigers were composed of several categories of members: the hard-core, faithful-to-the-leader supporters of the football club the Red Star of Belgrade, and finally, auxiliary members,[13] who in turn were divided into several subgroups. Amongst them were Serbs from Croatia and Bosnia, forced to join the war effort, as well as Serbian volunteers from Serbia, engaging in ethnic cleansing. Many of them were already part of the world of crime and had connections with more central members of the Tigers in the Belgrade underworld. Janko was part of the outermost circle, namely the auxiliary volunteers who joined the Tigers. Unlike other participants, political affiliation to the Milošević regime, including that of the unit, had no importance for him. He became involved for the nationalist cause, in particular to help his "brothers" in Bosnia. His affiliation with the Tigers was thus circumstantial. As such, he cannot be considered representative of that unit. Prior to his involvement in the violence, Janko worked in a transport company, a profession he was still in at the time of our meeting.

As is apparent from their stories, even though they were operating mainly outside the institutionalized structure of violence,[14] these individuals were active on the frontline of ethnic cleansing as "auxiliary nonstate actors." Thus, it is as irregular perpetrators of mass violence that they fall into the category of war veterans. So, without further ado, let us analyze the first dimension of their "reintegration" into the community. This shows a reconfiguration of the economy of social relations at the local level, which tends to crystallize a postconflict order in which these individuals make up the new elite.

Collectivity and Postviolence Transition: An Accumulation of Prestige

An "outsider" entering the social sphere of those former perpetrators would be struck by an observation: these men, who claim to have been involved in massacres, have nevertheless a clear symbolic capital and, paradoxically, are strategic actors within their local community. However, their prestige is both the by-product and the consequence of their war experience. First, the ethnography shows that in the postconflict context, these four men have capitalized on the transposition of a register, or symbolic figures, revolving around the image of the patriotic hero. Correspondingly, a transformation can be observed in the perception that they have of themselves and the reshaping of their "matrix of perception, awareness and action"—to return to the concept of the habitus. The metamorphosis of these normative grids, or horizons, from which the actors interpret the events they have experienced, in its turn accompanies a "redistribution of the markers of morality."[15] To illustrate this last point, the killings are no longer perceived as criminal acts but as a by-product of the pursuit of a "superior" goal such as the defense of the Serb nation, for example. These new moral standards are shared with the local population through a structure of closely woven relationships. This structure is underpinned by both a local pattern underlying social relations, as well as the crystallization[16] of a new mafioso-type of regulation and local distribution of resources, resulting from the social networks constructed by the four men during the war. This is discussed later in this chapter.

Remodelling of the Modes of Subjectivation and Inscription of Violence in the Mythical Tradition

Fifteen years after the events, Radislav, Ivan, Nenan, and Janko situate their war experience—both as perpetrators and as witnesses—in the tradition of the Serbian patriotic heroes who fought throughout the ages for the preservation of the quiddity of the group. A transposition of the symbolic repertoire of the celestial warrior in the postconflict context is in operation here. In parallel, at the collective level, this phenomenon aligns with the concerns, beliefs, and local representations, respecting an assertion of identity and a nationalist and traditionalist *imaginaire*.[17] In fact, the presentation of oneself as a defender of the Serbian quiddity is echoed in a large part of the community. This "happy" coincidence is exploited by the four men and allows for a capitalization of their past experiences. This logic, as will be showed in this section, plays a key role in the emergence of idiosyncratic standards of morality within the community. In other words, these individuals enjoy local protection because of their conferred status of hero.

From the start of our discussions, Radislav situated his experience of violence in the framework of a legitimate action to defend the interests of the Serb populations living outside Serbia, and this from the first signs of any tension or aggression against them by Croats or Muslims. As is the case for many others,[18] in his discussions the Croats became "*Oustachi*," and Muslims the "*Turks*,"[19] reactivating both the rhetoric and the frames of reference used in the darkest moments in the history of the relationship between these three ethnic groups. But, this is just a symptom of a larger phenomenon, as became evident from the fieldwork. It consists of presenting the violence—and thus justifying it—as a parallel consequence to safeguarding the very quiddity of the Serb nation—defined as the land, religion, and culture. Therefore, the project they were involved in cannot be reduced to a single individual responsibility thus "exculpating" individuals who acted for the preservation of the Serbian nation. This is what emerges from Ivan's comments: "We fought to save our land, our religion and our culture. This territory is Christian not Muslim. They have no business being on our lands [Croatia and Bosnia-Herzegovina]. You Europeans, you think that we're crazy, but you just don't understand the dangers of the spread of Islam. We acted in the name of Christianity [...]. These people had to be eradicated, it was war, we had no choice."

Inscribed in the mythical tradition of the defense of the Serbs throughout the ages, their commitment is associated with the actions of past warriors who fought for the same cause: the defense of Orthodoxy, the frontiers of the kingdom, and the Serbian culture. In this tradition, these warriors of the past have been elevated to paragons of national defense and transformed into mythical and decisive figures in the rhetoric and nationalist frames of reference.[20] A famous case that was mentioned several times in discussions is Miloš Obilić, considered to be one of the fathers of the nation. He was a knight who, according to legend, murdered the Sultan Murad, head of the Ottoman Empire, during the famous Battle of Kosovo on June 28, 1389. Obilić was executed the following day by the Ottoman clan, making him a martyr and a symbol of sacrifice for his people and his country. The Chetnik is also a recurring symbol in the frame of reference of the four men as well as in the community where our fieldwork was conducted. The Chetniks fought against the Communist "Partisans" of General Tito and against the allies of the Axis alliance during the Second World War[21] in order to defend the regime of Karađorđević, head of the Kingdom of South Slavs (1921–1941). The Chetnik is an important figure in the Serbian Renewal Movement. The Serbian Renewal Movement proposed the establishment of a purely Serb army, modeled on the Chetnik, in order to defend the interests of the monarchy of the Karađorđević dynasty with the objective of the country being led by a member of that dynasty. For example, Radislav says: "What we wanted [in 1990], was the rehabilitation of the true fighters of Serbia, I mean by that the Chetniks who fought against the Oustachis and the Communists during the Second World War."

Radislav, Ivan, Nenan, and Janko relate to and confirm having followed in the footsteps of Obilić and the Chetniks during the 1990s. Since then, and as was the case for Obilić in his time, their involvement in the war is in the context of self-sacrifice for the good of the many. The violence resulting from this commitment is thus minimized: rather than being an objective in itself, it is presented as an inevitable consequence of the preservation of Christianity against Islam. As Ivan added: "I don't feel bad about what I did. People portray us as crazy killers but they don't know the reasons for our actions. We are the front line in the battle and the clash of civilizations."

In these terms, and according to our interviewees, the people involved in these massacres had a legitimate and noble reason for becoming involved: the preservation of the group and of its culture. But also, this involvement makes them the only people capable, in their eyes, of fully grasping the meaning of their actions, and therefore, of judging them. This rhetoric not only plays a role in transforming the way these participants see themselves, but also the moral standards in the local sphere.

In the postconflict context, this nationalist tradition of defending the Serb quiddity is observed not only in discussions but it also occupies the space shaped by their daily practices and customs. A belief in religion was confirmed by Radislav and Nenan who, since their return, respect the rules of their religion in a very disciplined way, including fasting and regularly attending church. At Radislavs' home, there are decorative objects that refer to the symbolic universe of the heavenly warrior and protection of the Serb quiddity: a portrait of Dragoljub "Draža" Mihailović, leader of the Chetniks in the Second World War, icons of "warrior monks" who fought for the nation, and a discotheque and library full of the epic stories of Serb warriors. These figures inspire him in his daily decisions. The ethnographic approach enabled us to spend time with these men, accompanied by eulogistic songs celebrating the prowess of former Serb fighters. Discussions with Radislav about literature also helped us to grasp the extent to which these references are an integral part of his psyche.[22] Finally, we should note that even car trips were almost always punctuated by traditional Serb songs—translated by Radislav. These songs were about the great founding myths of the nation, which is sometimes presented as being the oldest on earth. In a postconflict context these mythical figures, and frames of reference are incorporated into the images, everyday habits, and behavior of these men.

We mentioned earlier that the postviolence transposition and updating of this symbolic celestial warrior by Radislav, Ivan, Nenan, and Janko coincides with the existence of a repertoire of beliefs and local representations—exploited by the men—whose interaction contributes to the genesis of idiosyncratic moral standards. No belief excludes or contradicts the possibility of exploiting it for personal gain by the actors. This is precisely what emerges from the relationship between the four men and the local population—something that became clear during the fieldwork. This local repertoire of belief revolves more broadly around a rejection—or perhaps fear—of Islam and a distrust of large urban centers (Belgrade in particular)[23] not to mention a contempt for everything that affects, or embodies, the countries of NATO, an organization responsible for the bombing of Serbia in 1999. There is also a rejection of social movements typically associated with the idea of progressivism: pro-choice associations, emancipation of gays, lesbians, and transgender people, or organizations defending human rights. The latter are often perceived as unpatriotic, as they target first of all veterans and "defenders of Serbian values" in the war in former Yugoslavia.

The juxtapositioning by Radislav, Ivan, Nenan, and Janko of the postconflict transposition of the symbolic directory of the figure of the patriotic hero and the "defenders" of the Serb quiddity on the one hand, with the beliefs and expectations of the local population—and the need for it to appoint local leaders able to ensure and represent its interests—on the other, results in a reshaping of the economy of legitimacy in the local arena. In fact, because of their involvement in the war, and therefore the "sacrifice" they made for the nation, these four men have a significant symbolic capital, which locally gives them the status of moral authority. This is precisely the process that is at the source of new frames of reference, but also what we have called earlier on, the emergence of idiosyncratic moral standards. These frameworks and standards shape discussions, strengthen identity, and finally, guide actions. In short, they provide perspectives *on* the world.[24] This partially explains how former war criminals become patriotic heroes in the eyes of local communities and in the post-conflict context and, as such, benefit from protection, both internal and external to the community, against any action perceived locally as a threat, including the judicial system. But the symbolic sphere does not fully explain why this accumulation of capital occurs—for that account needs to be taken of the economy of social relationships and exchanges put in place within the community after the war.

A New Economy of Material Resources in the Local Arena

This accumulation of capital is also the product of the crystallization of a new type of social regulation of the "mafia" kind. Within this, and through the development of social networks both during and after the war, Radislav, Ivan, and Janko, and to some extent Nenan, occupy a central position as *brokers*, or "intermediaries." This new order seeks to create a system of mutual benefit between multiple partners—veterans, politicians, and local community—that protects and also places a veil of secrecy over their past.

Our field investigations suggested that even before the war Radislav, Ivan, and Janko were already involved, albeit on a small scale, in illegal activities. These mainly consisted of illegal betting, trafficking, and money lending. These were part of more general practices not systematically perceived locally as intimidating. According to the four men, this business was essentially a parallel economy, with the delivery of both legal and illegal goods and services for the benefit of their community. Thus, rather than "crimes of predation," these individuals were involved in a local "alternative system" of resource distribution. This needs to be understood at the community level, given the benefits it brought to the entire local population rather than exclusively serving the interests of Radislav, Ivan, and Janko, despite their role as a communication channel.[25] They were still active in this business at the time of our fieldwork. These activities played an important role in the progression of their *career* in mass violence, be it only in the resources and social structures they have constructed that facilitated their involvement outside of the state organization. That's what this comment by Radislav suggests: "You know, before I was involved in the war, we were a group [from here] and we knew each other for a long time. We had pretty much the same ideas about everything and of course on politics. We raised hell, did lots of dumb things before getting involved [...] it was other guys that showed us the way. I think what lead us there were the petty thefts. We were hardened by petty crimes."[26]

This practice or these "small jobs," to use their terminology, consisted at the time of our meeting of small profits from gambling (bets and lottery scams) or trafficking used cars, for example. This represented a set of practices that on the one hand expanded their network of contacts, and, on the other, generated "resources-profits," many of which were "reinvested" in the local community.

This "placement" occurs in the name of a fundamental principle of solidarity, a factor in a larger set of social norms and practices regulating local trade and designated by the interlocutors as *komsije*.[27] The funds generated by the illegal business permit the philanthropic conversion of Radislav, Ivan, and Janko, who lend money at low rates or participate in the sale of used cars at unbeatable prices. In any case, they "subsidize" the local economy. But not all resources are exclusively monetary or material. The moral authority enjoyed by Radislav, Ivan, and Janko makes them the mediators of choice in local disputes. Their gain is also social, such as helping young people in trouble or struggling with drug problems. This is notably so in the case of a young man we met, whom Radislav helped by a form of sponsorship. This person told us that, in return, they were co-opted into the "local business" as an informant. Their job was basically to stay informed of discussions in cafés, bars, and nightclubs in the area and to let Radislav know about any threat to the "small jobs" group, whether from the police or from other clans.

Moreover, Radislav enjoys quite an interesting position in this organization that further strengthens his status of moral authority. At the time of our fieldwork, not only did he have a job in public sector but he also campaigned locally for a pan-Serbian political party. As such, according to the principle of open-handedness, he had significant power to influence the distribution of the budgets that the public administration and the party inject into the region. As is clear from discussions with community members, Radislav was considered the right man for the job in the eyes of part of the population.[28] If Radislav represents an important bridge of assistance at the "top" to the community, that is to say from the governmental sphere, in addition he has a key role "at the bottom" in the expansion of the popular base of political education for which he was active in the region. He is an important player in the local political machine. Indeed, it appears that the four men were not the only ones in the region to get involved in the war. Radislav claims that some of their close entourage were also involved in these events and now form the "social networks of war."[29] In the post-conflict situation, the transposition of these networks is characterized by strong solidarity and mutual aid. These are evidenced, for example, by the active support given to Radislav in promoting the political group that he supports. The resources of each member of the network (family, local government, infrastructure, etc.) are thus mobilized to promote this political group, remain silent about all the local "small jobs," or generate material resources, and thus maintain the trust that is essential in these kinds of activities.[30] Thus a new economy of legal and illegal resources—material and services—is set up that supplements or grafts itself onto the way in which the state distributes goods and services—often perceived as deficient in the local sphere. This recalls a very similar pattern to that observed in the study of the Sicilian Mafia by Diego Gambetta.[31] It is largely a result of the action of the four men, who have developed "[...] a set of organizational solutions and action strategies enabling organized force (or organized violence) to be converted into money or other valuable assests on a permanent basis"—a definition of the entrepreneur of violence by Vadim Volkov.[32] In turn, these organizational solutions and strategic actions influence the perception the actors have of themselves, making them conscious of playing a crucial role in the community. This is apparent from Radislavs' comments: "People know me and they know I'm one of them. Some lost their family in Bosnia or in Croatia because of the war and they know they can trust me because they saw me act to save the Serbs. You can now understand that thanks to my position here [referring to the 'little jobs'] and my political party I can pull together 200 men in no time and intervene if other Serbs are threatened."

The men did not just perceive themselves as patriotic heroes but also as local figures of authority. They have succeeded in converting a criminal past, and a marginal social position within the community before the conflict, into an upward shift in their social, criminal, and political position. They have become brokers—or middlemen. As such, they are strategic players in the local governance of an economy of mutual benefit operating at the interstices of the community, political, and illegal spheres. This economy extends locally to players in each of these three spheres that then generate symbolic and/or unimaginable or impossible material benefits, even if they rely exclusively on the state sphere for the distribution of goods and basic services. The political context reinforces its legitimacy; the community finds itself with privileged access to scarce resources, or resources poorly distributed by the state, and so these four men have become pillars of the political, social, and local economy. It is this strategic position that gives them support and protection from formal social or institutionalized controls.

From the foregoing, it is evident that the authority enjoyed by these four men does not draw its origins exclusively from the exploitation of the framework of symbolic references, such as the patriotic hero. In addition to idiosyncratic moral standards, it is the development and crystallization of a wider range of uses related to the redistribution of capital and maintaining mutually beneficial links between themselves and the community and political spheres, that makes these men strategic actors. It is through their position as brokers, and the exchanges this permits between the different spheres critical to local governance, that one can explain the authority and the symbolic capital enjoyed by these four men. Therefore, Radislav, Ivan, Nenan, and Janko occupy a special place in the exercise of local power since their position makes them actors able to "govern" locally—in the sense of Michel Foucault, that is to say "structure the possible field of action of others"[33] and to be sure of their "consent," namely their silence on an incriminating past.

At the Individual Level: An Ambivalent Relationship With Violence

The advantages achieved in the collective sphere, such as social status and a strategic position within a trusted network that protect Radislav, Ivan, Nenan, and Janko contrast with the costs of the experience of mass violence experienced on an individual and personal level. Indeed, the remodeling of self-image in this sphere does not show the same *success story* as their rehabilitation at a collective level. At times cracks appear despite their past actions being inscribed in the tradition of protecting country and nation, linking them to the pantheon of mythic Serb heroes. These cracks appear in their speeches, their emotions, and their *hexis*, or the assimilation of their experience into their body. The intimacy permitted by an ethnographic approach facilitates the discovery of a relationship with themselves that is a less unequivocal aspect of their commitment, one that is not inevitably seen as a *necessary* sacrifice for the nation.

Their relationship with violence enables this phenomenon to be understood. It is ambivalent and varied considerably during the time spent in their company. This link to violence needs to be addressed through the prism of a fundamental distinction, as it appeared in the ethnography. According to a now classic categorization, it is useful to distinguish a potentiality for violence (or *mythical* violence) from an act of violence (or violence lived). The former is seen in its virtual or fantasy aspect and refers to *fantasized consequences* of its being exercised, without it actually taking place. Mythical violence refers to a teleological awareness, that is to say, as a means to an end. It is not generally perceived as problematic by participants as long as it is justified in the name of an objective considered legitimate by the actors. Generally, this violence is inscribed in a mythical global frame activating the nationalist representations described earlier. As for violence in action, or violence lived, this refers to the *consequences experienced* from its past exercise, and which are expressed in the present context under certain conditions that we shall return to in more detail. Unlike mythical violence, this type of violence is often relived by participants in a traumatic way, at times provoking strong reactions.

Mythical Awareness of Violence

During a discussion about the presence of Islam in the Balkans, Radislav rebelled against the desire—and the right—of a group of local Muslims to build a mosque in the area. Announcing that he would prevent this, we asked how he would achieve this. He replied: "I'll tell you what will happen, I'll let them built it, complete it, even inaugurate it and then...I'll contact two or three people who you've met [...] and ask them to set fire to it...It's as simple as that. They'll understand that they are not welcome here."

Negotiation is seen as a waste of time since the physical destruction of this mosque enables him, in his eyes and the *idea* that he has of it, to obtain complete satisfaction. The potentiality for violence, or mythical violence, as a means of achieving his goals, is reflected in the vision that Radislav has of children's education. He considers it important that they become familiar with it because "it's what makes men of them." Also, some people in his entourage, including Ivan, were active at one time in a combat sport, and the features on some of the faces suggest a journey into the grips of physical violence. The potential for violence—or as a potential means of achieving one's objectives—is a way of perceiving oneself but also presenting oneself to others. For those participants it is a mark of distinction. Showing a readiness to violence, or showing that it is not to be feared, also fits more broadly into the economy of local relationships and the maintenance of a position of authority. It enshrines those who are socially engaged—whether by war or combat sports—and gives them if not that of leader, at least the status of a man. Man is always fashioned in the image that these participants create. From a potentiality for violence that is not problematic in the eyes of these participants, the feeling grows, for the *outsider*, that it could explode unexpectedly. Two examples may serve to explain this.

After the slaughter of a pig, a popular local dish, Radislav, in the tone of a joke, took advantage of us being foreigners, to try to convince us that, according to local tradition, anyone witnessing the killing of a pig for the first time brings bad luck to the farmer. He tells us with complete seriousness that the only way to remedy this is to slaughter a beast in turn. We refuse categorically to do this but he tries to convince us saying: "But don't worry, you may be surprised at yourself," clearly referring to the act of slaughter. At another time during the fieldwork, when we were all sitting around a table in a bar and the discussion turned to the activities of the men of Naser Orić in the region of Srebrenica in 1991,[34] Ivan suddenly got up from the table and announced: "Come on guys, let's all get in a car, cross the border and slit some throats."

These examples provide a window on a "sustainable and replicable, system of transposition that functions as a matrix of perception, of awareness" that would seem to support the hypothesis of a transposition of a violent habitus. However, to assert that there is a direct transposition in a context of peace of a violent habitus[35] developed during war should be treated with caution. Nonetheless, even though these examples were not translated into reality, these episodes referring to a violent act enable a transition to be made to the second element of this fundamental distinction, namely the relationship with violence *enacted* or lived.

The Traumas of Violence Experienced

If potential for violence is valued, this attitude contrasts with a violence enacted, or lived—that participants experienced as perpetrators or as witnesses—which, for some, is experienced in a traumatic way. For example, and to take one of the examples described above, Radislav asked us one day to go with him to a farm, where he ordered a pig to be killed and prepared: "You who do research on violence and who want to know how it was during the war, you must accompany me tomorrow morning." While we are witnessing the killing of the beast,[36] he acknowledges: "Did you see that? Did you notice the precise gestures, the disciplined people? Each one knew what they had to do and everything happened in silence. It is with people like that that I worked with in Croatia. I don't like to see that—it reminds me of difficult things."

Radislav admits that this killing brings back pictures of scenes of violence whose postconflict survival—and out of the frameworks of violence that were then the action—cause moments of anxiety and panic that he has difficulty controlling. Fieldwork was punctuated by moments when it was clear that violence in action was seen in a traumatic way. Its exercise was ravaging its author. For example, one evening, when we had talked a lot about Radislav's experiences in Croatia, he said he needed some air and would step outside for a moment when in the discussion he suddenly said: "You know since you came here I haven't been sleeping, I dream every night [...], I think there are many of us who regret what happened. We didn't have any choice it's true, it was our Serb brothers who were being killed in Croatia, in Bosnia, in Kosovo. Enemies must be eliminated. But even so, lives were broken, families destroyed [...]."

Unlike the mythical violence, violence lived is not commonplace, and these comments show that Radislav is not indifferent to the fate of the victims. This seems to be confirmed not only by his recognition of the pain felt by the families of victims, but also because he would not rule out the idea of participating in a truth and reconciliation commission with the families of those who died. Just as Nenan was also to admit that the memory of the victims haunts him and he finds great difficulty in speaking about it. His experience did not "numb" him and his anguish and moments of panic show that it was part of his psyche, forming a *hexis* experience of violence. It is this that tends to a rejection of the hypothesis of "post-war brutality"[37] as far as he is concerned. His difficulty in tracing the thread of his own story, as well as the stages of his career and the reasons leading to this violence, is a mystery even to him. It is a reason why he abandoned his prewar occupation. He claims that after the killings—for which he made use of knowledge acquired in his civilian life in order to "spare the suffering"—it was no longer possible, from his moral viewpoint, to resume his prewar profession. The situations of Nenan and Radislav contrast however with the case of Janko, who does not show the same compassion for the people who were killed.

This experience of violence marks a major change in their professional careers, notably that of Radislav. In the intimacy of the ethnographic observations, it appears that violence in action also marks a break in his personal journey. Participation in violence develops over time and is a succession of events, or ordered sequences. However, from the standpoint of the perpetrator, it is very difficult to trace *post facto* the coherence of the events that led him to such violent acts and to an understanding of how he came to commit them. It is this linkage between the objective (the events and circumstances affecting the career) and the subjective (changes of perspectives, decisions, and motivations of the actor)[38] dimensions, as operated in each phase, or event, and which determines the next step that the participants struggle to retrace. Although it was never expressed in this way, a break in his journey is also observable in the case of Nenan, who wanders the Balkans with no fixed employment, even though he once had a steady job as a professional soldier. Thus, positive and beneficial identity reconfigurations, triggered by the remnants of war in a collective way are offset by a great difficulty in making sense of such an investment in violence on an individual and personal level. This ethnography reveals the importance of distinguishing between the collective mode from the individual or personal mode, of the transposition of the remnants of the experience of violence and reconversion of these veterans.

Finally, the description of the violence lived allows us to return more generally to the mythical awareness, as defined above. The apparent traumas described suggest that regardless of a macho environment, they constitute a means by which these individuals are able to handle, in a postconflict context, actions that were unjustifiable. In other words, by claiming that they acted for the good of the nation, we could hypothesize that such participants, in accordance with a principle of denial as proposed by Stanley Cohen,[39] develop such a metamorphosis in their perception of themselves that they eventually develop new beliefs and moral standards, including that of the merits of a mythical violence. The perception of their past actions as a sacrifice as part of a semantic framework, related to the preservation of the nation, may, in this respect, be considered as a means—conscious or otherwise—to manage the violence lived and its traumatic effects.

The Transposition of the Register of Violence and the Question of the Violent Habitus

Is it possible to talk of a constitution of a *habitus of war* or *violence*? If this notion is interesting, what has been discussed in this chapter and although admittedly based on a small sample, and, moreover, principally on the account by Radislav, it nonetheless allows us to make three concluding remarks. These tend to relativize a *direct* transposition of a habitus of violence into the context of a transition from war to peace.

First, if we observe the presence of a nonproblematic mythical violence, violence in action, or lived as an author or witness does not leave the person unscathed. As such, and given the traumatic way in which this is experienced *post facto*, it is important to stress even more the role played by denial in these individuals with that of a construction of a "structured system of lasting behaviors." While the mythical violence appears to result from a transposition of wartime experiences, which is implicated in the metamorphosis of their perceptual frame, their understanding and their actions, as far as the violence lived is concerned seems to highlight a critical look on such behaviors, a phenomenon hardly compatible with the construction of a habitus.

Second, our fieldwork provided a number of clues suggesting that they were already familiar, before the war, with the gestures used to kill—generally using knives. If we take the example of the farmers who slaughtered the pig, executions such as these inevitably took place before the war. Since these farmers and the four interviewees may well have been part of the same social network, one might presume that these methods of slaughter were familiar to them. This would have made them more assured in the acts of violence against their victims. This seems to suggest a certain similarity of *gesture*. The practice of a martial art before the conflict taught Ivan how to neutralize or immobilize a person physically, and so on. In addition, the development of a habitus of violence, a concept to which this chapter alone cannot do justice, does not see itself a priori in the "only" passage in mass violence, so to say, but more importantly in the larger or global world of these actors, and those who perpetuate it, as shown in the foregoing.[40] This requires a detailed reconstruction of these lives, or careers, and that means having sufficient data. Fieldwork into acts of mass violence, and especially where militiamen are involved, detracts from the need to collect detailed information and to trace the life history of those involved, even though this generates a more systematic and broader knowledge base.

Finally, it is clear that investment in the violence of war contributed to the metamorphosis of these individuals into strategic actors in their community. This transformation, and the maintenance of that status, are also the products of a postconflict mode of management of their past that plays a part in the interaction of these actors with their local community. In other words, in the case of the four men described in this chapter, the experience of war, and the resulting behaviors acquired, can only be converted into symbolic capital as a consequence of a social, political, and community conjuncture likely to give these players the status of patriotic heroes. Translated by Gillian Pritchett.

Notes

1. In this context normalization refers to an absence of systematic violence in the relationships between the actors.
2. P. Bourdieu, *Esquisse d'une théorie de la pratique. Précédé de trois études d'ethnologie kabyle* (Geneva: Librairie Droz, 1972), 178.
3. These are pseudonyms. This research is based on two field studies conducted in Serbia in the mid 2000s. This amounted to two weeks of complete immersion with four individuals

claiming to have been involved in the mass violence that occurred in Croatia in 1991 as well as in Bosnia-Herzegovina between 1992 and 1995.
4. For a more detailed analysis of this question, see M. Glamocak, *La transition guerrière yougoslave* (Paris: l'Harmattan, 2002).
5. For a detailed analysis of the genesis of the political conflict between the SPS and the SPO and the main issues of this conflict, see D. Stojanovic, "The Traumatic Circle of the Serbian Opposition" in N. Popov (ed.), *The Road to War in Serbia. Trauma and Catharsis,* (Budapest: Central European University Press, 1996), 449–478.
6. This commitment is part of a broader dynamic of legitimacy of war between the two major parties that sought to win the hearts and minds of the Serbs in Croatia in view of the possible elections if the Serbian region of the country achieved independence. The commitment of Radislav, like that of Nenan and Ivan, is part of a wider policy of creating a Greater Serbia, by the nationalist opposition leader, Vuk Drašković. For a more detailed analysis of these dynamics, see M. Glamocak, *La transition guerrière yougoslave*.
7. Vasiljković was born in Belgrade in 1954 but left Yugoslavia for Australia in 1969. He was military advisor in several African wars—Tanzania and Angola. He was often associated with mercenaries. When the conflict threatened to erupt in 1990, he returned to Yugoslavia and immediately joined the Serbian Renewal Movement. For more information about Vasiljković, see his testimony on February 19, 20, and 21, 2003, at the trial of former president Slobodan Milošević (IT-02-54).
8. For a detailed chronology of these events, the reader should refer to the excellent book by L. Silber and A. Little, *The Death of Yugoslavia,* (London/New York: Penguin Books/BBC Books, 1995).
9. "Originally developed in studies of occupations, the concept refers to the sequence of movements from one position to another in an occupational system made by any individual who works in that system." H. S. Becker, *Outsiders: Studies in the Sociology of Deviance* (New York: Free Press, 1963), 24.
10. For a general description of the events that marked the fall of Vukovar, and in particular the type of violence that accompanied it, see *The Prosecutor of the Tribunal against Mrksic et al.,* International Tribunal for the Former Yugoslavia, Case IT-95-13a, "Vukovar Hsopital," third consolidated amended indictment, November 15, 2004.
11. These events are all documented in: *Le Nouvel Observateur* and *Reporters sans frontières, Le livre noir de l'ex-Yougoslavie: purification ethnique et crimes de guerre* (Paris: Arléa, 1993).
12. *The Prosecutor of the Tribunal against Momcilo Krajisnik et Biljana Plavsic,* International Tribunal for the Former Yugoslavia, Case IT-00-39 & 40 PT. Nenan states that he was only in this area from Summer 1992.
13. C. R. Stewart, *Hunting the Tiger: The Fast Life and Violent Death of the Balkans' Most Dangerous Man* (New York: St Martin's Press, 2007); F. Foer, *How Soccer Explains the World: An Unlikely Theory of Globalization* (New York: Harper & Collins, 2004).
14. If one takes account of the fact that Nenan was no longer a professional soldier at the time of events in Vukovar.
15. R. Banégas and J. P. Warnier, "Nouvelles figures de la réussite et du pouvoir, " *Politique Africaine* 82 (June 2001): 5–23.
16. Crystallization at the local and community level is what institutionalization is at the state or societal level: the establishment of a stable and permanent order. If institutionalization is consequential to the development of legal rules external to the groups making up society—where every group must abide by a criminal code—crystallization relies on negotiated and implied standards that result from interactions between members of the group. They are continuously reupdateable and reupdated by the group or the community.
17. For a more systematic examination of the concept of imaginaire, see J. Sémelin, *Purify and Destroy: The Political Uses of Massacre and Genocide* (New York: Columbia University Press, 2007).
18. This was particularly shown in the analyses of X. Bougarel, *Bosnie, anatomie d'un conflit* (Paris: La Découverte, 1996).
19. Xavier Bougarel defines Oustachi as follows: "The term 'Oustachi' (*ustasa,* pl. *ustasi*) means insurgent. Originally, it had no national connotation, might designate a hajduk, and is sometimes used during the Balkan wars to describe...the Serbian Chetniks! It only gets its current meaning of Croatian nationalist extremist during the Second World War." Ibid., 34. As for the concept of "Turk," this is used to pejoratively designate Muslims of the former Yugoslavia and

relates back to the various invasions of Serbian territory by the Ottoman Empire and the many wars that have characterized relations between the two groups.
20. For a detailed analysis of this dimension, see I. Colovic, *Politics of Symbol in Serbia: Essays in Political Anthropology* (London: Hurst & Company, 2002).
21. This is only a very schematic presentation of the participation of the Chetniks. Numerous alliances between the different sides have been highlighted. For example, these warriors fought briefly both as allies of the Axis forces and as Tito's partisans. For a more comprehensive analysis, see Jozo Tomasevich, *The Chetniks: War and Revolution in Yugoslavia, 1941–1945* (Stanford, CA: Stanford University Press, 1975).
22. A good example is Dobrica Ćosić, a Serbian writer who was president of the Federal Republic of Yugoslavia (Serbia & Montenegro) from 1992 to 1993, before being ousted by Milošević. He had been expelled from the Communist Party by Tito in 1968 because of his writings promoting the Serbian nationalism.
23. This distrust is especially motivated by a sense that the region has been abandoned by the central government even though it faces enormous economic and social challenges, including a high unemployment rate. In addition, with the exception of certain individuals who became rich during the war, the majority of the population lives very modestly.
24. R. Brubaker, *Ethnicity Without Groups* (Cambridge: Harvard University Press, 2004).
25. Nenan did not have any involvement in these "little jobs."
26. It seems surprising that as a health professional Radislav was involved in such activities. However, we hypothesize that it is in the prism of his local integration, his relationships with his friends, and as a member of his community, that these activities should be considered rather than from the angle of criminal intent *as such*.
27. Like any system of regulation, the *komsije* empowered, where there was, for example, assistance to individuals in need, participation in both happy and unhappy events that some families lived through, invitations to and participation in family religious festivals. But it constrained, or subjugated also, and its standards exert pressure to conform. Indeed, any alternative, whether ideological or behavioral, is made difficult and ostracizes. Strategies guilt or humiliation encourage adherence to codes of interaction. Consequently, the actions of members of the community do not systematically result from individual preferences. They may be the result of a need—or necessity—of integration or compliance. This tight, almost organic web that underlies these social ties constitutes the fabric of an extremely efficient *informal* social control enabling community members to be informed of any deviation by an individual. The *komsije* are thus simultaneously aware of methods of local subjectivation; it tends to homogenize the representations, expectations, and preferences of community members.
28. It should be noted nonetheless that the ideas of Radislav and the other men are not endorsed by the entire community. But from the perspective of a population that has literally felt abandoned by Belgrade for several years, Radislav is seen as someone who is active and who is concerned about the future of the community.
29. The majority of these individuals did not wish to answer questions. The fact remains that ethnography accompanying Radislav in his travels around the region have revealed an extensive network of contacts and active support in his efforts to promote the ideas of this political party.
30. For a more detailed analysis of the role of social networks and the links of support and confidence that these promote, see C. Tilly, *Trust and Rule* (New York: Cambridge University Press, 2005); R. V. Gould, *Insurgent Identities: Class, Community and Protest in Paris from 1848 to the Commune* (Chicago: The University of Chicago Press, 1995).
31. Diego Gambetta, *The Sicilian Mafia: The Business of Private Protection* (Cambridge, MA: Harvard University Press, 1993).
32. Vadim Volkov, *Violent Entrepreneurs: The Use of Force in the Making of Russian Capitalism* (Ithaca, NY: Cornell University Press, 2002), 27.
33. M. Foucault, "Le sujet et le pouvoir," in *Dits et écrits II, 1976–1988* (Paris: Gallimard (Quarto), 2001), 1056.
34. For more information on the actions of these men, see *The Prosecutor of the Tribunal against Naser Oric*, International Tribunal for the former Yugoslavia, Case IT-03-68, Indictmnent, October 4, 2004.
35. Of course, this does not systematically imply acting on it. Let us remember that for Pierre Bourdieu practice does not occur in the strict transposition of a habitus but rather in the conjuncture of a situation and the habitus. The habitus does not systematically imply violent behavior.

36. This event involved three men and proceeds in the following way (according to our field notes): "The three men are focused, they talk for a few seconds and then the father makes a sign to the third guy to get the animal. From there, events unfold quickly: the man comes back from the barn with the pig, an animal of a good size, and leads it to the execution site; the son deals a sharp blow with a solid object attached to a long stick, the animal slumps trembling on its side. The father, positionned behind it, immediately puts his left arm around its neck, and with the right hand slits its throat in an extremely fast gesture. The incision is such that the animal did not have the time to struggle [...]."
37. In contrast to the results of the postconflict brutality in advanced societies put forward by G. L. Mosse, *Fallen Soldiers. Reshaping the Memory of the World Wars* (Oxford: Oxford University Press, 1990).
38. H. S. Becker, *Outsiders,* 47. It is here that a difficulty is felt by Radislav and the relationship he has with himself and the killer within since his current preferences and prospects do not have much to do with those from the time of his actions. But the traces of this experience remain present in his everyday life, and it seems, in a traumatic way.
39. S. Cohen, *States of Denial: Knowing about Atrocities and Sufferings* (Cambridge/Malden: Polity/Blackwell Publishers, 2001).
40. This is notably a position defended by N. Mariot in "Faut-il être motivé pour tuer? Sur quelques explications aux violences de guerre," *Genèses* 53 (2003): 154–177.

CHAPTER EIGHT

Museveni's Best Enemies: Dilemmas and Political Uses of the Reintegration of Former Lord's Resistance Army (LRA) Commanders in Northern Uganda[1]

SANDRINE PERROT

Abstract

The return to northern Uganda after 2003 of adults and commanders of the Lord's Resistance Army (LRA) in a no peace no war context has posed legal, political, and security challenges for the Ugandan government. This chapter shows that by encouraging and politically exploiting the successful reintegration of a few high ranking ex-commanders, the Ugandan government has been trying to win over—or at least control—this stronghold of political and military opposition. However, by perpetuating war hierarchies, chains of command, and mobilization networks, the political use of LRA chiefs by the government is simply putting off the "civilianization" of former combatants and the pacification of the political arena, in other words, the demilitarization of political relations between northern Uganda and the central government.

Microcosm

September 2005. Gulu. It was the first time I had met Brigadier K. B. one of the oldest commanders of the LRA. The gardens of the Acholi Inn where he told me to meet him were host to a very unusual clientele for anyone who had been following the developments of the northern Uganda conflict. Among humanitarian workers, UN agency representatives, researchers, passing journalists, and other city personalities, the former Ugandan minister and mediator for the latest peace talks Betty Bigombe, Colonel Charles Otema, head of military intelligence for North Uganda and owner of the hotel, several Acholi dignitaries and Brigadier K., former LRA emissary, all sat at the same table. K. quickly walked away from our table after having greeted us. He had just politely declined my request for an interview: "I may accept... If I want to...," he quipped with a smile, without my being able to tell whether it was provocation on the part of a commander raised a few months prior to the status of "VIP" or cautious detachment from the game of questions and answers with which he had little familiarity and that could have compromised his safety and recently acquired status.

Since they had come out of the bush, several of the former LRA commanders had joined the quarters of the Ugandan army's Fourth Division. Others lived at the hotel at the government's expense. They had become the government's ostentatious guests in the small city's luxury residence. The scene would have been unthinkable two years before. The LRA was known for its forced conscription of child-soldiers and its attacks against civilians—the very same people with whom it was now supposed to cohabit. But especially, the government and the army hardliners who were staunch partisans of a military option since the conflict began in 1987, refused at the time to engage in talks with the "remaining elements" of a group of "criminals," "bandits," and "thugs." Seizing an opportunity to align itself with US policy, Kampala had managed to get the LRA placed on the state department list of terrorist organizations in December 2001. The disconcerting microcosm of the Acholi Inn was revealing of several major changes at once in the course of the war, in the range of scenarios envisioned to exit it and in the treatment granted to former LRA combatants. Their demobilization raised military, legal, and political challenges. How would the government handle the reintegration of the most senior LRA commanders in a context where several hundred, maybe even thousands, of LRA combatants were still in the bush?[2] Under pressure from associations of parents of abducted children, religious and human rights organizations, and local officials, the government passed an amnesty law in 2000 that was to facilitate the defection of combatants and the return of children abducted by the rebels. But was it also applicable to those who bore criminal responsibility for the atrocities and war crimes committed? And what role would former combatants and their leaders play during the referendum campaign on the return of multipartism, the 2006 presidential election, and the future transition to peace? Did the government have reason to fear political radicalization in the northern region through a convergence of the political opposition and the former military opposition?

This chapter sets out to demonstrate that through the differential treatment received by certain senior commanders for their reintegration, the government was working in part to restore security in the north. But it was also, and perhaps especially, trying to conquer politically—or at least control—this opposition's stronghold. In this context, the measures set up by the government to demobilize and reintegrate former LRA commanders were less a tool for the return to civilian life than an instrument of domination and political clientelism.

LRA Commanders: "Returnees" Unlike The Others

The process of demobilizing former LRA commanders was carried out in a context of neither war nor peace. Despite the start of peace talks in Juba in July 2006 and the signing of a ceasefire agreement in August of the same year, no peace accord has yet been signed to date (March 2011) between the Ugandan government and the LRA. Security has now returned to northern Uganda, but the LRA has since deployed in the northeast of the Democratic Republic of Congo, southern Sudan, and eastern Central Africa, where it has established new bases.[3]

No national disarmament, demobilization, and reintegration (DDR) program had been implemented in the North. Since the 1990s, the large majority of those that in the North were euphemistically called "returnees"[4] (often translated in the North, in Acholiland, as "our children") were children forcibly conscripted by the LRA. Adults who trickled back following a facedown with the army or after fleeing the LRA were scarcely taken into account by local and international programs, which focused their efforts on child-soldiers and child-mothers.[5] The Amnesty Commission, however, provided those who applied for amnesty (the "reporters"), with materiel support (mattress, blanket, plastic tub, jerry can, hoe, etc.) as well as financial support (approximately $150). The World Bank Multi-Country Demobilization and Reintegration Program (MDRP) had taken charge of managing the reintegration programs as of January 2005, mainly to buttress the work of the Amnesty Commission. But many former combatants, out of fear of reprisal or simply lack of information, returned home directly without bothering to go through the reception centers, making their return go unnoticed.[6]

Operation Iron Fist and The Return of Former Commanders

Operation Iron Fist, launched in 2002, by the government's Uganda People's Defense Forces (UPDF) against the LRA's rear base in southern Sudan hastened the flow of demobilizations—forced or voluntary—and considerably altered the profile of the demobilized. Starting in 2003, it brought about a wave of returns not only of children, but also, quite unexpectedly, of adult combatants as well as middle-ranking and senior commanders.[7] Faced with heightened military pressure in late 2003–early 2004 and the tarnishing of LRA leader Joseph Kony's spiritual aura, commanders began deserting in greater numbers.[8] Lacking weapons and ammunition and later food and medicine, worn-out fighters surrendered "not to die in the bush."[9] According to army figures, at least 1,000 LRA combatants surrendered between January and November 2004, including 84 commanders, in the months of June and July 2004 alone.[10] Other figures also provided by a military source cite 46 officers (of the rank of second lieutenant and higher) between April and mid-August 2004,[11] some returning accompanied by several dozen simple soldiers and other members.[12] The Resident District Commissioner (RDC) in Gulu gave the figure of 1,431 persons of all ranks that came out of the bush for the period from December 2003 to mid-July 2004 alone, including one lieutenant colonel, three majors, 12 captains, 18 lieutenants, and 18 second lieutenants.[13]

These contradictions and approximations in the accounting matter little. The war had been raging since 1987 without anyone ever knowing the precise numerical strength of the armed group or the number of its victims.[14] On the ground, the return of huge numbers of combatants was clearly perceptible. The reception centers were full to capacity. The Amnesty Commission accumulated delays in processing the former combatants and issuing their reinsertion packages.[15] Healing or cleansing ceremonies organized by traditional Acholi chiefs (*rwodi*), or clan chiefs, to facilitate the return of former combatants were more and more frequent. In groups of sometimes nearly one hundred, returnees submitted to these rituals that had been modernized with the support—and sometimes instigation—of international donors, in keeping with the current enthusiasm for traditional justice.

Each "big catch" was moreover highlighted in the army's press releases. A few days after coming back, Brigadier B.'s return was conspicuously exposed in the media as a major army capture. Commander Onen Kamdulu, around age 30 at the time, suspected of several serious crimes such as having ordered the massacre of 27 persons in the village of Olupe in the Pader district on October 22, 2002, and having the victims hacked to pieces and cooked in pots, had defected just after B. was captured. He was later exhibited as a hero in the rear of a vehicle before presenting himself as a liaison officer between the government and the still active members of the LRA.[16] Others had been interviewed upon their return on the local radio Mega FM; still others were greeted as stars at political rallies. All this agitation surrounding LRA military officials reflected both the hope of an exit to the conflict suddenly made possible by the return of these senior officers, but also the particular place they occupied in the scheme of managing returnees.

Government Management of Returnees

Up until then, the Ugandan government had been little involved in the process of reintegrating former combatants. It had left it up to NGOs and other international programs to manage the reintegration of the younger combatants, officially devoting its effort to financing the modernization of the army and the prosecution of the war. For many years, it had been reluctant to pass an amnesty law. The Amnesty Commission was moreover funded mainly by the World Bank. But beginning in 2003, the North had become a considerable source of irritation in relations between Uganda and its financial backers. They finally questioned the government's military capabilities and especially its political determination to resolve the war in the North, which had become an instrument of containment of the opposition and a source of profit for a part of the army high command. The conflict furthermore had acquired renewed international visibility after the visit of Jan Egeland, UN undersecretary-general for humanitarian affairs, in November 2003, cast it into the spotlight.[17]

But the defections, both partial and massive, of LRA adult members and ranking officers posed the Ugandan government internal and external challenges. External, because the donors and the outside world had to be convinced that the government was doing something. Internal, because the attempt to resolve the conflict in the North was part of the government's strategy to reconquer this opposition stronghold. The army's objective was to deprive the LRA of a portion of its armed command and divide the remainder of the leadership still active in the bush. But most of all, the preelection context further sensitized the issue of demobilizing and reintegrating former combatants. Throughout the North, over 80 percent of the opposition to the regime voted for the challenger to incumbent President Museveni in the 2001 presidential election, a percentage that had grown constantly since 1996. For a long time, the northern vote had had little influence on the country's political balance, easily dominated by President Museveni's Movement (formerly National Resistance Movement, or NRM). But recent cracks in the block of support for the movement in its historic southwest bastion and risks of an alliance between southern and northern opposition leaders made the government nervous as the 2006 presidential and legislative elections approached. Reintegration of former LRA commanders was to serve as one of the starting points to mobilize the northern electorate that had deserted it since 1996.

The return of adult LRA members also led to a reinterpretation of the nature of the armed group, a far cry from the idealized image of child-soldiers grouped around a charismatic leader. The problem at hand was no longer minors abducted or forcibly conscripted by the LRA only but also commanders, some of which had voluntarily joined the LRA, sometimes as early as 1987. Others, after their abduction, had gradually climbed the ranks of the armed group, consolidating their warmongering habitus over the long years spent in the bush.[18] This led to partially revising the qualification of the conflict, which the regime in power had until then euphemized and depoliticized. Moreover, the political-military nuisance capacity of the adult *returnees* with regard to the government was much greater than that of the child-soldiers. Their political opposition to Museveni was more articulate, the officers' wish to set up in the big cities (for lack of demobilization centers) rather than their home villages was stronger and hence their ability to organize and mobilize greater and more visible.[19]

The returnees' own relationship to the atrocities perpetrated and thus to reprisals and legal proceedings were consequently altered. It was more difficult for officers than for the rank and file to plead legal irresponsibility for the war crimes and crimes against humanity committed.[20] The terminology used in northern Uganda reflected the fragmentation of the group of former combatants. Instead of the neutral expression of "returnees," the Amnesty Commission preferred the technical and administrative approach of "reporters" (those who reported to the Commission). The passive notion of "ex-abductees" took hold through NGOs and reception centers for children abducted by the LRA. But contrary to this victimizing rhetoric, senior ranking officers were referred to as "ex-commanders" or "ex-rebels," thereby retaining a trace of their military past, when such terms did not take on more insulting forms for a given individual.

The complaint filed in December 2003 by the Ugandan government before the brand new International Criminal Court underscored this gradation of responsibility of the former combatants in the armed conflict. It highlighted the government's ambiguous position with regard to the legal status of the LRA commanders and the constantly renegotiated tension between prosecution and amnesty. For nearly two years, until five international warrants for arrest were issued against the main LRA leaders in October 2005, the regime officials' double discourse had shrouded in uncertainty the fate of LRA officers, including those who had been demobilized or defected and already obtained a government amnesty.[21] Such prevarication was, at least at first, part of a strategy of government and military takeover of the demobilization and reintegration process of the former LRA commanders. The government intended to keep the most senior commanders as its exclusive domain. Having realized the stakes of conflict resolution and postconflict in northern Uganda, it then engaged in a selective policy of promotion and co-optation of certain LRA commanders.

A Selective Reintegration Policy

Upon their return from the bush, some ex-LRA commanders had been held up as symbols of a conflict on the way to being resolved. Their presence in town was to attest to the military effectiveness of Operation Iron Fist although the latter was criticized for the humanitarian consequences it had caused.[22] It also served as a basis for the governments double counterinsurgency policy, which involved making a clear distinction between combatants who opted for peace, who were given physical, material, and legal security, although depending on the circumstances and renegotiable according to the army's and central government's pleasure, and those who remained in the bush, for whom a military solution was required. However, in the space of a few months, within the very group of former combatants who had come out of the bush, a subtle game of inclusion and exclusion would take hold through a careful selection of beneficiaries of government privileges. The imposition of emblematic reintegration examples offered a means of concealing the failed trajectories of other veterans and imposing official mouthpieces of success in matters of reintegration.

Emblematic Reintegration Examples

"To treat [all former commanders] the same way is difficult. People who are stubborn can not be treated the same way."
Interview with F., former LRA combatant, Gyda reintegration center, December 2006[23]

"One year ago, I was shaking. But these days, it is okay."[24] This laconic statement made during our second meeting nevertheless well reflects Brigadier B.'s trajectory over a year and a half. Most commanders had been demobilized or integrated into the army with no ado.[25] Many of them had joined the 105th battalion, an army unit made up exclusively of former LRA members and the spearhead for counterinsurgency operations conducted against their former armed group. Some were even promoted to higher ranks.[26] Only a few commanders enjoyed privileged status, receiving a vehicle and, in the early days, a military escort in addition to a monthly army salary. B., the LRA's former military strategist, in his sixties at the time, was one of the closest and especially longest advisors of LRA leader Kony. He was one of the first to enjoy such preferential treatment.[27] His post-LRA trajectory was probably one of the most successful undertakings to convert the resources of violence into social, economic, and symbolic capital. His capture had a major psychological impact on the LRA combatants as much as on the outside actors present in the North.[28] It was interpreted (prematurely) as the signal of the imminence of a postconflict era that UN agencies were already busy preparing.[29]

B., a former helicopter pilot trained in the USSR, had served in Idi Amin's army before joining the Uganda National Liberation Army (UNLA), the former national army, at the end of the 1970s. It was at that time that he allegedly became the escort for then minister and future President Museveni.[30] He claimed to have been forced to join the LRA in October 1987 after the LRA threatened to execute his family.[31] He remained in the bush for 18 years. He was captured while commanding a group of some one hundred combatants in northern Uganda. Lack of food and medical care had weakened him physically. For our first meeting in 2005, he hobbled out of his residence located in the military quarter.

He wanted to wait for L., the star emcee of the local radio program *Dwog Cen Paco* (Come back Home), devoted to former LRA combatants, before starting the interview. After a brief and informal check of my identity and function, the latter then called for "respect" for the former commanders who had to be considered as "human beings" and stressed their fragile financial condition and the need to help them, without going into detail as to how to go about it. Leaving the table a few minutes later, he left Brigadier B. tense and wary of the slightest rustle of leaves that the sudden wind had caused to stir. The tea shared at the end of our interview restored to our meeting the strange and off-beat charm of a conversation in high society: "I have a family, a wife and children in Great Britain you know. I could have a life there," he then confided to me.

Yet, one year later, B.'s desire to leave the country seemed far away. I found him in better health and fluttering from one table to the next at the Boma, a newly built luxury hotel in Gulu where, gauging from the number of people he greeted before reaching my table, he was a regular customer. Although his name at first appeared on the list of those to be indicted by the International Criminal Court, he had secured an amnesty right after he was captured. "We haven't asked for an amnesty. We got it automatically," says another senior commander.[32] The former LRA commander then said that Museveni himself had assured him that despite the ICC indictment, his immunity would not be called into question.[33] B. had indeed quickly become the government's model for the successful reintegration of former combatants to the extent that members of parliament were mystified as to his official status: "This B[.], Sir, I do not know what his status is. Is he a prisoner of war, or is he somebody that is going to be prosecuted because when you watch television, he is being treated like a VIP. He goes all over the place and waves to people and so forth. Now, if he was a prisoner of war, I do not think that he would be receiving the kind of treatment that he is receiving right now," declared MP Mwondha.[34]

Other returns had been brilliantly supervised or at least staged by the army. Brigadier K., former police officer in his 40s upon his return, was also one of the rare privileged returnees. Former LRA spokesman in the negotiations held with mediator Betty Bigombe in late 2004, K. had defected in mid-February 2005 after disobeying a command from Kony ordering him back to Sudan. He was exfiltrated by an army helicopter after he had found out that Kony was threatening to arrest him. Closely connected to Bigombe's team, he mixed with UN circles and spoke regularly in various conferences on the conflict and the means to resolve it. More discreet and less flamboyant than B., for over a year K. hedged about what he would do in his new civilian life. He had returned to his studies to become an economist and worked a farm in the new Amuru district. "I hope Government will support me and the rest who need special treatment so that we can study. This is also one of the best ways for me to have national or international reconciliation with all categories of people," he commented after receiving his school's best score for his Uganda Advanced Certificate of Education in 2008.[35] Lieutenant Colonel A. Joseph Kony's Chief escort, had been interviewed in tears a few days after his capture, thanking the army for not killing him. A former member of the Ugandan army under Museveni's regime, he had joined the LRA at age 34 after a stint in prison for treason in 1996. He had been captured 40 km from Gulu with two of his young wives, a baby, and two adolescents.[36] He since exhibits the scar in his abdomen where three bullets were removed thanks to a Gulu military hospital doctor who had thus saved his life. He had become head of a former combatants association that used to meet regularly in the offices of the army's Fourth Division Unit for Child Protection headquartered in Gulu. All of these figures had become as it were civilian officers for the UPDF. B. had also become the leader and virtually official spokesman for former combatants in Gulu. With a handful of others, he played a pivotal role in the process of reintegrating former combatants.

Officially, the reintegration of former commanders was used as a test for the entire demobilization and pacification process. These demobilizations were used as a reintegration showcase aiming to reassure the remaining combatants about their future and convince them to come out of the bush. In this regard they had a "pull-out effect" on still-active LRA members. "The reintegration can't fail. We tested it with the top commanders. They wouldn't have walked in the streets in the very first days and see now," pointed out Colonel A., in charge of civil-military relations for the UPDF.[37] In fact, by selecting its interlocutors from within the LRA high command, the government and the army had above all imposed official and exclusive models of success spotlighted by a controlled media campaign and financed by structures of mobilization and control.

Government Creation of Structures of Mobilization and Control

The popular local radio station, Mega FM, financed by the British Department for International Development (DFID) and based in Gulu, was one of the instruments of selection and control of the official mouthpieces of reintegration. Through the program *Dwog Cen Paco* launched in December 2003 to broadcast returnee testimonials, radio MC L., whose relations with the military intelligence services were ambiguous, became the privileged interlocutor, even the overseer of former LRA commanders. The program was originally intended to defeat the LRA line of argument claiming that those who wished to flee the movement would be killed by the army or lynched by the population on their return to Uganda. It broadcast news of combatants' families and exhorted those who were still active to come out of the bush. But the program also hushed up failed social and economic attempts at reintegration of the majority. "We don't have access to Mega. They won't let us talk about what's really happening out there. Mega is the government's radio station. They don't want us to criticize it," one former rank and file combatant who was discontent with his social and economic situation noted.[38] Commanders sponsored by the army and the government were those who were interviewed, who were asked to participate in workshops, who were paraded in the districts, sponsored former combatant associations to raise funds and were invited to the State House, President Museveni's official residence. The song *Lukeme* by Acholi singer Guti Kwaro praised these muses of reintegration and called on the commanders still in the bush to follow their example.

Veterans associations that financed these imposed models of success were used as vehicles of both mobilization and political and economic exclusion. It was partly to handle the influx of veterans and the return of adult officers that the first former combatant associations had cropped up. Their official aim was to help former combatants achieve economic independence and give them a voice in the postconflict economic and social reconstruction process.[39] Several hundred of them had been formed since 2004, on the initiative of the veterans themselves but also at the government's instigation. The terms "child-soldiers" and "peace and reconciliation" had become the magic words to secure subsidies from the Northern Uganda Social Action Fund (NUSAF), funded by the World Bank. The largest, most structured and most financially endowed associations were run from the big cities (primarily Gulu) by former LRA commanders. They smacked of heavy government and security service involvement (from the army and military intelligence) in their genesis as much as in their operating mode. Other associations on the contrary, no sooner had they been formed, were disbanded by military intelligence on the pretext that they had not been initiated or approved by the army services.[40]

From that standpoint, the Labora Farm project was probably the most controversial. The government's nomination of Brigadier B. to head the project provoked a general outcry from humanitarian organizations, which pointed to accusations of sexual exploitation (particularly of very young girls) hanging over B. NGOs and UN agencies put pressure on the World Bank to make it alter the project organization chart. Shortly afterward, Brigadier B. officially left the project leadership but continued to have considerable influence over the program behind the scenes. This controversy reflects the dual process of reintegration that took hold in Uganda: on one hand, the process managed by international NGOs designed for the *abductees* (children kidnapped by the LRA) that was based on a psychological view of reintegration dealing with treating posttraumatic symptoms of violence and allied with a criminalization of the LRA commanders; on the other, the process managed with greater opacity by the political and military authorities geared toward a small number of former LRA commanders, which blended co-optation policies and clientelism and hinged around favor and disfavor.

The Case of Labora Farm

"This is just like Labora farm. The process of reintegration in Uganda is a situation that is not in a UN peace of mind. There were a lot of debates about Labora Farm. The main resistance came from NGOs that had a particular interest in maintaining control over the returnees. But there is no established structure. B[.] is not very influential. We want to have a radio program to say that Labora farm is not a classified file. There is no better alternative. What does Hunger Alert do for the returnees?"

Interview with the then Public Relations Officer of the UPDF's Fourth Division, October 2005.

The 200 hectares of Labora Farm are located on government land a few kilometers from Gulu, on the Opit road. The project, with an initial budget of 400 million Shillings (about €175,000 at the time), had been designed by the defense minister and funded by NUSAF, a World Bank funding scheme. In 2005, the farm counted 120 workers. At first, the farm grouped together three agricultural production subprojects, all run by middle-ranking officers: *Lubanga Tek* headed by Captain Ray Apire, known as "Bishop," Kony's former spiritual advisor who had defected in June 2004; *Ribe aye Teko*, headed by Major Jackson Acama; and *Upela* by Innocent Ocan. The land was farmed jointly by former LRA combatants, more precisely young women having been associated with the LRA, and by villagers from nearby camps of displaced persons.

The project's stated goal was to set up the returnees and their families with a perspective of becoming independent.[41] But Labora did not fail to raise both ethical and structural problems of demobilization: first, the question of women employed on the farm and maintained under economic dependence to their former kidnappers and "husbands" in the bush provoked such protest that UNICEF, although a leading force in the reintegration of child-mothers, had refused to sponsor the project. Second, the means of remunerating former LRA members remained opaque. Having the status of community workers, the former LRA combatants were not paid. They were theoretically compensated with a share of the profits from the sales of farm produce. The paid workers from the nearby camp of Te-Tugu, however, received a wage, albeit minimal, of 700 Ush (€0.30) per *katala* (a term of measurement corresponding to a little more than a meter of land) on average. The child-mothers in addition received food aid from the World Food Programme. But during the first two years, the sharing of profits remained opaque. Profits from the sale of the first harvest were supposedly reinvested without anyone knowing the details of where the money went. Third, farm management responsibilities appeared as a reward for the former leaders of the armed group and de facto replicated the LRA hierarchy.[42] Interestingly enough, LRA power dynamics and military hierarchy had been replicated and perpetuated on Labora Farm, under the government's impetus but also more informally within the psychosocial support groups, former combatant associations, in the army and even within the reception centers. The pyramid structure of Labora Farm made it easier for a small group to take over the funding networks for the reintegration of former combatants. Confiscation of these financial flows by the few LRA figures co-opted by the government easily enabled it to control the inclusion–exclusion policy by setting up a financial bottleneck. The internal displacement of 90 percent of the population in the North, the lack of economic opportunities there, the meager parallel financing, and the lack of management experience of the other veterans heightened the effectiveness of this grip on the allocation of resources.

Accused of rewarding the former "criminals of the LRA," the minister in charge of the North, Grace Akello, justified the government's action at the time by the need to build peace, trust, and reconciliation in northern Uganda:

> (…) the Shs 400 million (…) was not given to B[.] as a person. We are (…) in the process of building peace in northern Uganda, and Brig. B[.] has behind him some 20,000 people who came out of the bush, some of them mere children in one way or the other. (…) in the process of building peace, these people must be resettled, these people must have a stake, they must feel that they have something that they own, they must eat, they must be dressed, they must have somewhere to sleep and Brig. B[.] has led them into projects. (…). So, I want to persuade, Capt. Byaruhanga, that this is peace building we are doing, we are not rewarding anybody for anything. (Applause).[43]

It must be admitted a contrario that Labora Farm crystallized combatant identities for those who took part in the project. Contrary to what was initially planned in terms of mixing, former LRA members and villagers farmed separate plots of land, not together but side by side. In this way, better control over the premises and access to the places where resources were accumulated could be exercised. Accumulation of financial and symbolic resources via veterans associations would help build the former commanders' status as "big men." In the space of a few months, former LRA officers established themselves as the inevitable sponsors of the various projects geared toward former combatants. They became the nexus, the "gatekeepers," between the former combatants and their families on one hand, and the government, NGOs and donors on the other, thereby accumulating considerable social and economic capital.

Conversely, the trajectories of failure experienced by other veterans (junior commanders, women, the handicapped), eking out a living sometimes merely as a *boda-boda* (bicycle-taxi operator), turned away by their family or feared by their neighbors, were overshadowed. Not a word was spoken either about the most recalcitrant LRA commanders sent to a reeducation program in an army barrack in the South.[44] A number of former combatants and even former officers excluded from the government's and the army's official clientele networks had been left to their own devices without support or financing. Very often those who were excluded from *Dwog Cen Paco* broadcasts were also those who had not managed to get themselves registered on the list of beneficiaries of reintegration programs or join former combatant associations. After having been associated with the Labora Farm project, Major A., allied with the opposition and at odds with the other senior commanders, had formed his own association, Former Child-Soldiers Development Association (FOCSODA). Betty Akech, former Security Minister and Member of Parliament representing Gulu at first had thrown her support behind him. But wanting to shake off official LRA tutelage bore little fruit. The association collapsed for lack of access to funding.[45] Government promises were not kept. "Betty Akech had promised Ush 30 million but she only got us 15. I saw the check, but I know nothing about the money, bitterly comments N., a former combatant."[46] Capt. A. also feels neglected and betrayed by the government: "(...) When we came back, the government also made us promises: to build homes for the returnees, oxen, seeds. But I only got $100 in my reinsertion package, 260,000 shillings."[47]

Alice had been a lieutenant in the LRA. Since then she has sold coal on the market in Gulu. "The commanders made a list to know who would work on the farm, but my name wasn't on it. I wasn't able to go on NUSAF projects. I don't know why." Then, bitterly pointing out the contradictions of the former commanders' militarized return to "civilian" life: "The names of women on the list were the wives of the ones who worked for the government. When you work for the government, your wife's name appears on the list (...). Why create this sort of tension? They work with the military, I'm a civilian (...). There was no need to bother anyone [with that]. You stay like that and you suffer (...). Life in the bush was the same as today. The only difference is that in the bush, you don't sleep in a house."[48]

The highly selective and politicized success of former LRA commanders, in addition to causing frustration, also raised questions about the role of the international community in fashioning these combatant identities and the funding of these imposed models. In a few months, Labora had become a "model farm," the guided tour of which—led by former LRA commanders—was paced by a well-rehearsed speech on the successful reintegration of former combatants. It had also drained portion of NUSAF funds as well as other international reintegration program funding. "I'm not satisfied [with my life since my return] but with my intelligence, I've managed to make a little money, otherwise I would have gone back to the bush. There's not much business here but the *bazungu* [white people] give money," recounts Lt. Col. A., former LRA commander.[49]

A memo issued by a consortium of NGOs and UN agencies circulating in Gulu in June 2005 criticized Labora Farm as "indicative of the government's absence of ideas in regards to the key concerns of reconciliation and re-integration." In private, NGOs even used words such as "exploitation," "unethical," and "an outrage."[50] None of them, however, offered any real alternatives for commanders, aside from the judicial route.[51] In addition, the international community favored conflict resolution and reconciliation. From this standpoint, as this former commander well understood, the reintegration of former commanders back from the bush had to succeed.

- Former commander: Just after we came back, there was a strong jubilation. People thought that it would be the end of the war. But then, those who lost loved ones can feel bad and ask for a compensation.
- Author: What will you do if you are asked for a compensation?
- Former Commander: We'll ask donors to give money. For us, we won't have anything to pay. For us, we'll probably have to pay only for the girls who were with us in the bush. We'll have to compensate their families for them" (December 2006).

He nevertheless regretted in March 2009 that most of the funds were now attributed to "ex abductees only." "For total peace to prevail and the reintegration to be effective, treat us as the other returnees because we are also incapacitated," he added.[52]

Paradoxically, international funds had sharpened inequalities in the treatment of former combatants. They also in passing and for little cost fed the Movement clientele networks in the north of the country. For beyond pacification of the region, government co-optation of former LRA commanders was also part of a plan for the political capture of this traditional bastion of the opposition.

The Scheme to Gain Political Control of a Traditional Opposition Stronghold

Reintegration of former LRA commanders indeed fit within the broader set of issues of the military-political transition to conflict resolution then being prepared in northern Uganda. Since the early 1990s, attacks against civilians had finally weakened local support for the LRA. Only a few small traders who profited from the armed group's plundering still gave them residual support. But in the absence of effective political opposition to the government, the grievances brought up by the LRA had converged with those of the local population.

The first public appearances of former commanders left little doubt about what political utilization the government intended to make of them. Just a few days after his return—and a stint in the UPDF camp—Brigadier B. received an invitation from the political and military authorities. With the first meetings, he started singing *"Ekisanja,"* the song written by

Bebe Cool in favor of the very controversial constitutional amendment allowing Museveni to run for a third term. Decked in yellow t-shirts (the Movement's color) during the referendum campaign in early 2005, he had also appeared alongside Brig. K. getting out of an army helicopter. Surrounded by the military and regional officials, he briefly apologized for crimes committed before calling on the crowd gathered at Gulu's Pece Stadium to support Museveni's candidacy. One witness points out that it was "a quick turnaround" for people who only a few weeks before were still fighting against the government: "The two of them were undoubtedly under considerable pressure to toe a particular partisan line, but the crowd did not like it. People started to laugh and jeer. A friend muttered to me 'they need to be careful. If the UPDF were not there, they could end up getting themselves lynched.'[53]

No question indeed of "reconciliation" here. What was at stake was the reconfiguration of postconflict power, the relations between the army and the state and the redistribution of economic, political, and symbolic resources.[54] For lack of political mobilization, the presidential party's strategy involved broadening his clientele networks in the North. Reintegration of former LRA commanders was part of the game that involved dividing the Acholi political scene to prevent it from forming the point of convergence among opponents to the regime. Museveni had already co-opted several Acholi MPs who until then had formed the core of opposition to the regime. He was trying to divide the traditional leaders by advocating at once restoration of the Acholi royalty and the creation of a council of elders to offset royal power. He later appointed these political allies, who had lost the 2006 local elections in Gulu and Kitgum, Resident District Commissioners in these same two cities.

Several former LRA commanders had held rallies, particularly all over Pader district, in the company of the commander of the fifth division, the minister in charge of the North and the deputy political commissar. Flanked by a military escort, certain former commanders promised to denounce collaborators of the LRA and those who had lied about the conditions in which former LRA members had been welcomed and who had therefore postponed their return to civilian life, going so far as to give their phone numbers. They thus prolonged the war by other means, transposing the divisions of the war on the post-conflict Acholi society of the future.[55]

> Okwalero told the people that, "The reason why most of us spent a long time in the bush was because of wrong reports that we were getting from you people who are outside, who were seeing light." He even threatened to go and pick some of the collaborators who were seated in the crowd. He said, "if you feel that I am telling you lies, there were some collaborators who were giving us good information, but there were some of you collaborators who were giving us wrong information that 'If you come out, Museveni is there with a

very sharp knife, he will kill you there and then.' Therefore, if you think that I am telling lies, now I am walking.'" He said to the crowd that was seated, and some people felt very cold (...).[56]

"Now, this is the man who is saying there are some leaders who set from Pader here, they agree causing you problems, trying to insinuate that some of us are responsible for their delay in the bush, which is not right. These people move in a convoy of 30 UPDF soldiers, tankers and mambas they are forced to say anything except abusing their mothers (...)," complained the Hon. Odonga Otto, MP for Aru county in Pader district.[57] Far from the process of "cultural demobilization" that might consolidate peace[58] by deeply altering the bellicose rhetoric, collective representations of the enemy, and combatant identities, former commanders were in fact used to buttress the theory that the local population collaborated with the LRA.

Along the same lines, the young Colonel Alfred Onen Kamdulu came to fuel the government's confrontational policy toward an opposition it was seeking to discredit. He was instrumentalized in the legal action taken by Museveni against his main opponent in the presidential election, Kizza Besigye. This opposition figure had been accused of high treason along with 22 other men in 2005 (in the middle of the election campaign) before the Supreme Court in Kampala. Several witnesses had been called against the leader of Forum for Democratic Change, including Kamdulu, who had come to back up the accusation of collusion with the armed group.

The conflict in northern Uganda was an unfinished war at the time. At stake in the government's handling of former LRA combatants was its ability to establish itself as the true and only victor of the war, as much in the eyes of its financial backers as the populations in the North. The narrative of the conflict was in the process of being written. It would determine the historic truths that would hold sway. Thus "culture of war" discussed by John Horne, and which is characterized by the tendency to create a Manichean world that enhances the image of each camp "by demonizing the adversary,"[59] was the very one that still presided over the government's definition of the demobilization-reintegration program (or lack of one).

Conclusion

Demobilization is generally perceived as the mechanism that is preliminary to establishing peace and a pacified political arena. In Uganda, the return of former combatants in their original communities meant for some mixing with their own victims, for others with their torturers, and interacting day by day in a society undergoing a process of recomposition. It took place in a context of deep transformations of societies by war, the effects of which we are only beginning to gauge (90 percent of the population displaced during the war; changes in social hierarchies; recomposition of the geographic space, as well as power dynamics due to the progressive dismantling of displaced persons camps or the presence of satellite camps in the process of being institutionalized; interference of representatives of the Acholi diaspora in the constitution of a political branch of the LRA; etc.). Officially, the demobilization and reintegration process was supposed to continue in the broader framework of the Stabilization and Economic Reconstruction Program under the Peace, Recovery and Development Plan for Northern Uganda (PRDP) developed by the Ugandan government and backed by the United Nations Development Program (UNDP). In reality, the reintegration of former commanders was dealt with on a case-by-case basis without any systematic solution being proposed, or perhaps even being feasible. But above all, at no time in northern Uganda was there mention of forming a new political order that would modify the norms of political control and domination to propose a more inclusive recomposition of the state apparatus and transform relations between the opposition to the regime and the central authorities. The strategy implemented in northern Uganda neglected the process of civilianization[60] of former combatants by maintaining the LRA chains of command and perpetuating the control exercised by the LRA leaders over former combatants. It was based on a misguided interpretation of the Acholi political scene, which was perceived as the counterpart of the military branch of the LRA. The military decorum surrounding the former commanders was an obstacle to the normalization of political life and jeopardized the demilitarization of political relations between the North and the Ugandan central government, prerequisites for a long-term resolution of the conflict. The latest presidential campaign, in 2011, which for the first time took place in a context of restored peace, once again gave President Museveni the opportunity to sustain the confusion between his opponents in the opposition and members of the LRA. During a meeting presided by Brigadiers Sam K. and B., he praised the "former LRA commanders" and their "collaborators" (sic) for having joined the Movement's Acholi Solidarity Mobilization Team "to counter and expose the lies that opposition politicians have for years used to confuse and intimidate the population in northern Uganda in order to make them support opposition politicians and political parties," a government press release specified. He then added,

> he [the President] was disappointed that some politicians in Northern Uganda selfishly used the war situation to tell lies about the NRM Government instead of saying the real and true cause of the war in the North. (...). "I salute you for uniting to fight the psychological slavery of the people of Northern Uganda so that they can make their political decisions free of fear." He assured them that Kony will never come back to terrorise people of Northern Uganda as the Uganda People's Defense Forces (UPDF), is strong enough to counter any

negative force [in presidential speeches, the opposition is included among the "negative forces"] that tries to destabilize Uganda.[61]

Five years after the restoration of security in northern Uganda, the demobilization of stereotypes and beliefs about military force is still not on the government agenda.

Translated by Cynthia Schoch.

Notes

1. This article presents the results of three field studies conducted in Uganda between September 2005 and March 2008 among simple combatants (a majority of them child-soldiers and young adults), middle-ranking commanders, including one woman, and senior commanders. For security reasons, the names of the informants have been abbreviated or changed. My research assistant Tony Labol translated the interviews from Luo into English. I am grateful to him for his precious help and advice.
2. It is hard to evaluate the number of LRA combatants still active. Estimates vary between a few hundred and several thousand.
3. S. Perrot, "The Campaign Against The LRA: Old Wine in New Bottles?" in D. Richards and G. Mills (eds), *Victory Among People: Lessons from Countering Insurgency and Stabilising Fragile States*, (London: RUSI/Brenthurst, 2011), 295–312.
4. The term "returnees" underscores the informal nature of the demobilization. It includes the return of combatants and other forces, whether they were captured, liberated (as in the case of abducted children), or who surrendered to the local political and military authorities of their own accord.
5. Human Rights Focus (HURIFO), *Falling through the Net: The Challenges for Returning Adult Ex-Combatants in Northern Uganda*, HURIFO/Conciliation Resources, 2004; Conciliation Resources, Quaker Peace and Social Witness (QPSW), *Coming Home: Understanding Why Commanders of the Lord's Resistance Army Choose to Return to a Civilian Life*, 2006.
6. T. Allen and M. Schomerus, *A Hard Homecoming: Lessons Learned from the Reception Center Process on Effective Interventions for Former "Abductees" in Northern Uganda, An Independent Study Commissioned by USAID and UNICEF*, May–November 2005 [Revised April–July 2006], 22.
7. According to Colonel Acoka, "most returnees are those who were released or captured by the army. Defections are very rare, maybe 0.1 % of returnees." Interview with Major A., in charge of civil-military relations for the UPDF, December 2006.
8. Several of them had been killed during the LRA's unsuccessful incursion in the Teso region, breaking up the chain of command: the movement's second in command, Charles Tabuley, was killed in October 2003, the LRA overall army commander Tolbert Nyeko in January 2004, Col. Opiro Anaka in June 2005, and Raska Lukwyia, in charge of supplies and logistics and promoted to the rank of Major General in April 2005 when four LRA brigades were reorganized in August 2006.
9. Interview with a former LRA commander, Gulu, September 2005.
10. These figures were given by Amama Mbabazi, minister of Defense at the time, quoted by Integrated Regional Information Network (IRIN), "Uganda: Radio Programme that Touches Hearts of Rebels," *The Monitor* and *The New Vision* (July 30, 2004)), http://www.reliefweb.int.
11. Archdiocese of Gulu, *Justice and Peace Newsletters*, August–September 2007, http://www.archidioceseofgulu.org/JPC/Newsletter0904.htm (Accessed on May 2008).
12. Conciliation Resources, QPSW, *Coming Home*, 3.
13. Interview with the then Gulu's Resident District Commissioner, Gulu, July 11, 2004.
14. Several observers played with the official figures of the number of LRA combatants announced by the army, counting the number of combatants demobilized, captured, or killed, and arriving at the conclusion that if the official figures were accurate, the armed group would have been decimated long ago. The official discourse at the time was meant to underestimate the number

of combatants still active in North Uganda and its rear bases in southern Sudan. In fact, no serious observer has the capacity or the means to confirm or disprove the army's figures. On this issue, see S. Perrot, "Les sources de l'incompréhension: production et circulation des savoirs sur la Lord's Resistance Army," *Politique africaine* 112 (December 2008): 140–160 (English version to be published).

15. The MDRP, funded by the World Bank and implemented in Uganda by the Amnesty Commission, was closed on June 30, 2007. Over 16,000 former combatants were demobilized in this framework; 15,000 received aid for their reinsertion. MDRP, "Uganda fact sheet," March 2009, http://www.mdrp.org/PDFs/MDRP_UGA_FS_0309.pdf; Moses Draku, Public Relations Officer, Amnesty Commission, Kampala, "Uganda's Amnesty Commission in Final Phase of Issuing Resettlement Packages to Ex-Combatants," *News and Noteworthy*, no. 12 (May 18, 2006), http://www.mdrp.org/PDFs/N&N_12_06.pdf.

16. Charles Odongtho, "What Form of Justice Will Kony Face? LRA Leader's Victims Want Him To Be Brought to Account—But Aren't Sure How," *Institute for War and Peace Reporting, Africa Reports* (June 15, 2007), http://www.iwpr.net/?p=acr&s=f&o=336356&apc_state=henpacr. As soon as Kamdulu surrendered, the LRA attacked a camp of displaced persons from Gulu district, probably to try to kill Kamdulu's mother and take revenge for this defection. Kamdulu was also injured in an attack in June 2007 by three men who robbed him. But the real cause of this attack remains obscure. Chris Ocowun, "Former LRA rebel Kamdulu attacked in Gulu," *The New Vision*, June 7, 2007. Kamdulu was recently arrested for armed robbery. Charles Akena and Patience Aber, "Uganda: Ex-LRA Boss Kamdulu Jailed," *The Monitor*, November 13, 2007.

17. The visit made by Jan Egeland, UN under-secretary-general for humanitarian affairs, in November 2003 was a major turning point in the internationalization of the conflict. Egeland had in fact called the northern Uganda conflict the "world's worst forgotten humanitarian crisis." This international indictment was followed by enormous political and financial involvement of donors, UN agencies, and other NGOs working toward a rapid resolution of a conflict that has now been going on for 20 years. See S. Perrot, "Northern Uganda: A 'Forgotten Conflict,' Again? The Impact of the Internationalization of the Resolution Process" in T. Allen and K. Vlassenroot (eds), *The Lord's Resistance Army, War, Peace and Reconciliation*, (London: Zed Books, 2010), 187–204.

18. As the most recent statistical studies show, LRA abductions were not always permanent. Some children and young adults were kidnapped only for short periods, sometimes only for carrying the booty of the plunder committed by the LRA. See Allen and Schomerus, *A Hard Homecoming*.

19. Upon the return of former adult combatants, particularly to the town of Gulu, many rumors of urban crime began circulating, most of them unsubstantiated. According to the Gulu regional police commander, no statistical data corroborated such claims. There were, however, a few isolated cases of armed robbery in which the culprits were found carrying amnesty certificates. Interview with the Deputy Police Commander of Gulu, Gulu, September 2005.

20. T. Allen, *Trial Justice, The International Criminal Court and the Lord's Resistance Army* (London/New York: Zed Books, 2006); Office of the United Nations, High Commissioner for Human Rights, *Making Peace Our Own, Victim's Perceptions of Accountability, Reconciliation and Transitional Justice in Northern Uganda* (New York: United Nations, 2007).

21. The ICC prosecutor began his investigations in northern Uganda in a highly controversial context. Concerning the debates between international and local justice, see T. Allen, *Trial Justice*. Five warrants were issued in July 2005 for the principal LRA leaders.

22. Operation Iron Fist had provoked a backward surge of LRA combatants from their rear bases in South Sudan to northern Uganda and led to the worst humanitarian crisis the area had known since the beginning of the war.

23. Interview with F., Association Gyda, Gulu, December 2006.

24. Interview with Brigadier B., Senior commander de la LRA, Boma Ground, Gulu, December 2006.

25. Former LRA combatants were grouped into two battalions, the 105th and 106th (formed later in September 2005), a total of 1,300 men according to official figures. All kept their rank, thereby perpetuating the LRA chain of command, under UPDF supervision. "These people used to be thugs. Now you bring them to order and you want them to behave in a certain

manner. That's why the leadership is from UPDF (even if some LRA commanders kept the rank they had in the bush)." Former Public Relations officer of the UPDF's Fourth Division, Gulu, October 2005. Some former combatants were invited to work with the Chief Military Intelligence (CMI).
26. In August 2005, 112 former combatants from armed groups, including 48 from the LRA, completed six months of training at the Jinja Military Academy and were promoted in rank. Anne Mugisha, "Ex-rebels Rewarded," *The New Vision*, August 29, 2005.
27. This version is subject to controversy, as is the true position he occupied in the LRA.
28. After he was captured, several other commanders surrendered, including Major Isaiah Luwum, one of the first LRA combatants, as well as Col. Onen Kamdulu. IRIN, "Uganda: Senior LRA commanders captured by the army," *Irinews.org*, July 15, 2004, www.globalsecurity.org/military/library/news/2004/07/mil-040715-irin01.htm (Accessed on May 2008).
29. In 2004, an emergency plan had been set up with the help of the World Food Programme and UNICEF to provide shelter and food for the some 3,000 combatants and people accompanying them in northern Uganda. Wholesale demobilization of the LRA never took place. Interview with UNICEF Field Coordinator, Gulu, September 2005.
30. IRIN, "Uganda: Senior LRA commanders captured by the army," July 15, 2004, www.globalsecurity.org/military/library/news/2004/07/mil-040715-irin01.htm (Accessed on May 2008).
31. John Goddard, "A 'grandfatherly' killer," *Toronto Star*, May 8, 2006. Interview with Brigadier B., Gulu, September 2005.
32. Interview with Lt. Col. A., former LRA commander, December 2006.
33. Remarks reported by Goddard, "A 'grandfatherly' killer."
34. Question from Hon. Mwondha to Defense minister Amama Mbabazi during a ministry declaration on the security situation in northern Uganda, *Hansard*, July 29, 2004.
35. Dennis Ojwee, "Uganda: LRA Ex-chief Kolo excels in S6," *The New Vision*, March 11, 2008.
36. Alfred Wasike, Chris Ochowun, "Kony Spy Caught," *The New Vision*, June 28, 2004.
37. Interview, Gulu, December 2006. Some commanders in fact were afraid of physical threats made by some LRA victims. Certain former combatants and former children abducted by the LRA were lynched on their return to their home village as punishment for crimes perpetrated against their own family or some of their neighbors.
38. Interview with a group of young former LRA combatants who became bicycle-taxi operators, Gulu, December 2006.
39. Where possible, younger children were reintegrated in their families. The reintegration of adolescents and young adults (including young female ex-combatants) proved to be more difficult due to their refusal to return to a subaltern social status, their unsuitability for the school reintegration programs that had been set up and the families' concern about taking them in (cost of additional food supplies, changes in behavior, vagueness of the torturer/victim status...).
40. In 2005, the army burst into the meeting of a former commanders association that was just being formed and asked the leaders to immediately cease gathering together former combatants. The reasons for this military intervention have not been clearly established. Although security concerns have been put forward, political reasons may also explain the closing down of this association run by an opposition supporter. Interview with T., former chairman of a veterans association, Gulu, March 2007.
41. Interview with Commander A., former LRA commander, Labora Farm, December 2006.
42. Allen and Schomerus, *A Hard Homecoming*, 22. The reception centers handled this problem in a different manner: CARITAS, for instance, decided not to accept combatants who had rank in the LRA; World Vision created two additional centers to separate children, child-mothers, and adults.
43. Answer from Grace Akello, State Minister for the North, Ugandan Parliament, *Hansard*, March 22, 2005.
44. "They picked me. Even my LC didn't know they had picked me. That means that you are still in the army. There are many who came out and haven't been taken. I was with 11 people. We got political and military education. I spent 5 months in Kaweta Wakaseke, close to Luwero." Interview with a former LRA lieutenant colonel, December 2006.
45. Interview with N., former LRA combatant, Gulu, December 2006.
46. Ibid.
47. Interview with Major A., December 2006.

48. Interview with A., Gulu, December 2006.
49. Interview with a former LRA lieutenant colonel, December 2006.
50. Tristan McConnell, "Model farm or concentration camp?," *African Business* (August–September 2005).
51. See HURIFO, *Falling through the Net*, and QPSW, *Coming Home*. The UNDP also conducted a study on child-mothers and devised a support plan for former combatants, nevertheless focusing on girls. Even if the UNDP had proposed a more comprehensive project, it also lacked realism: "The UNDP policy is: why should we reward the killers only? We don't want any favourite treatment. The reintegration program has to include ex LRA, some [Internally Displaced People] IDPs and some members from the host communities" without giving any more details as to the selection of displaced persons and the communities that would host the former combatants. Interview with Takeste Aderhom, UNDP representative in charge of former combatant reintegration programs, June 2005.
52. Cornes Lubangakene, "Ex-LRA Officers Ask to Be Treated as Former Abductees," *The New Vision*, March 25, 2009.
53. D. Newton, "Quakers in Britain," *Journal Letter*, Uganda, June 2005, http://www.quaker.org.uk/Templates/Internal.asp?NodeID=91013
54. R. Marchal and C. Messiant, *Les chemins de la guerre et de la paix. Fins de conflits en Afrique orientale et australe* (Paris: Karthala, 1997).
55. Newton, "Quakers in Britain," *Journal Letter*.
56. Speech before Parliament by Hon. Santa Okot, State Security minister, *Hansard*, March 22, 2005.
57. Ibid.
58. J. Horne (ed.), "Démobilisations culturelles après la Grande Guerre," in *Revue 14-18 Aujourd'hui* (Paris: Editions Noésis, 2002).
59. J. Horne, "L'invasion de 1914 dans la mémoire (France, Grande-Bretagne, Belgique, Allemagne)," Proceedings of the conferences *Traces de 14-18*, testimonials, Carcassonne, April 24–27, 1996, available at http://www.imprimerie-d3.com/actesducolloque/invasion.html.
60. M. R. Berdal, "Disarmament and Demobilisation after Civil Wars: Armed Soldiers and the Termination of Armed Conflicts," in *Adelphi Paper 30* (Oxford: Oxford University Press for IISS, 1996).
61. Translation of: Uganda Media Center, "President Commends Former Rebel," available at http://www.mediacentre.go.ug/details.php?catId=4&item=1096.

PART 3

*From Military Combat to Political Struggle:
Reconversion or Continuity?*

CHAPTER NINE

From the Great War to Democracy: Former Combatants and the Sardinian Autonomist Movement[1]

CHRISTOPHE ROUX

> **Abstract**
>
> This chapter, a study of Sardinian veterans in the aftermath of the First World War, describes a mobilization by ex-combatants that led neither to totalitarianism nor authoritarianism, but on the contrary to the beginnings of a democratic construction. The chapter describes the situation in the region after the war, how veterans first organized in an association and how the association developed into an autonomous political party with universal male suffrage before the rise of fascism in Italy.

The objective of this chapter is to bring to light the role played by former combatants' organizations in the emergence of the autonomist movement in Sardinia in the wake of the First World War.[2] This region of Italy provides a very pertinent case for anyone interested in former combatants in postconflict situations. Indeed, as early as 1918, the island saw its demobilized citizens organize themselves into a specific association for the defense of their particular interests, before entering the political struggle with the formation of an autonomist party[3] that would go on to have significant electoral success. Such a trajectory is undeniably worth examining—particularly as it came about at the same time as the birth of Fascism in Italy. On one hand, it shows how violent conflict may function as a matrix for the politicization of the different social groups that come together under the same banner in combat; however, it tends to challenge the inevitability of the trend toward the "brutalization of society" proposed in Europe by George L. Mosse.[4] The title of this chapter deliberately turns the American historian's formulation on its head. Of course, women did not yet have the vote and Fascism was spawning, but the period of the First World War nevertheless represents a passage to universal male suffrage (comparable, say, to 1848 in the French context). It was also marked by the emergence of the first mass parties (Socialist and Christian-democrat), which had been absent up until then. Above all, the movement of ex-combatants in Sardinia (we will see its significance for the rest of Italy) was transformed from their associative structure into an autonomist political party embedded in the representative mechanism.

This entry into political life was widely noticed, and would have undoubtedly been impossible only a few years earlier. The island had a reputation for political backwardness (with local notables organizing electoral clienteles in the absence of structured political parties or clearly identifiable public opinion) and the general apathy of an amorphous society marked by misery, mutual distrust, and the absence of collective action.[5] Suddenly, however, it became the site of powerful contestation. In order to understand this shift, it is necessary to take into account the effects of the First World War and the return of combatants to civilian life. This stands out as an essential element in the explanation of the birth of the "Sardist" movement. The period of the war is generally considered by political scientists (but rarely by historians) as a political parenthesis in which everything "was asleep"; as such, its study is left to military historians or specialists of international relations. However, it appears to us essential to underline the fact that this dramatic change, through its direct impact on the lives of civilians, was able to create a "critical conjuncture," likely to profoundly disturb the fundamental structures of any given political configuration. Through the demonstration of an "ex-combatant spirit" in Sardinia, we will show here how this "spirit" was extended into a collective organization, then into a political party, and how it eventually disappeared from regional politics under the weight of Fascism.

The Birth of an "Ex-combatant Spirit" in Sardinia

Sardinia made a heavy contribution to the Italian war effort. It is true that the intersocial violence that reigned in the region—so strong that it justified the establishment of a parliamentary inquiry in 1896—may have led one to think that, as long as they were supervised, the soldiers mobilized from the island (and especially its internal regions) would be valiant. As one French observer reported at the end of the nineteenth century, "they say that the Sardinian troops, Sardinian hunters, are among the best in the Italian army. They are extremely courageous and enthusiastic, they are strong and restrained, so they can always be counted on and can be put in the front line when it is dangerous."[6] The implication of these island soldiers in the First World War was indeed very significant; most of them were sent to infantry regiments composed mostly of soldiers from rural areas (as was the case in many regions). According to figures provided by the historian Manlio Brigaglia,[7] Sardinia mourned the loss of some 13.9 percent of its soldiers (against a national average of 10.5 percent), with some 40,000 soldiers killed. On the front line, the battle feats of regiments with many decorated Sardinian soldiers gives certain credence to the representation of Sardinians as "good soldiers."

It is worth mentioning here one of the specificities of the Italian military organization: the establishment of an essentially regional recruitment unit, the "Brigade Sassari," in 1915. From the following year, this unit was, along with the alpine units, the only one in Italy to be based on territorial selection (whereas in theory the mobilization was supposed to mix recruits from different regions). Still active today and deployed in recent years to countries where Italy provides military support, this brigade was made up of two regiments of infantry (the 151st and 152nd) and continues to excel, its feats lauded in the national press.[8] Although not all Sardinians were sent to the Brigade and although "only" one in six fallen soldiers were from this unit, it is nonetheless true that the Brigade benefited from a particular aura, both during the conflict and immediately afterwards. This is still visible today in the street names and square names that are dedicated to the Brigade in numerous towns and villages on the island.

The social and political consequences of the traumatic experience of the front line have been established by many different studies. What we observe in Sardinia is no different from the general trends documented in Italy. The state of mind of those called up, which of course denoted a certain patriotism, was not that exalted nationalism that could be observed far from the front line; indeed, Italian soldiers were less than enthusiastic at the announcement of the beginning of hostilities in 1915.[9] Italian combatants were above all characterized by their incredible ability to resist tough ordeals, by their simple solidarity in the face of death (without this being "naive" fraternity, exempt from tension), and by an evolution in representation, which was similar to that observed elsewhere in Europe.[10] In the moments of calm, all their attention was focused on the memory of familiar places, the private sphere, and their homeland. This sentiment was particularly strong among the soldiers in the ranks of the Brigade Sassari; these men were living a three-fold experience in terms of society, politics, and identity.

From the perspective of identity, deployment to the front line in the ranks of the Brigade reinforced and exalted the feeling of national belonging, constructed in the preceding 50-year period. It also confirmed the reality of local belonging but, above all, it *revealed* regional identity by giving it a concrete consistency. This is important given that the form of political engagement undertaken by the Sardinian ex-combatants would be that of an autonomist party aiming to defend the specific interests of Sardinia in the face of successive Italian governments. The "Sardinian people," in the name of whom the party would claim to speak, were "discovered" during the war, which imposed an initial geographic mix between soldiers from different areas of the island, who were assembled under the banner of a specific Sardinian unit.

A second mix, social this time, was also a result of the war. Peasants and shepherds found themselves alongside members of the bourgeoisie on the front line together, united by their circumstances. It is nevertheless important not to overstate the ability of the war to make people forget social hierarchies, particularly given that those at the bottom of the hierarchy were not those who left testimonies of their experiences. Yet we undeniably observe a rapprochement, to a certain extent, as the "bourgeois" discover "the people." This created the possibility of a connection between individuals who until then had never shared the same social experiences and who lived in separate worlds. This is clear in the testimony of one of the principal Sardist leaders between the wars, who describes his experience in the Brigade in both social and identity terms:

> [With] a love never felt before, we loved our brothers of blood and spirit in the shepherds and peasants of Sardinia. In their pain and ours, we felt the pain of the island that we were learning to love. Today we thank the army command which, with its brash circulars, imposed the formation of our legendary regional unit, thus accelerating our spiritual fusion and leading our regional identity to ripen in the face of the most difficult ordeals. The Brigade Sassari was the biggest and most profound collective sacrifice that Sardinia has ever accomplished [...]. The shared suffering made us understand all the importance of the unity of the race. The actions we accomplished together showed the strength and the ability of Sardinia in collective action, they spoke persuasively for its necessity; they tightened a knot that will never be undone. We clearly saw the unity of the language. There is a Sard language. The infinite forms and diversity of sound and cadence seem to us to be the necessary harmony of dialects, which serve to make up this idiom. The student, the independent worker, all cultivated men recognized in the shepherd and the peasant their same soul. They spoke and thought in the same language, on their lips was the same melodious refrain [...]."[11]

Finally, a third aspect of this experience of armed conflict in the Brigade was that of the progressive appearance of the beginnings of new politicization. Sociologically this phenomenon can be defined in general terms as a "process of re-qualifying a range of social activities, which results from a practical agreement between social agents inclined, for a variety of reasons, to transgress or to question the differentiation of spaces of activity."[12] Thus explained, this definition refers to two central points, as Camille Hamidi says "the reference to the general principles that should govern a society" and "the recognition of the controversial dimension of the positions adopted (in the sense that the speaker recognizes the existence of cleavages on the question, and not in the sense that they necessarily mobilize a dissenting or protesting discursive tone)."[13] This is exactly what the former members of the Brigade describe, when they talk of the emergence of a new critical perspective on political and social institutions overall. Here too this trait is not typical of the Sardinian experience, as Giovanni Sabbatucci[14] has demonstrated. The experience of the trenches is idealized as an allegory of sacrifice for the common good, above all other concerns: it is the embodiment of the respect for the *res publica* at the risk of one's life. However, in the trenches the men develop a veritable hatred of the institutional categories that stand in their eyes in opposition to their moral uprightness. It was not only the rich capitalists who were assimilated to these categories, but also the factory workers and "this aversion ended up involving more or less everyone, the senior army command, the government, the nationalist media, delegates and the political class in general, and finally the whole civil society."[15] This is precisely the process that is at work in the case of the Sardinian brigade, as the testimony of Emilio Lussu illustrates. Lussu (1890–1975)[16] was the leader of the Sardist movement until it was marginalized and eventually joined with the Italian Socialist party in 1948, which then led to the birth of new dissent within the ranks of the army:

> Another unprecedented occurrence: for the first time [the soldiers of the Brigade] had observed, from the first day of fighting and from then on without rest, that the Colonels and the Generals, who they had previously considered as monuments of authority and science, didn't understand anything. They really didn't understand anything, to the point where they seemed to [be] there by mistake, and that this wasn't really their job. Then certain heinous actions, without military or common logic and used on purpose to have the soldiers needlessly massacred, showed that, in reality, they were the real enemy. But who was leading Italy? The fundamental criticism shifted onto the political field: the King's government. In the village, the Mayor, the pharmacist, the tax-collector, the Marshal (of the *carabinieri*) were all part of the King's government. Were they enemies too? All enemies. Unheard of. The myth of the King crumbled.[17]

This passage shows how the difficult conditions led the soldiers to look for causes in the decision-making processes that acted upon them, and led them to question military and civilian authority. This is all the more important given that, overall, the conflict also represented a form of politicization, as described by an Italian contemporary at the end of the war:

> We'd had the war which, with the mobilization of millions of workers from far-flung regions, who came together in the offices, in the barracks, in the camps and the trenches, had brought them new ideas,

provoked discussions between them, led them to read pamphlets, handouts, and newspapers they had never seen. Overall, it opened up a new horizon in millions of heads, such that probably a large part of them would no longer have been able to feel removed from the electoral campaign, and would have participated and helped with the meetings and putting their vote in the ballot box.[18]

This critical reaction did not immediately bear fruit; the movements toward insubordination were curbed, and the Brigade continued its exemplary performance in the conflict. Nor did it lead to a more formal or articulate political project—this only happened progressively in the postwar period. On the other hand, this mindset was important in the new conjuncture of the return to civilian life. The combat seems to have predisposed a certain number of individuals to engagement, according to a psychological mutation that took place on the front line amongst the young men who would go on to become the leaders of the party. This is illustrated by one of the leaders in the north of Sardinia, Luigi Battista Puggioni:

> None of us [...] knew life in its tangible harshness, in its struggles and its disappointments. What an amorphous life was ours. Without much pain, it's true, but also without the tumult of deep passions, without vital struggles, without young joy in life. War, abandoning home and domestic habits, books and school, material commodities, for us it was like a violent slap in the face. [...] Going from home to the barracks or directly to the trenches, we came to know something we didn't know before, the sense of responsibility. Responsibility for ourselves, for things and people entrusted to our care or our directive. We didn't know how to keep or defend these things, how to lead men, we didn't know at all. And yet, in little time, we understood and we learned by the force of events [...] to understand the men, and to guide them.[19]

This particular state of mind is very important for the context of the return to civilian life. It indeed supposes that the criticism leveled at the elites, which was in fact nothing more than the expression of resentment, was prolonged by positive action attempting to compete with and correct the errors or shortcomings of the past. This passage to action thus consists in a reconversion of practices and knowledge learned on the front, to the area of mobilization. This is exactly what was observed at the end of hostilities.

Structuring the Association

At the end of the conflict, the enjoyment in life that had been cultivated in the moments of rest on the front line was transformed into a desire for concrete action, first expressed in solidarity toward the victims of the war.

In light of this, associations for those wounded, widowed, and orphaned by the war flourished, as did those defending the rights of demobilized troops. The latter indeed encountered particularly difficult conditions in their return to civilian life, which was often difficult and sometimes cruel. In economies ravaged by the war, where soldiers had often lost their professions, their reinsertion met with a certain indifference. Those returning home were forced to realize that their deprivation and sacrifice did not provoke the gratitude they had expected. In order to have this gratitude, they had to "lobby" local public authorities in a protest action born of the frustration at the gap between the collective devotion shown on the front line and the disappointment encountered at the return of peace. Rapidly a fracture emerged between the former combatants on one hand (whose action had the form of a genuine mass movement of several million members) and society on the other. Society was symbolized by a whole range of groups accused by the former soldiers who claimed to have come up against them: "profiteers" who had gotten rich from the war, "stowaways" who had reneged on their military duty, and "decision-makers," the politicians and diplomats who had led the country to tragedy. Full of these idealized ambitions and accustomed to commanding troops, the officers took poorly to the difficulties of reinsertion (unemployment, low-paid jobs, lack of recognition in spite of services rendered to the motherland), which corresponded to so many aspects of social downgrading, an important source of frustration.

It was in this context, in peace-time, that the first demonstrations of action by former combatants appeared. Through the logic of the association, the future protagonists of the Sardist movement took control of the running of the "ex-combatants" association. Like in France, this movement initially appeared with the objective of defending specific interests (ex-soldiers interests), and the first association (*l'Associazione dei reduci della trincea*, which could be translated as the "Association of those returned from the trenches") was created in Sassari in November 1918. The newspapers that appeared over the course of 1919, *La Voce dei Combattenti* ("Soldiers' Voice") in Sassari and *Il Solco* ("The Furrow") in Cagliari, quickly came together within the latter, the future official organ of the Sardinian Action Party, to speak with a single voice, transcending the traditional territorial cleavages between the two provincial administrative centers. The association brought together most of the former combatants and was for a time affiliated with the National Association of Combatants (ANC) (between May 1919 and August 1920).[20]

The "combatant" publications of this period thus show the multifaceted nature of this group. On one hand they transmitted the initiatives of the associative movement, combining them with reflections on the lives of ex-combatants. However, they took their remarks further with the analysis of the society in which the action of the former combatants' movement was embedded. The movement allowed itself the right to comment on the general running of Italy in the postwar years, on the way the country had been governed since unification and since the end of the fighting. This represented a generally critical perspective on the overall running of affairs, sometimes based on concrete testimonies provided by correspondents at the local level,[21] sometimes expressed in more general terms, as in the text entitled *Sardinian Autonomy,* published in 1920:

> Everyone now knows the long list of wrongs Sardinia has suffered following her union with Italy. Passively, we have made a very large contribution to the blood spilt in all the wars of national independence and all the colonial adventures; moreover, the absence of fiscal adjustment born of abusive and shortsighted fiscal policy. As Sardinians, we have been pillaged in every imaginable way by the Italian Government, and our island has been repeatedly up for auction. Actively, we have no roads, no railways, no ports, no improvements, nothing. Our island has the highest rates in Italy of malaria and tuberculosis, the lowest for the number of schools, post offices and telegraphy.[22]

These negative appraisals found an echo in the calls for reform that took the shape of an autonomist platform for Sardinia, the basis of a purely political shift. This platform had several ambiguities, most notably on economic and social issues, which reflected the heterogeneity of the movement. However, it found its base in two key ideas: firstly, that Sardinia suffered from conditions of economic and social backwardness compared to the most developed parts of Italy; secondly, that this situation was the product of the disinterest of the Italian government, of which the regional representatives were just passive intermediaries. Regional autonomy thus appeared to be the way to tackle the unresolved problems of the island head-on (poverty, isolation, illness, and so on), by entrusting most of the responsibilities to those who had demonstrated their ability and trustworthiness on the front line, but without cutting the link to Italy. This is how the combatants' movement became the Sardist Party.

It is worth emphasizing two major characteristics of this phenomenon. First, the identity of the ex-soldiers was only the basis for a reform movement that was much larger, so the structure of the association was destined to be replaced. According to the leaders of the movement the "combatant spirit" was not to be the privilege of only those who had fought on the Venetian fronts, it was to be the source of inspiration for a new way of taking on political responsibility and thus required moving beyond the frame of the ex-combatants. Second, as Salvatore Sechi has demonstrated,[23] the strategy of the Sardist leaders was part of an *Italian* movement that was looking to constitute a political project for deep reform at the level of national politics. The message of the renewal of the nation, to remedy its numerous malfunctions and injustices, or of the struggle for the general interest against the defense of individual interests, was clearly characterized by its pacifism and its skepticism toward the nationalism that was present in different forms in Italy during the postwar years. This is particularly true for the contestation that emerged (timidly it is true) with the appearance of the *fasci di combattimento* in March 1919, precursor to the National Fascist Party (PNF) led by Mussolini. In the Sardist publications there are no calls to continue any war effort. Like other ex-combatants' movements in the South, as portrayed by the dissident historian and socialist Salvemini, they instead displayed an ethic of responsibility, a moderate tone and called for the respect for institutions. Indeed, the ANC (to which, as noted above, the former Sardinian soldiers were for the most part affiliated) was never considered a subversive organization—as demonstrated by the Prefects' reports—showing itself instead to be fundamentally legalist, in spite of political accusations leveled at it on these grounds by representatives of the local political class. Many of the leaders of the Action Party would later be found in the Resistance, and after the Second World War, alongside the anti-Fascists who claimed to be inspired by liberal socialism.

Thus the prolongation of the ethos of the ex-combatants into civilian life was essentially the work of officers (along the lines of the wartime structure). These officers generally came from the petty-bourgeoisie, and discovered peasants who were neither interventionist nor particularly patriotic, but who were valorous in combat and capable of stoically putting up with the greatest suffering. In their eyes, the rural soldiers acquired "a noble moral stature, and seemed inestimably better than the incompetent general, the garrulous politician, or the lecturing superintendant."[24] Hence this particular state of mind that led the officers to position themselves at the head of the ambitions for specific treatment, and as candidates for running the country: "the history of the ex-combatants' movement, in its early years, consisted precisely in [...] petty-bourgeois officers attempting to set themselves up as the new leading class, and an alternative both to the old conservative liberal-democrats as well as to the socialists, by drawing on these peasant masses who until then had remained excluded from political live and from the unitary process itself."[25]

However the formal cohesion of the ANC concealed a wide range of ideological and strategic divisions; the rivalries between the different factions were apparent from the first congress of the association in August 1920. Several representatives declared their withdrawal from the ANC and formed autonomous regional federations, declaring that they constituted, "on the basis of ideal—and moreover moral—intransigence, the Italian Action Party."[26] Amongst them were the regional sections of Molise, Puglia, and under the leadership of Camillo Bellieni, Sardinia. Originally, Sardism was simply the Sardinian branch of the veteran's movement at the national level. It was thus part of a movement of which the platform included nationwide reform of the institutional relationship between the center and the periphery by moving beyond the unitary formula established in Italy in 1865. The wrongs done to Sardinia were considered to be akin to those in other regions of Italy, particularly in the South, which like the island had an essentially agricultural economy and a critical regard toward politics and administration. Some years later, in 1931, in the middle of the anti-Fascist struggle, one of the exiled Sardinian leaders, Emile Lussu, confirmed this view—but not without some rhetorical exaggeration:

> [W]hen we say "Sardist," we don't mean a campanilist or nationalist position at all, nor do we mean a particularist position in a struggle distinct from that which is underway in Italy. Autonomy is not a claim made only in Sardinia; it is a general claim that has taken over the whole problem of the construction of the Italian state. Autonomy must be the key idea behind the anti-fascist democratic revolution. [...] So much so that when the "Sardists" speak of autonomy in Sardinia, it means they want it in Sardinia because they live there but that they would want it anywhere else in Italy if they lived elsewhere. And even anywhere else in the world, because autonomy is really a universal claim and a universal idea.[27]

As the historian Luigi Nieddu notes, this dimension suggests that the autonomist contestation seems to be a national mobilization successful at the regional level: "Bellieni's understanding was [...] not the inheritance of centrifugal forces then present in central Europe ranging from certain regions in the ex-Austro-Hungarian Empire and Germany, extending to the United Kingdom and France, but instead the fruit of the conviction that only in this way [i.e., through autonomy] could national unity be reconsolidated, the basis of a new path, for Sardinia also."[28]

In this context, in support of their claims, the testimonies by Sardists themselves consistently emphasized the weight of the experience of war. Bellieni frequently speaks of the Brigade Sassari as the "[Sardinian] people in uniform" (*"il popolo in divisa"*[29]), an image that is reminiscent of the revolutionary concept of the nation in arms, promoted in the peninsula during the 1870s. The success was remarkable because, by mid-1919, the Sardinian branch of the ANC already had some 30,000 members, a considerable number for an island, which had little more than a million inhabitants at that time, and where political parties and union movements were still in their infancy. The ex-combatants' movement was also characterized by its ability to spread densely through the territory as a result of intense activism, in which the solidarity of the trenches that was potentially present in many towns was activated by a series of tours. Bellieni himself took part in these tours, going from village to village around Sassari to address former soldiers and convince them to prolong their efforts in the war through mobilization in civilian life.

The Transformation of the Movement into a Party

The independence of the Sardinian combatants' movement at the time of the ANC implosion was followed by its transformation into a regional political party. In itself this transition from one form of public action to another is not unusual in this type of movement because the organizational structure paves the way for this. Indeed, as René Rémond observed in an early overview that essentially focused on the interwar period, "any ex-combatants' association was inclined to consider politics as the natural extension of its own action. The reunion of former combatants quickly stopped being sufficient reason, they became a force that the leaders were tempted to use for the general interest; it was felt they had the right to do so; better yet, that they had the mission to do so. The maxims of military society were consequently applied to civilian life, and without wanting it, without even realizing it, they found themselves involved in politics along a certain line of thought."[30]

Once the Sardinian ex-combatants' movement was independent from the ANC, the Sardinian Action party, an emanation of the Italian Action Party, called for by the regional delegates who had broken away from the ANC, rose from this movement. The party was defined as being "fundamentally regional, adopting the economic program of the former combatants [who] proposed to promote a renaissance for Sardinia and to protect the interests of the island by way of regional organisms [...] to be created; in order to obtain economic and administrative autonomy [...]."[31] The appearance of an autonomist political party modified the meaning of the political debates that the liberal era had presented as being "the Sardinian question." In previous decades, this expression had essentially applied to the local aspect of an essentially "southern question," which was seen as a lack of social and economic integration and which had been a concern for Italian elites since the beginnings of unification. This "question" was address by successive governments through the first regional development policies, some of which affected the island.[32] With the Sardinian Action Party (PSdAz), the "Sardinian question" appeared more as a problem of political confrontation, manifest in the specific regional claims carried by organizations that were mobilized on these issues against the Italian state.

The founding meeting of the PSdAz took place during the fourth congress of the Sardinan ex-combatants association, a symbol of the united action between this movement and the newly formed Sardist party. It thus led to an formal assembly of all the representatives of the island in a town that is only of moderate administrative importance (Oristano, administrative center of the *circondario*, situated approximately halfway between the major towns), but which is the capital of the zone that corresponds to the former *giudicato* of Eleonora d'Arborea, independent Sardinian territory at the time of external domination in the fourteenth century. Significantly, all members of the Sardinian ex-combatants' association automatically became members of the PSdAz without paying a membership fee. The party organization envisaged setting up local party cells able to adapt their action to specific local events within the framework of the overall party line. The desire to maintain a strong presence on the ground was clearly present.

Thus during this period, conditions finally seemed favorable for the production of large-scale collective action in Sardinia. The configuration that we have sketched above evokes the importance of the social embeddedness of these groups, which brought their mobilization to life.[33] The concept of *catnet*, developed by Charles Tilly,[34] is useful in the analysis of the emergence of the PSdAz: the *category* mobilized is that of the ethnic group "Sardinians," which is activated through an associative *network*—the ex-combatants' movement—that was powerful, hegemonic, and active as early as 1918, and tended to ideally take on the exact form of the category to be mobilized—because of its essentially regional composition. However, this match was not perfect. As Manlio Brigaglia observes, not all Sardinians or Sardist leaders went through "*la Sassari*," far from it. As many of the citations in this chapter suggest, the entire discursive enterprise of the leaders was aimed at building an allegorical equivalence between the two groups. This assimilation presented several advantages because it extended the apparently natural hierarchical relationship that favored the organization (the leaders of the movements appeared to have the same relationship with the members as the officers had previously had with their soldiers) and preserved the social hierarchy that it was based upon (the rural bourgeoisie leading the peasant masses). The automatic membership for the former combatants of the PSdAz further extended the strong incentives to mobilize, both material (defending ex-combatants' rights in a very difficult economic climate) and symbolic (gratification obtained from the reiteration of values shared on the front line: courage in the face of danger, solidarity between brothers-in-arms, fulfillment of patriotic duty). In return, the movement gained legitimacy by profiting from the unanimously recognized virtues of the Sardinians and their bravery during the war. Overall, these sociological effects of the collective action shed light upon the central role played by the ex-combatants' movement in the matrix of the autonomist mobilization, and help to explain its ongoing success.

Indeed this embeddedness would ultimately be extended by the successful entry of the party into the political arena. After a certain number of debates regarding the opportunity to play the electoral game, the movement officially proclaimed its attachment to the representative system.[35] This is all the more understandable given that the Party knew it could count on substantial support; a good indicator was the number of members in the ex-combatants'. A Sardinian specificity emerged here, within the Italian context, in the form of the unprecedented strength of this movement compared to the more modest success of other candidates running under the same banner in other regions. Within the framework of a confrontation that had been prepared for by political socialization during the war, and that was often quite rough,[36] the electoral impact of the PSdAz was clear during the legislative elections of 1919 and 1921 (which were the least irregular[37]).

During the legislative elections of 1919, marked by a high turnover rate (nearly two MPs out of three were not previously in office, against a fairly stable rate of one out of three since the early 1890s), the Sardinian combatants' movement obtained 26.8 percent of the vote and three MPs out of the 12 that Sardinia sends to the Chamber of Deputies. If the 12 deputies represented 2.4 percent of the total number of MPs in the lower house, the island also provided 15 percent of the members of the ex-combatants group (three out of 20).[38] During the legislative elections in 1921, the Sardinian Action Party took up the reins in the island, presenting itself as the successor to the soldiers' movement. At the regional level, the liberal coalition list obtained the relative majority with 47.3 percent of votes, and five MPs; the PSdAZ came in second with close to 28.8 percent and four elected (a third of the representatives for Sardinia), before the Socialists with 12.5 percent (one MP) and the "Populars," precursors to the Christian-Democrats with 11.5 percent (one MP). In the rest of Italy, the combatants' movement obtained only 1.7 percent of the vote and 10 MPs, with Sardinia representing 40 percent of this trend. In 1924, part of the combatants' movement had been absorbed by the Fascist Party (which obtained 61.5 percent and eight MPs in Sardinia), and the PSdAz ran its own candidates in the island (where it obtained 17 percent and two MPs; the other parties coming in under 10 percent) and in Latium (where it obtained 522 votes, that is about 0.1 percent).

The information available on the leaders of the PSdAz is extremely patchy,[39] as Eugenia Tognotti has pointed out, as are most of the internal party documents. This is in fact the major obstacle for any detailed study of the daily functioning of either the association or its political extension. We must therefore be contented with an overview, which is not without significance. The biosocial variables suggest a shared intergenerational enrollment (at the beginning of the 1920s many were young men in their 20s and 30s, affected by the Great War). We observe a diversity in geographical origins within Sardinia between the three principal regions of Sassari, Cagliari, and Nuoro. Historians of the Sardism have emphasized the role of lawyers, occasionally rural landowners, sometimes even nobles or those with links to the Freemasons. In other words, the personnel of the Sardist movement had significant social capital at its disposal, to the point where it resembled in many regards the political class it meant to fight and replace.[40] It seems that, in the absence of detailed evidence, this type of confrontation also explains how the leaders of the PSdAz were sometimes able, through their professions, to mobilize durable support via the transformation of their professional clientele networks into political obligations—notwithstanding their own criticisms of this kind of practice. As a result, coming into a field already occupied by the leaders of the coalition, concentrated in the urban areas, they were only able to engage with those who were the most autonomous with regards to the preestablished clientelist relations: the shepherds and peasant landowners. This is what the ecological analysis of the Sardist vote in 1921 suggests, emphasizing the connection between the PSdAz's areas of electoral success and the areas where these rural activities were based—making most of the future Nuoro province into a Sardist stronghold, while most of the Sassari region remained impermeable to the PSdAz message.[41]

In any case, this success, unique in Sardinia because of its scope, can largely be explained by the way the ex-combatant movement functioned as a moral and material matrix for mobilization. However, this is not the only factor. It is important to mention that, like in other southern regions, there was an absence of competition from workers' parties (whose presence was limited to the mining zones in the south of the island), as well the particular social structures of the island. Antonio Gramsci, who was himself Sardinian, observed that the specificities of the island, compared to other regions of the Mezzogiorno, were the result of its socioeconomic configuration: "The only region where the ex-combatants' movement took on a more precise profile, and succeeded in creating a more solid social structure, was Sardinia. And this is understandable. Precisely because in Sardinia the big landowner class is very exiguous, carries out no function, and does not have the ancient cultural and governmental traditions of the mainland South. The pressure exerted from below, by the mass of peasants and herdsmen, finds no suffocating counterweight in the higher social stratum of the big landowners."[42] The combination of the strong structuration of the ex-combatant and then Sardist mobilization, with the weak organization of their traditional political adversaries, thus explains the particular impact that this phenomenon had on the island.

Conclusion

We have summarized the parable of Sardism, identifying the beginnings of political socialization during the war, the organization of the association, and then the transformation of the Sardinian ex-combatants movement into an autonomist party. This provides a very illuminating case of the multiplicity of forms that the trajectories of combatants can take in the wake of a conflict. Rather than directly feeding the ranks of those driven by extreme-right ideology, and adopting violent practices as a means of exerting or conquering power once the conflict is over, as has historically been the case elsewhere, the Sardinian case shows how their engagement within an emerging democratic framework is also possible. This possibility supposes that a range of specific historical conditions are met, concerning both the resources of the movement—owing to a certain extent to chance (such as the choice of the Italian general staff to form a unit like the Sassari Brigade)—and the absence of obstacles such as preexisting political movements, likely to be competitors. It also suggests that the experience of combat serves as a point of reference for political morals, but that its protagonists accept that it has been overtaken by other more general forms of participation. It is thus presented as a basic resource and no longer as a limit that would imply the exclusion of those who have not participated first hand in life on the front line.

It is of course important not to excessively idealize this predemocratic mobilization. In the subsequent phase of the arrival of Fascism, Mussolini attempted to infiltrate the movement after trying to overcome it by force. During this period, the reference to combat, although still present, lost its impact as the goal of territorial conquest became an element of the foreign policy of the regime, under the influence of Fascism. In this, it was complexified beyond the desire to engage in immediate military action; it became an objective that was prepared over the long term and that drew on means of influence associated with seizing power.[43] There is not enough space here to go into the details of the interaction that would lead to "Sardist-Fascism," a recuperation attempt that presented itself as a synthesis around the objective of breaking away from the political class and practices of liberal Italy.[44] We will limit ourselves to the observation that this concerned the lower ranks of the autonomist organization more than the leadership. Certain Sardist leaders (such as Paolo Pili, Antonio Putzolu, or Antonio Cao di San Marco) accepted the Fascist agreement, but many others refused it (such as Emilio Lussu, Camillo Bellieni, Francesco Fancello, Pietro Mastino, Luigi Oggiano, Dino Giacobbe, or Luigi Battista Puggioni). We nevertheless have no estimation as to the size of the exchanges, although Lussu has tended to support the idea that they were massive for low-responsibility positions.[45] Following this, the contiguity of combat experiences may have facilitated the Fascist recuperation of the base, given that they were unsuccessful with the leaders. It is most likely to be this uncoupling that explains the waning relevance of the combat reference in the historical vicissitudes of the Sardinian Action Party. After the fall of Fascism, the glorious heritage of the Brigade (although it was occasionally mentioned) was not what earned the party its driving role in the regional democratic reconstruction. Instead it was the engagement of a certain number of its leaders in the constitutional arc that brought together different forms of anti-Fascist forces. Translated by Katharine Throssel.

Notes

1. This chapter originates from a paper presented at a conference entitled "Les Anciens combattants dans les transitions de la guerre à la paix" (Lyon, April 10–11, 2008). The text benefited from the comments of the editor and anonymous reviewers, whom I wish to thank. Naturally, any shortcomings in the current text remain the responsibility of the author alone.
2. A former Spanish colony, the island became part of the Kingdom of Piedmont-Sardinia in 1720; it abandoned its institutional specificities, which had fallen into disuse after the granting of the "Albertine Statute" in 1848, and became "Italian" with the declaration of national unity in 1861. Initially divided into two provinces, the island is today an autonomous region composed of eight provinces. For a general historical framework, see M. Brigaglia, A. Mastino and G. G. Ortu (eds.), *Storia della Sardegna*, 2 vol. (Rome/Bari: Laterza, 2006). On the specific period examined in this chapter see, G. Sotgiu, *Storia della Sardegna dalla Grande Guerra al fascismo* (Roma: Bari, 1990).
3. The Sardinian Action Party, which is still active. See C. Roux, "Des difficultés de la contestation nationalitaire dans le Mezzogiorno. Le cas du Parti Sarde d'Action," *Pôle Sud* (May 20, 2004): 147–164.

4. G. L. Mosse, *De la Grande Guerre au totalitarisme. La brutalisation des sociétés européennes* (Paris: Hachette, 1999).
5. This reputation was subsequently verified by a prominent school of research influential in English-speaking scholarship, following the work of Edward Banfield and those who came after him; see E. C. Banfield, *The Moral Basis of a Backward Society* (Glencoe: The Free Press, 1958); G. Almond and S. Verba, *The Civic Culture* (Boston: Little & Brown, 1963); R. Putnam, *Making Democracy Work* (Princeton, NJ: Princeton University Press, 1993). Banfield's research, cleared of the pejorative connotations of the influence of the family sphere in sociopolitical interactions, would be taken up for the case of Sardinia by L. Pinna, *La famiglia esclusiva* (Bari: Laterza, 1967).
6. J. H. Benett, *La Corse et la Sardaigne. Etude de voyage et de climatologie* (Paris: Assadin, 1876), 209.
7. M. Brigaglia, "La Brigata Sassari come problema storiografico," in G. Fois (ed.), *Storia della Brigata Sassari* (Sassari: Gallizzi, 1981), 2.
8. See G. Mazzoni, "Nobile sangue," *Il Giornale d'Italia*, December 19, 1915, cited in "Per una storia della Brigata Sassari," in Fois, *Storia della Brigata Sassari*, 30; more broadly we can refer to the publication during the conflict of the bulletin *Pro Sardegna* discussed in the panorama presented by P. Marica, *Stampa e politica in Sardegna* (Cagliari: La Zattera, 1968).
9. The Italian situation can be compared to what Becker describes for France. J. J. Becker, *1914: comment les Français sont entrés dans la guerre* (Paris: Presses de la Fondation Nationale des Sciences Politiques, 1977).
10. See for the French case: A. Prost, *Les Anciens Combattants, 1914–1940* (Paris: Gallimard, 1977); A. Prost, *Les anciens combattants et la société française, 1914–1939*, vol. 3 (Paris: Presses de la Fondation Nationale des Sciences Politiques, 1977); H. Peres, *Individus entre village et nation. Une expérience identitaire dans la formation de la France républicaine*, Doctoral Thesis in Political Science, Bordeaux, University of Bordeaux I, 1993; A. Becker and S. Audoin-Rouzeau, *14-18, retrouver la Guerre* (Paris: Gallimard, 2000).
11. L. B. Puggioni, "Il Partito Sardo d'Azione. Travaglio di rinascita nella gara eroica," *Il Solco*, November 27, 1919, republished in L. Nieddu (ed.), *Luigi B. Puggioni e il PSdA (1915–1955)* (Cagliari: Fossataro, 1959), 37.
12. J. Lagroye (ed.), "Les processus de politisation," in *La politisation* (Paris: Belin, 2003), 360.
13. C. Hamidi, "Eléments pour une approche interactionniste de la politisation. Engagement associatif et rapport au politique dans des associations locales issues de l'immigration," *Revue Française de Science Politique* 56, no. 1 (February 2006): 10.
14. G. Sabbatucci, *I combattenti nel primo dopoguerra* (Bari/Rome: Laterza, 1974).
15. Ibid., p. 5.
16. On Lussu, see E. Vial, P. De Capitani, and C. Mileschi (eds.), *Emilio Lussu (1890–1975). Politique, histoire, littérature et cinéma* (Grenoble: Publications de la MSH-Alpes, 2008).
17. E. Lussu, "La Brigata Sassari e il Partito Sardo d'Azione," *Il Ponte*, a. VII, 9–10 (September–October 1951): 1078–1079.
18. A. Schiavi, "Il numero e l'idea", in A. A. Quaglino, *Chi sono i deputati socialisti della XXV legislatura (156 biografie)* (Turin: Artale, 1920), cited by M. Ridolfi, "'Partiti elettorali' e trasformazioni della politica nell'Italia unita," in P. L. Ballini and M. Ridolfi (eds.), *Storia delle campagne elettorali in Italia* (Milan: Mondadori, 2002), 78–79.
19. L. B. Puggioni, "Il Partito Sardo d'Azione," 35–36.
20. See G. Sabbatucci, *I combattenti nel primo dopoguerra*.
21. See C. Roux, *Les "îles sœur." Une sociologie historique comparative de la contestation nationalitaire en Corse et en Sardaigne*, Doctoral Thesis in Political Science/ Comparative and European Politics, University of Lille II/ Siena, 2005.
22. E. Pilia, *L'autonomia sarda. Basi, limiti e forme*, Cagliari, 1920, republished in S. Sechi (ed.), *Il movimento autonomistico in Sardegna (1917–1925)* (Cagliari: Fossataro, 1975), 104–105.
23. S. Sechi, *Dopoguerra e fascismo in Sardegna* (Turin: Einaudi, 1967), 225.
24. Sabbatucci, *I combattenti nel primo dopoguerra*, 7.
25. Ibid., 8–9.
26. *La Nuova Sardegna*, August 25, 1920.
27. Speech by Emilio Lussu in Paris, November 29, 1931, published in 1932, in the text by *Giustizia e Libertà* entitled *La rivoluzione antifascista*; republished in M. Brigaglia (ed.), *Per l'Italia dall'esilio* (Cagliari: Ed. Della Torre, 1976), 112–113 for the quotation.

28. L. Nieddu (ed.), "Introduzione," in *Camillo Bellieni: Partito Sardo d'Azione e Repubblica federale. Scritti 1919–1925* (Sassari: Gallizzi, 1956), 39.
29. Quoted by M. Brigaglia, "La Brigata Sassari," 3.
30. R. Rémond, "Les anciens combattants et la politique," *Revue Française de Science Politique*, 5, no. 2 (April 1955): 279.
31. Article 3 of the *Statuto provvisorio del Partito Sardo d'Azione*, 1921, republished in S. Cubeddu, *Sardisti. Viaggio nel Partito Sardo d'Azione tra cronaca e storia. Documenti, testimonianze, dati e commenti. Volume I (1919–1948)* (Cagliari: Edes, 1993), 179–180, note 3.
32. As shown in C. Roux, *Les "îles sœurs,"* Chap. 2.
33. A. Oberschall, *Social Conflicts and Social Movements* (Engelwood Cliffs: Prentice Hall, 1973).
34. C. Tilly, *From Mobilization to Revolution* (New York: McGraw-Hill, 1978), p. 62.
35. *Il Solco*, July 5, 1922.
36. In Usini (south of Sassari), despite the intervention of the Mayor, the future Sardists prevented two candidates from speaking and a car leaving the village was stoned. In Nuoro, three combatant candidates prevented the socialist candidate from speaking and a general brawl was only narrowly avoided. In Dorgali (on the west coast, in the Nuoro province), the Town Hall was very nearly swamped (*Telegram no. 1221 from the Prefect of the Sassari province to the Minister of the Interior, October 29, 1919*, ACS, Ministero dell'Interno, Direzione generale della pubblica sicurezza, Ufficio riservato, b. 96, f. E1 Elezioni politiche Sassari).
37. The 1924 elections occurred just after the accession of Fascism in a context of near total suffocation of pluralism and under the impact of the 1923 Acerbo electoral law, which gave unequal preference to the winning list for the Chamber (the list that obtained a relative majority of at least 25 percent of votes, obtained 75 percent of the seats available in the house).
38. Compared to 3 out of 23 for Calabria, 1 out of 17 in Liguria, 1 out of 39 in Tuscany, 1 out of 46 in Veneto, 1 out of 47 in Campania, 4 out of 23 for Abruzzo and Molise—especially in the latter—and 1 out of 52 in Sicily; none in other regions.
39. E. Tognotti, "La base sociale del PSd'A nel primo dopoguerra. Note introduttive," in Istituto Sardo per la Storia della Resistenza e dell'Autonomia (ISSRA), *Lotte sociali, antifascismo e autonomia in Sardegna. Atti del convegno du studi in onore di Emilio Lussu* (Cagliari: Edizioni della Torre, 1982), 48.
40. L. Nieddu, "Sulla composizione sociale del movimento degli ex-combattenti e del primo Partito Sardo d'Azione", in ISSRA, *Lotte sociali*, pp. 127–130.
41. E. Tognotti, "La base sociale del PSd'A,." 47.
42. A. Gramsci, "Alcuni temi della quistione meridionale" (1926), reprinted in the anthology by G. Melis (ed.), *Antonio Gramsci e la questione sarda* (Cagliari: Edizioni Della Torre, 1975), 239.
43. This was analyzed for the Corsican case in Roux, *Les "îles sœurs."*
44. On the relationship between Fascism, anti-Fascism, and Sardism in the island, see L. Marroccu, "Le origini del fascismo in Sardegna," in M. L. Plaisant (ed.), *Dizionario della Resistenza. Volume primo: storia e geografia della Liberazione*, (Turin: Einaudi, 2000), 65–71; M. Brigaglia, "Per una storia dell'antifascismo in Sardegna," in M. Brigaglia, F. Manconi, A. Mattone and G. Melis (eds.), *L'antifascismo in Sardegna. Vol. 1.* and G. Melis (Cagliari: Ed. Della Torre, 1986); Plaisant, "Sardegna"; Roux, *Les "îles soeurs."*
45. E. Lussu, *Marche sur Rome et autres lieux* (Paris: Ed. du Félin/Arte Editions, 2002 [first pub. Paris, Gallimard, 1933]).

CHAPTER TEN

The Postwar Period in Chechnya: When Spoilers Jeopardize the Emerging Chechen State (1996–1999)

AUDE MERLIN

"After the war, the worst thing was not the destruction, it was not even the dead and the injured... it was the veterans."
Usam, Chechen youth, Nazran, March 2000

Abstract

This chapter deals with the way in which the period between the two Chechen wars (1996–1999) was sabotaged by spoilers. Maskhadov, who was head of the Chechen army in Ichkeria—though elected President of Chechnya in 1997—was rapidly weakened by other Chechen ex-combatants, grouped mainly around the Islamists. Taking into account Moscow's influence on the young independent state of Chechnya and its possible collusion with spoilers inside the country, this chapter attempts to analyze how the nonreintegration of ex-combatants into the postwar social and political framework fostered the spread of violence and undermined the authority of the newly elected president. All this in a context of quasi-total destruction and the absence of a political tradition of the state in Chechnya, along with the growing power of the Islamists.

"We gave them a chance, we let them have their independence and look at what they did with it: chaos, hostage taking, criminality everywhere; in a word, the 'Afghanisation' of Chechnya." This kind of assertion, which featured heavily amongst Russian supporters of a resumption of the Chechen war in autumn 1999, mixed disappointment, a feeling of abuse, and also a contempt for Chechens who were very much perceived, in a culturalist approach, as a "savage people" (*dikij narod*) ontologically unfit for peace and social order. Stereotypes abounded: "they have war in the blood"; "it has always been like that," and so on. These rash judgments, largely fuelled by the Russian media reactivating entrenched stereotypes[1]—in particular since war resumed in 1999—disregarded the specific problems linked to the transition from war to peace.

The question of finding a way out of conflicts has generated a new genre of academic literature, which is supported by numerous case studies of conflicts that broke out during the Cold War or thereafter. However, Chechnya has often been treated separately, the emphasis being on the periods of open conflict (1994–1996; 1999–...)[2] and the issues related to the conflicts themselves.[3] The aim of this chapter is therefore to revisit the period between the two wars (1996–1999) and analyze the causes of the failed reintegration of veterans into the Chechen social fabric, an issue that soon hindered the construction of an independent Chechen state. This period indeed provides particularly interesting research material into the failing of a fragile newborn state (the Republic of Chechnya-Ichkeria),[4] the total destruction of a country, the glorification of the veteran seen as the "defender of the nation," and therefore a figure legitimizing a state coming into existence; all of this is combined with the ambiguous behavior of the former tutelary state, Russia.

In the multifaceted context of the demise of the Soviet Union as a state and the aftermath of an armed conflict as a factor in the destruction of whole sections of the social order,[5] political and military circumstances have had a decisive impact on the way that the interwar period was "negotiated." Even though it was Aslan Maskhadov, a former Soviet Red Army colonel, who, as the appointed "leader of the armed forces of Chechnya-Ichkeria,"[6] officially defeated the Russian troops in the summer of 1996, he was still to have great difficulty in exercising his political power in postwar Chechnya. Although he was elected President of Chechnya in January 1997 under the auspices of the Organization for Security and Cooperation in Europe (OSCE), he was soon weakened by the veterans, whose claims and grievances increased and whose political agenda sometimes overlapped with that of some of the Moscow elite, thus making the weakening of the Chechen state particularly easy. The "rule of force" then got the better of the attempt to impose the "rule of law" and of the gamble in placing politics as the continuation of war through pacific means. This chapter will analyze the specific context of interwar Chechnya as well as the tension between an attempt to build a state during the immediate aftermath of the conflict and the failed reintegration of veterans, who were to become spoilers.

An Ambiguous Way Out of War

At the end of July 1995, a first ceasefire avowing to end the conflict was obtained.[7] In general, negotiation efforts and endeavors to find a solution were real, particularly after the setting-up in spring 1995 of an OSCE mission in Chechnya, which contributed to getting the warring parties around the table. Among the July 1995 ceasefire clauses were mainly the disarmament of Chechen fighters (*boyeviki*). Joint Russian-Chechen brigades had even initially been planned but soon the ceasefire had been broken and war had resumed, more violent than ever.

The Khasav-Yurt ceasefire agreement was signed a year later on August 31, 1996. This time, the end of the conflict was part of a Russian political agenda that had been well orchestrated as the June–July 1996 presidential elections approached. In a context where war was deeply unpopular[8] within Russian society, businessmen and close advisers of Boris Yeltsin were anxious to get him reelected against Communist candidate Zyuganov; negotiations had already been ongoing for several months. In May and June 1996, a number of bilateral meetings took place, mainly in Moscow, with a delegation that included Yandarbiyev, the interim Chechen president, who had succeeded separatist Chechen President Dudayev, who was murdered in April 1996 during the war. In Nazran, an agreement was signed on June 10 in the presence of Tim Guldimann, the OSCE's special representative and an important actor in the monitoring of negotiations.

The Khasav-Yurt agreement was thus part of the political agenda of Yeltsin's supporters. Its signing was immediately contested by some segments of the fighting forces, Russian as well as Chechen. Perceived by most of the Russian military on the field as the theft of an imminent victory—in May 1996, Yeltsin had indeed congratulated the military forces on their "victory"—this agreement was also more and more criticized by former Chechen war chiefs who contested the way that Maskhadov tried to maintain links with Moscow, thereby lacking, from their point of view, true radicalism and intransigence in his negotiations with Russia.

Khasav-Yurt, An Unacceptable Compromise

In the joint declaration, on August 31, 1996, agreement stipulates that resorting to violence in order to resolve political disagreements between the conflicting parties is unacceptable. It also stipulates that, on the basis of universally recognized principles of the people's right to self-determination and equality of rights, parties, moved by the intention to unconditionally defend the rights and liberties of citizens—regardless of their national origins or religious loyalties—should draw up principles on which the future relations of the Russian Federation and the Chechen Republic can be built. The main fault incurring serious consequences lies in the nature of the Russian-Chechen relationship—a polite way of referring to the status of Chechnya. The Khasav-Yurt agreement stipulates that a settlement on the terms of the relations between the Russian Federation and the Chechen Republic must be concluded on December 31, 2001, at the latest. The Khasav-Yurt agreement seems very vague compared to the Matignon agreements ending the conflict in New Caledonia in June 1998, which stipulated that a referendum should be held within ten years.

The word "status" of Chechnya is not used, and a referendum is not mentioned. None of this contributes to a clarification of the context within which Chechen veterans should be reintegrated.

In the practical part of the agreement, it is mentioned that a joint commission, (including representatives from state institutions in both the Russian Federation and the Chechen Republic) must be put together before October 1, 1996. One of the objectives of this commission would be to verify the pull-out of Russian troops from Chechen territory. The disarmament of Chechen fighters[9] is, therefore, not mentioned, contrary to the text of the July 31, 1995 ceasefire; however, the August 1996 text stipulates that the commission would have to put measures into place aiming to fight criminality and terrorism and to prevent any manifestation of a conflict with an ethnic or religious character. Furthermore, it would have to initiate a program for the economic reconstruction of Chechnya and supervise the activities of the state institutions in the field of food and medical aid.

The reference to criminality and terrorism directly echoes the problem inherent in both the way out of war and the way that this war unfolded (the mention of terrorism only serves to recall the 1995 Basayev-directed hostage-taking episode in Budennovsk) as well as the return to a hypothetical "previous social harmony," to use Sandrine Lefranc's expression.[10] In reality, the withdrawal of Russian troops started on November 23, 1996, and ended on January 5, 1997, while parliamentary elections were scheduled for January 27, 1997.

The Khasav-Yurt agreement is a compromise that gave rise to the anger and/or the humiliation of the most radical factions from both Russian and Chechen sides. Yeltsin's sending of General Lebed in order to negotiate with Maskhadov took place despite the disagreement of the main Russian generals involved in the war,[11] whereas a number of Chechen fighters saw in it the end of the advantages that the state of war guaranteed them. Indeed, war allowed many leaders of armed groups to benefit, economically, symbolically, or politically, in a context where guerrillas granted them an autonomy, which was all the more important as it was combined with a historical lack of a Chechen state and therefore no tradition of centralized authority.

Behind the Chechen "Military Victory," The Political Defeat of "Moderate" Separatists

On August 6, 1996, the capital, Grozny, was recaptured by thousands of well-coordinated separatist fighters under the stunned eye of part of the Russian military.[12] This event carried great symbolism that would later infuse the collective narrative of an independence snatched from Russia in a David-vs-Goliath fight. This recapture of Grozny marked the re-legitimization of the separatist project, challenged by the 1991–1994 Dudayev experiment. The unbalance of power (there were about 15,000 Chechen fighters in the

"Ichkerian army,"[13] and more than 100,000 federal soldiers[14] on Chechen territory) only served to amplify the perception of the event: it was the heroic deed of a small nation in arms against an Empire, which was to sign the birth certificate of the young state. The ceasefire protocol signed in Nazran on June 10, 1996, planned the disarmament of Chechen fighters for August 7, 1996; the *boyeviki* invaded the town on August 6, obviously showing a willingness to prevent this disarmament.

On the Chechen side, the euphoria was therefore as great as the temptation to analyze the end of the war as a triumphant victory.[15] Grozny was recaptured by Chechen fighters and a ceasefire was declared that planned the withdrawal of Russian troops without explicitly necessitating Chechen disarmament (this clause being absent from the Khasav-Yurt agreement): everything seemed to indicate a Chechen military victory. But what was the political translation of this victory? Amidst the ambiguity of the end of the war loomed the weakening of the separatist camp embodied by Maskhadov, who would soon be caught between two enemies with converging objectives: former Chechen war chiefs on the one hand, and part of the Russian political and military power, on the other. The military victory barely hid the political defeat that was looming for the Chechen moderate side.

Breakup of the Separatist Camp and Maskhadov's Project Discredited

Maskhadov, the very man who led the armed resistance and embodied the victory that was celebrated with great pomp in autumn 1996,[16] soon found himself in a weak position, on the home front as well as on the away front.[17] The veterans who were more radical than he was called his legitimacy into question and, with him, the legitimacy of the state he was trying to set up. However, the Russian state did not support the Chechen president, even as the latter was asking for its help to fight the increasing criminality in the Republic, thereby encouraging the perceived continuing dependence upon the former colonial power, and therefore perpetuating some kind of blur around the status of the Republic. This behavior had a retrospective effect on the radical veterans who ended up contesting Maskhadov's authority even more.[18] Maskhadov was then trapped: the weakness of the Maskhadov state offered a privileged arena to the spoilers,[19] who, in return, kept on preventing this embryonic state from growing. This interaction therefore created a vicious circle, which carried the seeds of civil war. The conversion of the military victory into a political defeat of the moderate camp is also a by-product of Russian behavior, whether this behavior came from the political or the military power: the disagreement on the interpretation of Khasav-Yurt is patent.

Political and Legal Viewpoints Diametrically Opposed

Furthermore, a fundamental disagreement on the political status of Chechnya remained. Despite the overt support of part of the Russian elite to Maskhadov's candidacy in the run-up to the January 1997 election and the official recognition of his election by the Russian authorities,[20] the official Russian and Chechen views were diametrically opposed. While the separatists, in order to legitimize both their victory and the independence process, put forward the recapture of Grozny in 1996, the prospect of a Russian troop withdrawal as written in the agreement, and the non-participation of Chechens in the 1993, 1995, and 1996 federal elections, most of the Russian elite continued to view Chechnya as one of the 89 "federated subjects" of the Russian Federation, as described in the 1993 Russian Constitution. The lack of international recognition of independent Chechnya only served to strengthen their viewpoint.[21] Recognition by the international community was indeed one of Maskhadov's main concerns after his election,[22] whereas Moscow had the opposite goal. The humiliation experienced by the Russian military played a part in this refusal and led to a Russian wait-and-see policy.

Military Humiliation and a Russian Political Wait-and-See Policy

Talk of a "victory stolen by the politicians" grew among the Russian military forces.[23] Furious that the ceasefire agreements had, according to them, short-circuited a military victory that they had seen as imminent and real, the military forces unleashed their fury against general Lebed who they now perceived as a traitor. Statements issued by some Russian military figures and politicians[24] on the necessity of revenge actually heralded the possible resumption of war and, at least, an abandoning by the Russian elite of any support to the secular separatist Chechen elite. During the signing of the Khasav-Yurt agreement, when Lebed wanted a referendum to be organized rapidly on the status of Chechnya, the anger of the army stopped him. The signing of the agreement grouped together both Chechen and Russian elites looking for peace, the more radical factions developing on the extremes, contesting the way that peace had been obtained and concessions made. This is the classic scenario at the end of a war where the "doves" are condemned by the "hawks" on both sides. Nevertheless, the situation remained a minefield. A paradox typical of all national liberations gained through armed resistance prevailed: the veterans were legitimizing Chechen independence and running the risk of burying it at the same time.

The Veterans' Glory as an Integral Part of the Legitimization of Chechen Independence

In the collective narrative on the end of the war, it is truly the Chechen resistance that legitimates, even more strongly than the 1991 "Chechen national revolution," the emergence or reemergence of a Chechen "state." The veterans therefore have a particular aura. The resistance's active participation in the military defeat of the Russian army (including a few notable heroic deeds) is the object of a particular glorification within the society as well as within the elite that would constitute the new political team in power. The fact that the votes expressed in the 1997 elections were massively in favor of the supporters of an independent Chechen state, such as Maskhadov, Basayev, Yandarbiyev, Udugov, and Zakayev, was yet another proof. Even though unknown figures were running as candidates, the political program of a Chechnya that was part of Russia was de facto excluded from the debate[25]: the disputes within the Chechen camp were suspended and the independence project appeared to be consensual. The brutal methods used by the Russian forces in waging the war, in particular toward civilians, the extent of the destruction, and the heavy historical liabilities prior to what the Russian government euphemistically called "an operation of re-establishment of the constitutional order and disarmament of illegally formed gangs," amplified the perception among the population (both civil and fighting) that a new milestone had been reached on the long road toward decolonization.

At this stage, the disagreements and the potential factors that could trigger civil war were to be found not between the "pro-Russian" elements and the separatists, as under Dudayev, but within the separatist movement itself, therefore including veterans and in particular former war chiefs. However, at first, the consensus on the legitimacy of an independent Chechnya came together alongside a strengthening of the veterans' aura, backed up by the new institutions in power. The cultural sphere reflected the way in which the veterans' aura fitted into the social fabric, while the measures aiming to celebrate the memory of those killed in action, support their families and help the reintegration of those who had come back from the front, showed how the young state envisaged their place in a society in need of reconstruction.

The Cultural Sphere and the Veterans in the Place of Honor
It is against a backdrop of jubilation—parades of tanks captured like trophies, shots in the air to celebrate victory, warlike rhetoric—that the country, still devastated by war, was called upon to envisage a future "living together." While most symbols put into place in Maskhadov's Chechnya represented a continuity of the Dudayev period, the place of the "veterans" was obviously a new element. In a country where a warlike tradition and the armed resistance pervade the identity narrative, those who have taken up arms to resist an immensely larger country that had embodied colonial supervision for two centuries were held in a place of honor. A wall was therefore erected in Grozny, bearing the names of the martyrs, not very far from a memorial to the 1944 deportation erected, in his time, by Dudayev. The names of 3,000 fighters who died at the front were inscribed in golden letters. This symbolism feeds largely on the martyr symbolism of the Second World War, during which thousands of Chechens had fought the Nazi invader, but focuses this time on the blood that has been shed to obtain freedom. The fact that Maskhadov

himself was a war chief meant that the symbolism of the martyr-fighter was only strengthened, and there was a move from a "slotted-together" nationalism where Chechen identity and Soviet belonging could combine in times like the Second World War, to a patriotism built upon national liberation.

In the cultural sphere, books celebrating fighters were published, and theater plays were produced. Under the auspices of the minister of Culture Tamara Mazaeva, a book called *Glazotan blakhoï* (Jihad fighters) was published. It includes pictures of *boyeviki* killed in action. Among numerous faces, one can see the faces of Dudayev's two nephews, who both died in combat. Maskhadov published a book called *Honour is Dearer Than Life,* which also included pictures of commanders and *boyeviki.* In the theater, a symbolic play, *Otvergnutye geroi* (The rejected heroes), written by Makhal Sabdulaev, embodied the spirit of the time. The play starts at the beginning of the first war. Staging a dialogue between separatists and Chechens against Dudayev, who fear the price to pay for the declaration of independence, it is a glowing tribute to the defenders of the homeland and to their courage. The play was premiered a year after the Khasav-Yurt ceasefire, on September 6, 1997—the anniversary of the proclaimed independence in 1991—in the small room of Grozny's Great Theatre. The audience was made up of very important figures and almost all official representatives attended it. The show always sold out during the interwar period[26] and several different productions were made. The show *Sheikh Mansur* by Mimoa Soltsaev was also staged. It is an homage to the resistance organized at the end of the eighteenth century by the shepherd Mansur,[27] during the first colonization attempt by the Tsar's army. The songs of Imam Alimsultanov, a Chechen singer whose music supported the fighters, were still widely listened to. As a matter of fact, art and collective symbolism glorified the fighters, who generally inspired gratitude and admiration, although their image was to change considerably during the second war. Against the backdrop of this reaffirmed cultural support, the new Chechen state tried to put into place measures of material and financial support to veterans and to their families.

Material, Moral, and Financial Support for the Veterans from the Young Chechen State

The initiatives taken by the Chechen state in favor of the veterans and their families were along the same lines as the artistic production described above. A state commission for the "participants in the resistance movement" was created. Veterans received a badge bearing the initials of the phrase "Participants in the Resistance Movement" and were given the title of *"shahids"* (jihad fighters). They were given high-ranking positions, had better than average living standards, and were granted certain "privileges." The commission, which had regional branches, registered 1,347 people[28] and dealt with four categories of people: actual veterans; those who brought help, material, or moral support to the resistance; the relatives of soldiers killed in action; and the organizers and participants in meetings. The members of the first three categories were given a special card, the last a certificate. Free access to public transport and material help to unemployed veterans were some of the advantages given, as well as easier access to education (access to university was granted without an entrance exam in some fields) in order to avoid penalizing those whose studies had been largely amputated because of their participation in combat. A 10 percent quota in universities with an exemption of entrance exam was granted to veterans and active members of the resistance; a 5 percent quota to orphans.[29] War orphans, the children of fighters who fell on the frontline, were the subject of a statutory order decreed by Maskhadov, which also gave them priority access to education as well as, theoretically, to employment.[30]

These essentially symbolic initiatives did not constitute the only steps taken to resolve the question of reintegration. If this cannot be described as a DDR process strictly speaking (demobilization, disarmament, reintegration), part of the institutional project consisted in integrating the veterans into the structures of the official forces of the Chechen state. Far from allowing a monopoly of coercion to grow, this strategy would reveal the breaking up of the armed groups, the social importance of practices that developed during the war, and the persistence of tensions and infighting that had already been at play under Dudayev. Thereafter, the divergence between an ever-weaker state and increasingly powerful spoilers would grow.

Weakness of the State, Strength of the Spoilers

If the military victory legitimized the project of an independent Chechnya and signed its birth certificate, it also bore all the ingredients of the failure of this state, for the violence, which was legitimized during the conflict as long as it complied with a globally recognized political and military agenda—resistance against the occupier and fight for independence—did not meet enough constraints able to channel it, control it, and convert it into peaceful social relationships in civilian life. Thus, the military feats of someone like Khattab—a foreign commander of either Chechen, Saudi, or Jordanian origins depending on the source (when he heroically defeated a column of Russian tanks in Yarysh-Mardy during spring 1995)—have undoubtedly influenced the resistance and thus part of the population. His connections with Basayev and his ability to find foreign funds for the resistance, as well as the use of Islam as a means of galvanization, have simultaneously precipitated the shift within the resistance from a secular separatist basis toward an Islamist transnational matrix. The case of Khattab, once a hero useful to the resistance, later an undesirable intruder in the management of the after-war period, illustrates the paradoxical balance that rests upon a tension between legitimization through force on the one hand and necessity to affirm political authority on the other. The transition from isolated acts of violence, perpetrated by numerous actors and "violence entrepreneurs," to a centralized violence is of course the major issue. We see here the danger that the transformation of veterans into spoilers represents, to use Stedman's terminology.[31] The point here is therefore to question the persistence, even the importance of the logics of war and violence in the after-war period, and to see how the perpetuating of a warlike tradition resonated with the difficulty Maskhadov and his team had in creating a state with a claim on the monopoly on the legitimate use of violence, as defined by Max Weber. As Stedman writes, spoilers do not exist during wartime. They appear during the contractualization of an after-war period that means a loss of benefits. In this context, Maskhadov would quickly find himself caught "between a rock and a hard place."

A President Caught "between a Rock and a Hard Place"

September 6, 1996: Independence Day was celebrated with great pomp in Grozny against a backdrop of ruins. The general exaltation was only equaled by the barefaced pride of the fighters who had beaten the second most powerful army in the world. Pictures of the event show a general euphoria. A few tanks, recovered during or after the war, were parked on Grozny's central square. Perched on a car, Maskhadov extended his arm toward the crowd among shouts of joy. This euphoria masked the fragility of Chechen independence and the stumbling blocks that were strewn along the road to the construction of a state.

Maskhadov was already confronted with the necessity of finding arrangements with various war chiefs who strengthened their fiefs during the war and did not intend to submit themselves to a man who was nevertheless the leader of the Chechen army. In spite of his election in January 1997 with nearly 60 percent of the votes (against Basayev who harvested only 23 percent, and Yandarbiyev, 10 percent), and in spite of the validation of this election by the OSCE, which partly played the role of custodian,[32] his vulnerability is already perceptible. Faced with the Republic's general state of destruction (a decimated population, a destroyed territory, and mined fields, infrastructures in fragments, an unemployment rate close to 90 percent),[33] discussing the reintegration of war veterans would suppose the existence of a professional network that had survived the war or had already been brought back to life.

In post-war Chechnya, this situation was, in many respects, a matter for political fiction. The absence of jobs and economic reconstruction obviously amplified the abyss between an inactive population and profits obtained from various forms of reproduction of the violence, in the context of a lack of law and order (hostage taking, illegal securement of oil wells in particular). All the more, such a gamble requires the means as well as an unfailing determination.

(Re)integrating the Veterans into a Devastated Society... An Impossible Challenge

The difficulty in shifting from a segmented control of violence in the context of the self-organization of the fighter groups to an order imposed by a military hierarchy supposed to serve the monopoly on the legitimate use of violence is obvious in the Chechen case. The analysis of their (re)integration then presupposes a consideration of their various ways of functioning in the underground resistance movement, and the blurring of the boundaries between state of war and state of peace. This blurring was amplified by the geographical proximity between their homes and the front, unlike the Russian veterans of Chechnya once back "in Russia." Furthermore, the degree of addiction to the conflict and to the violence, the varying lengths of time spent in the underground resistance, cut off from civilian life, are some of the numerous criteria influencing the modalities of return, combined with the aura of the fighter mentioned above. Consequently, the policies implemented by the new power, itself stemming from the victory, had to deal with this reality.

The integration and the commitment of the fighters into power structures controlled by the new power is a cornerstone of Chechen strategy, all the more so in the context of almost total unemployment and where a feeling of general insecurity prevailed, widely fed by the lack of disarmament of the war veterans.[34] Maskhadov's Chechen army was created under the name of the National Guard and placed under the orders of former commander Magomed Khanbiyev, one of Maskhadov's supporters, then appointed minister of Defense. Several special departments or groups of people were connected with his ministry. Therefore, his official subordinate was Magomed Khatuyev, a war veteran who ruled the Department of customs and border police. The Interior Ministry also hired former *boyeviki* into the Chechen security forces: Makhachev, who was the supervising minister, had under his responsibility between 5,000 and 6,000 men dispatched in various police forces, a large number of which took part, briefly or for longer periods, in the resistance. A large-scale reintegration of war veterans into state structures would presuppose enough political support to curb the logic of fragmentation and rivalry. But within the Maskhadov government itself (Maskhadov was simultaneously President and Prime Minister) his support was fragmented. Though he was surrounded by a few faithful[35] supporters and was also able to take advantage of the support of some clans *(teips)*[36]—in particular the *teip* Aleroy to which he belonged, and the *teip* Akhchipatoy, who were limited in numbers—Maskhadov knew that he was far from controlling the whole territory. His support was essentially located in Grozny and in the region of Grozny, in Avtury, Atagi and some villages of the Vedeno district.

At the same time, among the forces that were not officially part of the emerging Chechen state, and in the face of which Maskhadov had to find a viable position that neither weakened him from the inside nor prevented him from governing, two sizeable "armies" with a significant capacity to make trouble for him were to be found. The respective leaders of these two armies, Raduyev at the head of the "Dudayev Army"—Raduyev is a nephew of Dudayev—and Basayev, kept their men outside the Maskhadov structures, in spite of Basayev twice accepting offers of political inclusion. Independently from periods during the course of which he was a minister of the Maskhadov government, Basayev maintained authority over various "battalions,"[37] an "official" part of which, made up of about 400 men, was based in Grozny; the unofficial part of it, equipped with tanks, was stationed in Vedeno and in the south of Chechnya. In Grozny, Raduyev organized parades that questioned Maskhadov's power—as soon as the war ended, he announced that Dudayev was still alive, denying Maskhadov any legitimacy, and organized the kidnapping of several leading Russian political figures as hostages. As for Basayev, he would be at the center of a raid in Dagestan in 1999. In this context, the steps taken by Maskhadov to obtain an agreement on economic relations, defense, and safety from Moscow made his questioning by his new opponents materialize. The vulnerability of the rising Chechen state allowed rival groups to develop. This consequently contributed to a further weakening of the state.

Fragmentation of groups, territorialization of fiefs, privatization, and criminalization of financial resources: threats to the transition toward peace, fuelled by the game of some Kremlin insiders

"The war was hardly finished and they were already dividing up Grozny and the rest of the country: to you that market and that district, to me the control of this district, etc."[38]

The setting-up of Chechen armed forces supposed to recycle the fighters was not enough to stop the consolidation of fiefs, which originated in the way the resistance was organized. As Sebastian Smith indicates, during the first war, "Real power was held by a group of about a dozen leaders, headed by Dudayev, Maskhadov, the top field commanders and intelligence chiefs. The field commanders were essentially warlords, controlling their home regions with private armies. [...] There were many lesser warlords, with correspondingly smaller units."[39] According to Charles Blandy,[40] provided it is possible to quantify the level of authority of Maskhadov's political and military forces, Maskhadov directly controlled 60 percent of the territory of Chechnya after the war, while claiming to be able to exert an indirect control over 30 percent of the territory, but admitted that 10 percent of the territory escaped him totally.[41] These assessments should be treated with caution, as the strength of the opponents cannot be effectively gauged by these figures. To oppose him, Basayev, Raduyev, and Udugov strengthened their fief, which was built partially on the traditional forms of substate solidarity: if Basayev enjoyed strong support in the cities and villages of Shali, Achkhoy-Martan, Urus-Martan in the plains, and Shatoy in the mountains, the clan membership cemented the forms of support, and the Tsentoroy, Kurchaloy, Gunoy, Gendergenoy, Varandoy, and Belgatoy *teips* were largely devoted to him. As for Raduyev, he found support in Nozhay-Yurt, Samashki, Gekhi-Chu and enjoyed solid allegiances in the Mialkhi and Orstkhoy-Tsekhoy *teips*. Furthermore, as a commander of the "Dudayev" army, he was able to mobilize about 4,000 men and benefited from the support of Lecha Dudayev, another nephew of Dudayev and mayor of Grozny. Gelaev also strengthened his troops.

This cluster of personalities coexisted with other increasingly radical figures, who systematically opposed the policy led—or envisaged—by Maskhadov but without being actual war veterans. As war chiefs or ideologists of the resistance, they supported the underground resistance movement but without getting involved physically. This was the case with Yandarbiyev, a poet who became an Islamist, or with Udugov, who would more easily be labeled an Islamist than a war veteran but who also developed into a spoiler. Udugov strengthened his support within the Party of the Islamic Way and in various districts of Argun, Gudermes, or in some villages of the Vedeno district. Besides, he had the support of Khattab at the beginning of the Maskhadov period.

The manpower of these groups evolved over time and, from one group to another, they varied from a few tens to, in some cases, some thousand fighters. The diversification of funding sources played a determining role in this fragmentation. Basayev built up connections from all sides—from the contacts he made during the 1992–1993 war of Abkhazia to those he made with Chechen businessmen in Moscow—and he also drew from resources accumulated during the 1991–1994 period of chaos, when economic predation was a way of redistributing resources. The protection that he assured Khattab was arranged in exchange for financial flows from the Arabic world. As for Udugov, he was particularly known for his connections with businessman Berezovsky,[42] which gave him access to sizeable funding and high-technology equipment used for Islamo-independent communication. Other forms of help, originating from Fatkhi, one of the first foreign Islamist clergymen who came to Chechnya,[43] and the Saudi and Pakistani Islamists, were also part of his capital, according to various sources.

Hostage taking was an increasingly common practice in Chechnya between the two wars.[44] It constituted a considerable source of income and fed the consolidation of fiefs, destroying Maskhadov's entourage: his vice-president, Vakha Arsanov, a former traffic policeman, was particularly known for this activity, like Arbi Barayev, whose Sharia regiment was part of the Ministry of Defense, or the Yamadayev brothers,[45] who were also widely known for their intense hostage taking activity.[46] Khultygov, for his part, seemed to benefit from his role as an intermediary in the liberation of hostages, in a context where the hostage-taking industry also concerned certain Kremlin insiders who did not hesitate to get involved in the ransom payments, as well as in the organization of some kidnappings.[47] The murder, in their sleep, of six members of the ICRC in December

1996 is doubtless one of these extremely violent acts that, regardless of their obscure nature, show the absence of control by Maskhadov over these groups, in spite of the creation of a serious crime squad.

Furthermore, the probable help of the Russian services to certain war chiefs was, it seems, still ongoing: Charles Fairbanks[48] mentions, among the presumed beneficiaries of help from the Russian services, Arbi Barayev, Vakha Arsanov, and Salman Raduyev. The Yamadayev brothers, who would be involved in the battle of Gudermes and claimed to be pro-Maskhadov at the time, or mufti Kadyrov, are also mentioned by Fairbanks as benefiting from the discreet support of the Russian services. Finally, the parallel oil trade guaranteed additional income to certain groups, as in Raduyev's case.

Diversifying resources dividing the leaders and the groups; although Moscow's political agenda was not explicitly to abort the attempt to build Chechen independence, the agenda of the Chechen spoilers and part of the Russian elite sometimes seem to converge to destabilize Maskhadov. In spite of his overt obsession of preventing the outbreak of a civil war, the activities of the Chechen President did not succeed in stopping its development, which accelerated during the first half of 1998.

Toward a Civil War?

> "An armed combat within the boundaries of a recognized sovereign entity between parties subject to common authority at the outset of the hostilities."[49]

This is Kalyvas' definition of civil war. July 1998: the peak of violence reached in Gudermes will doubtless remain in the Chechen history of the interwar period the episode in which the intra-Chechen civil war is the most tangible. In international law, the notion of civil war is used to describe both Russian-Chechen conflicts. This time, it is about defining the reverting to violence within Chechen society itself. Maskhadov then tried a strategy of political inclusion through the integration of spoilers by appointing them to official posts.[50]

Controlling Spoilers by Appointing Them to Official Posts: A Gamble Lost in Advance?

> "I remember, someone in the crowd told him, during a gathering in Grozny: Aslan, if you attack them, you have to go all the way! You must not stop halfway; otherwise it will be even worse. But he had an obsession: to avoid a civil war at all costs; I mean at all costs."[51]

In order to avoid civil war, Maskhadov's strategy was the integration of his enemies and rivals into Chechen state structures. This is how Basayev, one of the most powerful former war chiefs, was appointed twice in the Maskhadov government. The first time, in April 1997, he was appointed deputy Prime Minister where he dealt with Industry and was thus associated with the management of oil affairs. The second time, in 1998, he was appointed Prime Minister. While he was under a mandate of investigation from the Russian Prokuratura for the taking of hostages at Budennovsk, this appointment was perceived in Moscow as a provocation. This is how the Sharia regiment of Arbi Barayev (a particularly feared war chief, who would eventually be suspected of being at the origin of the beheading in October 1998 of four British and New Zealand immigrant workers) joined together with the Khanbiyev's National police. This is how Gelayev's forces came to be, provisionally, under the direction of the Ministry of Internal Affairs. As for Udugov, he was appointed leader of the negotiations with Russia in April 1997, which augured an orientation radically different from that privileged by Maskhadov during the 1996 ceasefire.

The constant tension between the moderate and the radical approaches; the repeated attempts by the elected President to assert an authority that the ballot boxes should have conferred him but that was constantly challenged by his richer opponents equipped with superior weaponry—who challenged the election to claim their "right" to use violence against the "rule of law"; the absence of a culture of political dialogue in a situation of massive economic and social destruction: all these elements were leading toward the outbreak of the very civil war, which Maskhadov wanted to avoid at all costs.

The Peak of Gudermes

The pitched battle in Gudermes marked the peak of the political and military crisis that troubled Chechnya in the interwar period. This was fought between various Islamist leaders, called "Wahhabis,"[52] who managed training camps in particular around Avtury and Serzhen-Yurt, and the armed guard of commander Sulim Yamadayev, who was in control of Gudermes and supported Maskhadov. This battle caused the death of several dozens of people, mostly in the Islamist ranks but not only: civilians and supporters of Yamadayev were also killed. While the Wahhabis received the support of Arbi Barayev and Mezhidov, who managed the military Sharia structures (Mezhidov was a minister of Sharia safety), the members of the guard were supported by the inhabitants of the villages around Gudermes and by the respected members of society in Naqshbandiya and Qadyriya brotherhoods. The ideological and religious conflict opposing both factions took the form of an armed confrontation, a proof that the issues of political orientation and the place of religion in the construction of a Chechen state had yet to be resolved and that ideology and power struggles were handled, if necessary, using weapons. Maskhadov, in reaction, demoted Mezhidov and Barayev, who had been decorated in the euphoria of the 1996 victory, from their rank of general,[53] and ordered that the Sharia structures they managed be dismantled. Foreigners working in

Sharia courts were declared personae non gratae but no massive dismissal of Wahhabis took place: they were protected by Vice President Vakha Arsanov and by Basayev personally. After the fightings at Gudermes, the Wahhabis moved their base near Starye Atagi, fief of Yandarbiyev, whom they asked to pursue and even to lead the fight against the authorities. Maskhadov's authority was left even more weakened.

The introduction of the "full Sharia regime" in February 1999, the enactment of a decree creating a presidential *Shura* (Islamic Council) with consultative status in order to repeat the strategy of the political integration of Islamist opponents, revealed an increasingly blocked situation of "double power": a formal power on the one hand, an increasingly real and threatening one on the other. The political crisis deepened: the Chechen Parliament elected in 1997 refused to recognize this decree, while the Islamist opposition set up its own Shura. The divorce was complete, and continually fuelled by the spoilers' connections with the outside world.

Outside Connections Further Weakening the Inside

The sanctuary represented by an "independent" Chechnya for Dagestani Islamists and the reservoir made up by Dagestan as a supplier of Islamist theologians show in a two-way relationship how an Islamo-militarized project directly involving former Chechen war chiefs was articulated. These connections not only strengthened former Chechen war chiefs but offered them opportunities for later action.

The army commanded by Raduyev was particularly involved in these connections. On December 20, 1997, it signed an agreement of mutual help with the Islamic Jamaat of Dagestan. On the same day, a Russian military unit was attacked by armed men near Buynaksk. At the end of 1997, a round table took place in Dagestan, in the district of Novolakski, at the instigation of Chechens Udugov and Yandarbiyev, and of the Lak of Dagestan, Khachilayev, who was chair of the Union of the Muslims of Russia, in order to create a Congress of the peoples of Ichkeria and Dagestan. At the end of January 1998, the leaders of the Islamic Jamaat of Dagestan met in Gudermes, where the relations between the radical Wahhabis of Dagestan and the Islamist war veterans of Ichkeria were reinforced. This assembly declared it was in a state of war against the pro-Russian authorities of Dagestan and proclaimed the "jihad against infidels." Chechnya was put forward as a territory-sanctuary for hunted Dagestani Islamists: all those who feared for their own lives or the lives of their close relations were invited to settle down in Chechnya with their "brothers of faith, where monotheist faith can be professed freely and safely." At the end of April 1998, the Congress of Peoples of Ichkeria and Dagestan met under the slogan "Ichkeria and Dagestan, a family, a future!" Spoilers and government members (these two kinds of status are not incompatible) were part of this "Congress that founded the peoples of Chechnya and Dagestan": there were Shamil Basayev, prime minister of Chechnya at the time, Movladi Udugov, president of the Congress called

"The Islamic Nation," Vakha Arsanov, the Chechen vice-president, and other members of the Chechen government.

Basayev proclaimed himself Emir of Dagestan and Chechnya in May 1998 and invoked Dagestani Islamist Bagauddin Kebetov's appeal to support three villages of Dagestan who proclaimed the Sharia to justify the raid of 2,000 Chechen and Dagestani fighters in Dagestan in August 1999. The war veterans were a good opportunity for Dagestan and Moscow alike, in a kind of waiting game and/or collusions with Islamists.

No consensus within the military elite after the first war; no redeployment of the war veterans and/or redeployment as "troublemakers"; extreme fragility of the secular separatist political project...Combined with the absence of help from Russia to Maskhadov (although he had been democratically elected) and the association of Islamists, fed by Dagestani-Chechen connections, this situation was to lead straight to the raid in Dagestan. The failure of the Chechen state was obvious and its initiatives no longer had any weight against its rivals.

Conclusion

Basayev and Khattab's incursion into Dagestan marked the resumption of war. This major, highly-publicized incursion corroborated the thesis that Chechnya was out of control between the two wars. About 12 years after war resumed and fighters returned to the underground resistance, violence has clearly not been eradicated. Despite the official announcement on April 16, 2009, of the end of the "anti-terrorist operation" (the official name of this second war), underground fighters are still being recruited. The official discourse developed in Chechnya today on Ichkerians (partisans of independent Chechnya) in general and on fighters in particular is unambiguous. All are described as bandits, hooligans, and terrorists. But these bandits, hooligans and terrorists can be found today in great numbers grouped around Ramzan Kadyrov. The methods used to recruit them, including torture, formal "amnesties," or job offers, show that the issue of the failed reintegration of veterans and its consequences is raised along with questions on "the economics of violence," to reuse the words from the title of Jean Hannoyer's book.[54] The distinction between two types of violence, one that "preserves the social order" ("systematically functional violence") and one that "destroys it" ("dysfunctional violence") may help us to comprehend in retrospect the differences but also the common points in the transition from war to peace in Chechnya after the first war and after the second war, while being very careful when considering a "second post-war period."

The "accordion" alternation between open war periods between Russia and Chechnya (1994–1996; 1999–2003) and periods of Chechenization of the conflict or political transactions within the Chechen camp (1991–1994; 1996–1999; 2003–...) raises a key issue: a united front happens when the external threat comes to cement together a society that is in reality already very fragmented, as long as there is resistance to an oppressor. As soon as this external threat is supplanted by a Chechenization of the conflict, the expression of violence between Chechens and the difficulty to regulate violence reappears. The question of the state is therefore central. The unachieved state of the Maskhadov period, weakened from the start and largely jeopardized, be it through the lack of recognition by other states and the absence of help from the Russian state, was unable to operate the monopoly on the legitimate use of violence. The state of Kadyrov, a kind of "State within the State," benefits from the support of Moscow, including in the use of violence in order to consolidate Kadyrov's terror. In both cases, finding a way out of the conflict lacks real programs of reintegration into civilian life. In both cases, the amount of violence remains very high. In neither case is it possible to talk about reintegration and civilianization of veterans, despite the differences in strategies and contexts. Translated by David Ranc, Martin Cruse and Catherine Librini.

Notes

1. See in particular John Russell, "Mujahedeen, Mafia, Madmen: Russian Perceptions of Chechens during the Wars in Chechnya, 1994–1996 and 1999–2001" in R. Fawn and S. White (eds.), *Russia after Communism,* (London: Routledge, 2002), 73–93. We would like to thank Nathalie Duclos and the anonymous referee for their advice, patience, and stimulating remarks.
2. The difficulty in dating the end of the second war, despite the official announcement of the end of the anti-terrorist operation by Russian President Medvedev on April 16, 2009, raises a major epistemological problem. Indeed, while reconstruction is real and has caused many deep changes in Chechnya since war resumed in 1999, there has been no negotiation between the warring parties and the political and historical dispute, which largely led to the first war, is denied today. See A. Merlin, "Tchétchénie, un après-guerre sans paix," in A. Merlin and S. Serrano (eds.), *Ordres et désordres au Caucase,* (Bruxelles: Editions de l'Université de Bruxelles, 2010).
3. See A. Le Huérou, A. Merlin, A. Regamey, and S. Serrano, *Tchétchénie, une affaire intérieure? Russes et Tchétchènes dans l'étau de la guerre,* (Paris: Autrement, 2005) and the bibliography.
4. The name of *Ichkeria,* used to define separatist Chechnya, has kept this connotation.
5. As explained in this chapter, the "social order" that existed before the first war was already very fragile, in the context of the Chechen declaration of independence in 1991 and of the collapse of the USSR giving birth to newly independent Russia. Before the collapse of the Soviet Union, the social organization in Checheno-Ingushetia was already very distinctive, strongly marked by the colonial dimension in a fringe of the Empire where sovietization was never fully accepted. The history of Russian-Chechen relations (up to the present day) cannot be understood without considering the colonial heritage, in particular the brutality of the conquest by the Russian Army in the nineteenth century, which met strong resistance, and of the memory of the 1944 deportation of the whole Chechen people to Central Asia. See M. Vatchagaev, *L'aigle et le loup. La Tchétchénie dans la guerre du Caucase au XIXe siècle* (Paris: Buchet Chastel, Paris, 2008); on deportation, see A. Campana, S. Tournon, and G. Dufaud (eds.), *Les Déportations en héritage. Les peuples déportés du Caucase et de Crimée, hier et aujourd'hui* (Rennes: PUR, 2009); A. Nekritch, *Les peuples punis* (Paris: Maspero,, 1982), in particular "La situation dans le Caucase du Nord et la politique d'occupation allemande," pp. 38–65; J.-J. Marie, *Les peuples déportés d'Union soviétique* (Paris: Questions au XXe siècle, Editions Complexe, "Questions au XXe siècle," 1995); J. Otto Pohl, *Ethnic cleansing in the USSR, 1937–1944* (Westport, CT: Greenwood Press, 1999).
6. A. Malasenko and D. Trenin, *Vremâ Ûga, Rossiâ v Čečne, Čečnâ v Rossii* (Moscow: Gendal'f, 2002).

7. This agreement planned the end of the conflict, the liberation of detainees, the disarmament of Chechen forces, the gradual withdrawal of the Russian Army, and the cessation of terrorist and diversionary acts. See Stasys Knezys and Romansas Sedlickas, *The War in Chechnya* (College Station: Texas A&M University Press, 1999), 196–197. The agreement was signed in the context of negotiations initiated after the taking of hostages in a hospital in Budennovsk in June 1995 by a group of fighters led by Basayev. The Russian Prime Minister of the time, Chernomyrdin, had then negotiated with Basayev in order to put an end to hostage taking. Several texts of ceasefire were later signed, the first one on June 21, 1995. See also Isabelle Astigarraga, *Tchétchénie, Un peuple sacrifié* (Paris: L'Harmattan, 1999), 285–287.
8. Anne Le Huérou, "L'opinion russe face à la guerre en Tchétchénie" in P. Hassner and R. Marchal (eds.), *Guerre et Société: État et violence après la guerre froide,* (Paris: Karthala, 2003) 165–191.
9. This is all the more interesting as the signing of a ceasefire protocol on June 10, 1996, in Nazran planned the disarmament of Chechen fighters for August 7, 1996.
10. Sandrine Lefranc (ed.), *Après le conflit, la réconciliation?* (Paris: Michel Houdiard éditeur, 2006), 13.
11. Numerous were indeed the interventions of Russian servicemen, who saw this as a treason, especially after Boris Yeltsin congratulated the Russian Army for its victory in Chechnya! See for example, 11 years later, the way certain members of the military hierarchy still saw this agreement: "Hasav-ûrt: k godovsine predatel' stva," (Khasav-Yurt: the anniversary of a treason), August 28, 2007, http://www.zvezda.ru/politics/2007/08/28/hasav yurt.htm.
12. This event, whose preparation was never secret, perplexed some observers. If the civilians were warned of the necessity of leaving Grozny, why Russian servicemen did not try to prevent this offensive more actively? We find a very detailed description of the troubles of spring and summer 1996 and all the initiatives taken thereafter to prepare peace in the chapter by A. Cherkasov in T. Lokshina (eds.), *Chechnya, Inside Out* (Moscow: Demos, 2007).
13. Malashenko mentions a contingent of 15,000 fighters in the Army of Ichkeria at the beginning of 1995 and of 10,000 to 11,000 at the beginning of 1999, adding that in both cases, 30,000 potential fighters could be raised to support this army. A. Malasenko and D. Trenin, *Vremâ Ûga, Rossiâ v Čečne, Čečnâ v Rossii* (Moscow: Gendal'f, 2002), 133.
14. The name "the federals" is frequently used by the Chechens to refer to the forces sent by Moscow to Chechnya.
15. For a narrative on the capture of Grozny by Chechen fighters on August 6, 1996, see Sebastian Smith, *Allah's Mountains: The battle for Chechnya* (London/New York: I. B. Tauris Publishers, 2001).
16. Interviews with L. G., journalist, Nazran, March 2000.
17. See for example, "Victory and Defeat, January 1996 to October 1998," in A. Lieven, *Chechnya: Tombstone of Russian power* (New Haven, CT: Yale University Press), 137–146.
18. See below.
19. See S. J. Stedman, "Spoiler Problems in Peace Processes," *International Security* 22, no. 2 (Fall 1997): 5–53.
20. Yegor Stroyev, president of the Council of the Federation, sent his congratulations to Maskhadov after his election, whereas President Yeltsin signed a peace agreement with him in May 1997.
21. Only the Afghan Taliban recognized Chechen independence; very late, though: this recognition took place in 2000, after the resumption of war. Russia had announced that they would break their diplomatic relations with any state recognizing independent Chechnya. See, for example, Rahim Kherad, "De la nature juridique du conflit tchétchène," *Revue générale de droit international public* (January 2000): 171; and the reference to the Hallstein doctrine.
22. Sebastian Smith quotes him: "In the afterglow of his victory, Maskhadov declared that 'Chechnya is an independent state...Only this remains: that the rest of the world, including Russia, recognise this independence.'" *Allah's Mountains*, 259.
23. See, for example, A. Cherkasov, "Stolen victory" in T. Lokshina (ed.), *Chechnya, Inside Out* (Moscow: Demos, 2007), 47–54.
24. Interview with M. B., December 8, 2008, on the topic of V. Lukin, still described as a personality with a liberal political orientation, particularly at the time. The testimonies on the comments made by the oligarch Berezovski at that time also showed a wish to get revenge.
25. Doku Zavgayev, the first Chechen appointed Secretary of the Communist Party of Chechnya-Ingushetiya in 1989, which had been restored by Moscow at the end of 1995, during the war, was opportunely appointed Ambassador of the Russian Federation in Tanzania.

26. Interview with Z. R., a Chechen actress who found refuge in Belgium, May 9, 2009.
27. On Mansur and the resistance to the first attempt of armed colonization, see M. Vatchagaev, *L'aigle et le loup,*. With the 1991 independence declaration, the central square of Grozny was renamed Sheikh Mansur Square.
28. See V. Tishkov, op. cit., p. 192.
29. Ibid.
30. Interview with M. V., Chechen historian and former spokesman of Maskhadov, February 1, 2009, Paris. See also I. Akhmadov, and M. Lanskoy, *The Chechen Struggle, Independence Won and Lost* (New York: Palgrave Macmillan, 2010).
31. See the definition in the general introduction. See Stedman, "Spoiler Problems in Peace Processes," and by the same author "Negotiation and Mediation in Internal Conflicts" in M. E. Brown (ed.), *The International Dimensions of Internal Conflict,* (Cambridge, MA: MIT Press, 1996).
32. S. Stedman mentions the role of international actors as *custodians of peace*. ("The crucial difference between the success and failure of spoilers is the role played by international actors as custodians of peace"), "Spoiler Problems in Peace Processes," 6.
33. Interview with the economist M. B., Paris, February 2002. See also Zura Altamirova, "Zizn' v poslevoennoj Cecne" (Life in Chechnya after the War) in D. Furman (ed.), *Chechnia i Rossiia: obshchestva i gosudarstva,* (Moscow: Publication of the Andreï Sakharov Museum, 1999), 308–309; and the interview of Aslan Maskhadov by M. Perevozkina, "Vive la Tchétchénie libre!," *Politique internationale* 75 (Spring 1997): 148.
34. The way armed militias were established some years later, with Akhmad Kadyrov, leader of the provisional administration set up by Moscow, then "president" of Chechnya from October 2003 to May 2004, and then with Ramzan Kadyrov, president in his turn since March 2007, testifies of the equation of the circulation of men in arms. In fact, the combined situation of mass unemployment, the absence of opportunities and the general feeling of insecurity is the axiom according to which the most plausible future for war veterans, usually young men, is to retrain as militants. From 2003 onwards, it became clear that the only way of escaping the raids and *zachistki* (mop-up operations) was to be enlisted in the militias of Kadyrov, called "*kadyrovtsy.*"
35. Turpal-Ali Atgeriyev was his first deputy prime minister, Kazbek Makhachev was deputy prime minister in internal affairs, Magomed Magomedov was deputy prosecutor, leader of the special anti-kidnapping brigade, and Mayrbek Vachagaev his spokesman.
36. Chechen society is divided into *teips*, communities of extended families among which solidarity plays out (in particular in economic matters). Marriages take place between members of two different *teips* and children will belong to the *teip* of the father. The *teip* was the object of a certain mobilization on the political level under Dudayev in particular. See M. Vachagaev, "Chechen Society Today, Myths and Reality," *Central Asia and Caucasus,* 2 no. 20 (2003): 14–21; and E. Sokirianskaia, "Families and Clans in Ingushetia and Chechnya," *Central Asian Survey*, 24, no. 4 (December 2005): 453–467. See also Huérou, Merlin, Regamey, and Serrano, *Tchétchénie, une affaire intérieure?*
37. The term of *battalion* is widely used in the Caucasus but does not necessarily refer to heavy artillery.
38. S. Y., Chechen writer, interviewed on May 20, 2009, in Brussels.
39. Smith, *Allah's Mountains,* 180.
40. Charles Blandy, "Chechnya: A Beleaguered President," Conflict Studies Research Center, 1998, http://www.ppc.pims.org/csrc/ob61.htm
41. Interview with Khadji-Murat Ibragimbekov, Dagestani historian, occasional adviser of Aslan Maskhadov, Moscow, April 20, 1998.
42. See A. Le Huérou and S. Serrano, "La Tchétchénie, miroir de la société russe," *Le Monde diplomatique, Atlas 2001 des conflits (Manière de voir* n°55) (January–February 2001); Huérou, Merlin, Regamey, and Serrano, *Tchétchénie, une affaire intérieure?* on the dangerous liaisons of Udugov and Berezovsky.
43. A Chechen from Jordan, Fatkhi took upon himself to put Chechnya back on the path to "true Islam." He was the first to organize a group of Islamist fighters (a *jamaat*) within the Chechen resistance and he managed to spread it out in several groups, in Urus-Martan, Argun, Gudermes, Makhketi. See M. Vatchagaev, "L'islam en Tchétchénie: sur fond d'aggravation,

analyse et témoignage," in B. Balci, and R. Motika (eds.), *Religion et politique dans le Caucase post-soviétique* (Maisonneuve et Larose: IFEA, 2007), 210.

44. The international media focused on foreign hostages kidnapped in Chechnya, but the main victims were Chechens, who were kidnapped in the hundreds, even in the thousands. However, the fact that eminent Russian personalities were among the hostages widely contributed to jeopardize the emerging Chechen state. Among these personalities, we find Valentin Vlasov, a messenger of Boris Yeltsin in Grozny, or Shpigun, chief warrant officer of the Russian Ministry of the Interior.
45. The Yamadayev brothers, "bosses" of Gudermes in both wars, turned around from supporting independence during the first war to a pro-Russian stand at the beginning of the second war, to finally become the arch-enemy of Ramzan Kadyrov, who organized their liquidation in Moscow or even abroad. Ruslan Yamadayev was murdered in September 2008 in Moscow, his brother Sulim at the end of March 2009 in Dubai.
46. Doku Umarov, who would become the leader of the resistance after the death of A. Kh. Sadulayev, himself a successor of Maskhadov after the assassination of Maskhadov in March 2005, was also supposedly largely involved in the taking of hostages, according to M. Vachagaev. Interview with M. V., Chechen historian, July 21, 2006, Paris.
47. The name of Berezovsky came up repeatedly in the payments of ransoms, for example, for the release of 22 members of the Federal Ministry of the Interior in December 1996, of the journalists from NTV in August 1997, and of two British hostages in September 1998.
48. C. H. Fairbanks, "Weak States and Private Armies" in M. Beissinger and C. Young (eds.), *Beyond State Crisis? Postcolonial Africa and Post-Soviet Eurasia in Comparative Perspective,* (Baltimore, MD: Johns Hopkins University Press, 2002), 138–139.
49. S. N. Kalyvas, *The Logic of Violence in Civil War* (Cambridge: Cambridge University Press, 2006), 17.
50. Especially as Maskhadov was to be the target of several attacks.
51. Usam Baysayev, journalist, interview in Nazran, 4 March 2000.
52. On the word "Wahhabi," see Huérou, Merlin, Regamey, Serrano, *Tchétchénie, une affaire intérieure?*; and A. Merlin, "Des usages de l'islam en Tchétchénie post-soviétique" in F. Nahavandi (ed.), *Mouvements islamistes et Politique,* (Paris: L'Harmattan, 2009), 115–134.
53. As Smith underlines, ranks were many within Chechen army, especially after the first war, when numerous veterans were awarded decorations.
54. Jean Hannoyer (ed.), *Guerres civiles: économies de la violence, dimensions de la civilité* (Paris: Karthala, 1999).

CHAPTER ELEVEN

A "Warrior" Generation? Political Violence and Subjectivation of Young Militamen in Ivory Coast

Richard Banégas

"These young people, after all that's going to happen, are coming back. Could they remain at the level of the army? These are young people that the government will no longer... after all that, the government will no longer be able to find positions for them. That's going to create still other problems, and we're going to experience the same problems tomorrow or possibly even in two or three years. A group of unruly youth, maybe a group enrolled in 2001 or 2002 starting a new war. Because, the government might not have held to something with them. Because it's always like that. The problem is going to stick around with those young people, it'll be around tomorrow. So, somehow, that rebellion... what's happening now—enrolling young people to do your dirty work—that can turn against you."[1]

Abstract

Since the outbreak of war in 2002, militia organizations have flourished in the southern regions of the country. This chapter analyzes the role of these militia since the official end of the war and examines their social and political influence. Studies of urban militia in the west of the country and in Abidjan show that since the official end of the conflict young recruits have gained considerable power on the local and national levels, thus disrupting intergenerational relations—though the chapter insists that the phenomenon

> is variable and contingent on groups and regions. Although some former fighters have become exemplary figures of social success, others feel the process of peace has left them behind. The chapter discusses the brutalization of Ivory Coast society and the subjectivation of youth by violence. It foresees the possible spread of a "war ethos," on the hypothesis that it is most likely linked to an (im-)moral ghetto economy dominated by the ambiguous figure of the urban "warrior."

Since the start of the armed conflict that, in September 2002, divided the country in two—the North under rebel control and the South under government authority—the Ivory Coast has entered into a multiform "militianization" of army and society (a word borrowed from Marchal and Messiant[2]). Under the government's auspices, this process has been especially intense in southern areas, where self-defense movements and "patriotic" militias have proliferated.[3] The signing of successive peace agreements, such as the one at Ouagadougou in March 2007, and the launching of various "demobilization" programs have not significantly affected this trend, whence a major question: what will become of these militiamen in the "post-conflict" situation? What social and political influence will they have in a "pacified" society?

From the start of rebel operations in the North and West during the autumn of 2002, President Gbagbo and his advisors realized that they could hardly count on the weak and divided national army to put up a fight and reconquer areas lost to the rebellion. To make up for the structural weakness of official security forces, they adopted a twofold strategy of "privatizing" the conflict and setting up paramilitary organizations. For one thing, they recruited foreign mercenaries (Angolese, South Africans, Ukrainians, Israelis, French, and so on), who mainly served as officers in intelligence, training, and supervision. For another, they sponsored the creation of paramilitary formations for opposing the rebels and consolidating the regime. These formations—urban militias operating mainly in southwestern Ivory Coast—and their "postconflict" predicament are the topic of this chapter.

The data presented herein comes from fieldwork conducted in southern areas, mainly in Abidjan, since the start of the conflict[4] but prior to the recent events leading to Gbagbo's ouster from the President's Office. Originally written in 2009, this chapter does not take into account the 2010–2011 postelection crisis. Since fieldwork was not conducted in the North, I shall leave aside the areas controlled by their proclaimed enemies, the rebel combatants in the Forces Nouvelles (henceforth, FN), the focal point of demobilization and reintegration programs.[5] This chapter concentrates on militiamen interviewed in the South, who too have been targeted by specific demobilization programs. However our fieldwork focused more on the enrollment of youth in the Young Patriot movement than on their demobilization.

What groups do we have in mind when talking about "militia" in the Ivory Coast? This word usually confusedly covers groups and actions of several types. To be brief, I might mention three in particular: paramilitary forces in the West; self-defense groups in villages; and urban militias along with the Young Patriots who have often made the headlines. Not all these organizations have taken an active part in fighting. Some are specialized in street actions, intimidation, and demonstrations, for instance the Abidjan Young Patriots and Fédération Estudiantine et Scolaire de Côte d'Ivoire (FESCI, a student union and one of the most influential forces backing the regime). Bear in mind that open conflict lasted for a short time, mainly between September 2002 and the summer of 2003 with a few episodes of sporadic violence thereafter (again, leaving aside the events leading to Gbagbo's ouster in 2011). Despite the extreme acts of violence committed in some areas during this "short war," the "veterans" discussed herein were, in comparison with others, not involved in fighting or at least not for very long. This typology is mainly analytical. In the field, these formations have porous boundaries, and are part of a loose agglomeration of parallel forces organized and funded by the inner circle of power around the President's Office. Though lacking in homogeneity and often in coordination, these parallel forces fit into the regime's paramilitary strategy of "privatizing" the conflict. They were especially active when the conflict broke out. Thanks to them, the regime remained in place. Afterwards, their fervor fluctuated depending on events. Some formations vanished or fell apart, whereas others changed their tactics and operations. Nonetheless, most of these formations, though dormant since the Ouagadougou Agreement, are a major cause of concern in the "postconflict" situation.

For the sake of convenience,[6] I shall use the term "post-conflict" to refer to the period following the open violence in 2002–2004, especially the period following the March 2007 Ouagadougou Agreement (but not the situation created by the electoral war of 2010-2011, nor the reconstruction undergone under the Ouattara's regime).

This chapter inquires into the social and political significance of militias in society by analyzing the trajectories of their members during and after the conflict. What social and political positions do these "veterans" hold since the end of hostilities? Are the militiamen new figures representing power and success? Or, on the contrary, has the peace process left them behind? Has the recourse to violence become a means whereby young men express political opinions and assert a sense of identity? What effects has this twofold process of militarization and militianization had on social relations, in particular on intergenerational relations? Is a "warrior ethos" being diffused? If so, what is its significance? To reply to these questions, I shall draw on an analysis of paramilitary and self-defense groups in the west of the country and make comparisons with the urban militias in Abidjan among whom I conducted fieldwork. By describing the historical and sociological development of militia violence, I shall try to formulate answers to two major questions raised in this volume: the question about the continuity/discontinuity of armed mobilization before and after the conflict; and the one about the "brutalization" of society formulated by historians of the First World War[7] and used in attempts by some sociologists to interpret the Ivorian case.[8]

The Politicization of Violence and "Militianization" of Politics: A Short History of The "Brutalization" of Social Relations

To understand the importance in ordinary social relations and politics of violence in general and of militia violence in particular, let us bear in mind a few facts. Although the Ivory Coast was long thought to be a haven of peace and stability, West Africa's economic hub plunged into a spiral of violence in the late 1990s.

A coup d'Etat in December 1999 put an end to the old political system set up by Houphouët Boigny under the Parti Démocratique de Côte d'Ivoire (PDCI). A civil war followed in September 2002. The putsch led by General Gueï marked a rupture with the relatively tranquil "passive revolution" and with the sociopolitical system for settling conflicts with its political ideology of peace and social cohesion. This putsch itself was a product of rising tensions since the early 1990s, when Houphouët Boigny was president and the democratic movement was fiercely quelled. This movement had been led—a point worth bearing in mind when analyzing later events—by Laurent Gbagbo's Front Populaire Ivoirien (FPI) and by FESCI.

State violence targeted the leaders of opposition parties and student groups; but in ricochet, it legitimated the recourse to force and street actions against the government. It signaled the start of the militianization of politics, as authorities abandoned any qualms about paying hooligans, *gros bras* (strong arms) or *vagabonds salariés* (vagabond wage-earners, who have left memories in several urban neighborhoods) to break up strikes and crush the opposition. As our interviews show, some episodes during this period still serve as landmarks in the saga of militia actions. The direct or indirect victims of this coercion, which was delegated to gangsters paid by the regime, often recall such episodes when justifying their own involvement. This especially holds true for FESCI members.

Tensions worsened after the "father of the nation" died in late 1993. The new pretender who emerged from the ranks of the former one-party system during this "war of succession" was Henri Konan Bédié. For political reasons, he opened the Pandora's box of *ivoirité*. This concept was initially intended to brush aside a major rival, former Prime Minister Alassane Ouattara, a native from the north. PDCI propagandists cast doubt on his nationality. The concept spread like wildfire in a country where more than a third of the population was of immigrant origins. Groups were lumped together, and citizens from the north—in particular, the Dyula, a merchant group scattered throughout West Africa—were stigmatized as "foreigners" in their own land or considered to be second- or third-class citizens by southerners who felt themselves to be "real Ivorians" (with reference to an ethnopolitical ideology formed during the colonial era).[9] In towns, where most jobs in the informal sector were held by immigrants or northerners, this ideology radically turned the rivalry for jobs into a fierce political fight for rights.

Sharpened by the competition between the PDCI, Gbagbo's FPI, and Ouattara's RDR (Rassemblement des Républicains), this struggle for rights took an ever more violent turn that soon "brutalized" urban society. The 1995 elections, boycotted by the opposition, was a key event in this politicization of violence and the enrollment of young people in partisan politics.

In rural areas in the west, land-related issues were a source of tension between natives, who deemed themselves in charge of the land, and nonnatives, who had come to farm there under the free-enterprise ideology of Houphouët Boigny's regime ("The land is for whoever works it"). The argument in favor of nativism thrived there, especially among young dropouts without jobs who had come back to their hometowns in search of a piece of land and had formed paramilitary and vigilante groups to "defend their territory" and drive out "foreigners." In the second half of the 1990s, well before the "official" eruption of armed violence, self-defense organizations and ethnically based movements against "nonnatives" were proliferating in the villages and small towns of southwestern Ivory Coast. Nonnatives, in turn, organized similar groups.

Roadblocks became a socially institutionalized game with its rules and players. Militia violence prevailed in certain areas, sometimes turning into pogroms, as in Tabou (near the Liberian border) in November 1999. A few years later, once war had broken out, some of these "roadblockers" joined village self-defense groups and thus they put their "know-how" in use in the patriotic struggle against rebel "assailants." This fieldwork, along with that conducted by the team of Jean-Pierre Chauveau and Samuel Bobo in western and central parts of the country, provides fragmentary evidence of this continuity.[10] Far from ending tensions, the military transition that began in December 1999 exacerbated them. Without describing in detail this "terrible year"[11] during which a referendum enshrined the principle of *ivoirité* in the constitution, it is worthwhile recalling that events during the transition under army rule shaped the processes of militarization and militianization.

Acts of political violence had occurred previously, under Houphouët Boigny and his successor (for instance during the Guebie counterinsurgency in 1970). They had even become a full-fledged part of the system, evidence of this being the numerous accounts left by the victims of fake conspiracies under Houphouët Boigny or of the repression exercised by Bédié. Apart from the aforementioned episodes during the 1990s, political violence was, however, not committed on a large scale nor staged for the public, as in some countries. It was downplayed and targeted. The regime's stability relied more on institutionalized patronage networks than on terror. True, the army held an important place in this arrangement, especially in the administration (in customs and through prefects) and public enterprises. Houphouët Boigny had always seen to it that the military machine was separate from the process for obtaining political legitimacy. The president-planter drew his aura from sources other than guns. Financially generous to his own army but mistrusting it, he heavily relied on "military cooperation" with France for the country's security. He saw to it that the country's armed forces (FANCI: Forces Armées Nationales de Côte d'Ivoire) remained a rump army of loyal officers confined to tasks of law and order.

The putsch in December 1999 broke with this historical pattern of neutralizing the army and set off a spiral of violence. Ever more attempts were made to stage a coup d'Etat, and the political crackdown was ever harsher. Three major consequences of relevance to the discussion herein are worth pointing out.

First of all, armed violence came to be the trump card in political compromises. Soldiers who broke ranks and young militiamen became middlemen in politics and kingmakers. They did not control the game by themselves, but Houphouët Boigny's political heirs could no longer govern without them.

Secondly, the military transition considerably sped up the militianization of army and society, which had started during the preceding decade. From the junta's first days, security services (including the gendarmerie reputed for its sense of discipline) disintegrated into factions, whose orders came less often through the official chain of command than through informal patronage networks and clans. In fact, this had already started under Bédié, who was unable to maintain the national army's cohesion as his predecessor had done. Noncommissioned officers from the west and especially the north, many in number and of low birth, were discontented with a situation that blocked their career prospects.[12] They overthrew Bédié in December 1999 and handed the reins of government to General Gueï. In the wake of the trend launched by the young mutineers in December 1999, relatively autonomous factions formed in the army and in parallel structures that would soon turn into urban militias. Each tended to be affiliated with a political leader but obeyed, in fact, only their military bosses, such as Lieutenant Boka Yapi and Staff Sergeant Ibrahim Coulibaly, the notorious "IB" who headed the rebellion in 2002 and was killed in 2011 by Soro's forces. Their mafia-like names (Camorra, Cosa Nostra, Red Brigades, Mafia, etc.) reflected this transitional regime's criminal drift. These groups looted and committed all sorts of acts of violence. General Gueï tried to restore order during the summer of 2000 by conducting brutal purges and exiling "IB." Nonetheless, he was unable to control these formations. The General-President was taken hostage by these "young people" who had made him king and now deemed themselves above the law.

The third effect of this "terrible year" was that violence spread rapidly throughout society. More importantly, those who used violence to accumulate wealth and power had an even stronger sense of impunity.

Far from reversing this trend, the election of the former opponent, Laurent Gbagbo, as president of the Second Republic in October 2000 paradoxically reinforced the idea that armed violence and street actions were now normal means for taking and keeping power. Evidence of this came from the October 2000 election when, despite Gueï's last-ditch efforts, the head of the FPI managed to win by relying on military factions and launching his troops on the streets of Abidjan. In turn, the RDR, considering that power was to be seized "on the streets," mobilized its activists. They clashed with the FPI's and were severely repressed by the new government. In Yopougon, a lower-class neighborhood in Abidjan and an FPI stronghold, 57 bodies were found in a mass grave, mostly northerners and Muslims close to the RDR. This massacre set off a shock wave through society. Many rebels referred to it when explaining why they joined the FN and justifying their own abuses of power against southerners and government representatives.

Legislative elections in December 2000 played out following this same scenario of urban violence, after Alassane Ouattara's candidacy was again declared invalid. Setting up the Forum of National Reconciliation in 2001 did not lessen tensions. Quite to the contrary, Gbagbo's regime adopted and adapted the ultranationalistic logorrhea about *ivoirité* and nativism. Like his predecessor, he pushed a large proportion of the population outside the pale of citizenship. Throughout 2001, plots brewed against a backdrop of insecurity and radicalization around the issue of new identity cards. In September 2002, an umpteenth putsch attempt spurred an armed rebellion that divided the country into two political and territorial units.

This overview of recent events in the Ivory Coast provides a time line and insight into the process of militarizing and brutalizing society. Far from being linear, these processes took place in fits and starts, depending on political events and, sometimes, very local circumstances, as in the southwest. During this phase preceding open warfare, these processes made headway less in line with the government's strategy for privatizing coercion than as a function of political quarrels and the splintering of public authority in a context of polarization around issues related to citizenship.

Protection and Extortion: The Formation of Militias in Rural Areas

This militia-based strategy was put to use after October 2002 in response to rebel operations. Applying a counterinsurgency policy, Gbagbo's government created paramilitary formations in the southwest. Parallel armies were formed, sometimes in a hurry, under loyalist forces (FANCI now the FDS, Forces de Défense et de Sécurité) in charge of supervising and training them. Though passing over details about the "transnationalization" of the conflict, I would like to point out that the tasks of staffing and recruitment were mainly in the hands of Liberians from LURD, a rebel group that would later overthrow Charles Taylor with Abidjan's support. The volunteers in these paramilitary groups who had no experience in using weapons were hardened for war by their Liberian "advisors." This direct experience with warfare and the massive atrocities committed in certain zones turned some of these men into killing machines. Combatants received accelerated training; and most of them also attended sessions for receiving "mystical" protection (*kanké*), whence their feeling, even nowadays, of power and invincibility.

This trend was not confined to areas near the Liberian border. It spread elsewhere. Throughout the south and central areas in the west, dozens of militias and self-defense groups emerged. War and the regime's superpatriotic propaganda radicalized "natives" and sharpened young men's determination to take land and crops from nonnatives. Even though this violence had deep roots running through local history and disputes, it was also directly linked to the paramilitary strategy of authorities in Abidjan and to the regionalization of the war. Advisors close to the President's Office organized and financed paramilitary groups, specifically: Kadet Bertin, a former minister of Defense and advisor of the head of state who also had family ties with Gbagbo; and Eloi Oulaï, the director of Radio Côte d'Ivoire.[13] Trained by commandos from the national army in cooperation with Liberian rebels, these groups maintained close contacts with loyalist forces and local administrative authorities, ties to which political leaders did not deny.[14]

The collusion between village militias and local officials is worth noting. Whether elected (to local authorities or parliament) or appointed (local representatives of the national administration: prefects, subprefects, and so on), these officials spurred the militias on and coordinated their activities in rural areas. These entangled rationales, administrative, and militias are evidence of an informalization process that led to a "militia state."[15] This state, once war broke out, increasingly relied on these parallel structures and on shadowy lines of command that inextricably mixed networks of political, economic, military, and paramilitary influence.

Paramilitary groups proliferated in the Ivorian "far west." The major one was the Forces de Libération du Grand West (FLGO) set up by

"General" Denis Maho Glofiéhi. This jumble of organizations also included: the Mouvement Ivoirien pour la Libération de l'Ouest de la Côte d'Ivoire (MILOCI) headed by "Pastor" Gammi, who claimed to be a reverend who had learned his trade in Liberia; the Alliance Patriotique Wê (AP-Wê) under Julien Gnan Monpého, alias Colombo; the Union des Patriotes pour la Résistance du Grand Ouest (UPRGO) led by Gabriel Banao, a former customs officer and *tirailleur sénégalais*; the FS Lima, a loosely knit group of Liberian mercenaries stationed in Duékoué that, headed by Maho Glofiéhi at the start, later became part of LURD; etc. To this nonexhaustive list, a somewhat different organization should be added: the Groupement de Patriotes pour la Paix (GPP), an urban militia in the south (in Abidjan and around San Pédro) that claimed to have several combatants in the southwest. In July 2005, Maho Glofiéhi became the official head of all these militias, going under the name Forces de Résistances du Grand Ouest (FRGO). This third assistant of the mayor of Guiglo sat on the FPI's central committee and had contacts with the President's Office in Abidjan (where he visited frequently). Furthermore, he had been installed as a traditional chief. The militia head had accumulated means and positions in pursuit of the strategy of "straddling" political and security organizations.[16]

In line with the FPI's paramilitary strategy, the regime also fostered the formation of village self-defense groups. Given the increasingly dangerous environment, these groups proliferated in nearly all rural townships. Similar to urban vigilante groups, these village militias mounted patrols. These initially informal groups were soon organized with help from local officials into Young Patriot rural groups. In many a locality, these patriotic organizations had a president, treasurer, supervisor, and other officers of activities related to security and demonstrations. Once these organizations had a political and administrative shape, volunteers were identified and enrolled. According to Bobo and Chauveau,[17] "each of them has an identity card bearing his name, age, and hometown and proving that he is a patriot serving his country. It serves as a pass, following instructions from the prefect." According to information gleaned during our fieldwork, a classical trend was taking place, one observed in other countries: the number of cardholders increased significantly as the time drew near for disbanding the militias and reintegrating their members in civilian society.

It is important to my argumentation to describe the sociological characteristics of these local militias and the methods they used. This is no easy task since empirical data are scarce or inaccessible and far from complete. International agencies active in the area, such as the German overseas volunteer service (GTZ), the Office International des Migrations (OIM) and peacekeeping forces (the United Nations Operation in Côte d'Ivoire, UNOCI, and Force Licorne), have "profiled" former combatants, but the results are not easy to find. The only academic studies are those: by J. P. Chauveau and S. Bobo in the central western area; by M. Chelpi-den Hamer in the west (in particular the areas of Guiglo under loyalist control and the rebel zone of Man); and by two members of our small team in 2008, Alain Toh in Duékoué and Guiglo, and Gnangadjomon Koné in Daloa. What information do these surveys provide?

Despite the difficulty of drawing general conclusions, the militias and self-defense groups were mainly made up of young men less than 30 years old at the start of the conflict. Recruits were of three sorts. Young "natives" (locals), the largest group, had joined to defend their village or "homeland" and "drive out nonnatives," regardless of whether the latter came from the north, from Mali or Burkina Faso, or were Baoule from the east of the country. Chelpi-den Hamer[18] insists that we should not overestimate this factor, a point discussed hereafter. According to Bobo and Chauveau,[19] persons experiencing problems in school or employment or involved in land disputes with Burkinan immigrants were often part of this "native" group. These two authors identified a second sort of militiamen-roadblockers: a few young "urbans" who had come back to their village in search of land but whose plans were blocked. Having become involved in politics or unions in the city (in particular on campuses), some of them tendered their "organizational" skills to the local patriotic movement. This background, though less common, is not to be overlooked, since these young men played an important role in the patriotic constellation of forces in local politics both during and after the war. Following an active initial phase in a militia, the men who held regular jobs gradually withdrew, it seems, thus leaving control in the hands of school dropouts who thus found a real opportunity for social climbing. A third category was less often present in the ranks of village self-defense groups: young men displaced by war, who had been the victims of violence and were seeking revenge.

Chelpi-den Hamer's survey of 200 militiamen and rebels provides a clear picture by dissipating false ideas about the militiamen's social backgrounds and their motivations for joining or quitting.[20] Unlike what is widely imagined, in particular by the international aid agencies that are funding the demobilization/reintegration process, not all these combatants—far from it—are illiterate, jobless persons who broke with their social environment. In the Guiglo-Bloléquin area, one of the places most affected by militia violence, 97 percent of the combatants in paramilitary formations were educated; half of them had even started secondary school.[21] These militiamen told Chelpi-den Hamer about how hard it had been for them to stay in school. Their schooling had been interrupted for various reasons, in particular because parents were unable to pay for it, a characteristic observed among former combatants elsewhere on the continent.[22] Far from being social misfits, most of them lived in a family, and some even headed households with children. The majority of these militiamen had held jobs before joining, often small trades in the informal sector and, above all, in farming. This is important for understanding how these men were being "reintegrated" after the war. During the relatively long phase of "neither war nor peace," many militiamen did not abandon their former jobs. Like "peasant combatants" in the north, who shifted back and forth from their fields to the battlefield, these militiamen went on tending to crops or small workshops. Statistically however, "only a minority takes back up the trade exercised before the war."[23] Before the outbreak of hostilities, many of these young men were in the precarious situation of looking for "contracts."

These surveys shed light on a recurrent trend that is not without significance: several militiamen who, before the war, were eking out a living in the city had to give up their means of livelihood and come back to their village to take care of an ageing parent, take charge of the family farm, or fill some other family obligation. Since "protecting parents" or kin in the very broad sense was important among the justifications mentioned for joining a militia, we wonder whether this rural vigilantism might be a continuation of the moral economy of the lineage-based societies in this part of the Ivory Coast.[24] This hypothesis merits further study on both the motivations for joining an armed group and the symbolic rewards accruing from joining once the war is over.

According to Chelpi-den Hamer, the explanations and motivations for joining were not directly tied to the search for resources and goods (in particular land), as is too conveniently advanced in the economic arguments discussed in the introduction to the present volume. In Guiglo, a more frequently mentioned motivation was "protection": 46 percent of interviewees said they joined to protect themselves and their kin; and 19 percent, to defend their region. These percentages were even higher among militiamen who farmed (54.3 percent and 21.7 percent, respectively). Although 46 percent of interviewees came from families that had experienced direct acts of violence, only 15 percent said that the death of someone close was a decisive factor for joining.[25] By way of comparison, very few mentioned the quest for resources or goods. Very few had joined because of a promise of rewards, apart from the fuzzy promise of an eventual incorporation in the army. Only 16,5 percent of respondents said they joined to vent frustrations related to specific events or their economic plight.

To make the argument convincing, Chelpi-den Hamer examines the combatants with rural origins, in particular the young "rurbanites" (rural-urbanites) who had come back to the village to work the land. As already pointed out, they were key players in local conflicts. A usual argument runs that the primary motivation leading young "natives" to join a militia was their predatory envy to push nonnatives off the land or keep them from acquiring land. However Chelpi-den Hamer's study shows that these young men did not, prior to the conflict, have more or fewer land problems than other groups:

"If the 'frustrated group' hypothesis were rooted in the unequal access to resources, we would expect that the majority of combatants would be young men who had been deprived of access to the land before the war or were involved in land disputes. But this is not the case. Access to the land does not seem to have been a significant problem in respondents' lives before the war. Although some had difficulty working their land, the reason had more to do with the complexity of family obligations and a lack of cash for making the investments necessary for starting a plantation than with any misunderstanding between two individuals from different ethnic origins. The civil war did have effects that worsened land disputes [...] but land issues were a problem before the war, will remain a problem after the war, and cannot be considered a major cause of the current conflict."[26]

However these factors should not be underestimated, according to the information from our interviews with militiamen in Duékoué and Guiglo and from more neutral local observers. Although a predatory appetite for the land of nonnatives was not a reason for joining a militia, it later became a reason, in several localities, for taking an active part in a militia.

The operations conducted by militiamen varied significantly from the start until the official end of the conflict. Rural Young Patriot organizations assumed several tasks in addition to the war-related activity of providing support to the army and paramilitary formations. Although motivations obviously varied depending on the situation, we usually detect a twofold rationale of protection and extortion. These organizations often sprang up as a more or less spontaneous response to insecurity. Elders conferred on youth the task of protecting the village, which initially involved filtering and controlling access to the village by setting up roadblocks. In many a case, local officials extended recognition to these young people for their duties of policing and checking identities. Security forces found them useful in the attempt to control the territory. More and more roadblocks were erected everywhere, with serious consequences for the freedom of movement.

This activity soon proved to be well paid. Although the first roadblocks, in 2002, were intended to prevent rebel infiltrations, they soon provided a means for racketeering passengers and vehicles following relatively fixed procedures. Roadblocking became, we might say, a "career." Without a doubt, some roadblockers thus became involved in a process of "primitive accumulation," whereby they gained the seed money for other activities.

When it was time to prepare for elections, local militias were assigned political chores. A journalist remarked:

> For want of an attack by ex-rebels, the militiamen's assignment has been adapted to the combat at hand. In forest zones in the southwest, clear instructions have been given to the militias. For one thing, they are to protect the zones in the ruling party's political grip against incursions by the opposition. In areas such as Gagnoa, Guibéroua, Divo [...], elective offices (MPs, mayors, local authority presidents) are to remain the FPI's exclusive property. For another thing, the government's militiamen have to chase opposition parties out of the zones where they hold political positions. [...] "In the upcoming

elections [a militiaman in Diégonéfla told the journalist] there will no longer be any PDCI or RDR mayor, MP or local authority president in our region. These parties are rebel parties, and we are going to stand in the way of their activists going to vote."[27]

During preparations for the election scheduled for November 2009 but postponed until November 2010, the pressure exercised by militiamen was less visible but not any less strong. Evidence of this was the pivotal role played by Maho Glofiéhi, the former paramilitary commander, whom all parties came to meet and court in his fief in Guiglo.[28]

Besides their "taxation" activities and involvement in partisan politics, rural militiamen were also delegated, during and after the war, power over the land with, as a consequence, an increase in expropriations. With the backing of local officials and persons from the region who held high positions in Abidjan, groups of Young Patriot vigilantes made terror reign in some areas in the west, where they drove "nonnatives" (northerners, Burkinans, and Baoule) off the land, which they then recuperated "legally" with the help of the aforementioned "big men" and local authorities. They were also, now and then, used to bring pressure to bear on an agribusiness conglomerate installed in the area and make it pay "licence fees" to the new landowners. The young militiamen used violence to extort the land, but significantly, they readily bedecked themselves with the "traditions" and "customs" from which, according to them, their parents had strayed: they laid claim to land rights as natives.

Ex-militiamen: Symbols of Social Success or New Misfits?

Through this description, we detect the complicated upheaval in power relations between generations that took place in the wake of the militia movement in the western Ivory Coast. This also occurred in Abidjan, where I conducted most of my interviews. Let us now examine the influence of young militiamen in the postconflict situation.

As for rural areas, Chauveau and Richard[29] rightly stated:

> By placing the ideology of nativism and the protection of "traditional" land rights at the center of the competition for power, politicians could mobilize the younger generations of rural "urbanites," who were very mobile and had contempt for the overly accommodating attitude of chiefs and elders toward foreigners. It is mainly (but not only) these young people who joined village self-defense organizations [...]. All young Patriots mentioned as stakes: putting a stop to the economic and political influence wielded by outsiders, Ivorian as well as non-Ivorian; pressuring chiefs and elders into returning to the moral economy of "intergenerational justice" associated with customs—all this without asking any questions about

customs but, if need be, by combating the persons who did not seem to live up to customary principles. Significantly, even though self-defense organizations were actively mobilized for a limited time during the conflict, there was continuous agitation in the Gbanland [in central areas in the west] where actions were organized by groups of young men who wanted to unseat a village chief or impose rites for exorcizing witchcraft that mainly targeted elders and, in many cases, authority figures. The surveys under way in these areas show that the young men participating in self-defense organizations were clearly aware that they could not effectively oppose the advance of heavily armed rebel forces and that their vigilantism mainly targeted "outsiders," most of whom were well-known. In fact, the roadblocks and self-defense organizations mainly seemed to be an occasion for ritualized performances during this period of mounting tensions as young people redefined bounds of identity and staged, for lineage and political authorities, their model of a social order and its underlying principles of justice, inclusion and exclusion.

The hypothesis I have pursued since the start of my research on the Ivorian situation is that these young men, owing to the conflict, have managed to claim, both in public and in their households, an increasingly autonomous, influential role as bearers of a new ethos and new model of social mobility.[30] The power seized by the Young Patriot movement in Abidjan is evidence of the upheaval in intergenerational power relations, as a fraction of young activists have staked out positions in the postconflict society and politics. Have these young men become figures of success and power in the Ivory Coast[31]? If so, to what extent has their "warrior ethos" spread through Ivorian society? By contrasting the data I collected from interviews with militiamen in Abidjan with the information from rural areas, I would like to try to refine the analysis by drawing attention to the diversity of situations and to the fragility and ambivalence of what is called "empowerment" in English.

Since the start of the conflict, violence has been a factor in the rising power of a new, politically active generation that has taken up a position in between the local and national levels. In villages as in neighborhoods in large urban agglomerations, the young are increasingly assertive, throwing off the yoke of age-based relations and trying to compel public recognition. This process of autonomy is not something new; nor should we set it down to the conflict alone. The war has, however, sped up the process by turning these activists into full-fledged political players. As the surveys in the west of the country, corroborated by other studies, suggest,[32] this trend is especially noticeable in villages where the elders gave young men, organized in self-defense militias and Young Patriot associations, weapons, and conferred on them responsibility for defending the community. As already pointed out, blocking roads endowed this youth, thanks to racketeering, with relative financial autonomy and, too, with authority for managing village boundaries. They were to control the movement of persons and merchandise, to settle land disputes or political differences (often through violence), and to see to the community's safety. The unbelievable has occurred: young people in the west have often led actions for unseating and replacing customary chiefs![33] They have acquired considerable influence within a few short years. In the San Pédro area, according to an NGO fieldworker[34]:

> There is no longer any respect between old and young throughout this zone. Since 1999, the young have been accusing the old of selling the forest. At the start, these young people wanted to take the land back by force [...] The whole Tabou subprefecture was organized. The young were given full mystical powers for opposing the rebellion. Now, this power cannot be taken back. Nowadays, Kru young people have no respect for the customary authorities who gave them all their secrets, all their mystical power, which used to inspire fear. Nowadays, young people have the monopoly over selling the forest. All young people in Bas-Sassandra now have the monopoly over selling the forest. Even in Soubré, that is what feeds them, land sales.

These young people, who "bared their chest for the republic," were claiming their due. They were demanding to be hired and often imposed their conditions on local authorities. The interviewee continued:

> The young people that fought there want to work for the port. They are usually part of the Patriot movement. During the president's state visit in San Pédro around December 2007, these young people asked to be integrated in the economy, in the San Pédro port in particular. In San Pédro, there is, too, a serious problem between Kru youth and administrative authorities. Nowadays, when a prefect or subprefect gives a permit for building on a lot without going through the young people, they come right away to break everything. They feel that San Pédro belongs to them, it's their land. They have even commandeered the local radio station to broadcast messages. [...] They say that anyone who wants to build on a lot from now on has to contact them. [...] In any case, they always have to have their share in it. They even have a word for showing that the land is theirs. It's widespread now in San Pédro: *a mô kö blô*, which, in Kru, means "The land belongs to us; we are the owners of the land."

The reconfiguration of intergenerational relations is important in rural areas, especially in localities in the southwest. Let us refrain from generalizing, however, and from concluding that this taking of power by former militiamen/roadblockers has been one-sided. Other examples reveal a more complicated situation. In Soubré (southwest) and Booda (central west), Samuel Bobo[35] has remarked that the young militiamen in the FBI

(Frères Bénis Invincibles) and GPP have acquired real power locally even though they have never fought. Initially, "military training and promises of incorporation in the regular army were seen by these young people as a way to be spared the limitations related to family landholdings and the tight control exercised by elders. [...] Joining was also motivated by their quest to find esteem by exercising a role of national interest (defending the nation). They were proud of having been mobilized for their country. [...] In Booda, military training has enabled young people to acquire esteem for their courage (*gwɛkõle*: force; or *gwiŋ*: the valiant)."

Militia power emerged gradually, challenging the legitimacy of local and customary authorities: "Several acts of defiance of administrative and customary authorities, civil servants, etc., were observed. [...] Despite the power struggle between militiamen and customary authorities over strategic issues, customary political authorities remained in control of the situation. The militias did not manage to impose a new order on local authorities. [...] The elders still wield political and economic power."[36]

The signing of the Ouagadougou Agreement in 2007 and the blocking of the demobilization/reintegration programs have weakened militias in the west. Like their counterparts in Abidjan, these men saw themselves as being left behind by the peacemaking process. The demobilization of militias has become a major factor impeding the return to normalcy, despite the programs foreseen under peace agreements (500,000 CFA francs per registered militiaman under the Ouagadougou Agreement). As of July 2009, a genuine start had not yet been made at disbanding militias. In the spring of 2007 in the west, shows were staged of paramilitary groups turning in their weapons. A symbolic bonfire was even organized in the presence of the head of state. But only 37 weapons of war were turned in during these ceremonies! The principal militia leaders met with the president's inner circle and signed pledges to demobilize their troops. They were paid a considerable amount: 500 million CFA francs, approximately €800,000; but part of this sum vanished. Tensions, instead of cooling down, flared up. The western militiamen felt frustrated and discouraged. Their acts of violence had made several of them persona non grata. They fled from their home areas to seek refuge in Abidjan, where they contributed to insecurity.

According to a local NGO member, who asked to remain anonymous: "The self-defense movements have lost the will to demonstrate in Duékoué and Guiglo. [...] Banao, the leader, said that he washes his hands of anything military or political. He no longer wants to be killed. His daughter's in Europe. She sent him a Mercedes. He said he prefers riding around in his Mercedes. He suspects that the military governor sent elements from the FDS to kill him during the recent militia uprisings. That's why he's decided to keep to himself. And he said that even if the Ivory Coast comes under attack, he doesn't give a damn. He told everyone that he's no longer ready to defend the Ivory Coast. The AP-Wê is made up of combatants who all come from Duékoué. They're not satisfied, but are afraid to demonstrate. Their leader, Maho, is a charismatic person whom the President's Office listens to. Every three months, he goes to Abidjan and comes back with a four-wheel drive. He's really rich and has a lot of luxury vehicles. His men are still hoping, they're all counting on the civic service. Everyone thinks that if he demonstrates, Maho's going to strike him off the list of those who are going to benefit from the civic service.[37] This is the hope that keeps the AP-Wê from demonstrating. There's no longer a movement in Duékoué because there's no leader. Colombo fled, and Banao has given up the fight. They're all fending for themselves. Combatants are on the point of begging for a livelihood. You feel pity for them."

In cities, the situation was far different since the relations between persons and between generations had already, well before the war, undergone major changes owing to several factors (urbanization, the economic recession, social mobility, and education). Nevertheless, something similar could be observed in Abidjan where, under the leadership of figures who attracted media attention, the Young Patriots took control on the streets. Within a few years, they forced recognition as not-to-be-slighted players in Ivorian politics. This movement in all its organizational, ideological, and sociological complexity illustrates most clearly the evolution of Gbagbo's regime during the war. Unable to depend on a strong army and on solid international alliances, the regime played the paramilitary card to strengthen its hand in politics.

The "patriot galaxy" represents a genuine social movement; its significance cannot be reduced to acts of violence.[38] According to several pundits, these organizations are puppets in the government's pay and have no influence other than what higher-ups want them to have. That is true to a large extent. Given the role that leaders from this "galaxy" (among others, Charles Blé Goudé and Damana Pickass) have played in national politics and that their lieutenants have taken in neighborhoods or municipalities, these organizations have gained considerable influence in public affairs. But what about the militiamen? What is their place in society since the end of hostilities?

In Abidjan as in the west, a slue of formations can, with reservations, be said to be militias in the government's pay: Charles Blé Goudé's COJEP (Congrès Panafricain des Jeunes Patriotes) and AJPSN (Alliance des Jeunes Patriotes pour le Sursaut National); CONARECI (Coalition Nationale des Résistants de Côte d'Ivoire) headed by Damana Pickass, a political advisor of the FPI's president; "Marshal" Eugène Djué's ULTCI (Union pour la Libération Totale de la Côte d'Ivoire); and the aforementioned student union, FESCI with its "combat section," the notorious Blindé created and headed by Kacou Brou, alias "Marshal" KB, who was also close to the FPI's president. But the group in the city that most resembled a paramilitary formation was the GPP (Groupement des Patriotes pour la Paix). The GPP and its militiamen (in the UMAS, Union des Mouvements d'Autodéfense du Sud) along with FESCI's Blindé were, we might say, the "patriotic galaxy's armed wing." My remarks concern the GPP.

Between 2006 and 2010, we conducted a dozen interviews, more or less in secret, with GPP members. Mostly staff persons and middle-rank "officers" accepted to be interviewed. For reasons having to do mainly with a political context that kept the GPP from acting in the open, it was not possible to talk with ordinary militiamen. The formation's hierarchy never allowed us into the "camps."

During our interviews, GPP members insisted on telling the difference between their movement, involved in the armed struggle, and the other patriotic organizations that "fought with words." Despite this emphasis, their rhetoric was similar to the Young Patriots. They described their combat as a heroic resistance to save the republic, a struggle for national liberation. They tended to see themselves as "uniformed corps" (*corps habillé*), which they actually were since, during most of the conflict, they wore uniforms identical to those of the loyalist soldiers who supervised them. They even had identity cards similar to those of the FDS.

The GPP was set up at the very start of the conflict as an army of "reservists" for backing up the FDS. Charles Groguhé, a former FESCI leader, created the GPP, but the movement slipped into the hands of Touré Zéguen, whom some militiamen still consider to be the actual leader. Following infighting and divisions, Bouazo Yoko Yoko replaced Zéguen as president. In the words of Bouazo Yoko Yoko during an interview conducted in Abidjan in September 2006:

> The spirit of the movement was created...what's the spirit of the movement?...Well, some people talk about militia, some cite all the names...that's the game. It might be descriptions...or well...a pejorative way of describing the movement. But what you have to know, I think, is that the GPP itself should not have existed since military service is compulsory in all former French colonies. Legally, it's compulsory. But...practically, it's been made optional. The country's under attack. Those who want to force themselves to think it's a crisis between Ivorians can do so. It's their right. But for us, we know for a fact that it's not a crisis between Ivorians. Our country's under attack. The fatherland's in danger. The reservists who should be there aren't there. The army has a limited number, grown old. What are we doing? That's the question answered by setting up the GPP. What are we doing? So, it's necessary to quickly form...this...this group of reservists for backing up the regular army. Besides, the way this crisis started...it attacks the civilian population more than the army, which means that it's not open warfare. So the point was to form self-defense committees, self-defense groups...that, given outside aggression, can form a rear base for the regular forces.

In Abidjan, the GPP recruited hundreds of young men whom the FDS supervised, armed and trained. Among them were several veterans and policemen whose jobs had taught them how to use weapons. In coordination with instructors from the loyalist army, they trained new recruits in camps in the city.[39]

The GPP in Abidjan was organized into a dozen companies, each in charge of a clearly delimited sector. The militiamen did not receive pay. They often resorted to racketeering. Their looting has caused many a conflict with inhabitants, for instance in Yopougon-Azito in November 2006. Frequent clashes occurred with the police who tried to restore order. In some cases, the police was routed and P. Mangou, the FDS head of staff, absolved the militiamen. Prime Minister Diarra even tried, without success, to dissolve the GPP. The organization was driven out of the Marie-Thérèse Institute but, as a consequence, dispersed throughout the city.

Once the Ouagadougou Agreement was signed, further steps were taken to curb the GPP. The government was forced to require more caution of it since its members were blamed for several acts of violence and racketeering. What caught our attention while studying urban militias was the utter destitution of their members. For many of these men, the first combat, day in day out, was to find something to eat. Once the state's cornucopia was no longer full, their principal preoccupation was a means of livelihood. In Abidjan as in the west, militiamen tended to see themselves as "cuckolded by Ouagadougou." They bitterly remarked that the "sacrifice" had not paid. "We bared our chest to save the republic [a frequent remark during interviews], we're less well treated than the rebels we fought, who are now in the ministries and ride around showing off in luxury four-wheel drives." The string of complaints and frustrations vented against authorities who have "forgotten their children" helps us understand the postconflict situation, fraught as it is with tensions and concerns for the country's stability.

In the words of A. G. a former combatant who ran a base (interviewed in Abidjan in March 2008): "To be frank, because... the man who's there and fights for... his country and then has nothing to eat... who doesn't even get a grain of rice... the one who... for whom he's fighting... it's hard. A lot are leaving, but they come back because, if you leave today, you've lost everything. Your family rejects you. But you, you said... you're military; you went to fight for the republic, now... you don't have a thing!"

Guy Roger Abialy, alias Sery Attention, former head of a GPP unit and member of FESCI's National Bureau, said during an interview in Abidjan in September 2006: "We asked them to... free the Marie-Thérèse Houphouët Boigny Institute in Adjamé. We were... in the logic of... of disarmament... So... everyone was... demobilized. Everyone, ah... everyone returned to their families. There was no camp... to receive people. [...] Everyone went home, like that! With nothing! Even though these people had military qualifications, not to say military actions to their credit, they were left like that."[40]

Since the official end of hostilities, most militiamen were living in squalid conditions while waiting for government aid. This might lead us to think that a modest financial effort would suffice to rally them behind the peace process, which they seem inclined to accept since "my president has set his foot in it."[41] Things are not so simple however.

First of all, these ex-combatants were seeking social and political recognition for their "sacrifices," their struggle to "save the republic." Here as elsewhere, the idea of a sacrifice, of giving oneself to the homeland, lies at the center of the militia ethos. It weighs heavily on the perceptions and procedures of pacification. Far from satisfying this desire for recognition, the Ouagadougou Agreement, whereby the leader of the rebellion became prime minister, frustrated the militiamen who think that their former enemies were better treated than them. The upward social mobility of former rebel combatants (some of whom, for instance Commandant Wattao, figure in success stories), the political visibility of former rebel leaders in Soro's first government, the compromises that these FN leaders made with Gbagbo, and the political and material benefits, all of this has, along with other factors, stoked the frustrations of former militiamen who feel that the republic has "forgotten its children."

Secondly, the war and violence have altered these men's relations to society, working, and money. The interviews with GPP members and persons who know them bear this out. These militiamen often saw no future other than a career using weapons in the "protection business." As might be expected, many militiamen, with nothing to do after the signing of the peace agreement, turned toward private security companies, which have thrived. Some companies were set up by persons near Gbagbo and the first lady[42] with the unstated goal of redeploying paramilitary groups. This provided these men with a new status at a time when there was less need of them and international pressure was mounting. It was also, of course, a way to form a private "reserve army" in case the political situation took a turn for the worse, as it did in 2010–2011. A job in the security and protection business was prized by the militiamen still in the camps. As we see through the interviews, they were for hire to whoever paid the most. The GPP militiamen, for instance, were increasingly hired to ensure the "safety" of firms (banks in particular) and security at private and public events in Abidjan in cooperation with the police. The head of the GPP, who had no other means for paying his troops, normally approved or even signed these "deals."

For all these militiamen in quest of a future, as for their counterparts in the FN, hope often boiled down to a single possibility: civic service. This service, an idea advanced by Laurent Gbagbo at the opening of direct talks with the rebels, was foreseen in the Ouagadougou Agreement. Authorities presented it as a miracle formula for absorbing former combatants and channeling their potential violence. It has received much publicity, and fostered high expectations among not only the combatants to be demobilized (some of whom want to remain in paramilitary formations) but also young people who, though they had not joined a militia, are attracted by the status of wearing a uniform. Given the absence of other programs, the civic service amounts to a public policy addressed to youth. Although the promises made risks not being kept, this policy has had one effect: it has kept the "nation under arms" and perpetuates the militianization of society in direct line with the period of war.

"The Ivory Coast Under Cover": The Warrior Ethos and Political Subjectivation Through Violence

Beyond the contingencies of demobilizing combatants, the armed mobilization of patriotic young people can be interpreted as an "emancipating subordination,"[43] a paradoxical process involving not only subordination to the regime's patriotic dogma and to militia discipline (of varying strictness), but also an emancipation of young men who violently grab power and try to compel recognition as full-fledged political players. Despite its ambiguity, this process reconfigures relations between generations and promotes a new political generation, who claims its due and exercises growing influence. To assess the place held by former combatants in a postconflict society, this sociological transformation of Ivorian politics must be assessed along with this advance by youth in public affairs.

Like FESCI activists, many of whom obtained positions in the administration, or like western militiamen who removed chiefs from office, the Young Patriots in Abidjan have experimented with "political subjectivation" through warfare, a process that has made them aware of their influence. Laying claim to power in society and to a "place in the world,"[44] this youth is determined to see to it that its rights are upheld even if this entails violence. Clear evidence of this is the looting that occurred when Young Patriots were mobilized in November 2004 or January 2006. Ultranationalism and looting combined in a single action of taking goods and asserting rights. This fits into what Achille Mbembe has called an "unprecedented culture of freedom as a mode of domination" and accumulation: "This domination consists of taking, appropriating and profiting in line with a logic whereby the course of life is likened to a game of chance and the present is dominant in the time frame. The freedom to encroach on others and on what belongs to them is not just part of a power struggle; it is part of an *art de vivre* and aesthetics."[45]

What effects will the militarization and militianization of Ivorian society have in the midrun? It is hard to say, since violence broke out again on another scale in 2010–2011. In working-class neighborhoods in Abidjan and in the west, militiamen have met with variable fates since the Ouagadougou Agreement. Some have, as a group, acquired significant power in local affairs. Others have, as individuals, managed matters to their advantage (for instance, the GPP commander of Riviera in Abidjan now an employee in the Cocody municipal administration). However the large majority are still in dire straits or have even lost social status. Despite the lack of empirical evidence, we know that these armed men have turned to criminal activities, whence the crime wave. Several firsthand accounts accuse former militiamen of being gangsters, whom the population increasingly holds in contempt. In fact, during the 2010–2011 postelection crisis, Gbagbo's regime remobilized them, thus fuelling the level of armed violence and repression.

Given the anarchic demobilization of militiamen, the "brutalization" of social and political relations has accelerated over the last ten years. The unprecedented crime wave, along with full impunity for crimes of all sorts committed since the start of the conflict, have reinforced the widely held opinion that legitimate values and social practices have come undone. People in working-class neighborhoods in Abidjan often say that, since the war, "the Ivory Coast is under cover" (*La Côte d'Ivoire est sous bâche*). In the darkness under cover, impunity: everyone can do what they want without any questions being asked. The militarization and militianization of the public sphere are obvious factors in this degradation of the established principles of urban civility. This degradation can also be seen in other forms. The *coupé-décalé* ("grab-and-run" in slang) fad in music is a symptom of this new mentality, which elevates as heros evildoers who accumulate money illegally (like the "419" Nigerians or the Cameroonian *feymen*). The "sagacity" of disc jockeys is measured by their conspicuous consumption of luxury goods, and "work" is no longer a way to earn money but, on the contrary, a synonym for squandering it ostentatiously.[46] This fad is presented as a genuine life philosophy. Having spread like wildfire around the planet, it is evidence that social norms have been overturned during a time of crisis.

I would like to hypothesize that to understand the ambivalent status and images of former militiamen—these new urban "warriors" who steal from and brutalize their neighbors—we must take into account this (im)moral economy of *coupé-décalé*, of force and dirty tricks. The "warrior" theme has a long history in the Ivory Coast. It saw the light of day in the ghettos of Abidjan during 1980–1990. At that time, it referred to hooligans (*ziguei*), "vandals," vagabonds (*nuchi*), and the forefathers (*vieux pères*), who, through violence, gained the stature of heroes, like street Robin Hoods.[47] In the urban ghettos portrayed so well in Éliane de Latour's film *Bronx Barbès*, social hierarchies and reputations were shaped by punches and knives. However the real "warrior" was the person, who, thanks to his "science" and cunning, was capable of bringing the spoils home to the ghetto and redistributing them to his "good little ones." To emancipate themselves from their elders, these little ones, in turn, have to prove themselves through their brutality as con artists. Owing to the crisis and certain cultural (in particular musical) fads, this philosophy of a vagabond life with its code and language has come out of the ghettos and permeated urban society, thus hallowing "values" such as courage, manliness (being a *garçon*, i.e. a brave male like Laurent Gbagbo is said to be), adventure, cunning, and dirty tricks. When inquiring into the diffusion of the "warrior ethos" borne by these former combatants, we must take into consideration this ghetto legacy in order to grasp the sense of what the phrase connotes in the postconflict situation in Abidjan. These former militiamen—most of whom have never been in a battle but who are now well trained in racketeering—are heirs to these ghetto "forefathers."

There is a significant difference, however[48]: the forefathers knew how to earn respect in the neighborhood owing to the moral economy of redistribution, whereas these ex-militiamen, through their manners and looting, have "spoiled the word warrior." Translated by Noal Mellott.

Notes

1. Somouss, a former "ghettoman," interviewed in Koumassi, Abidjan, in September 2003.
2. R. Marchal, and C. Messiant, *Les chemins de la guerre et de la paix* (Paris: Karthala, 1997).
3. See R. Banégas, "Côte d'Ivoire: les jeunes 'se lèvent en hommes.' Anticolonialisme et ultranationalisme chez les jeunes patriotes d'Abidjan," *Les Etudes du CERI*, no. 137 (July 2007).
4. During my last stint in the field in February–March 2008, two research assistants (Alain Toh and Gnangadjomon Koné) covered areas to the west, while I interviewed urban militiamen in Abidjan. I would like to warmly thank Alain Toh and Souleymane Kouyate for opening to me their lists of addresses, or rather telephone numbers.
5. Hardly any research has been conducted on the FN, apart from Moussa Fofana's survey (*Les déterminants de l'enrôlement des jeunes combattants de la rébellion du Nord de la Côte d'Ivoire*, Oxford: Crisis Working Paper, February 2008.) in the North and Magali Chelpi-den Hamer's PhD (2009) on rebels in the West, including the Man area.
6. I have not, herein, pursued the idea of "postconflict," a highly controversial word for conceptual and empirical reasons discussed in the introduction to this volume. Suffice it to say that it is hard to delimit what "post-conflict" means in the Ivory Coast for four reasons. First of all, actual warfare took place for a short time and affected localities variously, even sparing some fully. Secondly, the successive peace agreements signed from 2003 to 2007 did not fundamentally affect the matters. Thirdly, the situation has long been "neither war nor peace," which lends itself to all sorts of interpretations. Finally, according to data gathered during fieldwork in the general population, the people affected by the conflict usually refer to a very personal and local time scale that often contrasts with official chronology. The most frequently used phrase was: "The war found me..."
7. See G. Mosse, *De la Grande Guerre au totalitarisme: la brutalisation des sociétés européennes* (Paris: Hachette, 1999); and see the introduction to the present volume by Nathalie Duclos.
8. See C. Vidal, "La brutalisation du champ politique ivoirien," *Revue africaine de sociologie* 7, no. 2 (2003): 45–57.
9. See J. P. Chauveau and J.-P. Dozon, "Au coeur des ethnies ivoiriennes...l'Etat" in E. Terray (ed.), *L'Etat contemporain en Afrique*, (Paris: L'Harmattan, 1987), 223–224.
10. See S. Bobo and J. P. Chauveau, "La situation de guerre dans l'arène villageoise. Un exemple dans le Centre-Ouest ivoirien," *Politique africaine* 89 (March 2003): 12–33.
11. See M. Le Pape and C. Vidal (eds.), *Côte d'Ivoire, l'année terrible. 1999–2000* (Paris: Karthala, 2003).
12. See G. A. Kieffer, "Armée ivoirienne: le refus du déclassement," *Politique africaine* 78 (June 2000): 26–44.
13. See A. Marshall and C. Ero, "L'Ouest de la Côte d'Ivoire: un conflit libérien?," *Politique africaine* 89 (March 2003).
14. On May 8, 2007, Eloi Oulaï admitted this outright during a meeting of local officials in Bloléquin: "Tchéidé Gervais (vice-president of the local council in Guiglo), Daouho Benoît (mayor of Bloléquin), we are the ones who gave weapons to these young combatants and equipped them to push back the rebellion [...] If people are to be brought before the International Criminal Court, we're the ones. [...] The distribution of weapons and organization of various groups was done in my office. The organization of the visit by the head of state and the awareness campaigns for disbanding self-defense groups have to be our business" (*Le nouveau réveil*, May 9, 2007).
15. See R. Banégas, "Costa d'Avorio, lo stato delle milizie," *Limes* 3 (2006).
16. J. F. Bayart has reviewed the concept of "straddling" to explain state-building in Africa in *L'Etat en Afrique. La politique du ventre* (Paris: Fayard, 1989 [new edition in 2008]).

17. See Bobo and Chauveau, "La situation de guerre dans l'arène villageoise," 20.
18. See M. Chelpi-den Hamer, "Why We Fight? Perspective of Young Combatants in Western Côte d'Ivoire," contribution to the Workshop "Mobilisation for Political Violence. What Do We Know?," Oxford, Center for Research on Inequality, Human Security and Ethnicity (CRISE), March 17–18, 2009.
19. See Bobo and Chauveau, "La situation de guerre dans l'arène villageoise," 28–29.
20. The information in this paragraph comes from three studies by Chelpi-den Hamer from 2008, 2009, and "Le mythe du jeune désoeuvré: analyse des interventions DDR en Côte d'Ivoire" *Afrique contemporaine* 4, no. 232 (2009), who has graciously provided them to me.
21. In Man, on the rebel side, the rate was not so high (43 percent), a fact to be set down to regional differences in schooling in the Ivory Coast.
22. See P. Richards, *Fighting for The Rain Forest: War, Youth and Resources in Sierra Leone* (Oxford: James Currey, 1996).
23. See M. Chelpi-den Hamer, "Place de l'accès aux ressources des combattants avant, pendant et après le conflit," contribution to the seminar "Terre, ressources naturelles, conflits dans les sociétés du Sud," Paris, EHESS, December 2–5, 2008.
24. See J. P. Chauveau and P. Richards, "Les racines agraires des insurrections ouest-africaines. Une comparaison Côte d'Ivoire-Sierra Leone," *Politique africaine* 111 (October 2008): 131–168.
25. See Chelpi-den Hamer (2009), "Place de l'accès aux ressources des combattants," 20.
26. Ibid., 9.
27. See F. Konaté, "Bouaflé, Oumé, Diégonéfla, Hiré: les milices préparent un coup," *24 Heures*, (February 16, 2005): 4.
28. See D. Tade, "Tournée du Rdr dans le Moyen-Cavally, hier: Amon Tanoh et Mao Glofiéhi se sont parlé et se sont compris," *Le Nouveau Réveil*, July 18, 2009.
29. See Chauveau and Richards, "Les racines agraires des insurrections ouest-africaines," 151–152.
30. See Banégas, "Costa d'Avorio, lo stato delle milizie."
31. For a general discussion of changes in contemporary African success stories, see R. Banégas et J. P. Warnier (eds.), "Figures de la réussite et imaginaires politiques," special edition in *Politique africaine* 82(June 2001).
32. In addition to the previously cited studies by Bobo, Chauveau, and Chelpi-den Hamer, I would also like to mention the unpublished research carried out by Ousmane Dembele in the west for OCHA, and to thank him for allowing me access to his work.
33. See S. Bobo, "Le jeu politique autour des élections au village dans un contexte décentralisé. Entre autorités villageoises, ressortissants citadins et jeunes déscolarisés de retour au village," paper not published.
34. Y. B., a fieldworker in Bas-Sassandra for Search for Common Ground during an interview conducted by G. Koné on March 15, 2008.
35. See S. Bobo, "Les 'milices rurales' et la crise ivoirienne. Exemple du FBI et GPP (Soubré) et des 'jeunes combattants' de Booda (Oumé)," a paper submitted to the colloquium *Transguerre*, Montpellier, October 22–23, 2008.
36. Ibid., 7–9.
37. During the peace talks in Ouagadougou, President Gbagbo floated the prospect of demobilized combatants devoting a few years to military and civilian duties in a "civic service." This plan was continuously postponed after the signing of the peace agreements, thus leaving open the central issue of reintegrating soldiers in civilian life. Owing to the 2011 war, this issue has become all the more critical for Ouattara's new regime.
38. See R. Banégas, "Côte d'Ivoire: Patriotism, Ethnonationalism and Other Modes of Self-writing," *African Affairs* 105 , no. 421 (2006): 535–552.
39. The GPP had several camps in Abidjan: Vridi, Yopougon-Sable, Yopougon-Gesco, Abobo-PK 18, Bingerville, and even Cocody and Riviera)—places often taken by force (for instance, the Marie-Thérèse Institute in Adjamé).
40. A news report from one of the camps in the city confirmed this ("La vie des miliciens de Biabou II," *Nord-Sud Quotidien*, 792 (January 9, 2008): 2): "In Biabou II, the only worry that the thousands of young people involved in the 'liberation of the country' have is about their future. They say they do not understand why the policemen recruited in 2006, who merely heard about the war but do not know what it is, benefit from a bonus while those who fought on the front have been left behind. They also say they do not understand why the western self-defense

groups are bombarded with francs while those in the south are lavishly neglected. They feel it is time to stop discrimination. They have warned everyone, 'If we are not taken into account by civic service, the war that we are going to start will be serious.'"

41. S. R., commander of the AP-Wê camp in Duékoué, during an interview on May 26, 2007.
42. To readers unfamiliar with Ivorian politics, it should be pointed out that Simone Gbagbo was a major political figure: president of the FPI group in parliament and "godmother" of Young Patriot organizations. She had powerful personal networks and exercised considerable influence on the regime's "hawks."
43. An oxymoron borrowed from Xavier Audrain who, referring to Foucault, uses this phrase to describe Sheikh Modou Kara's young Mourid disciples in Senegal. By subjecting themselves body and soul to this marabout, they are emancipated from family oversight and assert themselves as moral and political subjects. See X. Audrain, "Terrain. Devenir *baay-fall* pour être soi. Le religieux comme vecteur d'émancipation individuelle au Sénégal," *Politique africaine* 94 (June 2004): 149–165.
44. James Ferguson's phrase refers both to a geopolitical, economic, and strategic category and to a widespread idea about Africa's "rank" in a global system. See J. Ferguson, *Global shadows: Africa in the Neoliberal World Order* (Durham, NC: Duke University Press, 2006).
45. See A. Mbembe, "À propos des écritures africaines de soi," *Politique africaine* 77 (June 2000): 42.
46. See D. Kolhagen, "Frime, escroquerie et cosmopolitisme. Le succès du 'coupé-décalé' en Afrique et ailleurs," *Politique africaine* 100 (2006): 92–106.
47. See E. de Latour, "Les ghettomen. Les gangs de rue à Abidjan et San Pédro," *Actes de la recherche en sciences sociales* 129, no. 1 (1999): 68–83.
48. I am grateful to Abou Kamate for drawing my attention to this.

Conclusion

Nathalie Duclos

In this collective work we hope to have shown the positive nature of an alternative approach to armed conflict—one which focuses on its main actors, the ex-combatants, and leaves in particular aside an exclusively negative vision of war produced for a large part by some economic analyses of armed conflict. Our intention has obviously not been to glorify military commitment either, but to try to objectivize after-war trajectories. The importance of depreciative a priori assumptions becomes apparent on reading historians' research on the after-war periods of the two World Wars, since their work contains no negative judgements regarding ex-combatants but on the contrary, has a tendency perhaps to view them with empathy. Doubtless this is because most of this research concerns ex-combatants of the authors' own or allied countries, thus nations at war with whom the latter sympathize. But it is certainly not insignificant either, that these studies concern interstate wars, and that the former combatants are either conscripts or career military, soldiers therefore, at the service of their state and not "rebels" defying the state. The ex-combatants one is inclined to consider suspect are those who engaged in a civil war, rather than those who fought in an orderly Westphalian framework. To avoid the biases inherent in preconceived notions of this sort, we have preferred to approach combat experience and that of postconflict with the tools of the social sciences, making particular use of the notion of trajectory and the concepts of collective action, engagement, and disengagement, socialization, etc., thus contributing, analytically, to a decompartmentalization of the war experience. It has also been our intention to extirpate the war experience from the temporal isolation to which it is confined in many analyses and to view it as a social experience in the context of previous experiences and later transpositions.

Rather than ask whether ex-combatants have reintegrated, the various contributions here have simply examined in an unbiased manner what became of these men (or women!) after the war, what paths they followed. Thanks to the "bottom up" approach adopted in this book, certain sociologic transformations (produced by the war and transposed after-war) have been pinpointed that show the importance of thinking about war and its effects on ex-combatants in sociologic terms, in an effort to view their postconflict trajectories with greater clarity. Some of these transformations seem particularly important. First of all, the fact that, after the war, combatants do not have the same status as before the war, and it is on the basis of this new status that they return to civilian life. Thus their return can only be understood in terms of a dynamic of interaction with the other sectors of society. This change of status operates on the micro level, in the space of family and social interpersonal relations, as well as on the meso and macro levels, concerning the group of ex-combatants in its social and political relations. Thus in this book we have shown how much the transformation in the status of certain ex-combatants contributed to the renewal of their relations with other social groups: we see this in the case of Peruvian militia who emerged from their state of second-rate citizens, in the case of the Ivory Coast's "Young Patriots," who emancipated themselves from the intergenerational relationships of the domination of elders, and again in the case of LRA renegades who can now envisage a national political career in Uganda.

Individual status is also modified, particularly in the family space, as we have seen with Second World War veterans returning home in Canada, or young recruits having taken part in the combats in Kurdistan, from then on seen as men. The context in which ex-combatants return to civilian life is a determining factor in how they are perceived: the status in society of the end of the war and the prevailing reading of it are imposed, *volens nolens,* on those who fought the war. Depending on whether veterans return victorious or defeated, on whether their war is perceived as shameful or "glorious," they are not seen in the same way, a fact which comes into play in interactions between ex-combatants and their families, friends, and colleagues on the micro level of daily interactions. The disapproval shown to Vietnam veterans, who sometimes felt perceived as plague-ridden, like the ex-soldier who described with bitterness how no one wanted to sit next to him in an airplane,[1] played an important role in the difficulties experienced on return by these men, who "went through an experience of 'transvaluation,'" in other words, a transformation of values, their war having become a "dirty war."[2] It is therefore in the context of a relational dynamic that the ex-combatant's trajectories evolve, trajectories that cannot be divorced from identitarian transformations caused by the war and resulting from this change of status after the war. For it is definitely an identitarian change that takes place after the war, because of the war experience and due to this change in status. Identity must be understood as the product of the transaction operating between the ex-combatant and the rest of society.

This brings us to the second major transformation, the renewal of the combatant's sociability networks brought about by the war. Many indestructible friendships are built or reinforced during combats, but there are also new everyday social relations that are an outgrowth of this common

CONCLUSION 269

experience—relationships often founded on solidarities that were a condition of survival during wartime, and which from then on rest on shared memories. Veterans' return to civilian life cannot be apprehended without taking the role of these new sociabilities into account. Many studies on the DDR express the view that the ex-combatant can only reintegrate if he breaks ties with his former "brothers-in-arms," those in particular who constituted the command chain.[3] This postulate is based on the tendency mentioned earlier to denigrate ex-combatants, and it appears unfounded when we approach "reintegration" from below, via empirical inquiries.[4] On the contrary, investment in these networks seems to be a constituent element of transaction modalities with the after-war, either via a new political action, as in Sardinia, where combat solidarities made up the framework of new regionalist solidarities[5] or, more prosaically, via regular friendly meetings and exchanges, which reactivate memories and provide an opportunity to seek meaning in shared experiences. In this sense, veterans associations play a central role, as was shown in the cases of Canada and Sardinia. Sometimes, as in the example of Serb militia, these relations between ex-combatants are maintained on a more informal basis, contributing to the perpetuation of a small, close-knit group, even if each of its members has found his place in civilian life. This sociability cannot be seen only as an obstacle to reintegration; it can in fact contribute to professional reinsertion, when the ex-combatant is good at social networking.

Our approach from the bottom up has also—unexpectedly, since it involves a macro issue—made it possible to show the importance to their return trajectories of public policies destined for ex-combatants. Not only DDR programs, designed more often than not from the viewpoint of security, but more generally, material and symbolic policies aimed at veterans—the first granting them specific benefits and the second a certain status in the nation, a sign of the official recognition of their contribution to a page of national history. When they exist, these policies play a role in the dynamic of return to civilian life in the sense that they contribute to the consolidation of this new status of the ex-combatant we have already emphasized, and heighten its impact on interactions with noncombatants. According to the case, public policies waver between official recognition or celebration (on one hand) and denial on the other. Often, they also show signs of the temptation to instrumentalize.

Several situations studied in this book illustrate the importance of official discourse, the cornerstone of symbolic commemoration policies led post-war—discourse celebrating the "heroism" of fighters, glorifying their contribution to the defense of a unified nation, mythifying the war and sanctifying its victims. At the opposite end of the scale, as in Russia and Turkey, denial of the reality of war (two major armed conflicts in Chechnya and Kurdistan) is an extreme case of (non)recognition of combat experience. The official position of euphemizing the war makes the return of ex-combatants more problematical: denied of their identity as fighters, their past experience becomes trivialized. Official discourse imposes a blackout, preventing any recognition, even of a symbolic nature, of sacrifices made, thus frustrating their expectations of gratitude and causing difficulty on return (at least if we believe the studies carried out on Vietnam and Afghanistan veterans confronted with this same issue). The symbolic dimension of official accompaniment of ex-combatants has a decisive effect on modalities of return. It contributes to giving meaning to the intimate experience of former combatants, one that more or less corresponds to their own subjectivity.

Equally important are concrete measures in favor of ex-combatants: material policies are undeniably an aid in their return, particularly in the case of those who interrupted their training because of the war. Thus the Canadian benefits program (scholarships for resuming studies, professional training, priority access to work, psychological programs, etc.) based on the US model facilitated the professional reinsertion of Canadian ex-combatants, helping them in a material sense to reintegrate. Material accompaniment also produces meaning and usually corroborates symbolic policies recognizing the "sacrifices" made by ex-combatants.

Nevertheless, beneath both symbolic and material policies, one can often discern the temptation to instrumentalize the memory of combat on the part of the political authorities, who, by seeking to impose meaning on the previous armed conflict, attempt to consolidate their power. Of this order are the material, as well as the symbolic policies led in Turkey: the glorification of war martyrs is one component that contributes to the construction of an inside enemy allowing the Turkish army to legitimize and pursue its interventions in Kurdistan. Directed toward aims other than the reintegration of ex-combatants, such instrumentalization compromises the return to civilian life, particularly when it rests on the denial of armed conflict.

Are combatants brutalized at the end of the war? Certainly there is not one answer, and we have seen the usefulness of sociologizing the questioning. Not brutalized, but not unharmed either, much depends on the modalities and context of the war: preparation for combat, exposure to violence, length of participation, type of violent acts, meaning of the conflict, and so on. Likewise, the modalities and context of the end of the conflict are decisive: victory, defeat, outside intervention, post-conflict political changes, the economic situation, and public policies aimed at veterans. Doubtless also that the war has not the same impact on everybody: combatants' sociocultural characteristics are definitely an essential filter. The pioneering research of Lazarsfeld showed early on that those most resistant to war violence were not the most physically valiant, as many had instinctively thought, but paradoxically, those with the highest level of education. Likewise, at the end of a war, the intention to join a union, political organization, or to an even greater degree a "civic club" is highest among those most educated.[6] Thus post-war transactions vary according to the socio-cultural dispositions of (ex-)combatants, which means that by studying from a sociological point of view those who become combatants, we will better understand the ex-combatants they become later on. Translated by Judith Andreyev.

Notes

1. P. L. Goldman, Tony Fuller, *Charlie Company: What Vietnam Did to Us* (New York: Morrow, 1983), 13.
2. F. Sironi, *Psychopathologie des violences collectives: essai de psychologie géopolitique clinique* (Paris: Odile Jacob, 2007), 112.
3. According to Joanna Spear, "peace requires breaking the command and control structures operating over rebel fighters..." in "Disarmament and Demobilisation," in S. J. Stedman, D. Rothchild, E. M. Cousens (eds.), *Ending Civil Wars. The Implementation of Peace Agreements* (Boulder CO: London : Lynne Rienner Publishers, IPA, 2002).
4. M. Humphreys and J. Weinstein show that ex-combatants who have lost all contact with their ex-brothers-in-arms do not reintegrate better than others, "Demobolization and Reintegration in Sierra Leone. Assessing Progress," in R. Muggah (ed.), *Security and Post-conflict Reconstruction: Dealing with Fighters in the Aftermath of War*, (London: Routledge,2009), 48.
5. Consider the role of solidarity incentives in mobilizations, well illustrated by A. Pizzorno in the sociology of social movements.
6. S. A. Stouffer, *The American Soldier. Vol II, Combat and Its Aftermath* (Princeton, NJ: Princeton University Press, 1965), 643.

BIBLIOGRAPHY

General Theory

Almond, Gabriel, and Verba Sidney. *The Civic Culture: Political Attitudes and Democracy in Five Nations and Democratic Stability*. Princeton, NJ: Princeton University Press, 1963.
Banfield, Edward. *The Moral Basis of a Backward Society*. Glencoe, IL: Free Press/Research Center in Economic Development and Cultural Change (University of Chicago), 1958.
Bayart, Jean-François. *L'Etat en Afrique. La politique du ventre*. Paris: Fayard, 1989 [new edition in 2008].
Becker, Howard Saul. *Outsiders. Studies in the Sociology of Deviance*. London: Free Press, 1966.
Bourdieu, Pierre. *Esquisse d'une théorie de la pratique. Précédé de trois études d'ethnologie kabyle*. Genève [Paris]: Droz, 1972.
———. *Questions de sociologie*. Paris: Éditions de Minuit, 1998.
Brubaker, Rogers. *Ethnicity Without Groups*. Cambridge: Harvard University Press, 2004
Cohen, Stanley. *States of Denial: Knowing about Atrocities and Suffering*. Cambridge, UK/Malden, MA: Polity/Blackwell Publishers, 2001.
Dubar, Claude. *La socialisation: construction des identités sociales et professionnelles*. 2nd edition. Paris: A. Colin, 1995.
Elias, Norbert. *La civilisation des moeurs*. [Repr.]. Paris: Calmann-Lévy, 1991.
———. *La dynamique de l'Occident*. Paris: Calmann-Lévy, 1991.
———. *La société des individus*. Paris: Librairie Arthème Fayard, 1991.
Foucault, Michel. *Dits et écrits. 1954–1988*. Paris: Gallimard, 2001.
———. *Il faut défendre la société: cours au Collège de France, 1975–1976*. Paris: Gallimard/Seuil, 1997.
———. *Sécurité, territoire, population: cours au Collège de France, 1977–1978*. Paris: Seuil/Gallimard, 2004.
Gaïti, Brigitte. "L'opinion publique dans l'histoire politique: impasses et bifurcations." *Le Mouvement social* 221(2007): 95.
Gambetta, Diego. *The Sicilian Mafia: The Business of Private Protection*. Cambridge, MA: Harvard University Press, 1993.
Van Gennep, Arnold. *Les Rites de passage: étude systématique des rites*. Paris: Picard, 1981.
Goguel d'Allondans, Thierry. *Rites de passage, rites d'initiation: lecture d'Arnold van Gennep*. Sainte-Foy (Québec): Presses de l'Université Laval, 2002.
Gould, Roger. *Insurgent Identities: Class, Community, and Protest in Paris from 1848 to the Commune*. Chicago, IL: University of Chicago Press, 1995.
Hamidi, Camille. "Eléments pour une approche interactionniste de la politisation. Engagement associatif et rapport au politique dans des associations locales issues de l'immigration." *Revue française de science politique* 56, no. 1 (2006).
Lagroye, Jacques. *La politisation*. Paris: Belin, 2003.
Lahire, Bernard (ed.). *L'homme pluriel: les ressorts de l'action*. Paris: Hachette Littératures, 2007.
Noiriel, Gérard. *Etat nation et immigration: vers une histoire du pouvoir*. Paris: Belin, 2001.
Oberschall, Anthony. *Social Movements: Ideologies, Interests, and Identities*. 2nd edition. New Brunswick: Transaction Publishers, 1997.

Peres, Hubert. *Individus entre village et nation. Une expérience identitaire dans la formation de la france républicaine,* PhD, Bordeaux, University of Bordeaux I, 1993.
Putnam, Robert D, Robert Leonardi, and Raffaella Y. Nanetti. *Making Democracy Work: Civic Traditions in Modern Italy.* Princeton, NJ: Princeton University Press, 1993.
Tilly, Charles. *From Mobilization to Revolution.* New York: McGraw-Hill, 1978.
———. *La France conteste: de 1600 à nos jours.* Paris: Fayard, 1986.
———. *Trust and Rule.* New York: Cambridge University Press, 2005.
Volkov, Vadim. *Violent Entrepreneurs: The Use of Force in the Making of Russian Capitalism.* Ithaca, NY: Cornell University Press, 2002.

War/Postwar

Audoin-Rouzeau, Stéphane, and Prochasson Christophe (eds.). *Sortir de la Grande Guerre: le monde et l'après-1918.* Paris: Tallandier, 2008.
Audoin-Rouzeau, Stéphane. *Combattre: une anthropologie historique de la guerre moderne, XIXe-XXIe siècle.* Paris: Seuil, 2008.
Audoin-Rouzeau, Stéphane, and Becker Annette. *14-18, retrouver la guerre.* Paris: Gallimard, 2000.
Barakat, Sultan (ed.). *After the conflict: Reconstruction and Development in the Aftermath of War.* London/New York: I.B. Tauris/Palgrave Macmillan, 2005.
Becker, Annette. "Compte-rendu de la traduction française du livre de Georges Mosse." *Annales* 1: (2000).
Becker, Jean-Jacques. *1914: comment les Français sont entrés dans la guerre: contribution à l'étude de l'opinion publique, printemps-été 1914.* Paris: Presses de la Fondation Nationale des Sciences Politiques, 1977.
Berdal, Mats R., and David M. Malone (eds.). *Greed and Grievance: Economic Agendas in Civil Wars.* Boulder, CO: Lynne Rienner Publishers, 2000.
Berdal, Mats R., and Wennmann Achim (eds). *Ending Wars, Consolidating Peace: Economic Perspectives.* Abingdon, Oxon: Routledge for the International Institute for Strategic Studies, 2010.
Bougarel, Xavier, Elissa Helms, and Duijzings Ger (eds). *The New Bosnian Mosaic: Identities, Memories and Moral Claims in a Post-war Society.* Aldershot: Ashgate, 2007.
Bourke, Joanna. *An Intimate History of Killing: Face-to-Face Killing in Twentieth-Century Warfare.* New York: Basic Books, 1999.
Brown, Michael. *The International Dimensions of Internal Conflict.* Cambridge, MA: MIT Press, 1996.
Bucaille, Laetitia. *Le pardon et la rancœur: Algérie-France, Afrique du Sud: peut-on enterrer la guerre?* Paris: Payot, 2010.
Cabanes, Bruno, and Piketty Guillaume (eds). "Sorties de guerre au XXe siècle." *Histoire@politique* (2007).
B. Cabanes, E. Husson (eds.). *Les sociétés en guerre. 1911-1946.* Paris: Armand Colin, 2003.
Cohen, Stanley. *States of Denial: Knowing about Atrocities and Suffering.* Cambridge, UK/Malden, MA: Polity/Blackwell Publishers, 2001.
Collier, Paul, V. L. Elliott, and Hegre Havard. *Breaking the Conflict Trap: Civil War and Development Policy.* Washington, DC: World Bank, 2003.
Collier, Paul, and World Bank. *Economic Causes of Civil Conflict and Their Implications for Policy.* Washington, D.C.: World Bank, 2000.
Collovald, Annie, and Sandrine Lefranc (eds). "La pacification des violences." *Politix* 80 (2007).
Crocker, Chester. *Leashing the Dogs of War: Conflict Management in a Divided World.* Washington, D.C.: United States Institute of Peace Press, 2007.
Darby, John. *The Effects of Violence on Peace Processes.* Washington, D.C.: United States Institute of Peace Press, 2001.
Darby, John, and Roger MacGinty (eds.). *Contemporary Peacemaking: Conflict, Peace Processes and Postwar Reconstruction.* Basingstoke: Palgrave MacMillan, 2008.

——— (eds.). *Contemporary Peacemaking: Conflict, Violence and Peace processes*. Houndmills, Basingstoke: Palgrave MacMillan, 2003.

Delpla, Isabelle, and Bessone Magali, eds. *Peines de guerre: la justice pénale internationale et l'ex-Yougoslavie*. Paris: Éditions de l'École des Hautes Etudes en Sciences Sociales, 2010.

Foer, Franklin. *How Soccer Explains the World: An Unlikely Theory of Globalization*. New York: Harper & Collins, 2004.

Fukuyama, Francis. *State-building: Governance and World Order in the 21st Century*. Ithaca, NY: Cornell University Press, 2004.

Galtung, Johan. *Peace: Research, Education, Action*. Copenhagen: Ejlers, 1975.

Hannoyer, Jean (ed.). *Guerres civiles: économies de la violence, dimensions de civilité*. Paris: Karthala-CERMOC, 1999.

Hardtwig, Wolfgang. *Politische Kulturgeschichte der Zwischenkriegszeit 1918–1939*. Göttingen: Vandenhoeck & Ruprecht, 2005.

Hassner, Pierre, and Marchal Roland (eds). *Guerres et sociétés: États et violence après la Guerre froide*. Paris: Karthala, 2003.

Hawk, Kathleen Hill. *Constructing the Stable State: Goals for Intervention and Peacebuilding*. Westport, CT: Praeger, 2002.

Holsti, Kalevi Jaakko. *The State, War, and the State of War*. Cambridge: Cambridge University Press, 1996.

Horne, John. "Guerres et réconciliations européennes au 20e siècle." *Vingtième siècle* 104, no. 4 (2009): 3–15.

Horne, John N. (ed.). *Démobilisations culturelles après la Grande Guerre*. Paris: Noésis, 2002.

Horne, John N, and Alan Kramer. *German atrocities, 1914: A History of Denial*. New Haven, CT: Yale University Press, 2001.

Horne, John, "Kulturelle Demobilmachung 1919–1939. Ein sinnvoller historischer Begriff?" In Wolgang Hardtwig (ed.) *Politische Kulturgeschichte der Zwischenkriegszeit 1918–1939*. Göttingen: Vandenhoeck & Ruprecht, 2005.

Human Security Center. *Human Security Report 2005: War and Peace in the 21st Century*. New York/Oxford/British Columbia(Canada): Oxford University Press, 2005.

Jones, J., "From The Thin Red Line." In P. Fussell (ed.) *The Norton Book of the Modern War*. London/New York: W. W. Norton, 1991: 325-334.

Kaldor, Mary. *New and Old Wars: Organized Violence in a Global Era*. Cambridge, England: Polity Press, 1999.

Kalyvas, Stathis. "New And Old Civil Wars: A Valid Distinction?" *World Politics* 54, no.1 (2001): 99–118.

———. *The Logic of Violence in Civil War*. Cambridge/New York: Cambridge University Press, 2006.

Keegan, John. *A History of Warfare*. New York: Alfred A. Knopf (Distributed by Random House Inc.), 1993.

Lefranc, Sandrine (ed.). *Après le conflit, la réconciliation?* Paris: M. Houdiard, 2006.

———. *Politiques du pardon*. Paris: Presses Universitaires de France, 2002.

Luttwak, Edward N. "Give War a Chance." *Foreign Affairs* 78, no. 4 (1999).

Marchal, Roland (ed.). "Justice et réconciliation: ambiguïtés et impensés." *Politique africaine* 92 (2003).

Marchal, Roland, and Christine Messiant Gerber. *Les chemins de la guerre et de la paix: fins de conflit en Afrique orientale et australe*. Paris: Karthala, 1997.

———. "Les guerres civiles à l'ère de la globalisation: nouvelles réalités et nouveaux paradigmes." *Critique internationale* 18 (2003): 91–112.

———. "De l'avidité des rebelles: l'analyse économique de la guerre civile selon Paul Collier." *Critique internationale* 16 (2002): 58–69.

Mariot, Nicolas. "Faut-il être motivé pour tuer?" *Genèses* 4, no. 53 (2003).

Mink, Georges, and Laure Neumayer (eds). *L'Europe et ses passés douloureux*. Paris: La Découverte, 2007.

Modell, J., and Timothy Haggerty "The Social Impact of War." *Annual Review of Sociology* 17, (1991): 205–224.

Mosse, George Lachmann. *Fallen Soldiers: Reshaping the Memory of the World Wars.* New York: Oxford University Press, 1991.
Münkler, Herfried. *The New Wars.* Cambridge: Polity, 2005.
Paris, Roland. *At War's End: Building Peace after Civil Conflict.* Cambridge: Cambridge University Press, 2004.
Richards, Paul. *No Peace No War: An Anthropology of Contemporary Armed Conflicts.* Athens, OH: Ohio University Press, 2005.
Pouligny, Béatrice. *Peace Operations Seen from Below: UN Missions and Local People.* London: Hurst & Company, 2006.
Pouligny, Béatrice, and Pouyé Raphaël. "Le state-building au secours de la sécurité internationale." *RAMSES 2004* (IFRI) (2004):47-60.
Prost, Antoine. "Les limites de la brutalisation. Tuer sur le front occidental, 1914–1918." *Vingtième siècle* 81 (2004): 5.
Rehn, Elisabeth, and Ellen Johnson Sirleaf. *Progress of the world's women 2002. Volume 1, Women, war, peace: the Independent Experts' assessment on the impact of armed conflict on women and women's role in peace-building.* New York: UNIFEM, 2002.
Reysoo, Fenneke. "Situations de conflits armés comme analyseurs de rapports de genre," in *Hommes armés, femmes aguerries. Rapport de genre en situation de conflit armé.* Ginebra, IUED, 2001.
Richards, David. *Victory among People: Lessons from Countering Insurgency and Stabilising Fragile States.* London: Royal United Services Institute for Defence and Security Studies, 2011.
Rozenberg, Danielle. "Mémoire, justice et...raison d'état dans la construction de l'Espagne démocratique." *Histoire@politique* 2 (2007).
Sémelin, Jacques. *Purify and Destroy: The Political Uses of Massacre and Genocide.* London: Hurst, 2007.
Sironi, Françoise. *Psychopathologie des violences collectives: essai de psychologie géopolitique clinique.* Paris: Odile Jacob, 2007.
Stedman, Stephen John. "Spoiler Problems in Peace Processes."*International Security* 22, no. 2 (1997): 5–53.
Stedman, Stephen John, Donald S. Rothchild, and Elizabeth M. Cousens. *Ending Civil Wars: The Implementation of Peace Agreements.* Boulder, CO: Lynne Rienner, 2002.
Stora, Benjamin. *La gangrène et l'oubli: la mémoire de la guerre d'Algérie.* Paris: La Découverte, 1991.
M. J. Zahar, "Reframing the Spoiler Debate in Peace Processes." In John Darby and Roger MacGinty (eds.) *Contemporary Peacemaking: Conflict, Violence and Peace Processes.* New York: Palgrave Macmillan, 2003.
Zartman, Ira William. *Collapsed States: Disintegration and Restoration of Legitimate Authority.* Boulder, CO: Lynne Rienner, 1995.

Soldiers/Ex-combatants/DDR

Alden, Chris. "Making Old Soldiers Fade Away: Lessons from the Reintegration of Demobilized Soldiers in Mozambique."*Peace Research Abstracts* 41, no. 1 (2004).
Allport, Alan. *Demobbed: Coming Home after the Second World War.* New Haven/London: Yale University Press, 2009.
Arnold, Matthew. "'This Gun is Our Food': Disarming the White Army Militias of South Sudan."*Conflict, Security Development* 7, no. 3 (2007): 361–385.
Bennett, Michael J. *When Dreams Came True: The GI Bill and the Making of Modern America.* Washington, D.C.: Brassey's, 2000.
Berdal, Mats R. *Disarmament and Demobilisation after Civil Wars.* Oxford: Oxford University Press, 1996.
Berdal, Mats R., and David H. Ucko (eds). *Reintegrating Armed Groups after Conflict: Politics, Violence and Transition.* London: Routledge, 2009.
Bonior, David, Steven M. Champlin, and Timothy S. Kolly. *The Vietnam Veteran: A History of Neglect.* New York: Praeger, 1986.

Boulanger, Ghislaine, and Charles Kadushin. *The Vietnam Veteran Redefined: Fact and Fiction*. Hillsdale, NJ: L. Erlbaum, 1986.

R. Branche, "La dernière génération du feu? Jalons pour une étude des anciens combattants français de la guerre d'Algérie," in B. Cabanes and G. Piketty (eds.), "Sorties de guerre au XXe siècle." *Histoire@politique*, no. 3 (November–December 2007).

Bucaille, Lætitia. "Introduction." *Revue internationale des sciences sociales: RISS* 189, no. 3 (2009): 459.

———. "Reshaping identities in post-conflict societies: ex-combatants, heroes and exiles."*International Social Science Journal* 58, no. 189 (2006).

Cabanes, Bruno. *La victoire endeuillée: la sortie de guerre des soldats français: 1918–1920*. Paris: Seuil, 2004.

———. "Le retour du soldat au XXe siècle. Perspectives de recherche." *Revue historique des armées* 245 (2006).

Cabanes, Bruno, and Guillaume Piketty (eds). *Retour à l'intime: au sortir de la guerre*. Paris: Tallandier, 2009.

Colletta, Nat, Markus Kostner, and Ingo Wiederhofer. *Case Studies in War-to-Peace Transition: the Demobilization and Reintegration of Ex-combatants in Ethiopia, Namibia, and Uganda*. Washington, DC: World Bank, 1996.

Davis, Diane E., and Anthony W. Pereira (eds). *Irregular Armed Forces and Their Role in Politics and State Formation*. Cambridge (UK)/New York: Cambridge University Press, 2003.

Demobilization and Reintegration of Military Personnel in Africa: The evidence from Seven Country Case Studies. 1993. Washington, D.C.: World Bank.

Duclos, Nathalie. *Le Kosovo Police Service, facteur de consolidation de la paix au Kosovo?* Paris: IHESI (Institut des Hautes Etudes de la Sécurité Intérieure), 2003.

Gamba, Virginia. "Managing Violence: Disarmament and Demobilization." In John Darby and Roger MacGinty (eds.) *Contemporary Peacemaking: Conflict, Violence and Peace Processes*. New York: Palgrave MacMillan, 2003.

Garibay, David. *Des armes aux urnes: processus de paix et réinsertion politique des anciennes guérillas en Colombie et au Salvador*. PhD dissertation. Paris: IEP, 2003.

Giustozzi, Antonio. "Bureaucratic Facade and Political realities of disarmament and demobilisation in Afghanistan."*Conflict, Security and Development* 8, no. 2 (2008): 169–192.

Glantz, Aaron. *The War Comes Home: Washington's Battle against America's Veterans*. Berkeley(LA)/London: University of California Press, 2009.

Goldman, Peter, and Tony Fuller. *Charlie Company: What Vietnam Did to Us*. 1st edition. New York: Morrow, 1983.

Granjo, Paulo. "The Homecomer: Postwar Cleansing Rituals in Mozambique."*Peace Research Abstracts Journal* 44, no. 3 (2007).

Helmer, John. *Bringing the War Home: The American Soldier in Vietnam and After*. New York: Free Press, 1974.

Higate, Paul. "Theorising Continuity: From Military to Civilian Life." *Armed Forces and Society* 27, no. 3 (2001).

Holm, Tom."Culture, Ceremonialism, and Stress: American Indian Veterans and the Vietnam War." *Armed Forces & Society* 12, no. 2 (1986).

Humphreys, Macartan. "Demobilization and Reintegration." *Journal of Conflict Resolution* 51, no. 4 (2007): 531–567.

International Peace Academy. *A Framework for Lasting Disarmament Demobilization and Reintegration of Former Combatants in Crisis Situations*. 2002.

Jennings, Kathleen M. *Seeing DDR from below. Challenges and Dilemmas Raised by the Experiences of ex-combatants in Liberia*. Fafo-Report, 2008.

———. "Struggle to Satisfy: DDR through the Eyes of Ex-combatants in Liberia."*International Peacekeeping* 14, no. 2 (2007): 204–218.

Kingma, Kees. *Demobilization in Sub-Saharan Africa: The Development and Security Impacts*. Basingstoke: Macmillan in association with Bonn International Center for Conversion, 2000.

———. "Demobilization of Combatants after Civil Wars in Africa and Their Reintegration into Civilian Life."*Sage Public Administration Abstracts* 25, no. 1 (1998).

Kingma, Kees, and Kiflemariam Gebrewold. *Demilitarisation, Reintegration and Conflict Prevention in the Horn of Africa*. London: Saferworld, 1998.

Knight, M., and Alpaslan Ozerdem."Guns, Camps and Cash: Disarmament, Demobilization and Reinsertion of Former Combatants in Transitions from War to Peace."*Peace Research Abstracts* 41, no. 6 (2004).

Kriger, Norma J. *Guerrilla Veterans in Post-war Zimbabwe: Symbolic and Violent Politics, 1980–1987.* Cambridge: Cambridge University Press, 2003.

Lazarsfeld, Paul. "The American Soldier—An Expository Review," *The Public Opinion Quaterly* 13, no. 3 (Autumn 1949).

Mc Mullin, Jaremey. "Reintegration of Combatants: Were the Right Lessons Learned in Mozambique?" *International Peacekeeping* 11, no. 4 (2004.): 625–643.

Mettler, Suzanne. *Soldiers to Citizens: The G.I. Bill and the Making of the Greatest Generation.* New York/Oxford: Oxford University Press, 2005.

Muggah, Robert (ed.). *Security and Post-conflict Reconstruction: Dealing with Fighters in the Aftermath of War.* London: New-York: Routledge, 2009.

Newman, Edward, and Oliver Richmond. *Challenges to Peacebuilding: Managing Spoilers during Conflict Resolution.* Tokyo/New York/Paris: United Nations University Press, 2006.

Özerdem, Alpaslan. *Post-war Recovery: Disarmament, Demobilization and Reintegration.* London: I.B. Tauris, 2009.

Porto, João Gomes, Chris Alden, and Imogen Parsons. *From Soldiers to Citizens: Demilitarization of Conflict and Society.* Aldershot: Ashgate, 2007.

Pouligny, Béatrice, and the Programme for Strategic and International Security Studies. *Les anciens combattants d'aujourd'hui: désarmement, démobilisation et réinsertion: The politics and anti-politics of contemporary 'disarmament, demobilization & reintegration' programs.* Geneva: Graduate Institute of International Studies, 2004.

Prost, Antoine. *Les Anciens combattants.* Paris: Gallimard, 1977.

———. *Les anciens combattants et la société française 1914–1939.* Paris: Presses de la Fondation Nationale des Sciences Politiques, 1977.

A. Prost, "Brutalisation des sociétés et brutalisation des combattants,"in B. Cabanes, E. Husson (eds.). *Les sociétés en guerre. 1911–1946.* Paris: Armand Colin, 2003.

Roynette, Odile. "La nostalgie du front," in Cabanes Bruno and Piketty, Guillaume (eds.). *Retour à l'intime au sortir de la guerre.* Paris: Tallandier, 2009: 51-65.

Sabbatucci, Giovanni. *I combattenti nel primo dopoguerra.* Bari: Laterza, 1974.

Schafer, Jessica. "Guerrillas and Violence in the War in Mozambique: De-Socialization or Re-Socialization?" *African Affairs* 100, no. 399 (2001).

———. *Soldiers at Peace: Veterans and Society after the Civil War in Mozambique.* New York: Palgrave Macmillan, 2007.

Stouffer, Samuel. *The American Soldier. Volume II: Combat and Its Aftermath.* New York/Princeton: Princeton University Press, 1949 [1965].

Themnér, Anders. *Violence in Post-Conflict Societies. Remarginalization, remobilizers and relationships.* London/New-York: Routledge, 2011.

De Zeeuw, Jeroen. *From Soldiers to Politicians: Transforming Rebel Movements after Civil War.* Boulder, CO, London: Lynne Rienner, 2008.

Countries

Russia/Chechnya

Akhmadov, Ilyas, and Lanskoy Miriam. *The Chechen Struggle: Independence Won and Lost.* 1st edition. New York: Palgrave Macmillan, 2010.

Astigarraga, Isabelle. *Tchétchénie: Un peuple sacrifié.* Paris: L'Harmattan, 2000.

Babchenko, Arkadi. *One Soldier's War in Chechnya.* London: Portobello Books Ltd, 2006.

Balci, Bayram, and Motika Raoul. *Religion et politique dans le Caucase post-soviétique: les traditions réinventées à l'épreuve des influences extérieures.* Paris/Istanbul: Maisonneuve & Larose/Institut français d'études anatoliennes, 2007.

Bannikov, Konstantin L. "Regimented Communities in a Civil Society."*The Journal of Power Institutions in Post-Soviet Societies* 1 (2004), http://www. pipss.revues.org/index40.html.

Beissinger Mark, and Crawford Young. *Beyond State Crisis? Postcolonial Africa and Post-Soviet Eurasia in Comparative Perspective*. Washington D.C./Baltimore, MD: Woodrow Wilson Center Press/ Distributed by Johns Hopkins University Press, 2002.

Blandy, Charles. *Chechnya: A Beleaguered President*. Conflict Studies Research Centre Royal Military Academy Sandhurst, 1998.

Campana, Aurélie, Grégory Dufaud, and Sophie Tournon (eds.). *Les déportations en héritage: les peuples réprimés du Caucase et de Crimée, hier et aujourd'hui*. Rennes: Presses universitaires de Rennes, 2009.

Cook, Amélie. *Les violences policières en Fédération de Russie: les pratiques policières violentes en Russie post-soviétique et leur constitution en enjeu politique et social*. Research thesis for a Master, directed by G. Favarel-Garrigues. Paris, IEP, 2005.

Daucé, Françoise, and Elisabeth Sieca-Kozlowski (eds). *Dedovshchina in the Post-soviet Military: Hazing of Russian Army Conscripts in a Comparative Perspective*. Stuttgart: Ibidem-Verlag, 2006.

Dmitrievskii, Stanislav, Bogdan Gvareli, and Oksana Chelyshev. *Mezhdunarodnyi tribunal dlia Chechni*. Nizhnii-Novgorod, 2009. Available with summary in English at http://www.tribunalchr.info/.

Edele, Mark. *Soviet Veterans of World War II: A Popular Movement in an Authoritarian Society, 1941– 1991*. Oxford/New York: Oxford University Press, 2008.

Evangelista, Matthew. *The Chechen Wars: Will Russia Go the Way of the Soviet Union?* Washington, D.C.: Brookings Institute Press, 2002.

Favarel-Garrigues, Gilles and Le Huérou, Anne. "State and Multilateralization of Policing in Post-Soviet Russie." *Policing and Society* 14, no. 1 (January 2004): 13-30.

Furman, Dmitri. *Chechnia i Rossiia: obshchestva i gosudarstva*. Moscow: Publication of the Andreï Sakharov Museum, 1999.

Galeotti, Mark. *Afghanistan, The Soviet Union's Last War*. London, England/Portland, OR: Frank Cass, 1995.

Holquist, Peter. *Making War, Forging Revolution: Russia's Continuum of Crisis, 1914–1921*. Cambridge, MA: Harvard University Press, 2002.

Human Right Watch Report. "To serve without health." 2003. Available at http://www.hrw.org /sites/default/files/reports/russia1103.pdf (accessed on June 2011).

Kherad, Rahim. "De la nature juridique du conflit tchétchène." *Revue générale de droit international public* 1 (2000.): 143–179.

Knezys, Stasys, and Sedlickas Romanas. *The War in Chechnya*. College Station: Texas A&M University Press, 1999.

Le Huérou, Anne. "L'opinion russe face à la guerre en Tchétchénie." In Hassner, Pierre and Marchal, Roland (eds.) *Guerre et sociétés: État et violence après la guerre froide*. Paris: Karthala, 2003.

Le Huérou, Anne, Aude Merlin, Amandine Regamey, and Silvia Serrano. *Tchétchénie, une affaire intérieure? Russes et Tchétchènes dans l'étau de la guerre*. Paris: Autrement, 2005.

Le Huérou, Anne, and Elisabeth Sieca-Kozlowski (eds). *Culture militaire et patriotisme dans la Russie d'aujourd'hui*. Paris: Karthala, 2008.

Lieven, Anatol. *Chechnya: Tombstone of Russian Power*. New Haven, CT: Yale University Press, 1998.

Lokshina, Tatiana. *Chechnia. Zhizn na voine*. Moscow: Demos, 2007.

———. *Chechnya, Inside Out*. Moscow: Demos, 2007b.

Malashenko, Aleksei, and Dmitri Trenin. *Vremia Iuga: Rossiia v Chechnie. Chechnia v Rossii*. Moscow: Gendal'f, 2002.

Marie, Jean-Jacques. *Les peuples déportés d'Union Soviétique*. Bruxelles: Editions Complexe, 1995.

Merlin, Aude, and Serrano Silvia (eds). *Ordres et désordres au Caucase*. Bruxelles: Editions de l'Université de Bruxelles, 2010.

Merlin, Aude (ed.). *Où va la Russie?* Bruxelles: Presses universitaires de Bruxelles, 2007.

Merridale, Catherine. "The Collective Mind: Trauma and Shell-shock in Twentieth-Century Russia."*Journal of Contemporary History* 35, no.1 (January 2000): 39–55.

Milicija mezhdu Rossiej i Chetchnej.Veterany konflikta v rossijskom obshchestve. [*Policemen in Limbo: Veterans of the Chechen Conflict in Russian Society*.] Moscow: Demos, 2007.

Markelov, Stanislas. "The Chechnya Syndrome and the Blagovechtchensk Case." 2007, http://www .robertamsterdam.com/2007/04/stanislav_markelov_russias_fil.htm (accessed on June 2011).

Nahavandi, Firouzeh (ed.). *Mouvements islamistes et politique*. Paris: L'Harmattan, 2010.

Nekrič, Aleksandr. *Les peuples punis*. Paris: Maspero, 1982.

Oushakine, Serguei Alex. *The Patriotism of Despair. Nation, War and Loss in Russia*. Ithaca, NY: Cornell University Press, 2009.
Pohl, J. Otto. *Ethnic Cleansing in the USSR, 1937–1949*. Westport, CT: Greenwood Press, 1999.
Prilepin, Zakhar. *Pathologies*. Paris: Editions des Syrtes, 2007.
Russell, John. "Mujahedeen, Mafia, Madmen: Russian Perceptions of Chechens during the Wars in Chechnya, 1994-1996 and 1999-2001." In Fawn, Rick and White, Stephen (eds.) *Russia after Communism*. London: Routledge, 2002.
Smith, Sebastian. *Allah's Mountains: The Battle for Chechnya*. New York: Taurus, 2005.
Sociology of Violence, Arbitrariness of Law Enforcement Bodies by the Eyes of People. Report and sociological study conducted by the Committee against Torture, Nizhni-Novgorod, 2006, http://www.pytkam.net/web/files/sociological.doc.
Sokirianskaia, Ekaterina. "Families and Clans in Ingushetia and Chechnya. A Fieldwork Report."*Central Asian Survey* 24, no. 4 (2005): 453–467.
———. 2009. *Governing Fragmented Societies: State-Building and Political Integration in Chechnya and Ingushetia (1991–2009)*. PhD dissertation, available at http://web.ceu.hu/polsci/dissertations/Ekaterina_Sokirianskaia.pdf.
Tishkov, Valery. *Chechnya: Life in a War-torn Society*. Berkeley: University of California Press, 2004.
Vatchagaev, Maïrbek. *L'aigle et le loup: la Tchétchénie dans la guerre du Caucase au XIXe siècle*. Paris: Buchet Chastel, 2008.
Vachagaev, Maïrbek. "Chechen society today, Myths and reality."*Central Asia and Caucasus* 2, no. 20 (2003).

Turkey

Ben-Eliezer, Uri. "L'armée, la société et la nation-en-armes." *Les cahiers de l'Orient* 54 (1999).
Berque, Jacques. *Le Coran: essai de traduction de l'arabe annoté et suivi d'une étude exégétique*. 2nd edition. Paris: Albin Michel, 1995.
Bougarel, Xavier. "Guerre et mémoire de la guerre dans l'espace yougoslave." In Stefanos, Yérasimos (ed.) *Le retour des Balkans: 1991–2001*. Paris: Autrement, 2002.
Bozarslan, Hamit. *Histoire de la Turquie contemporaine*. Paris: La Découverte, 2004.
———. *La question kurde: États et minorités au Moyen-Orient*. Paris: Presses de Sciences Po, 1997.
———. *Les Kurdes. L'autre front du Proche-Orient*. Paris: Autrement, 2009.
Ceyhan, Ayse, and Gabriel Périès (eds.). *Construire l'ennemi intérieur: nouvelles approches*. Paris: l'Harmattan, 2001.
Copeaux, Étienne. *Espaces et temps de la nation turque: analyse d'une historiographie nationaliste, 1931–1993*. Paris: CNRS, 1997.
Dieckhoff, Alain. "Où va Israël?" *Critique internationale* 16 (2002).
Dorronsoro, Gilles (ed.). *La Turquie conteste: mobilisations sociales et régime sécuritaire*. Paris: CNRS, 2005.
Grojean, Olivier. La cause kurde, de la Turquie vers l'Europe: contribution à une sociologie de la transnationalisation des mobilisations. PhD dissertation, Paris: École des Hautes Etudes en Sciences Sociales (EHESS), 2008.
Insel, Ahmet. "'Cet Etat n'est pas sans propriétaires!' Forces prétoriennes et autoritarisme en Turquie" In Dabène, Olivier, Geisser, Vincent and Massardier, Gilles (eds.) *Autoritarismes démocratiques et démocraties autoritaires au XXIe siècle: convergences Nord-Sud: mélanges offerts à Michel Camau*. Paris: la Découverte, 2008.
Kaplan, Alice. "Espaces publics, espaces privés, espaces intimes en sortie de guerre." In Cabanes, Bruno and Picketty, Gilles (eds.). *Retour à l'intime: au sortir de la guerre*, Paris: Tallandier, 2009.
Kaya, Sümbül. "La fabrique du soldat-citoyen." *European Journal of Turkish Studies* 8(2008).
Mater, Nadire. *Mehmedin Kitabı*, Istanbul: Metis Yayınları, 2001.
Picard, Elizabeth, "Armée et sécurité au coeur de l'autoritarisme." In Dabène, Olivier, Geisser, Vincent and Massardier, Gilles (eds.) *Autoritarismes démocratiques et démocraties autoritaires au XXIe siècle: convergences Nord-Sud: mélanges offerts à Michel Camau*. Paris: la Découverte, 2008.
Sourdel, Janine, and Dominique Sourdel. *Dictionnaire historique de l'Islam*.Paris: Presses universitaires de France, 2004.

Yıldırım Dursun, Özkül Çobanoğlu, Metin Özarslan. *Liseler için, Halk Bilimi*. 1st edition. Istanbul: Devlet Kitapları, 2004.
Official website of the Ministry of Interior devoted to martyrs and war veterans: http://www.sehitlervegaziler.gov.tr
Website of the Turkish armed forces: http://www.tsk.mil.tr
Website of the Mehmetçik Foundation: http://www.mehmetcik.org.tr
Website of war opponents: http://www.savaskarsitlari.org
Website of the Kayseri Prefecture: http://www.kayseri.gov.tr

Peru

Cadena, Marisol de la. "Las mujeres son más indias: etnicidad y género en una comunidad de Cuzco." *Revista Andina* 17 (1991).
Coral, Isabel. "Mujeres en la guerra: impacto y respuestas" In Marisol de la Cadena and Steve J. Stern (eds.) *Los senderos insólitos del Perú: guerra y sociedad, 1980–1995*. Lima: IEP, Instituto de Estudios Peruanos, 1999.
Coronel, José. 1996. "Violencia política y respuestas campesinas en Huanta," Degregori, Carlos Iván, "Cosechando tempestades: las rondas campesinas y la derrota de Sendero Luminoso en Ayacucho," and Del Pino Ponciano, "Tiempos de guerra y de dioses. Ronderos, evangélicos y senderistas en el valle río Apurímac." In Degregori, Carlos Iván (ed.), *Las rondas campesinas y la derrota de Sendero Luminoso*, Lima: Instituto de Estudios Peruanos.
Del Pino, Ponciano. "Los campesinos en la guerra o como la gente empezó a hacerse macho." In Degregori, Carlos Ivan, Javier Escobal d'Angelo and Benjamin Marticorena (eds.). *Perú, el problema agrario en debate*. Lima: Seminario Permanente de Investigación Agraria, 1992,
Henríquez, Ayin Narda, and Cecilia Reynoso Rendón. *Cuestiones de género y poder en el conflicto armado en el Perú*. San Borja/Lima: CONCYTEC, 2006.
Hurtado, Lourdes. "Después del municipio y qué? Las regidoras de Huanta. Un estudio de caso sobre las mujeres en los gobiernos locales." In *Ayacucho. Centralismo y desenctralización*. Lima: Ludwing Hubert, 2003.
Olano, Aldo. "Las rondas campesinas del Perú. Una brieve historia."*Oasis* 6 (2000).
Pérez, José Mundaca. *Rondas campesinas: poder, violencia y autodefensa en Cajamarca central*. Lima: IEP, 1996.
Taylor, Lewis. "La estrategía contrainsurgente, el PCP SL y la guerra civil en el Perú 1980–1996." *Debate agrario* 26 (1997).
Theidon, Kimberly. "Disarming the Subject: Remembering War and Imagining Citizenship in Peru."*Cultural Critique* 54, no. 1 (2003): 67–87.
———. *Entre prójimos: el conflicto armado interno y la política de la reconciliación en el Perú*. Lima: IEP, 2004.

Sources

Caballero, Gerardo. "Invertirán US 150 milliones en el desarrollo del VRAE." *El Comercio.*, February 27, 2007, http://www.elcomercio.com.pe/EdicionImpresa/Html/2007-02-21/ImEcPolitica0675302.html
Gastelmundi, René. "Guerra avisada: los ronderos y licenciados del ejército detrás de los conflictos sociales,"*Diario 16*, June 28, 2011.
Hidalgo María Elena. "Comando Conunto entrega armas a comités de autodefensa en el VRAE,"*La República*, March 21, 2011.
Truth and Reconciliation Comission, *Final Report*.2003, http://www.cverdad.org.pe/ingles/pagina01.php.

Colombia

Cinep. *Deuda con la humanidad, paramilitarismo de Estado, 1988–2003.* Bogotá: Banco de datos Cinep. 2004.

CNRR. Area de desmovilización, desarme y reinserción, *Disidentes, rearmados y emergentes ¿Bandas criminales o tercera generación paramilitar?* 2007.

Duncan, Gustavo. *Los señores de la guerra. De paramilitares, mafiosos y autodefensas en Colombia.* Bogotá: Planeta, 2007.

Echandía, Camilo. *El conflicto armado y las manifestaciones de violencia en las regiones de Colombia.* Bogotá: Presidencia de la República de Colombia, Oficina del Alto Comisionado para la Paz, 1999.

Fernández Carlos, García Durán Mauricio, and Sarmiento Fernando. "Movilizaciones por la paz en Colombia, 1978–2002." *Controversia* (February 2004).

Fundación Seguridad y Democracia. "La reinserción paramilitar, un balance."*Coyuntura de seguridad* (March 14, 2008): 14–20.

Fundación Seguridad y democracia, and Rangel Alfredo (ed.). *La batalla perdida contra las drogas: Legalizar es la opción?* Bogotá: Intermedio, (2008): 18.

Gallego, Medina C. *Autodefensas, paramilitares y narcotrafico en Colombia.* Bogotá: Editorial Documentos Periodísticos, 1990.

Programa Presidencial de Derechos Humanos y Derecho Internacional Humanitario, Vicepresidencia de la República. *Situación de derechos humanos y de derechos internacional humanitario,* 2007.

MAPP-OEA. *Décimosegundo informe trimestral del secretario general al Consejo Permanente sobre la misión de apoyo.* Bogotá, February 2009, OEA/Ser.G CP/doc. 4365/09 corr 1. Available at: http://www.acnur.org/secciones/index.php?viewCat=1412

MAPP-OEA. *Décimoprimer informe trimestral del secretario general al Consejo Permanente sobre la misión de apoyo.* Bogotá, March 2008. Available at: http://www.acnur.org/secciones/index.php?viewCat=1412

Pécaut, Daniel. *Les FARC, une guérilla sans fins?* Paris: Editions lignes de repères, 2008.

Springer, Natalia. *Desactivar la guerra, Alternativas audaces para consolidar la paz.* Bogotá: Aguilar, 2005.

Theidon, Kimberly, and Paola Andra Betancourt. "Transiciones conflictivas: combatientes desmovilizados en Colombia."*Analisis político* 58 (2006).

Tobón, Ramírez W. "Las Autodefensas, un tema difícil."*Coyuntura política* 15 (1999).

Verdad Abierta, Claudia Lopez, and Oscar Sevillano. *Balance político de la parapolítica.* Bogotá: Investigadores Observatorio del Conflicto Armado, Corporación Nuevo Arco Iris, 2008.

Articles
Canada

Bourque, Gilles, and Jules Duchastel. *L'identité fragmentée. Nation et citoyenneté dans les débats constitutionnels canadiens. 1941–1992.* Research Chair of Canada on Globalization, Citizenship and Democracy, 1996.

Le Breton, David. "Jeux symboliques avec la mort." *Religiologiques* 16 (1997).

Fahrni, Magda. "The Romance of Reunion: Montreal War Veterans Return to Family Life, 1944–1949."*Journal of the CHA/Revue de la SHC* 33, no. 3 (2007).

Fussell, Paul. *Wartime: Understanding and Behavior in the Second World War.* New York: Oxford University Press, 1989.

Morton, Desmond. *A Military History of Canada.* Toronto: McClelland and Stewart, 1999.

Nathan, Tobie. "La migration des âmes." *Nouvelle Revue d'ethnopsychiatrie* 11 (1988).

Neary, Peter, and J. L. Granatstein. *The Veterans Charter and Post-World War II Canada.* Montreal: McGill-Queen's University Press, 1999.

Soby, Alice. *A Study on Demobilization and Rehabilitation of the Canadian Armed Forces in the Second World War, 1939–1945.* Army Headquarters, 1960.

Stanley, George. *Canada's Soldiers: The Military History of an Unmilitary People.* Revised edition. Toronto: Macmillan of Canada.1960.

Sources

Richard, Béatrice.. "Entrevues avec les membres des Fusiliers Mont-Royal et quelques autres." Fonds Béatrice Richard 1(96/11), Défense nationale, La Direction—Histoire et Patrimoine (National Defense, Directorate of History & Heritage Library), 1995–1996.

France

Buton, Philippe. *La joie douloureuse: la Libération de la France*. Bruxelles/Paris: Complexe/IHTP-CNRS, 2004.
Cabanes, Bruno, and Guillaume Piketty. "Introduction" and "De l'ombre au grand jour: l'identité résistante en question."In *Retour à l'intime: au sortir de la guerre*. Paris: Tallandier, 2009: 11–34, 149–163.
Lagrou, Peter. "La Résistance et les conceptions de l'Europe, 1945–1965. Le monde associatif international d'anciens résistants et victimes de la persécution devant la Guerre froide, le problème allemand et l'intégration européenne." In, Antoine Fleury (ed.) *Le rôle des guerres dans la mémoire des Européens: leur effet sur la conscience d'être européen*. Berne: P. Lang, 1997: 137–181.
Lagrou, Pieter. "Le martyr national." In *Mémoires patriotiques et Occupation nazie: résistants, requis et déportés en Europe occidentale: 1945–1965*. Bruxelles: Complexe/IHTP-CNRS: 203–237, 2003.
Spire, Alexis. *Etrangers à la carte: l'administration de l'immigration en France, 1945–1975*. Paris: Grasset, 2005.

Serbia

Bougarel, Xavier. *Bosnie: anatomie d'un conflit*. Paris: La Découverte, 1996.
———. "L'ombre des héros: après-guerre et anciens combattants en Bosnie-Herzégovine." *Revue internationale des sciences sociales: RISS*. 189, no. 3 (2009).
Colović, Ivan. *The Politics of Symbol in Serbia: Essays on Political Anthropology*. London: Hurst & Co., 2002.
Foer, Franklin. "How Soccer Explains the Gangster Paradise." In *How Soccer Explains the World: An Unlikely Theory of Globalization*. New York: Harper & Collins, 2004.
Glamočak, Marina. *La transition guerrière yougoslave*. Paris: Harmattan, 2002.
Le livre noir de l'ex-Yougoslavie: purification ethnique et crimes de guerre. Documents gathered by *Le Nouvel Observateur* and *Reporter sans frontières*. Paris: Arléa, 1993.
Stojanovic, D. "The Traumatic Circle of the Serbian Opposition." In Nebojša Popov (ed.) *The Road to War in Serbia: Trauma and Catharsis*. Budapest/New York: Central European University Press, 2000.
Silber, Laura, and the British Broadcasting Corporation. *The Death of Yugoslavia*. London/New York: Penguin Books/BBC Books/Penguin Books, 1995.
Stewart, Christopher. *Hunting the Tiger: The fast Life and Violent Death of the Balkans' Most Dangerous Man*. 1st edition. New York: St. Martin's Press, 2008.
Tanner, Samuel. "Crimes de masse et justice en ex-Yougoslavie: la perspective de quatre anciens exécuteurs serbes" In Isabelle Delpha and Magali Bessone (eds.) *Peines de guerre: la justice pénale internationale et l'ex-Yougoslavie*. Paris: Éditions de EHESS, 2010.
Tomasevich, Jozo. *The Chetniks: War and Revolution in Yugoslavia, 1941–1945*. Stanford, CA: Stanford University Press, 1975.

Uganda

Allen, Tim, and the International African Institute. *Trial Justice: The International Criminal Court and the Lord's Resistance Army*. London: Zed in association with the International African Institute, 2006.
Allen, Tim, and Mareike Schomerus. *A Hard Homecoming, Lessons Learned from the Reception Center Process on Effective Interventions for Former "Abductees" in Northern Uganda*. USAID and UNICEF, 2006.

Allen, Tim, and Koen Vlassenroot (eds). *The Lord's Resistance Army: Myth and Reality*. London: Zed Books, 2010.
Amnesty Commission. "Uganda's Amnesty Commission in Final Phase of Issuing Resettlement Packages to Ex-Combatants." *News and Noteworthy* 12 (2006): http://www.mdrp.org/PDFs/N&N_12_06.pdf.
Archidiocese of Gulu. *Justice and Peace Newsletters*, August/September 2007, http://www.archidioceseofgulu.org/JPC/Newsletter0904.htm(Accessed on May 2008).
Borzello, Anna. "The Challenge of DDR in Northern Uganda: The Lord's Resistance Army."*Conflict, Security Development* 7, no. 3 (2007): 387–415.
Conciliation Resources, Quaker Peace and Social Witness (QPSW). *Coming Home: Understanding Why Commanders of the Lord's Resistance Army Choose to Return to a Civilian Life*, 2006.
Human rights focus (HURIFO). 2004. *Falling through the net. The Challenges for returning adults ex-combatants in Northern Uganda*. HURIFO/Conciliation Resources.
Odongtho, Charles. *What Form of Justice Will Kony Face? LRA leader's Victims Want Him to Be Brought to Account—but Aren't Sure How*. Institute for War and Peace Reporting, 2007.
Perrot, Sandrine. "Les sources de l'incompréhension. Production et circulation des savoirs sur la Lord's Resistance Army." *Politique africaine*. 112 (2008): 140–160.
———. "Northern Uganda: a 'Forgotten Conflict,' Again? The Impact of the Internationalization of the Resolution Process." In Allen Tim and Koen Vlassenroot (eds.). *The Lord's Resistance Army: Myth and Reality*. London: Zed Books, 2010.
———. "The Campaign against the LRA: Old Wine in New Bottles?" In David Richards and Greg Mills (eds.) *Victory among People: Lessons from Countering Insurgency and Stabilising Fragile States*. RUSI/Brenthurst, 2011: 295–312.
Refugee Law Project (RLP).*Whose Justice? Perceptions of Uganda's Amnesty Act 2000: The Potential for Conflict Resolution and Long-Term Reconciliation*. RLP Working Paper (15), February 2005.
Rodriguez, Carlos. *Seventy Times Seven, The Impact of the Amnesty Law in Acholi*. Acholi Religious Leaders' Peace Initiative, 2002.
United Nations Office of the High Commissioner for Human Rights. *Making Peace Our Own: Victims' Perceptions of Accountability, Reconciliation and Transitional Justice in Northern Uganda*. United Nations Office of the High Commissioner for Human Rights, 2007.

Sardinia

Bennet, James. *La Corse et la Sardaigne: étude de voyage et de climatologie*. Paris: P. Asselin, 1876.
Brigaglia, Manlio. *Per l'Italia dall'esilio*. Cagliari: Edizioni Della Torre, 1976.
———. "La Brigata Sassari come problema storiografico." In Guiseppina Fois (ed.) *Storia della Brigata Sassari*. Sassari: Gallizzi, 1981.
———. "Per una storia dell'antifascismo in Sardegna." In M. Brigaglia, F. Manconi, A. Mattone, and G.Melis. *L'Antifascismo in sardegna*. Cagliari: Edizioni Della Torre, 1986.
Brigaglia, Manlio, Attilio Mastino, and Gian Ortu Giacomo. *Storia della Sardegna*. Roma: Laterza, 2006.
Cubeddu, Salvatore. *1 Sardisti. Viaggio nel Partito Sardo d'Azione tracronaca e storia. Documenti, testimonianze, dati e commenti (1919–1948)*. Sassari: EDES, 1993.
Fois, Giuseppina. *Storia della Brigata Sassari*. Sassari: Gallizzi, 1981.
Lussu, Emilio. *La marche sur Rome: et autres lieux*. Paris: Arte Editions/Editions du Félin, 2002.
Marica, Pasquale. *Stampa e politica in Sardegna 1793–1944*. Cagliari: La zattera, 1968.
Marroccu, L. "Le origini del fascismo in Sardegna." In M. L. Plaisant (ed.) *La Sardegna nel regime fascista*. Cagliari: Cuec, 2000.
Melis, Guido. *Antonio Gramsci e la questione sarda*. Cagliari: Edizioni Della Torre, 1975.
Nieddu, L. "Introduzione." In Luigi Nieddu (ed.) *Camillo Bellieni: Partito Sardo d'Azione e Repubblica federale: scritti 1919–1925*. Sassari: Gallizzi, 1956.
———. *Luigi B. Puggioni e il P.S. D'A. (1919–1955)*. Cagliari: Sarda, 1960.

———. "Sulla composizione sociale del movimento degli ex-combattenti e del primo Partito Sardo d'Azione." In Istituto Sardo per la Storia della Resistenza e dell'Autonomia (Issra), *Lotte sociali, antifascismo e autonomia in Sardegna: atti del convegno di studi in onore di Emilio Lussu: Cagliari, 4-6 gennaio 1980.* Cagliari: Edizioni della Torre, 1982.

Pinna, L. *La famiglia esclusiva*. Bari: Laterza, 1967.

Plaisant, M. L. "Sardegna." In *Dizionario della Resistenza. Volume primo: storia e geografia della Liberazione*. Turin: Einaudi, 2000.

Ridolfi, M. "'Partiti elettorali' e trasformazioni della politica nell'Italia unita." In Luigi Ballini Pier and Ridolfi Maurizio (eds.) *Storia delle campagne elettorali in Italia.* Milan: Mondadori, 2002.

Roux, Christophe. "Des difficultés de la contestation nationalitaire dans le Mezzogiorno. Le cas du Parti sarde d'action." *Pôle Sud* 20 (2004).

———. *Les "îles soeurs": une sociologie historique comparée de la contestation nationalitaire en Corse et en Sardaigne.* PhD dissertation. Lille: University (Law and Health), 2005.

Sechi, Salvatore. *Dopoguerra e fascismo in Sardegna: il movimento autonomistico nella crisi dello Stato liberale, 1918–1926.* Torino: Fondazione Luigi Einaudi, 1969.

Sechi, Salvatore (ed.). *Il Movimento autonomistico in Sardegna: 1917–1925.* Cagliari: Fossataro, 1975.

Sotgiu, G. *Storia della Sardegna dalla Grande Guerra al fascismo.* Rome/Bari: Laterza, 1990.

Tognotti, E. "La base sociale del PSd'A nel primo dopoguerra. Note introduttive." In Instituto Sardo per la Storia della Resistenza e dell Autonomia. *Lotte sociali antifascismo e autonomia in Sardegna: atti del convegno di studi in onore di Emilio Lussu*, 1982.

Vial, Éric, Patrizia De Capitani Bertrand, and Mileschi Christophe. *Emilio Lussu, 1890–1975: politique, histoire, littérature et cinéma.* Grenoble: Publications de la MSH-Alpes, 2007.

Ivory Coast

Audrain, Xavier. "Terrain. Devenir *baay-fall* pour être soi. Le religieux comme vecteur d'émancipation individuelle au Sénégal." *Politique africaine.* 94 (2004): 149–165.

Banégas, Richard. *Côte d'Ivoire: les jeunes "se lèvent en hommes": anticolonialisme et ultranationalisme chez les jeunes patriotes d'Abidjan.* Paris: Centre d'Etudes et de Recherches Internationales (CERI-Sciences Po), 2007.

———. "Côte d'Ivoire: Patriotism, Ethnonationalism and Other African Modes of Self-Writing." *African Affairs* 105, no. 421 (2006): 535.

Banégas, Richard, and Jean-Pierre Warnier (eds). "Nouvelles figures de la réussite et du pouvoir." *Politique africaine* (82), Paris: Karthala, 2001.

Bobo, Samuel Koffi, and Jean-Pierre Chauveau. "La situation de guerre dans l'arène villageoise. Un exemple dans le centre-ouest ivoirien." *Politique africaine* 89 (2003): 12–33.

Chauveau, Jean-Pierre, and Jean-Pierre Dozon. "Au cœur des ethnies ivoiriennes…l'État." In Emmanuel Terray (ed.) *L'Etat contemporain en Afrique.* Paris: L'Harmattan, 1987.

Chauveau, Jean-Pierre, and Paul Richards. "Les racines agraires des insurrections ouest-africaines. Une comparaison Côte d'Ivoire-Sierra Leone." *Politique africaine* 111 (2008): 131–168.

Chelpi-Den Hamer, Magali. "Le mythe du jeune désoeuvré: analyse des interventions DDR en Côte d'Ivoire." *Afrique contemporaine* 4, no. 232 (2009): 39–55.

Ferguson, James. *Global Shadows: Africa in the Neoliberal World Order.* Durham, NC: Duke University Press, 2006.

Fofana, Moussa. *Les déterminants de l'enrôlement des jeunes combattants de la rébellion du Nord de la Côte d'Ivoire.* Oxford: Crisis Working Paper, 2008.

Kieffer, Guy André. "Armée ivoirienne: le refus du déclassement." *Politique africaine* 78 (2000).

Kohlhagen, Dominik. "Frime, escroquerie et cosmopolitisme: le succès du 'coupé-decalé' en Afrique et ailleurs." *Politique africaine* 100 (2006).

Konaté, Franck. "Bouaflé, Oumé, Diégonéfla, Hiré: les milices préparent un coup." *24 Heures* (2005).

De Latour, Elaine. "Les ghettomen: Les gangs de rue à Abidjan et San Pedro." *Actes de la Recherche en Sciences Sociales* 129, no. 1 (1999): 68–83.

Marshall Anne, and Comfort Ero. "L'Ouest de la côte d'ivoire: un conflit libérien?" *Politique africaine* 89 (2003): 88–101.

Mbembe, Achille. "À propos des écritures africaines de soi." *Politique africaine* 77 (2000).

Le Pape, Marc and Claudine Vidal (eds). *Côte d'Ivoire: l'année terrible, 1999–2000*. Paris: Karthala, 2002.

Richards, Paul. *Fighting for the Rain Forest: War, Youth & Resources in Sierra Leone*. Portsmouth, NH: Heinemann, 1996.

Tade, Dieusmonde. "Tournée du Rdr dans le Moyen-Cavally, hier: Amon Tanoh et Mao Glofiéhi se sont parlés et se sont compris." *Le nouveau réveil*, July 18, 2009.

Vidal, Claudine. "La brutalisation du champ politique ivoirien." *Revue africaine de sociologie* 7, no. 2 (2003).

CONTRIBUTORS

Richard Banégas is Professor of political science at Sciences Po-CERI and co-director of the Joint African Studies Program (Columbia University/University Paris 1). Until 2012, he was Director of the Master of African Studies at the Department of Political Science of the University of Paris 1-Panthéon-Sorbonne. He is also director of the academic journal *Politique africaine*. His research focuses on the issues of citizenship and political violence in Western Africa and the Great Lakes. He is the author of *La démocratie à pas de caméléon. Démocratisation et imaginaires politiques au Bénin* (Karthala, 2006) and *The Recurring Great Lakes Crisis. Identity, Violence and Power* (co-edited with J. P. Chrétien, Hurst, London, 2008). During the past decade he has been investigating on the role of youth in the crisis of Côte d'Ivoire. He is the author of a dozen articles on the subject as well as a book scheduled for publication in 2013 (La Découverte).

Camille Boutron, has a PhD in sociology and is postdoctoral fellow at the Institut de Recherche pour le Développement (IRD). Her doctorate thesis embraced a gender perspective in order to describe the implication of women in Peruvian armed conflict (1980–2000), and to highlight the sexual dimension of the "post-conflict" social space. She is currently postdoctoral fellow at the IRD where she pursues her researches on the role of informal social organizations in the resolution of different kind of crisis (disaster, armed conflict, poverty and marginality), insisting particularly on a gender perspective. Her publications include articles in a book on the aestheticism of genders published in 2009 at Nouveaux Mondes publishers and in *Pandora* review.

Sophie Daviaud is a professor at the IEP (Institut for Political Studies) of Aix-en-Provence and also a member of the CHERPA. Her doctorate thesis pertains to the importance of fundamental rights in the Colombian conflict. The focus of her work is on the struggle for human rights in Latin America during internal armed conflicts. Her current researches relates to the question of transitional justice and Colombian victims.

Nathalie Duclos is senior lecturer of political science at the University of Tours. Her current research focus is on international policies in post-conflict situations, peacebuilding missions, especially DDR and the reintegration of KLA's (Kosovo Liberation Army) former combatants. She has published a report *Le Kosovo Police Service, facteur de consolidation de la paix au Kosovo?* [The KPS, factor of peacebuilding in Kosovo?] (2003) as well as many articles, including "Pacification sans réconciliation. Les apories de la politique de réconciliation des Nations-Unies au Kosovo" [Pacification without reconciliation. Limits of UN peacebuilding policies in Kosovo], in Sandrine Lefranc (ed.), *Après le conflit, la réconciliation?* [After the conflict, Reconciliation?] (Paris, Michel Houdiard, 2006).

Sümbül Kaya is a PhD candidate in Political Science at the University Paris 1-Panthéon-Sorbonne. She is also Assistant Lecturer in Political Science at the University Lumière of Lyon 2. She is preparing a dissertation on the conscription in Turkey since 1980. Her publications include "Making 'soldier-citizen' through Conscription in Turkey" in *European Journal of Turkish Studies*, Thematic Issue 8, 2009, "Surveiller, normaliser, réprimer", http://www.ejts.org/document2922.html.

Anne Le Huerou has a PhD in sociology (Russian Studies), she is a research associate at the CERCEC (Russian and East European Studies, EHESS/CNRS, Paris), and works as a coordinator of Russian/CIS programs at Fondation Maison des Sciences de l'Homme, Paris. She has conducted research on various issues concerning contemporary Russian Politics and Society, and is currently working on a project on various aspects of violence in contemporary Russia (http://russiaviolence.hypotheses.org), focusing on police violence and on the consequences of the war in Chechnya on Russian society. Her publications include " La société civile en Russie face à la guerre en Tchétchénie [the Russian Civil Society in front of the War in Chechnya]", in Aude Merlin (dir.) *Où va la Russie?*, (Bruxelles, Presses Universitaires de Bruxelles, 2007), Together with Aude Merlin, Amandine Regamey, Silvia Serrano, *Tchétchénie : une affaire intérieure ? Russes et Tchétchènes dans l'étau de la guerre*, [Chechnya: An Internal Problem? Russians and Chechnyans in the Grip of War] (Editions Autrement/CERI, 2005). She has directed together with Élisabeth Sieca-Kozlowski the book *Culture militaire et mobilisation patriotique en Russie* (Karthala, 2008).

Aude Merlin is a lecturer, at Université Libre de Bruxelles, CEVIPOL (www.cevipol.be), in charge of the Russian chair. Her research focuses on the North Caucausus as a region emblematic of a series of social, political, and identity transformations in Russia, and the role of the two post-soviet Chechen conflicts in these transformations.

Sandrine Perrot is a research fellow at Sciences Po-CERI, her focus is on Uganda. Her current research focuses on armed conflicts and violent phenomena in sub-Saharan Africa. She is particularly interested in the sociology of armed groups, militias, and paramilitary groups South of the Sahara. She is the co-director of *Research in Question*, member of the editorial board of *Politique africaine* and associate researcher at the Centre d'Études des Mondes Africains.

Contributors

Béatrice Richard is an associate professor at the Royal Military College of Canada. She specializes in cultural studies of warfare and military issues with a specific interest in French Canadians' attitude toward wars and military institutions. She was awarded the C. P. Stacey prize for best Canadian military history publication in 2004 for her book *La mémoire de Dieppe, radioscopie d'un mythe* (Montréal, VLB éditeur).

Christophe Roux is a senior lecturer of political science at the University of Montpellier and a member of the South European Centre for Political Studies (CEPEL, UMR 5112 CNRS—LEA ETAPES). His research focuses on regional nationalist mobilizations in Europe and the political systems of Southern Europe. He is co-editor (with N. Conti and F. Tronconi) of *Parties and Voters in Italy: The Challenge of Multi-Level Political Competition*, a special issue of *Modern Italy*, 14, no. 2 (May 2009).

Élisabeth Sieca-Kozlowski has a PhD in Sociology and is editor in chief of *The Journal of Power Institutions in Post-Soviet Societies*, Research Associate at CERCEC (Centre des mondes russes, caucasien et centre-européen), Paris. In 2006, in partnership with Françoise Daucé, she co-edited *Dedovshchina in the Post-Soviet Military: Hazing of Russian Army Conscripts in a Comparative Perspective* (Stuttgart, Ibidem-Verlag, 2006). In 2008, she co-edited, and co-authored with Anne Le Huérou *Culture militaire et patriotisme dans la Russie d'aujourd'hui* (Paris, Karthala). Her current research focus is on veterans of the Chechen wars and their involvement in official patriotism, minorities in the post-Soviet army, and the ROSTO predraft training organization.

Samuel Tanner holds a PhD in criminology. He is assistant professor at the School of criminology, University of Montréal. His interests focus both on participation of militias and armed bands in mass violence, as well as transnational policing, postconflict security, and participation of police in international peace operations (UNPOL). His latest publications include: with Samuel Tanner, "Towards a Pattern in Mass Violence Participation? An Analysis of Rwandan Perpetrators' Accounts from the 1994 Genocide," *Global Crime* 12, no. 4 (2011): 266–289; and a forthcoming book, co-edited with Benoit Dupont (2012). *Maintenir la paix en zones post conflits : les nouveaux visage de la police.* (Montréal : Les Presses de l'Université de Montréal).

Fabien Theofilakis defended his PhD on German POWs in France and their repatriation into Germany (1944–1949) at the University of Paris Ouest Nanterre and the University of Augsburg (Germany) in 2010. It has received several prizes and is going to be published by Fayard Edition next year. He has published several articles on the captivity of prisoners and their repatriation to Germany, as well as the results of a French-German symposium on the Dachau concentration camp (2005). He is currently a teaching assistant at the University of Paris Ouest Nanterre.

INDEX

1929 Depression, 120

Abductees/ex-abductees, 182, 186, 190
Afghanistan war, 31, 38, 41, 48n48,
    49n54, 51n110, 118, 131, 134n2
    Afghanisation, 219
    Afghanistan veterans, 29, 35, 37–38,
        41, 45, 49n63, 270
    Union of Veterans of Afghanistan/
        Associations of Veterans, 37, 42,
        49n63, 51n105
Algerian war, 5, 18n24, 20n62/72,
    48n48, 134n13
Alimsultanov, Imam, 226
American dream, 117, 119, 122–123, 131
Amnesty, 83, 92n25, 97, 108, 110,
    178–182, 184, 195n19
    Amnesty Commission, 179–182,
        195n15
    amnesty law, 178, 181
Andes, 89
    Andean areas, 88
Antelme, Robert, 137, 145
Anthropology, 1, 16n2
    anthropologists, 6, 82, 89, 103
    ethnography/ethnographic/ethnologist,
        14, 128, 157–160, 162, 165, 169,
        172, 175n29
Apurímac and Ene rivers (VRAE), 76–77,
    80, 82–83
Armistice, 1, 5
Army, 3, 9–10, 12, 16, 19n53, 25–27, 31–33,
    36–39, 42, 44–46, 49n67, 53, 56,
    58–60, 73, 75–78, 80–81, 84, 89, 91,
    97, 107, 109, 122–124, 134n4, 140,
    160–161, 164, 177–186, 188–189,
    191, 194n7/8/14, 196n40/44, 202,
    204–205, 219–220, 223–224, 226,
    228–231, 234, 236n5, 237n7/11/13,
    239n53, 241–243, 245–246, 248,
    251–252, 256–258, 260, 270
Arsanov, Vakha, 231–232, 234–235
Ashaninka, 89
Association(s), 20n62, 28, 36–38, 44,
    47n22, 49n57/58, 62, 83, 91, 103,
    112n17, 135n36, 139, 143, 145–147,
    150–151, 165, 178, 185–186,
    188–189, 196n40, 201, 206–209,
    211, 213–214, 235, 254
    former combatant(s)/ex-combatants
        association(s), 185–186, 188–189,
        207, 211
    veterans association(s), 10, 19n56,
        36–38, 43, 45, 126, 130, 186, 188,
        196n40, 269
Atagi, 229, 234
Atatürk, Mustafa Kemal, 54, 62–63, 71n57
Aushev, Ruslan, 25, 46n2, 49n53
Autodefensasunidas de Colombia (AUC),
    97–98, 100, 103, 107–108
Autonomist movement/party, 201, 203, 214
    Sardinian Autonomy Movement, 201
    "Sardist" movement, 202
"Auxiliary non-state actors," 162
Avtury, 229, 233
Axis alliance, 164

Babchenko, Arkadi, 33
Balkans, 161, 169, 172
Barayev, Arbi, 231–233
Basayev, Shamil Salmanovich, 30,
    222, 225, 227–228, 230–232,
    234–235, 237n7
Becker, Howard, 1, 16, 21n82, 174n9,
    176n38
Bédié, Henri Konan, 245–246

Belgrade underworld, 162
Bellieni, Camillo, 209–210, 215
Berezovsky, Boris Abramovitch, 231, 238n42, 239n47
Blagoveshchensk, 34, 36, 46n7
BléGoudé, Charles, 257
Bobo, Samuel, 245, 249–250, 255
Boche, 12, 142–143, 145, 151
Boevoe Bratstvo, 27, 36–37, 49n57
Bosnia-Herzegovina, 159–161, 163, 173n3
   Eastern Bosnia-Herzegovina, 162
   Srebrenica, 170
   Sarajevo, 161
"Bottom up" approach, 6, 267
Bourdieu, Pierre, 13, 69n11, 173n2, 175n35
Bourke, Joanna, 21n76, 118, 134n11
Boyeviki, 221, 223, 226, 229
Brigaglia, Manlio, 203, 212
Broker, 166, 168
Brothers-in-arms, 117, 212, 269, 271n4
Brutalization, 5–6, 11–14, 18n26, 23, 26–28, 32–33, 39, 46, 47n21, 95, 202, 242, 244, 262
   Ensauvagement, 5, 18n26
   "Post-war brutality," 171
Budanov, Yuri Dmitrievich, 36, 46n8
Budennovsk, 222, 233, 237n7
Buynaksk, 234

Cabanes, Bruno, 14, 18n24/34/40, 20n68/76, 21n77/79, 70n16, 119, 134n10/11/13/16, 136n47
Canada, 14, 117–118, 120–123, 127, 129, 131, 134n19, 268–269
Canadian armed forces, 120
   Canadian Royal Air Force, 124
   Lieutenant-General Roméo Dallaire, 126
   Dieppe raid, 124, 129, 134n12
Canadian benefits program, 270
Capital, 166, 168, 188, 213, 231
   symbolic capital, 161–162, 166, 168, 173, 183
Cease-fire, 1, 6
   Khasav-Yurt (ceasefire) agreement, 15, 221–224, 226
Central Council for Veterans Affairs (TsSDV), 42, 50n94

"Champ d'honneur," 14
Chauveau, Jean-Pierre, 245, 249–250, 253
Chechnya, 13, 15, 25–36, 38, 40, 44, 47n12/14, 50n102, 219–231, 233–235, 236n2/4, 237n11/14/21, 238n34/43, 239n44, 269
   "Chechen syndrome," 25–27, 30, 32–34
   Chechenization, 235–236
   Chechnyan war, 13
   Grozny, 30–31, 38, 47n27, 222–226, 228–232, 237n12/15, 238n27, 239n44
   Gudermes, 231–234, 238n43, 239n45
   Republic of Chechnya-Ichkeria, 220
Chelpi-den Hamer, Magali, 249–251, 263n5
Chernokozovo, 30
Child-soldiers, 178–179, 181, 186, 189, 194n1
   child-mothers, 179, 187, 196n42, 197n51
Christian/Christianity, 163–164, 202, 213
Citizenship, 8, 84, 88, 121, 247
Civil Chamber, 37
"Civvy" street, 122
Claims, 57, 88, 160, 195n19, 210–211, 220
   grievances, 4, 89, 190, 220
Clausewitz, Karl Philip Gottfried von, 11
Clientelism, 179, 186
Cohen, Stanley, 172
Collapse/weakness/failure of the state/ failed states, 3–4, 16n3, 227, 230, 236
Collective action, 45, 75, 87, 202, 204, 211–212, 267
Collier, Paul, 8, 17n20, 19n50
Colombia, 15, 19n49, 95–98, 101–103, 106–111, 112n34/36
   MAPP OEA: OEA's mission to support the peace process, 97, 99–102, 109, 113n40
Command chain/military hierarchy, 32, 160, 177, 187, 193, 194n8, 195n25, 229, 237n11, 246, 269
Commemoration/commemoration policies, 119, 269
   commemorative ceremonies, 5, 61–62, 66–68, 129
   funeral ceremonies/funeral rites, 63–64, 68

INDEX

Commission Nationale de RéparationetRéconciliation (CNRR), 100
Communists, 164
  (Communist) "Partisans," 164, 175n21
  General Tito, 164
Community, 10, 14, 27, 41, 60, 68, 74–83, 85–89, 91, 102–104, 117–120, 123, 128–132, 157–159, 162–164, 166–168, 173, 174n16, 175n26/27/28, 187, 189–190, 224, 254
ConfédérationGénérale du Travail (CGT), 149
Conscript, 18n30, 32, 42, 48n32, 53–60, 66–68, 69n10/15, 71n55/56, 72n70, 152n5, 267
  conscripted, 120, 179, 181
  conscription, 178
Continuist hypothesis, 10, 19n58
Continuity, 61, 84, 87, 152n2, 199, 225, 244–245
Copp, Terry, 124
Counter-subversive Civilian Defense (Decas), 76
Counter-subversive struggle, 75, 77, 84, 87–89, 91
Crimes against humanity, 97, 100, 182
Criminality, 13, 21n76, 219, 222–223
  crime rates in postconflict societies, 158
  criminalization, 74, 108, 186, 230
  criminals, 43, 166, 178, 188
  drug-trafficking, 76, 82
  illegal activities/parallel economy, 166
  organized criminality, 4, 9
Croatia, 159–163, 168, 171, 173, 174n6
  Croats, 160, 163
    autonomous Serbian region of Krajina, 161
    Knin, 161
    Oustachi, 163–164, 174n19
    Vukovar, 161, 174n10/14
Crystallization, 146, 163, 166, 168, 174n16
Culture of war, 5, 18n30, 105, 118, 192
  cultural remobilization/cultural mobilization, 140, 145, 147, 150
  culture of violence, 32, 41
  military culture, 49, 74

Dagestan, 30, 230, 234–235
DDR programs/DDR policies, 3–4, 7–8, 16, 17n7, 18n42, 19n46, 74, 95–97, 104, 109, 111, 179, 227, 269
  maximalist programs/minimalist programs, 4
  World Bank Multi-Country Demobilization and Reintegration Program (MDRP), 179, 195n15
Dedovshchina, 32
Defeat, 9, 14–15, 46, 60, 185, 222–224, 270
Demilitarization, 15, 77, 121, 177, 193
Demobilization, 2–3, 5–7, 10–11, 14, 74, 80, 82–84, 91, 95–96, 98–101, 103–104, 108, 112n5, 113n34, 115, 118–123, 131, 137–138, 141–142, 144, 178–179, 182, 185, 187, 192–194, 194n4, 196n29, 227, 242–243, 250, 256, 262
  cultural demobilization, 5–6, 10–11, 96, 103, 112n5, 115, 118, 137–138, 141, 144, 192
  of ex-combatants, 3
  experience, 122
  machinery, 122
  (para)military demobilization, 6, 82, 95–96, 100–101, 142
  programs, 2, 242–243
Democracy, 73–74, 201
Denial, 35–36, 172–173, 269–270
Department of National Defense, 131
Destabilization, 2
Drašković, Vuk, 159, 174n6
Dudayev, DzhokharMusayevich, 221–222, 225–227, 230–231, 238n36
Durable peace, 3

Economy, 11, 15, 57, 101, 103, 105–106, 111, 118–119, 129, 157–158, 162, 165–168, 170, 209, 242, 251, 253, 255, 262–263
  economy of social relations, 162, 166
Elias, Norbert, 11, 13, 70n42
Engagement, 19n47, 32, 75, 77, 82, 84, 141, 206, 214–215, 267
  disengagement, 19n47, 32, 37, 41, 267
  political engagement, 203
Ergenekon, 68, 72n74
Ethnic cleansing, 162

Ethnicity, 88–89
Ethos, 53–56, 68, 69n11, 209, 242, 243–244, 254, 260–262
  military ethos, 56
  security ethos, 53–55, 69n11
  warrior ethos, 243–244, 254, 261–262
Ex-combatants/former combatants, 1–4, 6–16, 16n4, 18n44, 19n46/56/59, 21n76/79, 35, 39–40, 44–45, 53–55, 57, 59–63, 68, 75, 89, 91, 137–139, 141–151, 158, 177–186, 188–190, 192–194, 195n15, 196n25/26/37/39/40, 197n51, 201–203, 207–212, 214, 219, 249–250, 260–262, 267–271, 271n4

Fatkhi (Sheikh), 231, 238n43
Fédération Nationale des Déportéset Internés Résistants et Patriotes (FNDIRP), 139
FédérationEstudiantineetScolaire de Côte d'Ivoire (FESCI), 243–244, 257–259, 261
FédérationNationale des DéportésetInternésPolitiques (FNDIP), 145
FédérationNationaledes PG (FNPG, National Federation of Prisoners Of War [POWs]), 139, 150
Fighter, 3, 12, 29–30, 39, 87, 89, 91, 95–99, 101–105, 108–109, 138–139, 159, 164–165, 180, 221–223, 225–231, 235, 237n7/8/13/15, 238n43, 242, 267, 269–270
Forbes, Charly, 124
Forces ArméesNationales de Côte d'Ivoire (FANCI), 246, 248
Forces de Défenseet de Sécurité (FDS), 248, 256, 258–259
Foucault, Michel, 141, 152n18, 153n34, 169, 265n43
Frame, 34, 68, 163–166, 169, 173, 208, 261
France, 1, 5, 10, 14, 16, 19n56, 20n62/72, 66, 119, 137–140, 143, 145–146, 148–151, 207, 210, 216n9, 246
Fujimori, Alberto, 73–74, 83, 86, 88

Gambetta, Diego, 168
Gbagbo, Laurent, 242–245, 247–248, 257, 260–262, 264n37

Gbagbo, Simone, 265n42
Gelaev, Ruslan (Hamzat), 231
Gender, 74–75, 77, 80–81, 86, 89, 91
Generation(s), 42, 100, 132, 138, 241, 253–254, 257, 261
Gennep, Arnold van, 128
Germany, 5, 14, 66, 123, 127, 140, 142–143, 148, 153n23, 210
Ghetto, 242, 262
Gramsci, Antonio, 214
Great Britain, 14, 184
Greed, 4, 8, 17n20
  predation/predatory, 4, 166, 231, 251–252
Gromov, Boris, 37
Groupement de Patriotes pour la Paix (GPP), 249, 256–261, 264n39
Gueï, Robert (General), 244, 246–247
Guerrillas, 9, 15, 31, 53, 55, 66–67, 76, 95–96, 98–99, 106–107, 109–111, 112n8, 222
  Latin American Guerrillas, 9
  Shining Path guerrillas, 76
  Turkish Kurd guerrillas, 53

Habitus, 13, 23, 33, 62, 70n42, 73, 84, 95, 103, 117, 119, 124, 131, 157–159, 162, 170, 172–173, 175n35, 181
  national habitus, 62, 70n42
  war habitus (habitus of war)/habitus of violence (violent habitus), 13, 23, 33, 157–159, 170, 172–173
  warmongering habitus, 181
  warrior habitus, 73, 84, 95, 103, 117, 119, 124, 131
Hexis, 169, 171
History, 1–2, 7–8, 60, 61, 134n9
  historian(s), 2–6, 10–12, 18n30, 19n51, 20n60, 61, 82, 96, 124, 134n1, 202–203, 209–210, 213, 238n30/41, 239n46, 244, 267
  historicity, 88
  national historiography, 55, 60–61, 66–67
HouphouëtBoigny, Félix, 9
Human rights violations, 83, 92n25, 95–96, 98, 108
Hypermasculinity, 89

INDEX 295

Identitarian change, 268
  national identity, 61, 63, 66–67
  warrior's identity, 84, 119

Identity, 3, 10, 13–14, 61, 63, 66–68, 70n42, 84, 86–89, 91, 118–119, 121, 124, 150–151, 158, 163, 166, 172, 184, 203–204, 208, 225–226, 243, 247, 249, 254, 258, 268, 270
  identity reconfigurations, 172
  identity reconstruction, 118
Idiosyncratic moral standards, 165–166, 168
Independence, 15, 19n53, 30, 61–62, 64, 174n6, 186, 208, 210, 219, 222, 224–228, 232, 236n5, 237n21/22, 238n27, 239n45
Indigenous people, 89
Inside enemy/enemy within, 48n44, 55, 58, 61, 66, 68, 270
  "fifth columnists," 67
Instrumentalization, 41, 270
  instrumentaliz(ed), 9, 40–41, 53, 192, 269, 270
Interaction, 9, 165, 173, 174n16, 175n27, 215, 216n5, 223, 268–269
Intergenerational relations, 242, 243, 255, 268
International Committee of the Red Cross, 139
International relations, 2–3, 16n1, 21n80, 202
Invisibilization, 74, 91
Irregular groups, 3
Islam, 64, 69n9, 164–165, 169, 227, 238n43
  Islamists, 60, 68, 219, 231, 234–235
  Muslims, 19n54, 163, 169, 174n19, 234, 247
  "Turks," 163, 174n19
Italy, 127, 201–203, 205, 207–210, 213, 215
  Brigade, 203–206, 215
  Brigade Sassari, 10, 203–204, 210, 214
  Italian army, 202
Ivory Coast/Côte d'Ivoire, 9, 241–245, 246–249, 251, 253–254, 256–257, 261–262, 263n6, 264n21
  Young Patriot, 243, 249, 252–254, 257–258, 261, 265n42, 268

Jones, James/*The Thin Red Line*, 124
Justice, 3–4, 11, 17n16, 27, 32, 34, 36, 74, 77, 84, 96, 101, 108, 110–111, 151, 173, 180, 195n21, 253–254
  International Criminal Court, 182, 184, 263n14
Justice and Development Party, 68–69

Kadyrov, AkhmadAbdulkhamidovich (Mufti), 232, 238n34
Kazantsev, Viktor Germanovich, 31
Kebetov, Bagauddin, 235
Kemalists, 60
Khanbiyev, Magomed, 229, 233
Khattab(Ibn al-), 30, 227, 231, 235
Kingdom of South Slavs, 164
  monarchy of Karađorđević, Alexander, 164
Komsije, 167, 175n27
Kondopoga, 29
Kontraktniki, 32
Kony, Joseph, 179, 183–185, 187, 193
Kosovo, 16n4, 19n53, 21n81, 160–161, 164, 171
  Battle of Kosovo, 164
  Sultan Murad, 164
  Obilić, Miloš, 164
Kriger, Norma, 7, 18n43
Kurdistan, 14, 53, 55, 268–270
  Kurd separatists, 14
  Kurdish nationalist movement, 53
  Kurdistan Workers' Party (PKK), 53, 55, 57, 64, 66–67
  Öcalan, Abdullah, 53, 57

L'Associazionedeireducidellatrincea, 207
Lazarsfeld, Paul, 270
Legitimacy, 3, 6, 63, 67, 76, 81, 96, 138, 149, 165, 168, 174n6, 212, 223, 225, 230, 246, 256
Local distribution of material resources, 158
Lord's Resistance Army (LRA), 9, 177–193, 194n2/8/14, 195n16/18/21/22/25, 196n26/27/28/29/37/42/44, 197n51, 268
Low-intensity conflict, 4, 19n47, 26
Loyalty(ies), 3, 10, 29, 54, 221
  loyal/loyalist, 246, 248–249, 258
Lussu, Emilio, 205, 210, 215

Mackenzie King, William Lyon, 121
Mafia/Sicilian Mafia, 107, 166, 168, 247
  mafioso-type, 163
Makhachev, Kazbek, 229, 238n35
Maoist Shining Path-Communist Party of Peru (PCP-SL), 73–74, 76, 78–80
Martyrs, 14, 53–55, 58–68, 70n30/41, 71n47/55/56, 140, 145, 225, 270
Maskhadov, Aslan, 30, 219–236, 237n20/22, 239n46/50
Mater, Nadire, 59
Mbembe, Achille, 261
Mehmetçik Foundation, 66
Memory(ies), 11, 20n62, 41, 61, 71n60, 73–74, 91, 105, 119, 124, 126–127, 129–130, 145–146, 150, 151, 171, 203, 225, 236n5, 244, 269, 270
Mihailović, Dragoljub ("Draža"), 165
Militarization, 45–46, 54, 74–75, 83–84, 86, 91, 243, 244–245, 261–262
  militarization of society, 45, 54, 84, 261
  (para)military combat, 102, 199
Military service, 29, 31, 38, 42–43, 51n104, 53–58, 63, 69n10/12/15, 71n55/56, 258
Militia, 6, 9, 30, 104, 109, 150, 160, 241, 243–245, 248–253, 256, 258, 260–261, 268–269
  militianization, 242, 243, 244–246, 260–262
  Peruvian militia, 268
  "patriotic" militias, 242
  Serb militia, 269
Militiamen, 9–10, 157–159, 173, 242–243, 246, 250–263, 263n4
  Serbian militiamen, 9, 157–158
Milošević, Slobodan, 160–161, 174n7, 175n22
Milošević regime, 159–160, 162
Minister of Pensions and National Health (Canada), 121
Ministry of Defense, 38, 42–43, 231
Ministry of Internal Affairs (MVD), 31–32, 37–40, 42–43, 49n63, 50n81/87/98
Ministry of Urgent Situations, 32
Mobilization (for war), 5, 10, 15, 21n79, 43–45, 50n101, 81–82, 106, 120, 142, 146, 185–186, 205–206, 210, 212, 244, 261

Monopoly on coercion/(monopoly of) legitimate physical violence, 2–3, 6
Moral authority, 140, 142, 166–167
Moral economy, 118–119, 129, 251, 253, 262–263
Moral Recognition, 128
Mosse, George Lachmann, 5–6, 11, 14, 20n76, 21n79, 46, 47n21, 66–68, 71n60, 96, 103, 202
Mozambique, 14, 130
  civil war in, 130
Museveni, Yoweri, 177, 181, 183–186, 191–193
  President Museveni's Movement, 181
Mutual benefit, 166, 168
"Myth of the War Experience"/"War myth," 5, 54, 60, 66
Mythical, 10, 158, 163–165, 169–173
Mythical tradition, 163–164
Mythologization, 60, 63

Naqshbandiya, 233
NaserOrić, 170
Nathan, Tobie, 128
National Association of Combatants (ANC), 207, 209–211
National interests, 68
National Resistance Movement (NRM), 181, 193
National sentiment, 61
Nationalism, 54, 66, 175n22, 203, 208, 226
  Great Serbia, 10, 174n6
  nationalist and traditionalist *imaginaire*/defense of the Serb nation, 163
  Serbian nationalist tradition/Serbian nationalist arena, 158, 160
  ultranationalism, 261, 263n3
NATO, 134n2, 165
Nazism/fascism, 5, 46, 66, 142, 145, 147, 149, 201–202, 215, 217n37/44
"Negative peace," 3
Network, 9, 31, 45, 76, 81, 95–96, 103, 107–109, 122, 140, 163, 166–167, 169, 173, 175n29/30, 177, 188–191, 212–213, 228, 246, 248, 265n42, 268–269
  sociability networks, 268
  social networks of war, 167
  social networks, 81, 109, 163, 166, 173, 175n30, 269

INDEX 297

New armed groups / illegal armed groups, 95–97, 99, 101, 108, 111
New elite, 162
Nieddu, Luigi, 210
Noiriel, Gérard, 61–62
Nongovernmental Organization (NGO), 74, 84, 87, 90–91, 180, 182, 186–190, 195n17, 255–256
Normalization, 2–4, 7, 30, 75, 82, 129, 148, 173n1, 193
Northern Uganda Social Action Fund (NUSAF), 186–187, 189
Novikova, Asmik, 33, 40

OMON, 27–28, 48n30/40
Operation Iron Fist, 179, 182, 195n22
(Operation) to restore constitutional order, 13, 35
Opportunities, 15, 121, 188, 234, 238n34
ORB-2, 30
Organization for Security and Cooperation in Europe (OSCE), 220–221, 228
Orthodoxy, 164
Ottoman/Ottoman Empire, 61, 164, 174n19
Ouattara, Alassane, 243, 245, 247, 264n37
Oushakine, Serguei Alex, 35

Pacification, 2, 5, 7, 15, 81–83, 138, 143, 177, 185, 190, 260
Pacifism/pacifist movement, 14, 19n56, 208
Pan-African, 10
Paramilitary(ies), 6, 15, 19n49, 95–105, 107–111, 111n3, 112n20
  ex-paramilitary, 101–102, 109, 111, 253
  (narco-)paramilitarism, 100, 106, 108–111
  paramilitary activity, 96
  paramilitary influence /(narco-)paramilitary influence, 103, 108, 111, 248
  paramilitary organizations/groups/forces/formations, 95–100, 104, 106–107, 109, 111, 242–245, 248, 250, 252, 256–257, 260
  paramilitary strategy/paramilitary card, 243, 248–249, 257
  paramilitary structures, 96
  paramilitary techniques/paramilitary crime, 105–106

Para-political, 109
Partisan recompositions, 15
Pastrana, Andrés, 96
Patriotic Education Program(s), 41–42
Patriotic heroes, 163, 166, 168, 173
Patrols, 40, 73–74, 77, 86, 92n2, 249
"Peace and Development" plan, 77
Peace plan, 1
Peace-building, 4, 188
  liberal peace, 8
  nation building, 4
  state reform, 3
  state-building, 4, 263n16
Pensions, 39, 83, 121, 124
Perpetrator, 58, 158, 162–163, 171–172
Peru, 8, 73–77, 82–84, 88, 90–91
Poilus, 12
Police force, 3, 25–26, 30–32, 45, 229
Political careers/career military, 15, 90, 267–268
Political sociology, 1–3, 16n1, 158
Political struggle, 199, 201
Politicization, 10, 151, 201, 204–205, 244–245
Prost, Antoine, 12
Psychic disorders, 31–32
Psychologists, 40
(material and symbolic) Public policies (for veterans), 13–14, 101–102, 269–270
  celebration, 129, 269
  glorification, 68, 220, 225, 270
  gratitude, 207, 226, 270
  official recognition, 269
Puggioni, Luigi Battista, 206, 215
Putin, Vladimir, 40–42, 44

Qadyriya, 233
Quiddity/Serbian quiddity, 163, 165

Raduyev, Salman, 230–232, 234
Raznjatovic, Zeljko (Arkan), 159
Rebel(s), 3–4, 17n6, 18n44, 19n49, 73–74, 76, 82, 97, 105, 178, 182, 242–243, 245, 247–248, 250, 252–255, 259–260, 263n5, 264n21, 267, 271n3
Reception centers, 179–180, 182, 188, 196n42

Recognition, 6, 13, 35, 37, 39, 62, 81, 83, 88, 90, 104–105, 112n8, 128, 137, 142–143, 147–148, 171, 204, 207, 224, 236, 237n21, 252, 254, 257, 260–261, 269–270

Reconciliation, 4–5, 16, 74, 84, 96, 171, 185–186, 188, 190–191, 243, 247

Reconversion, 151, 157–158, 172, 199, 206

Recovery of arms/disarmament, 3, 7, 95, 179, 221–223, 225, 229, 237n7/9, 259

Red Star of Belgrade, 162

"Redistribution of the markers of morality," 162

Reengaging (in combat), 15

Rehabilitation, 28, 35, 37, 39–40, 112n5, 118–119, 121–122, 128, 164, 169
  psychological rehabilitation, 37, 39
  rehabilitation program, 118, 122

Reinsertion, 75, 80, 82, 91, 97, 100, 102, 104, 111, 112n8, 119, 125, 158, 180, 189, 195n15, 207, 269–270
  professional reinsertion, 269–270

Reintegration, 2–4, 7, 9, 14–16, 19n49, 38, 96, 99, 101–103, 105, 115, 118–119, 129–130, 138, 158, 162, 177–193, 196n39, 197n51, 220, 225, 227–229, 235–236, 242, 250, 256, 269–270
  civilianization, 3, 14, 117, 119, 121–122, 131, 177, 193, 236
  readaptation to civilian life, 118
  return to civilian life, 1–3, 7–8, 14, 33, 45, 54–57, 122, 179, 191, 206–207, 268–270

Relational dynamic, 268

Rémond, René, 211

Repertoire of action, 13

Reporters, 179, 182

Resistance/*Résistants*, 73, 88, 99, 138–146, 148–151, 187, 209, 223–227, 229–231, 235–236, 238n43, 239n46, 258, 270

Returnees, 179–182, 184, 187, 189–190, 194n4/7
  middle-ranking and senior commanders, 179

Richards, Paul, 10, 18n41, 19n58, 264n22/24

Rite of passage, 69n15, 86, 119, 127–128

Rituals/cleansing rituals, 5, 14, 117, 119, 129–130, 136n68, 180
  cleansing ceremonies, 180

Ronda campesina, 75

Ronderas/*ronderos*, 73, 76–77, 82–84, 86–87, 89–90

ROSTO – DOSAAF (Russian Defence Sports-Technical Organization), 43–44

Russia, 13, 32–34, 36, 37–30, 40–41, 44, 46, 220–222, 225, 229, 233–236, 237n21/22, 269

Russian Orthodox Church, 44

Rwandan genocide, 126

Sabbatucci, Giovanni, 205

Sacralization, 66, 68

Sardinia, 10, 21n79, 201–204, 206, 208–211, 213–214, 215n2, 216n5, 269

Sardinian Action Party (PSdAz), 207, 211–215, 215n3

Sardist Party, 208, 211

Schafer, Jessica, 10, 19n59

Sechi, Salvatore, 208

Security, 2, 4, 9, 15, 27, 29–30, 45, 53–55, 59–60, 62–63, 66–68, 69n9/11, 71n56, 77, 83–84, 91, 96–98, 101, 112n6/7, 121, 140, 143–144, 147–148, 153n18/34, 177–179, 182, 186, 194, 196n34/40, 229, 242, 246, 249, 252, 260, 269
  national security, 54, 66
  national security regime, 53–55, 59–60, 63, 67–68, 69n9
  security dilemma, 4
  security mindset, 54–55, 59–60, 67
  security regime, 54
  security sector, 4
  Security Sector Reform, 16n4
  security transition, 2

Self-defense, 9, 15, 74–80, 82, 84, 86–87, 89–91, 98, 104–107, 109, 242–245, 248–250, 253–254, 256, 258, 263n14, 264n40
  self-defense committees (SDC), 74–75, 77–78, 80, 82, 87, 91, 258
  self-defense groups, 9, 15, 98, 104–107, 243–245, 248–250, 258, 263n14, 264n40

"Self-help," 160
Separatism/Separatists, 3, 14, 221–227, 235, 236n4
Serbia, 159–160, 162–165, 175n22
　Belgrade, 162, 165, 174n7, 175n28
　Chetniks, 159, 164–165, 174n19, 175n21
　Serb fighters/Serb warriors, 165
　Serb forces, 161
　Serbian culture/traditional Serb songs, 164–165
　Serbian Guard, 160
　Serbian nation, 158, 160, 163, 175n22
　Serbian patriotic heroes/mythic Serb heroes, 163, 169
　Serbian values, 165
　Serbs, 160–162, 164, 168, 174n6
Serbian Renewal Movement, 159–161, 164, 174n7
Šešelj, Vojislav, 159
Shamanov, Vladimir, 44, 50n102
Sironi, Françoise, 13, 20n73, 35, 39, 48n48/49, 49n72, 271n2
Social mobility, 89, 254, 257, 260
Socialization, 13, 20n74/75, 26, 32–33, 59, 158, 212, 214, 267
Solidarities, 269
Spoilers, 4, 15–16, 18n44, 158, 219–220, 223, 227–228, 232, 234, 238n32
Status, 6, 12, 35, 39, 41, 56, 59–60, 69n15, 83, 87, 89–90, 103–105, 120, 128, 140, 143, 148, 151, 157–158, 163, 166–167, 169–170, 173, 178, 182–184, 187–188, 196n39, 221–224, 234, 260–262, 268–269
　"transformation of social statuses," 6
Strategies
　rational actor, 15
　strategic actors/strategic players, 162, 168, 173
Subjectivation, 163, 175n27, 241–242, 261
Symbolic figures/mythical figures, 162, 165

Terrorism, 13, 29, 34–35, 53, 55, 59–60, 62, 65, 67, 70n30, 111, 222
　antiterrorism/antiterrorist operations (or laws), 25–26, 29, 35, 235, 236n2
　struggle against terrorism, 13, 35
　terrorist(s), 18n44, 28–31, 34, 47n27, 58, 68, 78, 90, 237n7
　terrorist organizations, 171, 178

Tigers, 159–162
Tilly, Charles, 175n30, 212, 217n34
Tognotti, Eugenia, 213
Total institution, 56
Trajectories, 1–2, 7, 14–16, 25, 91, 183, 188, 214, 243, 267–269
Transactions, 235, 270
　postwar transactions, 270
Transitions from war to peace, 138, 158, 160
Transmission of the narrative of war, 125
Transvaluation, 268
Traumatic, 13, 31, 35, 40, 58, 62, 123, 169, 171–173, 176n38, 203
　posttraumatic stress disorders (PTSD), 20n64, 40, 50n81, 124, 130–131
TravailleursCivilsLibres (TCL), 148–149, 151
Troshev, Gennady Nikolayevich, 44
Truth and Reconciliation Commission, 74, 84, 171
　Comisión de la Verdad y Reconciliación (CVR), 74, 81, 84, 86
Tupac Amaru Revolutionary Movement (MRTA), 73–74
Turkey, 13–14, 53–54, 59–61, 65–69, 69n12, 71n63/66, 269–270
　Anatolia, 53–54, 61
　Dardanelles war, 61
　Kayseri, 54, 56, 63–65, 67, 71n46/47, 72n70
　South-East syndrome, 55
　war of independence, 61–62, 64
Turkish army/Turkish armed forces, 53, 55, 60, 62–64, 66–68, 71n56, 270

Udugov, MovladiSaidarbievich, 225, 230–231, 233–234, 238n42
Uganda, 9, 177–183, 185–188, 190, 192–194, 195n15, 268
　Acholi/Acholiland, 177–180, 186, 191, 193
　Gulu, 177, 180, 184–187, 189, 191, 194n13, 195n16/19
　Labora Farm, 186–189
　Northern Uganda, 177, 179, 182–183, 186, 188, 190, 192–194, 195n17/21/22, 196n29/34

Uganda People's Defense Forces(UPDF), 179, 185, 187, 190–193, 194n7, 195n25
Ulman, 36
Uminsky, Gennady, 38
United Nations (UN)/UN agencies, 3, 8, 16n4, 47n22, 177, 181, 183–184, 186–187, 189, 195n17
   United Nations Children's Fund (UNICEF), 187, 196n29
   United Nations Development Programme (UNDP), 3, 193, 197n51
   United Nations Protection Force (UNPROFOR), 161
Uribe Vélez, Alvaro, 95–98, 106, 108, 110–111, 113n50

Vasiljković, Dragan("Captain Dragan"), 161, 174n7
Vedeno, 229–231
Velasco's agrarian reform in 1969, 88
Veterans/war veterans, 1, 10, 13, 19n56, 20n64, 25–27, 29–30, 33–46, 47n9/14, 48n48, 49n63, 50n87/88/98, 53, 55, 57–68, 70n30, 71n47/55/56, 83, 117–131, 134n12/16, 135n24/36/37, 136n65, 137, 158, 162, 165–166, 172, 183, 186, 188, 201, 219–220, 222–229, 231, 234–236, 238n34, 239n53, 243, 258, 268–270
   Canadian veterans, 118–119, 125, 129–130, 135n24
   Native American veterans, 129
   Veterans Charter (Canada), 120–122
Victims, 4, 11–12, 26–27, 29–31, 36, 47n10, 58, 74, 87, 89, 91, 96, 101, 103, 105–106, 142, 147–148, 150, 171, 173, 180, 192, 196n37, 206, 239n44, 244, 246, 250, 269
Victory, 4, 9, 14–15, 21n80, 98, 109, 140, 221–225, 227, 229, 233, 237n11/22, 270
Vietnam, 20n64, 26–27, 75, 125, 130, 268, 270
   Vietnam veterans, 20n64, 268
   Vietnam War, 27, 130
Violence, 2–4, 6, 9–14, 18n26, 19n59, 20n60/62, 21n76, 25–30, 32–35, 39, 41, 45–46, 47n21, 48n44, 53, 58–59, 62, 66–69, 73–77, 80–82, 84–91, 95–99, 101, 103, 105–106, 108, 111, 112n5, 119, 138, 142, 157–166, 168–173, 173n3, 174n10, 183, 186, 202, 219, 221, 227–229, 232–233, 235–236, 241–248, 250–251, 253–257, 259–262, 270
   armed violence, 75, 77, 82, 87, 245–247, 261
   continuation of armed violence/continuity of the violence, 75, 84
   domestic violence/family violence, 14, 73, 75, 84–89
   entrepreneur(s) of violence, 33, 168
   interpersonal violence, 89
   intersocial violence, 202
   mass violence, 157–159, 162, 166, 169, 173, 173n3
   militia violence, 244–245, 250
   mythical violence, 10, 169–173
   political violence, 73–74, 76, 84–86, 88–91, 241, 246
   state violence, 68, 142, 244
   transfers of violence, 14
   trivialization (of violence)/trivialized, 5–6, 13, 32, 34, 59, 66–68, 270
   violence enacted or lived/violence in action, 169, 170–173
Volkov, Vadim, 168
Volunteers, 1, 29, 44, 120, 160, 162, 248–249

War, 1–16, 18n26/30/44, 19n46/48/50/51/56/59, 20n72/74/75, 21n76/79, 25–46, 47n21, 48n48, 54–69, 71n55/56/60, 79, 87–88, 95–97, 103–106, 108–109, 117–121, 123–132, 134n14/15/16, 135n19/24/39, 137–151, 152n2/13/18, 157–168, 170–173, 174n6/7/19, 175n23, 177–182, 184, 190–193, 195n22, 201–214, 219–235, 236n1/2/5, 237n21/25, 238n33/34, 239n45/53, 241–245, 247–248, 250–254, 256–258, 260–262, 263n6, 264n37/40, 267–270
   civil war, 19n59, 130, 223, 225, 232–233, 244, 252, 267

cold war, 4, 106, 148, 151, 220
dirty war, 268
First World War, 5, 10, 12,
    21n79, 47n21, 56, 61, 66, 138,
    201–203, 244
interwar period, 211, 220, 226,
    232–233
new wars, 2, 4, 12, 19n48
Second World War, 5–6, 10, 14, 42,
    118, 121, 130, 134n8, 135n24/39,
    136n68, 164–165, 174n19, 209,
    225–226, 268
  Canadian Second World War
    combatants, 10, 118, 129–131
  German war prisoners, 10, 137–141,
    143–146, 148–151, 152n13,
    153n24, 154n38
  Great Patriotic War,
    35–36, 41, 43
social construction of the war, 55,
    61, 67
war criminals/war crimes, 166,
    178, 182
war experience, 5, 10, 13–14, 19n46,
    20n74, 25–28, 32–34, 126, 130,
    132, 142, 151, 157, 159, 162–163,
    267–268
war martyrs, 270

Warrior, 14, 73, 84, 95, 103–104,
    117–119, 124–126, 128, 130–131,
    134n15, 163–165, 175n21, 241–242,
    243–244, 254, 261–263
  celestial warrior/symbolic celestial
    warrior, 163, 165
  past warriors, 164
  "warrior monks," 165
Weber, Max, 3, 228
Welfare state, 117, 119, 121
West-African soldiers/French colonial
    army, 10
Winnipeg general strike, 120
World Bank, 3, 179, 181, 186–187,
    195n15

Yandarbiyev,
    ZelimkhanAbdumuslimovich,
    221, 225, 228, 231, 234
Yanesha, 89
Yarysh-Mardy, 227
YedinayaRossiya, 37
Yugoslavia/Yugoslav federation/
    former Yugoslavia, 157, 161, 165,
    174n7/19, 175n22
  Yugoslav Peoples' Army, 161

Zakayev, Ahmed, 225